The DevelopMentor Series
Don Box, Editor

Addison-Wesley has joined forces with DevelopMentor, a premiere developer resources company, to produce a series of technical books written by developers for developers. DevelopMentor boasts a prestigious technical staff that includes some of the world's best-known computer science professionals.

*"Works in **The DevelopMentor Series** will be practical and informative sources on the tools and techniques for applying component-based technologies to real-world, large-scale distributed systems."*
—Don Box

Titles in the Series:

Essential XML
Beyond Markup
Don Box, Aaron Skonnard, and John Lam
0-201-70914-7

Programming Windows Security
Keith Brown
0-201-60442-6

Advanced Visual Basic 6
Power Techniques for Everyday Programs
Matthew Curland
0-201-70712-8

Transactional COM+
Building Scalable Applications
Tim Ewald
0-201-61594-0
12/5/00

Debugging Windows Programs
Strategies, Tools, and Techniques for Visual C++ Programmers
Everett N. McKay and Mike Woodring
0-201-70238-X

Watch for future titles in The DevelopMentor Series.

Programming
Windows Security

Keith Brown

Addison-Wesley

Boston • San Francisco • New York • Toronto • Montreal
London • Munich • Paris • Madrid
Capetown • Sydney • Tokyo • Singapore • Mexico City

The publisher offers discounts on this book when ordered in quantity for special sales. For more information, please contact:

Pearson Education Corporate Sales Division
One Lake Street
Upper Saddle River, NJ 07458
(800) 382-3419
corpsales@pearsontechgroup.com

Visit us on the Web at www.awl.com/cseng/

Library of Congress Cataloging-in-Publication Data

Brown, Keith
    Programming Windows security / Keith Brown.
        p. cm.
    Includes bibliographical references and index.
    ISBN 0-201-60442-6
    1. Computer security. 2. Microsoft Windows NT. 3. Computer programming. I. Title.

    QA76.9.A25 B78 2000
    005.8–dc21

                                                                                00-033148

ISBN 0-201-60442-6

Text printed on recycled paper.
1 2 3 4 5 6 7 8 9 10 – CRS – 04 03 02 01 00
First printing, July 2000

To my wife, Kathy; my sons, Colin, Nathan, and Aidan; and my mother, Carol. Thanks for your enduring patience and love.

Contents

Preface

As with most of my friends, I learned to program Windows by reading Charles Petzold's classic tome, *Programming Windows*. I then moved on to Jefferey Richter's seminal book for systems developers, *Advanced Windows NT*.[1] Finally, I moved into the realm of objects with Kraig Brockschmidt's *Inside OLE 2*.[2] With the release of Windows NT 4.0, I started using (and eventually teaching) COM as a way to build distributed applications. Until this point in my life, I'd been able to safely ignore security, and had long since suppressed the pangs of guilt I used to feel when passing NULL for `LPSECURITY_ATTRIBUTES`. Little did I know that my life was about to change forever.

It was a beautiful sunny day in Bellevue, Washington, when I drove up to the offices of Saros, a software development company where I was scheduled to give my first on-site presentation of Essential COM, DevelopMentor's flagship COM course that included coverage of the relatively new Windows NT 4.0 feature called DCOM. All the students in the class had packed in their own

---

[1] At least I think this was the title way back then…

[2] Like many early adopters, I started off with a laser-printed draft copy of Kraig's first edition, crying in my beer over what had happened to the operating system that I knew and loved.

computers (these students were worn and grizzled Windows programmers, some of whom had lost the covers to their machines long ago). What made the situation interesting was that some of the students had machines belonging to various Windows NT domains, whereas others had standalone machines not associated with any domain. One student was even running Windows 95. It was a recipe for disaster. Everything had been going smoothly, and the students (and myself) were thoroughly enjoying the class, but the radical configuration in the classroom put quite a crimp in the DCOM lab exercise that morning. Virtually all the students were getting E_ACCESSDENIED and various and sundry error codes, and of course they all looked to me to fix the problem. I failed miserably that day, and had to admit to myself (and the students) that I didn't yet have a good enough grasp of Windows security to solve their problems. I've rarely felt so small.

Shortly after this soul-wrenching experience, I dedicated myself to the pursuit of a deep and practical understanding of Windows security. I solidified my commitment by agreeing to write a new course for DevelopMentor about services and security, and proceeded to spend three months of virtually uninterrupted time studying and experimenting with the Windows security APIs. I never knew that I'd end up falling in love. Since then, I've learned loads more and answered hundreds of questions on the DCOM mailing list regarding security issues, and reached thousands of students, conference attendees, and readers of *Microsoft Systems Journal* (now *MSDN Magazine*) with the message that security is a fascinating and approachable topic.

As the culmination of my effort, this book attempts to fill the gaping hole in the Windows systems programming canon by providing a reference for programmers that covers Windows security from the basics of principals, authorities, logon sessions, and DACLs all the way through COM+ security, one of the most subtle and sensitive beasts you'll encounter as a Windows programmer.

As a side effect of my predilection for distributed programming, this book is unique in that it addresses security with the distributed systems developer in mind; in fact, the original title of the book was *Distributed Security in Windows NT*. Of course, Microsoft's decision to rename their (beta, at the time) operating system from "Windows NT 5.0" to "Windows 2000" didn't bode well for my original title. Frankly, *Distributed Security in Windows NT/2000* sounded really goofy. Thus the new title.

In any case, if you're a programmer who, not unlike myself a few years ago, feels a hollowness in the pit of your stomach as a result of being asked to add a security-related feature or debug a security-related problem in an application, I hope you'll find that this book completes you.

Which Windows?

This book covers security programming on Windows 2000 and Windows NT 4. Therefore, to avoid crossing the reader's eyes with "Windows 2000/NT" or similar nastiness, I'll simply refer to both of these operating systems as *Windows*. If I find the need to say anything specific about a distinct operating system (including Windows 9x), I'll use the full name.

Who Should Read This Book

This book was written for professional software developers involved in systems programming on Windows. The third part of the book was written for the subset of these programmers developing distributed systems (especially those using COM).

The first part of the book (the first three chapters) intentionally has no code in it, and instead speaks to the big picture, introducing terminology and concepts that will likely be useful not just for programmers but also for technical managers and advanced Windows users. If you are a manager and want to get a better understanding of Windows security, borrow this book from one of the developers on your team and rip out the first three chapters for yourself. Sharing a common terminology will help you and your development team play better together.

What a Developer Should Already Know

I assume you have a basic understanding of Windows system programming; that is, you know the difference between a process and a thread, and you've written a DLL before and perhaps even written a service or two. I casually mention features such as *thread local storage* and assume that you know what I'm talking about. If you're unsure of your ability in this area, my favorite book on the subject is *Advanced Windows,* by Jefferey Richter (as of this writing the fourth edition is hot off the press).[3]

In the COM chapter (Chapter 9), I assume you feel comfortable with the basics of IUnknown and that you know what a proxy and stub are. If you're unsure, my favorite COM book is *Essential COM* by Don Box.

Much of the later material in the COM chapter talks about COM+ features in Windows 2000, which *Essential COM* doesn't address (as of this writing, *Essential COM* is in its first edition). My favorite COM+ book in print as I write this is *Programming Distributed Applications with COM and Visual Basic 6.0* by Ted Pattison.[4] Tim Ewald's book *Transactional COM+: Designing Scalable Applications* will likely be a must-read as well, although it's not yet gone to press as I write this.

Although this book often shows full declarations of Windows API functions, I won't always bother to tell you the details of what each and every parameter means if it's not relevant to the topic at hand. I hope you find that this book works well as a *complement* to the Windows API documentation, as opposed to a *replacement* for it.

How to Approach This Book

I know that most developers don't relish thinking about security issues, which is often why security ends up getting retrofitted into existing products (or left until the last minute in new products). Most of my students are really surprised to learn that security is actually quite an interesting topic, and they really enjoy sitting through DevelopMentor's security class. However, I'm aware that this is a self-selecting group; these folks have *chosen* to take the class, often because there is a distinct set of problems that they need to be able to solve, whether they like it or not. Whatever your predisposition is toward security, I designed this book to be readable front to back, but also to be readable in chunks.

Many people will buy this book because it contains (at least as of this writing) an exhaustive coverage of COM security, and will want to dive right in to the chapter on COM. However, you can't possibly understand COM security

---

[3] Although the title has changed to *Programming Applications for Windows,* 4th ed.

[4] Ted is working on a new edition as this goes to press, so keep your eyes peeled for it.

without having a basic understanding of the fundamentals, and no matter how much I urge folks to read Chapter 4, there will be a large group of people who don't have the time for this. If it's you I'm describing, do spend the time to read the first three (very short) chapters of this book before you start diving into the nitty-gritty details of COM security. These chapters will help you develop a more intuitive feel for how Windows security works and why it works the way it does.

This Is *Not* a Cookbook

In the vein of my last book project, *Effective COM* (coauthored with Don Box, Tim Ewald, and Chris Sells), I've purposely avoided making this a cookbook that provides lots of code for you to cut and paste to solve a particular set of problems that you may or may not be faced with. Instead, this book is about helping you understand how things work. I'd love to see a Windows security cookbook written. I find that cookbooks increase my long-term productivity once I have a basic understanding of the topic at hand.

The code snippets in this book should all compile correctly. However, although some of them might be appropriate for cutting and pasting into your projects, be aware that a number of them exist solely to foster insight and understanding and will necessarily be a bit more abstract than what you'd expect to find in a cookbook.

The Bad Guys

Often I'll refer to the "bad guys" when I want to indicate someone who may be trying to break into your system either to do malicious damage, or just for fun. The bad guys are the folks that we want to keep out, and the good guys are folks that we want to let in. I actually borrowed the terms "good guys" and "bad guys" from one of my favorite security books, *Network Security: Private Communication in a Public World* (Kaufman, Perlman, and Speciner 1995).

Code Sample Conventions

All the code samples in this book were built using Visual C++ 6 with the Platform SDK for Windows 2000. Each snippet was compiled, and all functional samples were tested as well. This occurred *before* they were copied into the manuscript, so any syntax errors you find are likely printing errors.

Download the code snippets from http://www.develop.com/books/pws to get the real thing.

I built all the code samples with the UNICODE macro defined; I didn't want to clutter the code with __TEXT macros when this book is all about programming Windows 2000 and Windows NT 4, where Unicode is the norm.

I use a consistent naming scheme for any functions that are my own, so that you can distinguish them from system calls. My functions (and constants) all start with a lowercase letter prefixed with an underscore:

```
_thisIsACallToMyFunction();
ThisIsACallToASystemFunction();
```

Let me warn you that the snippets I provide sometimes ignore error checking for brevity, except in certain cases where I have some special insight to offer or when I'm providing functions that are generally useful to be worthy of direct cut-and-paste. There are many ways of performing error checks (many wars have been fought over the correct way to do this), but virtually all error checking mechanisms obscure the system calls you're making to some degree, and it's these calls that I want to focus on in the code snippets.

Finally, I'm a real stickler when it comes to writing const-correct production C++ code, but I found that this doesn't work well in the limited space a book affords. (Much of the Windows security API is notoriously const-incorrect, and having you wade through oodles of const_cast operators wouldn't serve any good purpose.)

Yes, There Is No CD-ROM

I've been told that we live in the "information age," and I personally think it's silly to ship a CD with stale content when I am perfectly willing to provide up-to-date content via the Web. So please visit http://www.develop.com/books/pws to download real examples that compile and build (this includes all the code snippets from this book, plus lots of other goodies that I upload from time to time).

Errata

I've gone out of my way to research all the topics in this book, but as with any endeavor of this magnitude, there's bound to be a few rough edges. Please send any errata to me via my Web site (http://www.develop.com/books/pws). I'll publish all confirmed bugs online, and credit the first person to report the problem. Please check my Web site from time to time to keep abreast of any problems that may have been reported.

What to Expect

Part I: Model

These first chapters were written to give you a roadmap of the Windows security architecture. These chapters are designed to be as concise as possible so that a dedicated reader can consume them comfortably in one or two sittings. My goal is to introduce some basic terminology with an emphasis on how all the pieces fit together, without drilling down into the details. An effective way to use this part of the book would be to read through it once before diving into the other chapters in the book, and then revisit these chapters whenever you need to step back and see the big picture. There is no code in these chapters, so this is a great section to tear out and send to your manager to help bridge the communication gap that often develops on a project.

Chapter 1: The Players

This chapter focuses on the actors in a secure system. It introduces principals and authorities, authentication, domains, and the Local Security Authority (LSA). The chapter emphasizes that security eventually boils down to trust, and provides several examples.

Chapter 2: The Environment

This chapter focuses on the environment in which your programs run. It introduces logon sessions, tokens, window stations, and profiles.

Chapter 3: Enforcement

This chapter focuses on authorization and access control. It introduces groups, aliases, roles, privileges, security descriptors, and DACLs and SACLs, as well as some access control strategies and guidelines for picking an appropriate strategy for your application. The chapter ends with a discussion of the session-oriented nature of Windows security.

Part II: Mechanics

These next three chapters drill down into the details of each of the concepts introduced in Part I. Except where noted, you can read these in pretty much any order you like.

Chapter 4: Logon Sessions

This chapter delves into the details of logon sessions and tokens. Systems developers will feel much more comfortable designing and implementing applications with a good grasp of logon sessions. This chapter discusses the System logon session, as well as interactive and network logon sessions and how to call `LogonUser` to establish new logon sessions. It also shows how to make use of privileges at runtime and restrict privileges with job objects.

Chapter 5: Window Stations and Profiles

Many Windows developers have never even heard of a window station, but these seemingly obscure entities will eventually haunt you if you don't come to grips with them. This chapter includes a discussion of window stations and desktops, as well as a discussion of user profiles and how to manage them. To get the most out of this chapter, read the previous chapter on logon sessions first.

Chapter 6: Access Control and Accountability

This chapter shows how to create and manage security descriptors, including access control list (ACL) programming and auditing. ACLs in Windows 2000 change quite dramatically from those in earlier versions of the operating system, and these changes are covered in detail. The chapter also includes a discussion of how to manage and use private security descriptors for securing application-defined objects, including dealing with object hierarchies and ACL inheritance.

Part III: Distribution

Parts I and II deal with basic Windows security programming. Part III builds on this foundation by showing how distribution factors into the security model. Many companies are developing Windows-based distributed systems these days, and most of them rely on COM and HTTP as integral enabling technologies. This book therefore culminates in a discussion of COM and IIS security. Except where noted, you can read these chapters in any order you like.

Chapter 7: Network Authentication

The problem of proving one's identity to another across a public wire was the primary question that originally captivated me and initiated my love affair with security. It's a fascinating problem with many solutions, and this chapter provides an introduction to the core network authentication protocols used in Windows NT and Windows 2000, namely, NTLM and Kerberos. After describing and contrasting the two protocols, the chapter concludes by introducing the Security Support Provider Interface (SSPI), which abstracts the differences between various authentication protocols.

Chapter 8: The File Server

Using the Windows file system across the network is a very common practice, and this chapter is dedicated to exploring the sort of security programming problems you're likely to encounter in these scenarios. This chapter is all about understanding SMB (Server Message Block) security and how to bend it to your will. Because named pipes are built on top of the file server infrastructure, I've also included them in this discussion.

Chapter 9: COM(+)

This chapter draws on the basics introduced in earlier chapters to provide the foundation for a solid understanding of COM(+) security, one of the most misunderstood and oft-cursed features in Windows. I address COM+ security features and provide notes on differences between COM+, MTS, and base COM. You'll get the most out of this chapter if you've already read the first and second parts of this book (Chapter 4 is the most important chapter from the second part). I'd also recommend reading Chapter 7 before tackling this chapter.

Chapter 10: IIS

DCOM isn't a popular protocol for use over the Internet. In fact, just getting it to cross firewalls and network address translation layers is quite a feat of engineering. The Internet is about simplicity, and HTTP and SSL are the protocols of choice for reaching the broadest audience. Often a distributed system is built using DCOM in the middle tier, with HTTP used as a gateway to the client tier. This chapter first covers the basics of SSL and certificate-based authentication, and then turns and focuses on issues you need to be aware of when building Web applications with IIS, especially when coupling them with a middle tier of COM+ components. The latter parts of this chapter will make more sense if you've read Chapter 9.

Appendix: Some Parting Words

I've put together some tips for writing setup programs (how to install user and group accounts, configure privileges, and configure secrets such as the COM RunAs password). I've included a list of well-known SIDs that you can form programmatically, and a simple class for making this easy to do. I've also included a discussion of the three different group scopes in Windows 2000 (universal, global, and domain local). Finally, I've included a list of all the defined privileges in Windows along with as much insight as I could muster into how they really work (the documentation often is too vague to be of use).

Glossary

Throughout the text, new terms are called out in bold as they are introduced, and are summarized in the glossary. I hope you find this section helpful.

Bibliography

Any book or magazine articles I reference can be found in the bibliography.

What Not to Expect

Active Directory

I'll spend just enough time talking about the Active Directory Services Interface (ADSI) to get you started installing user and group accounts. An entire book could (and should) be written on programming the Windows directory. This is not that book.

Public Key Infrastructure

Although I discuss SSL authentication and the basics of how certificates work, any detailed coverage of what it takes to build a public key infrastructure is beyond the scope of this book. I provide several references in the bibliography for interested readers.

Acknowledgments

First of all, I want to acknowledge the tremendous sacrifice my wife and kids made while I struggled to get this book to press. I've hardly seen them at all for the last four months of this project. Thanks Kathy, Colin, Nathan, and Aidan. I've missed you so incredibly much.

I'd like to thank Don Box and Mike Abercrombie of DevelopMentor for providing an unparalleled environment for research and development, and for feeding my family while I hunkered down to finish the book. I've had a ton of fun working with you guys, and I look forward to many more years of collaboration.

Thanks to Bruce Schneier for writing an incredibly readable book on cryptography that captivated me. Reading *Applied Cryptography* was a turning point in my life, because I discovered what a fascinating game security really was.

Thanks to all the students in my security classes over the past couple of years who have listened to an evolving story and have provided their own unique input. This story wouldn't be the same without you.

Thanks to the reviewers who gave me feedback on this project: Saji Abraham, Richard Ward, Michael Howard, Bob Beauchemin, Ian Griffiths, George Reilly, Michael Nelson, Steve Rodgers, Thomas Deml, Henk de Koning, and Jefferey Richter.

Thanks to the staff at Addison Wesley: Kristin Erickson, for being an advocate and friend, Jacquelyn Doucette for pushing production through in record time, and J. Carter Shanklin for talking me into this thing in the first place.

Thanks to my copyeditor Cindy Kogut, who continues to amaze me with her ability to cover my prose with oodles of red ink. Cindy also retrofitted a healthy dose of consistency into a book whose conception spanned two years of my life.

And finally, thanks to Alice and Bob for just being you.

PART 1

Model

Chapter 1

The Players

As a developer, I've always been interested in the nitty-gritty details of whatever technology I'm currently in love with. However, that's not a great way to start talking about a topic that might be completely new to some people. This chapter begins a gentle introductory section that introduces some basic terminology and mechanisms. It pieces together a big picture that you can return to if you start to get mired down in the details later on. It provides just enough detail to keep you turning the pages, but if you start itching to drill down, follow the references to the various chapters and read at your own pace. Even experienced Windows developers should probably start with this chapter, however, regardless of what you choose to read next.

Principals

One of the major benefits of having a secure system is that it's possible to grant or deny access to unique entities (humans or other entities such as computers or services). In security parlance, each unique entity that we can securely identify is known as a **principal.** Each principal has a unique name and some way of proving its identity to other principals in the system. The mechanism by which one principal proves its identity to another principal is called **authentication.**

Once you identify the principals in a system, you can control which resources each principal is allowed to use and the ways in which each principal can use them. You can also audit the use of these resources at runtime to help refine the security policy and detect intrusion attempts. Without the concept of a principal, and without a mechanism for allowing a principal to prove its identity, most security policies that you could enforce would be either very limited or completely meaningless.

In a general-purpose operating system such as Windows, each principal is identified via both a human-readable name and a machine-readable identifier. The former makes human use and administration of a computer system feasible, and the latter makes the implementation efficient at runtime. In fact, if the machine-readable identifiers chosen are reasonably different in space and time, it may be feasible to introduce two completely disparate systems into the same working environment (for example, connect them via a network and allow principals in one system to access resources in the other) without too much disruption to either system.[1] This is an important feature for scalability, because most networks start small and grow with the organization.

Information about principals is stored in a security database (which is discussed later in this chapter). Each entry in the database is known as an **account**, and each account represents a principal.[2] Be sure to keep the distinction between an *account* (a record in the security database) and a *principal* (an authenticatable entity in the system) clear in your mind. This text mostly talks about principals; it will only discuss accounts when specifically referring to configuring security information in the database (for example, when resetting a principal's password, you modify the account for that principal).

---

[1] A more specific example of this would be connecting two different domains together via a trust relationship, so that principals in one domain can access resources in another domain. I'll talk about domains and trust later in this chapter.

[2] Although groups have not been discussed yet, each group is also represented by an entry in the security database (you may have heard the term *group account*). Groups are very different from principals; we can authenticate principals, but not groups. Groups are discussed in Chapter 3.

In Windows, each principal has a human-readable name that is guaranteed to be unique within a certain scope, but the machine-readable identifier is guaranteed to be globally unique.[3] The Windows term for this unique identifier is **SID,** for security identifier.

SIDs

Most Windows programmers are already familiar with another unique identifier, the globally unique identifier (GUID; also called a universally unique identifier, UUID), which is used by COM (Component Object Model) and DCE (Distributed Computing Environment) developers all over the world. The GUID generation algorithm guarantees uniqueness in space by using an IEEE 802 address, which is a 48-bit unique identifier assigned to each network card by a centralized authority; the algorithm guarantees uniqueness in time by using a combination of the computer's clock, a sequence number that is incremented whenever the clock is adjusted, and a monotonically increasing counter.[4] The benefit of using GUIDs is that they are extremely easy to use from a programmer's perspective; each GUID is always 128 bits long.

The SID is conceptually similar to the GUID, in that it also provides uniqueness in space and time. Uniqueness in space is statistically guaranteed by a 96-bit machine identifier that is generated at the time the Windows OS is installed. Its value is tucked away in the registry and is combined with a persistent, monotonically increasing counter to achieve uniqueness in time. However, this is where the similarity ends. SIDs are variable-length data structures, which makes using them more difficult for programmers. On the flip side, SIDs allow more flexibility because they have a structure that a programmer can depend

---

[3] Technically, this guarantee is based on statistical uniqueness, but the chances of collision are negligible. This also assumes that you've installed Windows in the traditional fashion as opposed to making a binary copy of someone else's image. (Clearly, unless you do something to change it, the security database will be an exact copy of the original in this case; the folks at http://www.sysinternals.com have some information on this in case you're looking.)

[4] This algorithm is documented in an (expired) Internet draft filed in February 1998 as draft-leach-uuids-guids-01.txt. Due to some silly pressure from popular media wonks who thought that GUID stood for "global user ID" back in 1999, Microsoft replaced the tried-and-true implementation of `UuidCreate` with a random number generator from the CryptoAPI. If you still want to use the familiar old algorithm, call `UuidCreateSequential` and party on.

on. A SID is composed of several parts, each of which combines to form a hierarchical naming structure that is quite useful in many cases at runtime.

This hierarchical structure becomes most apparent in the text form in which SIDs are often represented: *S-R-I-SA-SA-SA*, where S is the letter *S*, *R* is the revision number of the SID binary format (currently 1), *I* is a 48-bit **identifier authority** value, and *SA* is a 32-bit **subauthority** value.

The identifier authority represents the outermost scope of the name, and it identifies a unique namespace via a 48-bit identifier. One can only imagine the original intended use for this field; perhaps it was designed to allow 48-bit IEEE 802 addresses to be used to give any third-party vendor its own namespace. We may never know, however, because SIDs for all principals you create (at least as of this writing) are always issued within the NT Authority namespace, whose value is `0x000005`. Other interesting namespaces include the World Authority (`0x000001`), which is used for the well-known SID S-1-1-0, more commonly known as **Everyone.** Since the largest identifier authority value currently in use is `0x000005`, today it seems as if 45 of those bits are effectively wasted.[5]

Because the 48-bit identifier authority is clearly not enough to guarantee uniqueness for the issuer, it is combined with either a well-known subauthority (such as the **BUILTIN domain,** which is present on all Windows machines) or a set of subauthorities determined from the unique machine ID assigned when Windows was installed on the machine. As an example, here are two well-known principals that are automatically created whenever you install Windows on a machine:

```
Administrator: S-1-5-21-XXXX-XXXX-XXXX-500
Guest:         S-1-5-21-XXXX-XXXX-XXXX-501
```

In place of *XXXX*, you'll find the 32-bit subauthority values that compose the 96-bit unique ID of the machine that generated the SID. This virtually guarantees that two machines will not generate the same SIDs and thus will not have

---

[5] Given the mud that has been hurled at Microsoft over GUIDs having layer 2 network addresses buried inside them, perhaps this wasn't a bad move after all! See http://www.develop.com/dbox/guidgen.asp for a laugh.

embarrassing security principal conflicts when connected over a network. Following the subauthority values that define a unique namespace, you'll find a number that identifies the principal within the namespace. In the above example, the number 500 identifies Administrator, and the number 501 identifies Guest.

There is clearly a pattern that you can rely on here. For instance, the number 21 is used to prefix the three machine-specific subauthority values, and the number 501 always represents the special principal named Guest, no matter what machine you happen to be working on. Each of these well-known subauthority values is called a **RID** (relative identifier), and `winnt.h` includes definitions for the ones used by the core Windows OS. The appendix includes a list of well-known SIDs that you can form programmatically using these documented RIDs, which is important if you are writing internationalized code that will be localized for multiple countries. *Guest* is not spelled the same way in German as it is in Spanish, so instead of referring to well-known principals by name, it's much safer (and more efficient) to form the SIDs programmatically.

That being said, given an arbitrary SID or a human-readable principal name, the two functions `LookupAccountSid` and `LookupAccountName` can be used to map between them at runtime. An example of where these functions would be appropriate is in a user interface component that allows a human to type in principal names.

Credentials

So far this chapter has discussed the need to identify principals, but has not specified how to distinguish one principal from another at runtime in a secure fashion. Unless you trust everyone who could possibly get access to your system not to pretend to be someone he or she is not, either maliciously or by accident, you need to have a way to prove a principal's identity.

A principal who has the means to prove his or her identity is said to have valid **credentials.** Generally, there are three questions you can ask at runtime to verify identity:

1. What do you have?

2. What do you know?

3. What are you?

Asking a mixture of these questions makes the system more secure. For instance, when you start your car in the morning, you must have the car keys to prove to the car that you are a valid principal. This is an example of a system in which *what you have* (in this case, the car keys) determines your credentials.

There are two ways to break this system. The first way is to hot-wire the car, which is an example of simply going around the security system (this is generally the way most bad guys prefer to break in). Generally you'll avoid parking your car in places where it is likely to be stolen in this manner, but there's not a lot you can do to prevent this, other than driving an armored military vehicle. In a computer system, this is equivalent to protecting your corporate network via a firewall. To keep the bad guys from going around your security policy, you need to plug lots of little holes that tend to change from service pack to service pack.

The second way to break this system is to steal someone's keys. The beauty of this approach is that you'll probably be able to turn off the car alarm (by virtue of the fact that the remote control is attached to the keys), and you can steal the car from virtually any location. Most folks who see people getting into cars using a set of keys do not suspect them of being car thieves. In fact, this system is so easy to break that if the owner accidentally drops the keys in the parking lot next to the car, a bad guy can safely escape with the car even in a parking lot crowded with honest people. Generally it's bad when you can accidentally break a system by being careless, so to protect against this, you can add another question to the mix, as in the next example.

Consider an automated teller machine (ATM). In order to use an ATM, you must prove your identity to it by inserting *what you have* (your ATM card) and typing in *what you know* (your PIN code). If you accidentally drop your ATM card on the ground next to the machine, a bad guy typically has three chances to guess your PIN code before the ATM swallows the card (probably taking a photograph of the bad guy at the same time). In this case, the system is hard to accidentally misuse, and in order to have *any reasonable chance* of guessing your PIN code in three tries, the bad guy has to know some information about you, such as your birthday, address, phone number, or social security number. Of course, if you write your PIN code on the back of your ATM card, you'd qualify as an extremely careless principal, but the system couldn't stop someone else from impersonating you.

For systems that require maximal security, the third question is often imposed: What are you? This question inquires about biometric information, which may be collected via a retinal scan, voiceprint, or even a machine that measures the relative length of your fingers. These are all ways of identifying a particular human. When posed in concert with the other two questions already discussed, the only reliable way to break the system involves stealing a bit more than just an ATM card or a set of car keys; doing so would require one seriously *motivated* individual. Thinking of it in this light makes me prefer not to be a principal in such a system!

Passwords

In general-purpose operating systems such as Windows, passwords traditionally have reigned as the preferred mechanism for proving one's identity. They are simple to use and easy to administer, but passwords only ask the single question *what do you know,* so principals must choose their passwords wisely to avoid being impersonated by the bad guys.

Imagine for a moment how a password could be used to prove a principal's identity. Say Alice walks up to a machine named BobsMachine and attempts to log in. She provides her principal name, "Alice," and her password, "supercalafragalisticexpialidocious." BobsMachine must verify Alice's password in order to know who Alice is, but this means that BobsMachine must store Alice's password somewhere in long-term storage. This doesn't sound safe; if BobsMachine is compromised, a bad guy could learn Alice's password and impersonate her anywhere she uses that password.

Using cryptographic techniques, however, it is possible for BobsMachine to simply calculate a **one-way function** (**OWF**) (typically a **cryptographic hash**) of Alice's password and store `OWF(password)` instead of simply `password`. Because the password is only held by BobsMachine (in memory) until Alice is finished typing it, Alice might feel much more comfortable with this scheme. However, it is still possible to perform a **dictionary attack** against

`OWF(password)`. If the security database on BobsMachine is compromised, the bad guy only has to calculate `OWF(guess)`, where `guess` is composed of single words (and combinations of words) from a dictionary, until a match is found. In fact, these sorts of attacks are often taken offline by making a copy of the compromised security database and performing the attack from a safe location. In an offline password-guessing attack, the bad guy will use as much computing power as he or she can muster. Thus Alice needs to choose a good password (one that is long and that can't easily be guessed by a dictionary attack).

Most system administrators are well aware of guidelines and programs that can help enforce good passwords, so they won't be enumerated here. The important *conceptual* point is that even when BobsMachine stores Alice's `OWF(password)` instead of simply `password`, there is an implied measure of trust between Alice and BobsMachine. Alice trusts that BobsMachine won't attack or otherwise disclose information about her password.[6] Alice also trusts that BobsMachine won't allow other principals to masquerade as her without her consent.[7]

Now imagine that Alice wants to log in to several different machines on the network throughout the day. Must each machine store a copy of her password, or `OWF(password)`? If so, Alice is a very trusting individual, because if any one of those machines is compromised, her password could be subjected to an offline dictionary attack.[8] There must be a better way.

Authorities

Instead of having every machine on the network store a copy of Alice's password, you could design a scheme in which only one machine, acting as an

---

[6] Without administrative privileges and physical access to Bob, a bad guy would have a very difficult time stealing the security database in a system with a security-conscious administrator. This is not meant to frighten you, but to point out in a very concrete fashion the inherent trust that Alice must place in the operating system and the administrator of BobsMachine. Security is all about trust, as is discussed later in the chapter.

[7] If Alice has an account on BobsMachine, it is possible at any time for BobsMachine to masquerade as Alice (or allow someone else to masquerade as Alice). This concept is revisited in the section about trust.

[8] If Alice has chosen a good password, this may not be a problem. However, obtaining a password hash will allow an attacker to masquerade as Alice on the network (see Chapter 7).

authority, needs to have information about her password. In this manner, Alice's password only resides in two places: in her long-term memory and in the authority's database. Alice then only has to trust a single machine. Locking down one machine and watching it carefully to avoid compromise is much easier than locking down every machine on the network (most users get annoyed when system administrators start turning on security features that impede their daily work).

Let's call the authority Trent,[9] for "trusted authority." Trent is a principal (physically he is represented by a process running on a designated machine on the network), and his job is to help Alice prove her identity to other principals such as Bob. To make this work, not only must Alice trust Trent (not to attack her password), but Bob must also trust Trent, because if Trent says "that's Alice," Bob has no other way of verifying what Trent says. Details of how this might be implemented are found in Chapter 7, but for now, suffice it to say that Alice and Bob need to perform some sort of network communication with Trent to help establish each other's identity.

To avoid administrative (and runtime) nightmares, each authority has a namespace from which it can dole out principal names. In many general-purpose operating systems (including Windows 2000), principal names are often written "principal@authority". In earlier versions of Windows NT, principal names are written "authority\principal". Both written forms clearly indicate a scoped name. This translates into a SID that takes the form of S-1-5-21-*XXXX-XXXX-XXXX-N*, where the *X*s are replaced with the unique identifier for the authority, and the *N* is replaced with a unique 32-bit identifier (unique within that authority's namespace) for the principal. This scheme also clearly shows how the principal is scoped. The name Alice@foo.com is different from Alice@bar.com, just as Alice@foo.com is different from Bob@foo.com.

With Trent in the picture, if Alice wants to change her password, she doesn't need to synchronize this change with each computer in the network; rather, she can change it by simply talking to Trent. This is one obvious example of the benefits realized when introducing an authority into a network. As with most things

---

[9] In homage to *Applied Cryptography* (Schneier 1996), which was quite an inspirational book for me.

in life, nothing comes for free, though. Adding Trent to the picture makes the system less efficient at runtime, and it institutes a single point of failure. To solve these problems, Trent may provide service from several machines on the network (using a replicated security database). This means low latency and high availability to principals such as Alice and Bob.

Machines as Principals

I'd like to take a short interlude to make a point that developers really need to keep in mind. In the previous example, Alice (a human) logged into BobsMachine. Both Alice and BobsMachine are principals. It may seem strange to think of a machine as being a principal, especially if you've been used to running Windows NT 4.0 or earlier. If you run **User Manager,** you won't see any machines listed as principals in the system. However, try running **Server Manager** for your domain, and you'll see a list of machines. Machines are not first-class principals on Windows NT 4.0; in fact, although a machine *can* prove its identity to its authority (and is required to do so), a machine cannot prove its identity to any other principals. However, even with this limitation, machines are still principals of the domain, with a unique name and password.

Under Windows 2000, this limitation goes away, and machines are first-class principals. In fact, you'll see machine accounts listed along with user accounts when exploring the Windows directory or when editing per-object security settings (such as the permissions on a file).

Regardless of which of these operating systems you happen to be running, as a developer of distributed systems you should always think of machines as principals. This will help you distinguish between the human sitting behind the console and the machine with which the human is interacting. Failing to make this distinction is one of the many reasons that security programming seems so obscure to many otherwise confident and competent Windows developers.

Authentication

When Alice (a principal) wants to establish a secure channel with Bob (another principal), the system must use some form of handshake to give Bob a warm fuzzy feeling that he is really talking to Alice as opposed to a bad guy masquerading as Alice. Depending on several factors, the warm fuzzy feeling may even be mutual (Alice might be assured that she's really talking to Bob).

If Bob is a machine, and Alice is simply logging in interactively, the handshake might be as simple as Bob popping up a dialog to ask Alice for her password. Once Alice is logged in, anything she types at the keyboard will be implicitly private between her and Bob. Of course, this statement assumes that Bob is a local machine rather than a remote machine being exposed to Alice via some mechanism such as **Windows Terminal Services.**

This is an example of authentication. As mentioned earlier, authentication is the process by which one principal proves his or her identity to another principal. Sometimes we want to clarify the difference between the case in which Alice proves her identity to Bob but doesn't expect proof of Bob's identity and the case in which there is a mutual warm fuzzy feeling. This latter case is known as **mutual authentication,** which is clearly a desirable trait in a secure system. In our example, Alice can generally authenticate Bob by simply looking at the PC and verifying that it hasn't been tampered with or replaced with an imposter machine that would like to learn Alice's password.

What happens if Alice logs in to a machine named AlicesMachine (via the interactive authentication protocol previously described) and then starts a process that connects to Bob on Alice's behalf, across a network? Alice is once again talking to Bob, but mutual authentication and confidentiality are clearly going to be considerably more difficult to achieve. In this case, the authentication protocol that Alice and Bob must use cannot be implemented via a simple dialog box, for even if AlicesMachine collects the password from Alice, AlicesMachine cannot simply ship this password across the wire to Bob. A bad guy could be listening on the network using one of a number of freely available network sniffers (this is much easier and safer than physically replacing someone's PC). The protocol used in this case will be a **network authentication protocol,** which uses cryptographic techniques to introduce Alice and Bob and allow them to have an authenticated conversation with one another. If Alice and Bob so choose, they can even encrypt the packets they send back and forth to hide the contents from bad guys. Imagine for a moment how difficult this problem is, and you'll begin to appreciate what a fascinating subject network authentication really is.[10]

Throughout this text, the term *authentication* will generally be used whether the process occurs over a network or not, or whether it's mutual or not. Where the situation demands more clarity, the terminology will be more specific.

Establishing a Secure Channel

When Trent helps Alice authenticate Bob over a network, he also helps Alice and Bob establish a **secure channel.** As long as Alice uses this channel to communicate with Bob, the two principals can assure one another that their communications are authentic. Ensuring authentic communication can mean guaranteeing detection when a bad guy tampers with the data flow by changing, deleting, reordering, or injecting packets. In many cases, it can also mean that communication between Alice and Bob is protected from prying eyes. To make this work, Trent may provide Alice and Bob with a secret cryptographic key (known as a **session key**). This key is used to sign the data stream to allow the detection of tampering, and perhaps to seal the data stream (via encryption) to foil eavesdroppers.

Domains

The main function that a Windows **domain** provides is that of Trent: The domain is an authority that allows central storage of password material (either **cleartext** passwords or OWF passwords—it doesn't really matter from a conceptual standpoint). A domain is a scope within which principals may be created; it provides a database to store information about those principals, and it provides authentication services. For security purposes, a domain is a very convenient boundary within which security policies may be defined independent of other domains. Ultimately, a domain is a somewhat abstract concept.

Whereas a domain is abstract, a **domain controller** (**DC**) is a very concrete concept: It is a single machine that physically provides these services (authen-

---

[10] Understanding network authentication was a turning point in my life; it was only after gaining this understanding that I began to really enjoy security programming because it had become much more concrete.

tication, hosting of the security database, and so on). Sometimes a single domain controller will suffice; however, for large domains with thousands of principals, perhaps spread over a large geographic area, multiple physical machines (domain controllers) will be required to provide low-latency and high-availability service throughout the domain. Clearly this will require some form of replication of the database.

The way this replication works is important to a developer who wants to programmatically modify information in the security database. In Windows 2000, the database is physically managed in the **Active Directory,** and each domain controller maintains a replica of certain parts of the directory. The multimaster replication model in the directory makes updates quite easy: A programmer can simply contact the closest domain controller in the domain and make an update, and the changes will propagate (eventually) to the peer domain controllers (see Figure 1.1).

In earlier versions of Windows NT, there is no directory service. The database is stored in the registry of the **primary domain controller** (**PDC**), and replicated (read-only) copies are maintained on a set of **backup domain controllers** (**BDC**). Similar to Windows 2000, all domain controllers provide authentication services and access to the security database. However, as shown in Figure 1.2, without the directory service, any changes to the database must be made on the primary domain controller (the master); these changes will eventually be pushed to the backup domain controllers (the slaves). Other than

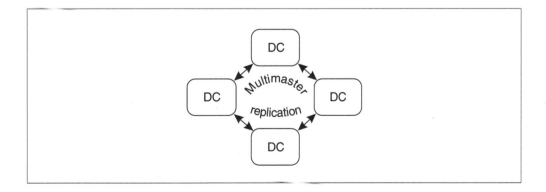

Figure 1.1   Windows 2000 domain controllers

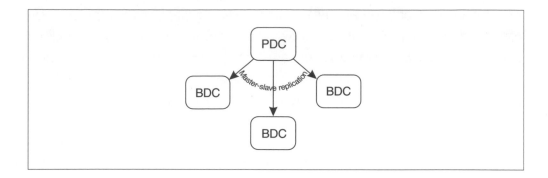

Figure 1.2. Windows NT 4 domain controllers

this difference, you can pretty much think of a domain controller without wor-
rying whether it is a PDC or a BDC (in Windows 2000, there is no such
distinction).

Organizational Units

In Windows 2000, it is possible to subdivide a domain into **organizational units**
(**OUs**). This doesn't change the way authentication works; the domain is still
the authority. An organizational unit is simply a smaller boundary with its own
security policy, making the administrator's job a bit easier. Often a domain
administrator will allow another principal to administer the resources and
security policy within a particular OU to help shoulder the load, but this really
doesn't affect the fundamental model of how security works in Windows. It's
just a more convenient administration model.

Local Security Authority

The **Local Security Authority** (**LSA**) is the subsystem in Windows that is responsible for performing the core duties of an authority, that is, providing authentication services. This subsystem runs in a separate, highly privileged process
(LSASS.EXE) on each Windows machine. That's right—each machine that
runs Windows has its own built-in authority. What this means is that you don't
need to have a sophisticated infrastructure in order to have security on any
given machine; rather, you can simply leverage the local authority and create

principals within its scope. In this case, the name of the authority is simply the name of the machine itself, and each account created within the authority's database is known as a **local account.**

What is really neat about the LSA is that it allows tremendous flexibility, making it easy for small systems to grow. An isolated machine has its own LSA and a private security database, and the administrator of the machine can define accounts for each principal that will need access to it. When the administrator decides to connect several previously isolated machines together (via a local area network [LAN], for instance), he or she simply needs to synchronize the passwords of the accounts on each machine. Even though there is no centralized authority, this will quickly provide a simple connected system that can perform network authentication.

To enable this feature for small networks, local accounts have a special characteristic that allows each LSA to authenticate a principal with a local account in a special way. Here's a concrete example: Imagine two machines, MAC1 and MAC2. If the administrator of these machines adds an account Alice to both authorities, you'll of course end up with MAC1\Alice and MAC2\Alice, which, as mentioned previously, represent completely separate principals because the authorities are different. (The SIDs are, of course, different as well.) However, if the passwords are the same on both machines, the LSA is designed to treat them as if they were the same principal (at least with respect to network authentication). So if Alice logs into MAC1 and then starts a process that connects to MAC2 on her behalf, the LSA on MAC2 can authenticate Alice and create a logon session for her, using MAC2\Alice as the principal. To reiterate, Alice is logged in as MAC1\Alice on MAC1, and she is now also logged in (via the network) to MAC2 as MAC2\Alice. This is incredibly convenient for small businesses that can't afford a domain controller. (To promote a machine to a domain controller, that machine must be running a more expensive version of Windows.)

As the system grows, this local account mechanism will start to break down (administration is difficult and the trust issue mentioned earlier starts to rear its ugly head). When the administrator is ready, he or she can promote one of the machines on the LAN to become a domain controller, which at a conceptual level simply increases the scope of its authority. For this discussion, let's say the administator promotes MAC2 to be a domain controller and calls the new domain DOMA. The LSA on MAC2 now provides services not only for the local machine but also for all machines that register as principals within DOMA. Each account that is created within the domain is a **domain account,** which means that DOMA\Alice will be different from MAC2\Alice or MAC1\Alice.[11]

As the system grows further, a potential problem is that security databases are normally stored in the registry, which limits their physical size. This is one reason why in Windows 2000, although *local* security databases are stored in the registry (as before), each *domain* security database is tucked away in the directory service, which scales much better.

At each stage of growth, the tools used to manage the security database are similar, reducing the learning curve for the administrator; the programming model is also the same, reducing the learning curve for the developer. The run-time model is the same as well because it is abstracted behind the LSA and programmatic interfaces that shield applications from the differences among various network authentication protocols. (The protocols used to authenticate principals represented by local accounts as opposed to domain accounts are different in Windows 2000.)

Trust

One obvious drawback of introducing a central authority (Trent) into a system is that if a bad guy quietly compromises Trent, he or she can force Trent to say things he wouldn't normally say. This is why we don't all belong to a single global authority. In practice, islands of authority form, with the boundaries being dictated by trust.

For example, take Microsoft and Sun, two fierce competitors.[12] Imagine the two companies relying on a single authority (Trent, say) to authenticate principals in both companies. Imagine a machine (with infinite computing power)

---

[11] One other back door eases the transition from small company to large enterprise: A principal logged in using a domain account on one machine may be authenticated using a local account on another machine that is not in the same domain, provided the principal names and passwords match. However, this is a special case; don't let mechanisms like this fool you into thinking MAC1\Alice is somehow related to DOMA\Alice. They are entirely different principals scoped by entirely different authorities.

[12] At least as of this writing, but Murphy's law dictates that by the time this book is on the shelves, they will have merged into a huge conglomerate.

that could act as the authority in this case. Would that machine be managed at Microsoft's or Sun's campus? Who would be the administrator of that machine, a Microsoft employee or a Sun employee? If Microsoft gets to administer the machine, Sun must trust the administrator at Microsoft not to impersonate Scott McNealy. If Sun gets to administer the machine, Microsoft must trust Sun not to impersonate Bill Gates.

Understanding trust is one of the keys to unlocking the mysteries of security programming. Commercial operating systems such as Windows are designed to be secure, but just what does this promise of security mean? Most developers don't bother to think about security, and many even scoff at it. One reason for this is that the overwhelming majority of Windows developers working in the commercial world happen to also be administrators of their own Windows machine. There doesn't seem to be any security constraints for administrators. To take an example, an administrator is allowed to look at the password stash in the registry where the passwords are stored for the machine itself as well as for any NT services and COM servers that run as distinguished principals.[13] What sort of security is this?

The crux of the issue is that there are no guarantees. The measure of a system's security, at least from a conceptual standpoint, is not an objective quantity. Rather, it is subjective and is proportional to the amount of trust that one places in the operating system itself and in the administrators who define the security policy. If you don't trust Trent, or the administrator who operates Trent, you shouldn't ask to become a principal in that system.

In fact, this idea of trust actually extends all the way down into the operating system itself. Consider, for example, a device driver. Code running in kernel mode on a Windows machine has tremendous power there and is not subject to any sort of security checks when accessing resources on the local machine. Device drivers are simply pieces of code that you must trust either to help enforce the security policy of the system or not to interfere or try to subvert that policy either maliciously or accidentally. Certain user-mode code

---

[13] Technically, as of Windows NT 4 Service Pack 4, administrators can no longer view the cleartext passwords for NT services (LsaRetrievePrivateData fails with an access denied error), but even in Windows 2000 as of this writing, COM servers and other secrets such as the machine account password are visible.

also must be trusted in this way because it's an integral part of the operating system.

The key is to define a boundary around all these trusted elements, and, in fact, there is such a definition. The **trusted computing base (TCB)** is defined by Federal Standard 1037C as follows:

> [The] totality of protection mechanisms within a computer system, including hardware, firmware, and software, the combination of which is responsible for enforcing a security policy. Note: The ability of a trusted computing base to enforce correctly a unified security policy depends on the correctness of the mechanisms within the trusted computing base, the protection of those mechanisms to ensure their correctness, and the correct input of parameters related to the security policy.

In the Windows operating system, kernel-mode code (device drivers, etc.) is considered part of the TCB. By installing an application as a **service**, an administrator can also add user-mode code to the TCB. What it boils down to is that the administrator of the system *defines the boundary of the TCB* on that system, and therefore becomes a very powerful entity indeed. The administrator of a given machine, at his or her discretion, can install good applications that provide well-needed functionality in a timely and correct fashion. The same administrator can install evil applications that try to guess your password and send nasty email messages to the first 50 friends you've listed in your address book.

The alternative to this is the military model of security,[14] in which mandatory access controls reign. If you think you feel constrained by Windows security, consider working at the NSA[15] (or its equivalent in your country of choice) for a week; a typical software developer will be dying to rejoin the ranks of the

---

[14] *Network Security* (Kaufman, Perlman, and Speciner 1995) has a very approachable discussion of the difference between commercial and military models of security (or more specifically, discretionary vs. mandatory access control).

[15] For those unfamiliar with the acronym, NSA stands for the National Security Agency, an agency of the U.S. government whose existence was for a long time hidden from even the highest-ranking government officials. The NSA is responsible for making and breaking cryptographic codes, and they guard their secrets with an iron fist.

commercial world in less than a day. In determining an appropriate security policy for any given system, the tension between ease of use and bulletproof security is often critical to its success; as in any engineering undertaking, there are trade-offs here that one must choose. Windows provides a very usable system that can be locked down (using discretionary, as opposed to mandatory, access control) to varying degrees of rigidity, but by definition, the administrator of the system ultimately determines the security policy and the boundary of the TCB.

Principal–Authority Trust

If BobsMachine is a member of the Trent domain, BobsMachine implicitly trusts Trent to vouch for (authenticate) principals in that domain. If Alice is a member of the Trent domain who wants to log in to BobsMachine (interactively, say), Trent will obtain proof of Alice's identity and indicate to BobsMachine that Alice is who she says she is. Because BobsMachine doesn't maintain a local copy of Alice's password, he must rely on the trust he has in Trent to feel comfortable that the user typing on his keyboard is really Alice (see Figure 1.3).

But what happens when Mary, a member of Trudy's domain, attempts to connect to BobsMachine? Bob trusts Trent, not Trudy. However, Trent may trust Trudy. In this case they can work together to help Bob and Mary authenticate

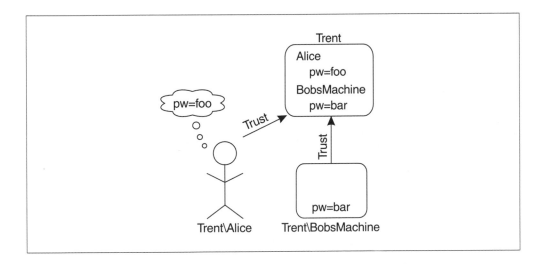

Figure 1.3. Principal–authority trust

one another (or perhaps they can just hang out together and read tongue-tangling paragraphs like this one).

Authority–Authority Trust

Because domains not only perform the role of Trent (by providing authentication services) but also act as boundaries for implementing security policies, it is often useful to divide an organization into several smaller domains rather than trying to force a single global security policy on the entire organization. Let's look at a concrete example to see how multiple domains in an organization can collaborate.

As an organization grows, one department (say, HelpDesk) might want principals in their domain (which has a security policy designed specifically for HelpDesk) to access resources in another domain (perhaps Sales). One way to make this work would be to move all the principals in HelpDesk over to the Sales domain. This would not only be painful from an administrative point of view, but also would completely change the topography of the security policy of the organization. Prior to the change, HelpDesk and Sales had separate domains with different security policies (perhaps HelpDesk had a very strict account lockout policy because people in the engineering department kept walking around behind the counter trying to guess the one password used by everyone at the desk so the engineers could log in and play pranks on them). After the change, there would no longer be two separate domains, and both departments would share a common security policy (assuming they weren't divided into two separate organizational units). This would make both departments rather unhappy—the Sales department prefers to have a more relaxed policy, whereas HelpDesk prefers a stricter policy. So let's leave HelpDesk and Sales in their own individual domains and find another solution.

Another option is to allow each individual in the HelpDesk domain to trust not only the HelpDesk domain but also the Sales domain. But once again, this would be an administrative nightmare. A much simpler approach to cross-domain authentication is simply to have Sales trust HelpDesk. In this case, when a principal in HelpDesk wants to talk to a principal in Sales, the two authorities cooperate in the authentication mechanism. In order for this collaboration to be secure, HelpDesk and Sales must authenticate with one another.

This is traditionally implemented by having HelpDesk register an account with Sales (complete with a password, just like any other principal) so that HelpDesk can prove its identity to Sales and establish a shared session key. If bidirectional trust is required, Sales will register an account with HelpDesk as well.

In Windows security jargon, these cross-authority accounts are known as **trust accounts.** You've already seen that any time a principal becomes a member of a domain, there is an implicit trust relationship: The principal trusts the domain. Machines may also join domains, but this is just another example of a principal joining a domain. So machines in a domain also implicitly trust the domain. All that has been done now is to extend this concept to authorities. One authority (Trudy) may establish an account with another authority (Trent) so that Trent's principals can authenticate with Trudy's principals.

Under Windows 2000, trust relationships are usually implicit. Most domains within an enterprise will typically reside in the same Active Directory **forest,** which allows Windows to set up implicit, bidirectional **transitive trust** relationships between the domains automatically, following their arrangement in the DNS hierarchy. *Transitive* means that if several authorities are linked via a path of trust, they all trust one another without having to explicitly set up trust relationships between each pair. Kerberos makes this possible (see Chapter 7).

In earlier versions of Windows NT, trust relationships must be configured manually, and because of the nature of the network authentication protocol on those platforms, these trust relationships are not transitive. This makes administration much more difficult in large enterprises. If a trust relationship is missing in this case, it means that there is a group of principals from one domain who will be completely unknown in the other domain and will not be able to authenticate, or establish a secure channel, with principals in that domain. Lack of trust relationships causes a significant percentage of the pain felt by distributed system developers. The discussion of network authentication protocols later in the book will explicitly show how these trust relationships are used and will help explain the importance of interauthority trust.

Figure 1.4 illustrates the difference between transitive and nontransitive trust relationships. Note that two trust relationships are required if two domains both want to trust each other. Clearly, transitive trusts are much simpler to maintain.

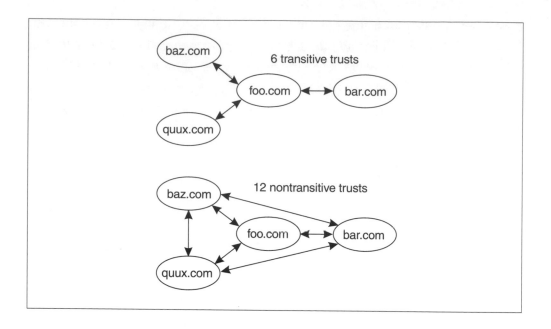

Figure 1.4. **Transitive versus nontransitive trust relationships**

Summary

- Principals are the entities in a system that can be distinguished from one another in a secure fashion.

- Each principal has credentials that, when presented, provide proof of the principal's identity. This usually takes the form of a password but can also be something more exotic, such as a smart card.

- The process of proving one principal's identity to another is known as authentication. *Mutual* authentication further ensures that *both* principals are authenticated to each other.

- Authentication enables the establishment of a secure channel so that the actual data being sent back and forth between the two principals can be verified as being authentic (that is, it hasn't been forged, or perhaps even seen, by a bad guy).

- Machines are also principals.

- Each principal is identified via a SID, which is a unique value that has a hierarchical internal structure that also indicates the authority that issued the SID. Well-known SIDs should be constructed programmatically to avoid localization issues.

- A domain is an abstraction that acts both as an authority and as a security boundary within which an administrator can set policies.

- The Local Security Authority (LSA) runs on each Windows machine, providing authentication services.

- Security in Windows is all about trust. Principals trust authorities to provide authentication services.

- Trust extends down into the operating system itself. The trusted computing base (TCB) includes all code that has the potential to enforce or subvert the security policy of a given machine. Administrators, by definition, control what goes in the TCB and what doesn't.

- A single global authority will likely never exist. In practice, islands of authorities form, and these authorities may trust each other so that interauthority authentication is possible.

Chapter 2

The Environment

Prior to coming to grips with Windows security, COM servers and services often seemed somewhat mystical to me—exactly what was it that allowed them to run in the background (even while no human was logged on to the machine)? Once I discovered how security dictates the environment in which a process runs (via logon sessions, window stations, and profiles), I quickly developed an intuition for the way Windows works that I would never have had otherwise. I now find systems programming on Windows much more comfortable because I can make predictions about how my programs will behave that I never would have even considered before.

If you are developing distributed applications (or even just services that run in the background on the local machine), you should make it a priority to know what "run in the background" really means. You should be aware that writing daemons is very different from writing interactive applications. This chapter, along with Chapters 4 and 5, aims to help you develop this intuition.

Logon Sessions

During my day-to-day life at DevelopMentor, I am occasionally called upon to teach a class on location at a client's site. At most organizations, each day when I arrive in the morning I am invariably required to prove my identity to the security guard at the front desk. The guard gives me a badge that I must wear during my stay and return before I leave. The security guard has authenticated me and given me the badge so that I won't have to suffer the authentication process (it's more rigorous at some organizations than at others) at the entrance to each room I need to traverse. The badge is simply a mechanism that promotes efficiency and helps prevent others from making mistakes, and therefore is a great analogy for a **logon session,** which basically does the same thing for principals in the Windows operating system. With a badge, anyone in the organization can quickly verify my identity and authorization level. With a logon session, any subsystem on the machine can quickly verify a principal's identity and **authorization attributes.**[1]

When Alice logs in to AlicesMachine in the morning, AlicesMachine challenges Alice to prove her identity by requesting a password. The operating system takes this information and hands it off to the LSA for AlicesMachine (the LSA is analogous to the security guard), which verifies the password (this may require communicating with Alice's authority over the network) and creates a logon session for Alice. The logon session is one of the cornerstones of the environment within which Alice works, and developers of distributed systems should have a clear understanding of its role.

A logon session has classically been a very abstract notion for most developers because there is no specific API that allows you to access its contents, and thus there is very little documentation on what it is or how it fits into the big picture. Physically, however, a logon session *does exist* and consists of a collection of information about a principal who has logged in to a machine. A 64-bit number uniquely identifies each logon session from all others on a given machine.

---

[1] When tokens are discussed later in this chapter and the next one, you'll see that authorization attributes are technically stored in a *token,* not in a logon session. However, a token is simply part of the surface area of a logon session; it's the part you can touch as a programmer, as will be discussed shortly.

Conceptually, a logon session represents a principal's appearance on a machine. In the example, Alice introduces herself to AlicesMachine by logging in interactively, and a logon session documents the fact that the LSA has successfully authenticated Alice. Alice's logon session allows Alice to use secured resources on the machine (assuming she has been granted the correct access permissions on those resources, of course). Without a logon session, Alice would have no chance of accessing those resources unless she somehow subverted the security policy of the machine.

Why a session? Imagine that Alice logged in to AlicesMachine, selected five text files via Explorer, and pressed Enter to bring up five copies of Notepad, each displaying one of the files. If not for the logon session, Alice would need to prove her identity to AlicesMachine each time the operating system opened a new file on her behalf. Imagine if a program that you were running needed to open several files on the local hard drive and therefore prompted you five times for a password so the system could discover who was really opening those files. Not only would you get sick of typing your password, but you would also quickly become desensitized to typing your password at random times throughout the day in response to a prompt from the operating system. Although this is great in that it continually guarantees that it's still you sitting behind the console, it also makes it really easy for a **Trojan horse** to prompt you for your password. You'd be so accustomed to typing in your password that, as a software developer, you probably would have written a piece of code that temporarily turns off the ES_PASSWORD style bit on the password edit control and automatically pastes in your password.[2] To avoid this problem, once the LSA authenticates the user, it constructs a logon session that acts very much like the badge mentioned earlier. The logon session represents the principal on that particular machine. As long as the badge exists, it can be used to open local resources on the principal's behalf.

---

[2] One of my students showed me the trick of turning off the ES_PASSWORD style bit to discover plaintext passwords in amateurish tools such as DCOMCNFG, which naively reads the existing password and uses it to populate a password edit control. (To be fair, you must be an administrator to run DCOMCNFG.) More sophisticated tools such as User Manager in Windows NT 4.0 populate password controls with spaces, and even better tools (such as the Windows 2000 account editor) don't even display such a control unless you explicitly request to reset or change a password.

So Alice has logged in to AlicesMachine and now has a logon session there. Let's say that a program (running under the auspices of Alice's logon session) tries to access a remote resource (a file share, COM server, etc.) on a remote machine named BobsMachine. BobsMachine now also needs a logon session for Alice. The LSA on BobsMachine doesn't necessarily trust the LSA on AlicesMachine to give it a badge that supposedly represents Alice, and even if it did, simply passing the badge across the wire would make it easy for a bad guy to record and replay those network packets at a later time in order to masquerade as Alice.

In this case, we need concrete proof of Alice's identity in order to safely perform authentication across the network. In order for the LSA on BobsMachine to create a logon session for Alice, she once again needs to prove her identity. Should AlicesMachine pop up a dialog asking for Alice's password in this case? What if Alice runs a program on AlicesMachine and it goes into a loop, accessing files on *many* different machines, not just BobsMachine. Should the operating system prompt Alice for her password to set up remote logon sessions on each of these machines? Probably not—it's a bad idea to get users in the habit of typing their passwords when prompted at seemingly random times.[3]

The solution to the problem is simple: If the logon session caches Alice's **network credentials**—whatever information is required to authenticate Alice over the network, her password or OWF(password), for instance—then it can automatically answer any network authentication requests for processes running under the auspices of Alice's logon session. This allows Alice to safely walk away from AlicesMachine while it is doing work on her behalf. In fact, Windows provides a user interface feature that allows Alice to lock the console of AlicesMachine if she plans on walking away from it, so a bad guy can't hijack her interactive logon session. When she goes home for the night, she logs off, which tears down any processes running under her logon session and destroys the session itself.

---

[3] Yes, EXPLORER.EXE does in fact pop up a dialog if authentication fails, asking for alternate credentials. Is this a good idea? The other alternative would be to allow the user to establish multiple interactive logon sessions, and although this is possible (see Chapter 4), it wouldn't appeal to those users who already have difficulty understanding overlapped windows. Such is the double-edged sword of trying to provide an operating system that is all things to all people.

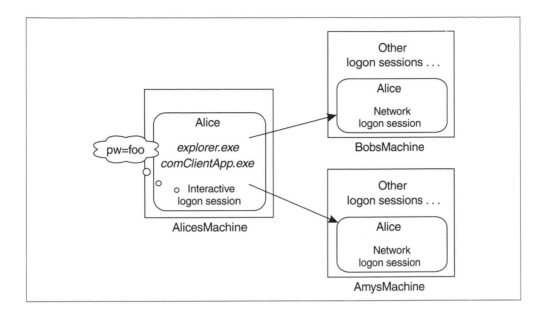

Figure 2.1. Network credentials

The beauty of the logon session is that applications launched on Alice's behalf can still do work for her, even across the network, without Alice needing to be physically present or even paying attention (see Figure 2.1). Alice can therefore be doing many types of work simultaneously, or just resting while her machine does work on her behalf. This model requires some responsibility on Alice's part, of course (she needs to remember to log out or lock her workstation when she goes to lunch), but it is very efficient and reasonable for a commercial operating system.

Having a firm grasp of logon sessions is critical for developers of distributed systems because the logon session dictates many elements of the environment within which a process runs. For instance, in the example mentioned earlier, Alice's interactive logon session on AlicesMachine has cached Alice's credentials in order to be able to satisfy network authentication requests automatically. However, Alice's network logon session on BobsMachine does not normally cache these credentials,[4] and thus processes running on BobsMachine that

---

[4] Under Windows 2000, using a Kerberos feature called *delegation*, this restriction may be relaxed, but only if certain knobs are turned just the right way in the security database (the details are covered in Chapter 7).

have access to Alice's logon session cannot use her credentials to access network resources on *other* machines on the network. Alice's credentials can normally be used only for a single network hop, and in this case that hop was from AlicesMachine to BobsMachine. This protects Alice, by the way, from BobsMachine misusing her credentials. Knowing which logon sessions have network credentials and which do not is critical in distributed application design and is a useful tool when debugging existing code.

Some of you may be wondering whether it's really safe to cache Alice's credentials in the logon session. Doesn't this make it possible for evil code in the system to impersonate you? The answer comes back to the issue of trust. If you don't trust the TCB of a particular machine, you should not log in to that machine. If the TCB on a machine has been compromised and you log in to that machine, it doesn't matter whether the system is caching your credentials or not, because a piece of evil code slipped into the TCB could simply record your keystrokes as you type in your password.

Tokens

Whenever Alice logs in to her workstation and the LSA creates a logon session for her, the LSA also creates something called a **token.** Each token is always associated with a single logon session, but a given logon session may have many tokens associated with it. Think of the tokens associated with a logon session as simply the surface area of the logon session: They are the things that you can see and touch via the Windows API as a developer. A token is an important level of indirection that allows individual processes to make localized changes to the security attributes for the logon session. Let me illustrate with an example.

Have you ever passed NULL for the `LPSECURITY_ATTRIBUTES` parameter when creating an executive object (for example, a process, thread, section, or semaphore)? Actually, I should probably ask if you've ever passed something *other than* NULL,[5] because most Windows developers have been trained from birth that NULL is the only appropriate value to pass for those parameters. If

---

[5] Many system-level developers pass in this data structure to control handle inheritance, but even in this case, most folks pass `NULL` for the `lpSecurityDescriptor` parameter, which I'm also categorizing as "passing `NULL`" for the purposes of this book.

you were expecting me to say "shame on you, get your act together," surprise! You've actually been doing exactly the right thing (even though you might sometimes have felt a little guilty about it). Passing NULL allows you to implement a consistent security policy by keeping your default security settings centralized in your application. Where are these defaults stored? In the token associated with your process.[6]

To see why tokens are needed, imagine a system without tokens. In such a system, each process's link back to the principal on whose behalf it was running is simply a handle to a logon session, and so the default security settings for new objects that you create (passing NULL for LPSECURITY_ATTRIBUTES) would logically be stored in the logon session data structure. This works fine if only one process ever runs under that logon session. However, if several processes were running simultaneously and one of them decided to adjust these default settings, the other processes would also be affected. Clearly we need a repository for volatile security settings associated with a logon session. The token provides this repository by acting as a localized extension of the logon session; this allows certain changes to be made without affecting other processes.

So when Alice logs in and launches several processes, those processes don't simply get a reference directly back to the logon session; instead, each process has its own copy of a token that links back to the logon session, thus providing each process with a certain amount of autonomy. Figure 2.2 shows an example.

It's also interesting to ask yourself this (somewhat remedial) question: Just what is a process anyway? A process is a collection of resources. It has a virtual address space and a handle table that is a collection of references to executive objects, and it contains one or more threads that bring the process to life, operating on the various resources in the process to get work done. Because Windows is a secure operating system, each resource you obtain clearly must be obtained in the name of a particular principal (so the system can perform access checks and audits as appropriate—the operating system doesn't just let you open random objects willy-nilly, as you are well aware). So ultimately, a process is a collection of resources that are being managed by a particular principal.

---

[6] Technically, both processes and threads can have tokens; a detailed discussion appears in Chapter 4.

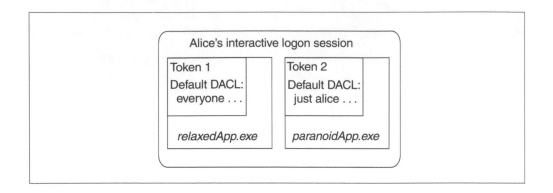

Alice's interactive logon session

Token 1	Token 2
Default DACL: everyone ...	Default DACL: just alice ...
relaxedApp.exe	*paranoidApp.exe*

Figure 2.2.   Each process has its own token

With this new perspective on what a process is, it's clear that a process simply cannot exist without an associated principal. And because principals manifest themselves on machines via logon sessions,[7] it's clear that each process absolutely must be associated with a logon session. To give the process some flexibility, each process has a token that links it back to the logon session, allowing threads within the process to make slight adjustments to the security settings for the process.

Let's go back to the original example of Alice logging in to AlicesMachine interactively. Once Alice provides her credentials to the logon process, the LSA creates a logon session and a token for Alice. The logon process then launches the shell for Alice, which is typically EXPLORER.EXE. The key is that Alice's token is attached to this new process, so that any work the process does (including any resources it obtains programmatically) will be "charged" to Alice. For instance, if the person sitting behind the console selects all the files on Alice's desktop and deletes them, and auditing has been enabled, *Alice* will be listed in the event log as having performed this action. In this case, EXPLORER.EXE performs all its work on Alice's behalf by virtue of the token attached to its process. The token is a piece of **out-of-band** information that developers don't normally bother thinking about (most folks can get away with

---

[7] Even the principal for the machine itself has a logon session, which is discussed in detail in Chapter 4.

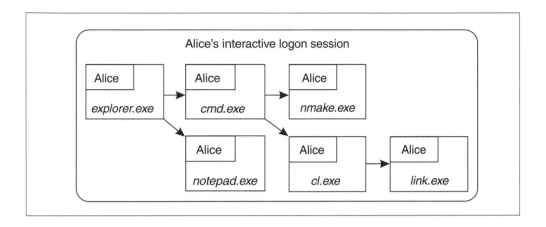

Figure 2.3.   Logon session propagation

this until they start writing distributed applications), but it keeps each process accountable for its actions by associating every action with a principal.

So the shell is happily chugging along under Alice's logon session, and now Alice double-clicks a text file. The shell detects the request and starts a new process by executing some routine that eventually calls `CreateProcess` to launch Alice's text editor, `NOTEPAD.EXE`. This new process must also be associated with Alice's logon session via a token, and therefore `CreateProcess` simply looks at the calling process's token (that is, Explorer's token) and duplicates it to create a new token for Notepad. Alice now has two processes, and each one is linked back to her single logon session via its own private token.

Imagine now that Alice starts a command prompt (`CMD.EXE`) via the shell, and from that command prompt, Alice runs `NMAKE.EXE` to build an app she's been working on, and NMAKE spawns a compiler and linker to perform the work. All these processes run within the same logon session and are linked back to it via their own individual tokens. It's so automatic that most developers never even think about it (see Figure 2.3).

The System Logon Session

Given this automatic propagation of Alice's token and logon session, it doesn't even seem possible to have multiple logon sessions running simultaneously on the same machine. However, remember the process that was running before

Alice even logged in? The logon process itself must run in some other logon session, right? The machine (remember, machines are principals too) also has a logon session, and a very special logon session at that. This logon session is created by the system at boot time, and it lasts until the machine is restarted or shut down.

This is the **System logon session,** and any process that runs within it is considered a trusted part of the operating system; in other words, that process lives inside the boundaries of the TCB. As a member of the TCB, a process running in this logon session can create other logon sessions (as the logon process did when Alice first logged on) as long as it has the correct credentials to present to the LSA. In fact, an API that will be discussed in more detail in Chapter 4, `LogonUser`, makes it quite easy to start up new logon sessions on the fly by simply presenting an authority/principal/password tuple.

Many systems developers need the capability to manage logon sessions programmatically, and because `LogonUser` cannot be called outside the TCB, they will typically want to have their code execute inside the System logon session. How can you get a piece of code to execute inside this special logon session? It's quite simple. Just like in the earlier example in which one process executing within a logon session called `CreateProcess` to launch an application running within the same logon session, you can do the same in this case. You just need a process *already running* in the System logon session to call `CreateProcess` on your behalf.

This is the job of the **System Service Control Manager** (**SCM**).[8] To bootstrap an application into the System logon session, you must write it as a **service** and install it by calling `CreateService` (see Chapter 4 for details). The System SCM can then launch your application so that the process runs in the TCB. Not just anyone can install services, for obvious reasons (if a bad guy can install a service on AlicesMachine, he can compromise the TCB of AlicesMachine). Remember who is responsible for defining the boundary of the TCB—the administrator of the machine. Administrators are allowed to install services at

---

[8] COM developers should note that the SCM referred to here is not physically the same as the COM Service Control Manager, although their roles are similar. In fact, I chose to call this entity the *System* SCM specifically to differentiate it from the COM SCM. Microsoft's documentation (as of this writing) doesn't make the distinction between the two.

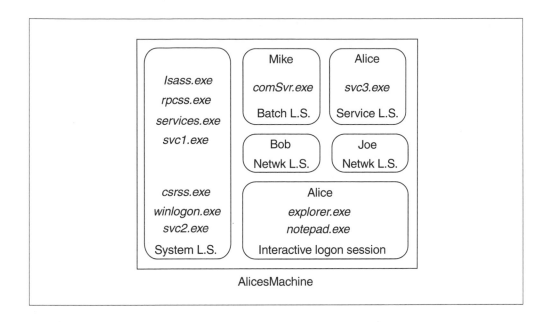

	Mike	Alice
lsass.exe	comSvr.exe	svc3.exe
rpcss.exe		
services.exe	Batch L.S.	Service L.S.
svc1.exe	Bob	Joe
	Netwk L.S.	Netwk L.S.
csrss.exe		Alice
winlogon.exe		explorer.exe
svc2.exe		notepad.exe
System L.S.		Interactive logon session

AlicesMachine

Figure 2.4. A typical collection of logon sessions

their discretion, and they must clearly trust any service they install into the TCB to help enforce the security policy, not to compromise it. It's all about trust! Figure 2.4 shows a typical example of what AlicesMachine might look like when Alice is logged on, including the various types of logon sessions that are discussed in Chapter 4.

Window Stations

Earlier an example was presented in which Alice uses the shell to select a bunch of files and delete them, and it was noted that even if Alice doesn't happen to be the person sitting behind the console (perhaps she left her desk without locking her console, and a bad guy took her place), it will be Alice's name that shows up in the event log as being charged with deleting those files. Well, wouldn't it be possible for a piece of code executing on Alice's machine to reach in and *programmatically* do the same thing? For instance, one could imagine a bad guy writing a piece of code that watches for an Explorer window to appear and then sends fake keystrokes (via `SendMessage` or `PostMessage`) to the window to simulate Alice deleting files. Alice would watch in horror as her work for the last three months was deleted. In fact, it's possible that the bad guy could initiate this remotely from a safe location (for instance, if it were written as a COM server).

Well, you might be thinking, surely each window has security settings associated with it to keep this sort of thing from happening. It turns out that this is not the case. For whatever reason (perhaps for backward compatibility with older platforms, but more likely for efficiency), each window does not maintain its own individual security settings. It's the environment in which each window lives that keeps it secure. A **window station** is a secure executive object that encapsulates an entire USER environment, complete with a clipboard, atom table, and a set of one or more **desktops.** Each window handle is only valid within the window station where it was created (akin to the idea that virtual addresses are only meaningful within a single process). By locking down an entire window station versus individual windows, we simply widen the boundary where security checks need to be performed, thus tremendously improving the performance of the system and simplifying the programming model for user interface developers.

Each process is always associated with a window station, and window stations are assigned at process creation time based on the logon session with which the process is associated (in fact, window station names are normally constructed based on the logon session identifier). To take a concrete example, before Alice logs in to AlicesMachine, there are several processes already running on AlicesMachine under the System logon session (for instance, system services such as the RPC subsystem). There is a window station for the System logon session that naturally hosts these processes. When a COM server is activated (say, from a remote client) on AlicesMachine, the COM Service Control Manager will normally run the server process in a distinct logon session, in which case the server process will run in a window station created specifically for that logon session.

When Alice logs in interactively, her logon session will be assigned to a special window station for the interactive user, named **Winsta0**, which is different from the other two window stations discussed so far. This window station is known as the **interactive window station,** and it's special because it's the only window station that can ever receive input from the user sitting behind the con-

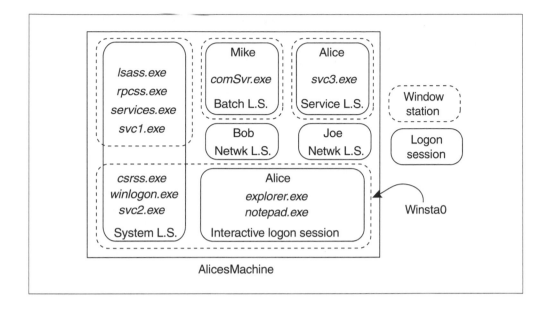

Figure 2.5.   A typical collection of window stations

sole. It's also the only window station whose windows will be displayed on the screen. This prevents the COM server (activated earlier) from being able to send messages to Alice's windows or create its own windows on Alice's window station (perhaps to prompt her for a password illegitimately). Because Alice has her own private window station, with her own private clipboard, she doesn't have to worry about that COM server stealing information from her clipboard or scraping her screen while she's working.[9] Figure 2.5 shows a typical array of window stations.

Whereas tokens are used to link processes to logon sessions, window stations are generally used to provide separate USER environments for each logon session. That being said, sometimes it is useful to have a process that is associated with an alternate logon session be able to display windows in Alice's window station or perhaps read Alice's screen. Imagine a screen-reader accessibility application that runs as a service in order to be part of the TCB.

---

[9] Technically, a process may dynamically attach to a different window station at runtime, but there are strict access controls on window stations (see Chapter 5) that keep Alice protected.

Normally, services that run in the System logon session would run under the window station assigned to the System logon session, not Winsta0. However, the System logon session is extremely privileged (being part of the TCB) and therefore has just as much access to Winsta0 as does Alice's logon session. This particular service might want to use a special option that causes the process to run in Winsta0 rather than the natural window station created for the System logon session. (The name of this option, when specified via the administrative tools for services, is "Allow service to interact with desktop.")

Any process you create can be forced to run in a particular window station. Although the details will be discussed later, for now be aware that window station assignment is normally a no-brainer when you're launching applications that all live in a single logon session. But whenever you take logon session management into your own hands, you'll need to be very aware of how window stations are assigned, lest you assign a process to a window station that doesn't grant access to the process's logon session.

The other gotcha with window station assignment hearkens back to the definition of Winsta0. This is the only window station whose windows can be seen or touched by humans; that is, Winsta0 is the only interactive window station,[10] and all others are considered **noninteractive window stations.** If you create windows in noninteractive window stations (for instance, the window station associated with the System logon session), you'll get a valid window handle, but no human will ever be able to see your window. So if you call `DialogBox`, for instance, and wait until someone presses a button to call `EndDialog`, you'll get a nasty surprise because nobody will ever be there to press one of the buttons. In fact, the thread that called `DialogBox` will never return, and `DialogBox` will patiently wait for input that will never come.

The most obvious answer to this problem is "Don't do that." Don't put user interfaces in code running in noninteractive window stations. Don't put user interfaces into components that run in the background as COM servers.

---

[10] Terminal Services for Windows 2000 (or Terminal Server for Windows NT 4.0) provides somewhat of a twist on this: There can be many client *sessions,* and each session has its own interactive window station, each of which is named—you guessed it—Winsta0. So the model is the same even when seen through a Terminal Services session. See Kim (1998) for details on how Terminal Services gets away with having multiple executive objects that share the same name.

But how many C and C++ programmers use the ASSERT macro to give their debug builds a really nifty user interface that puts up a dialog when an assertion fails that shows exactly which line of code failed and prompts the developer who is testing the build to ask whether the system should wrap a just-in-time (JIT) debugging session around the process? It's clear that debug builds of your applications should always run in Winsta0, unless you either never call ASSERT or you've written your own version that works correctly in a noninteractive window station (see Chapter 5 for an example). Even then, debuggers sometimes have difficulty attaching to processes running in noninteractive window stations in JIT debugging scenarios.

How can you tell whether a given process will run in an interactive or a non-interactive window station? It depends on many factors, but the key is to first become aware of the *existence* of window stations and understand why they are necessary. Chapter 5 covers the basic rules of window station allocation and shows you when it's appropriate to bend those rules.

Processes

We've already seen two of the most important aspects of a process's security environment: the logon session in which it runs (coupled with the token, which acts as an umbilical cord to that logon session) and the window station in which it runs. However, there are other elements that contribute to a process's environment. Consider, for example, what happens when an application opens a registry key under HKEY_CURRENT_USER. Clearly, the system must map this key onto a physical registry hive, but the mapping depends on the security context of the application. If a process running in Alice's logon session attempts to open this key, the system should clearly use Alice's registry hive to satisfy the request. If a process in Bob's logon session attempts the same thing, the system should use Bob's hive. Printer settings and the user's desktop directory are other settings that are principal sensitive. All this information is stored in a file system directory known as the *user profile.*

Programs that are designed to run in the interactive logon session will naturally require access to the per-user state that is maintained in the user profile. Daemon processes (specifically COM servers) should *not* rely on any information in the user profile because profiles weren't designed with this in mind and aren't automatically loaded for COM servers, because loading a profile can be a very expensive operation. Sophisticated applications that broker logon sessions will sometimes need to worry about loading user profiles, however. Chapter 5 discusses these details.

Summary

- A logon session represents the presence of a principal on a machine. A single principal may have several logon sessions on a particular machine simultaneously, but each logon session represents only a single principal.

- Each process is associated with a logon session. Always.

- Each process is connected to its logon session via a token.

- A token provides a link back to the logon session, but also allows customization of certain volatile security settings such as default settings for new objects. This allows the system to apply a consistent security policy when new objects are created from within the context of a particular process. Passing NULL for LPSECURITY_ATTRIBUTES is usually the right thing to do!

- There is exactly one System logon session on each machine, which is created when the operating system boots and is destroyed when the operating system shuts down. Code that runs in this logon session is part of the TCB.

- The way to bootstrap a process into the System logon session is to write your program as a service. Thereafter, calling CreateProcess will inject other processes into the System logon session.

- Try to run as little code as possible in the System logon session. Assume that any bug in your code will compromise the security of the machine.

- Each window station provides an entire environment for a user interface, complete with clipboard, desktops, and window handles.

- Window handles are window station relative, not machine relative as you may have thought. Avoid using window messages as an interprocess communication mechanism.[11]
- User profiles store principal-sensitive environmental information such as environment variables, registry hives, and shell settings.

---

[11] For those familiar with the way the single-threaded apartment (STA) works in COM, be aware that the window messages used to dispatch messages to an STA are purely there to support thread switching within a single process. COM does not use window messages to perform interprocess communication.

Chapter 3

Enforcement

This chapter introduces authorization attributes (groups and privileges) and provides a discussion of access control that covers the three most common strategies in use today, including role-centric security. Although this chapter *does* introduce security descriptors and DACLs, it defers most of these details to Chapter 6 and remains focused on concepts and application design. The chapter also addresses the session-oriented nature of Windows security and how this affects your applications.

If you're reading chapters out of order, I recommend that you read this chapter before moving on to Chapter 6.

Authorization

If authentication answers the question "Who are you?" then authorization answers the question "What can you do?" There are a number of ways of answering this second question, and in many secure systems (including Windows), the answer takes the form of **authorization attributes.** The most obvious authorization attribute is the principal SID, since it's possible to grant or deny access directly to individual principals. However, this doesn't scale very well when administering nontrivial systems, so another type of authorization attribute is needed, the **group.**

By creating several groups, and granting access permissions to these groups as opposed to individual principals, an administrator makes it very easy to add new principals (or remove old ones) while preserving a consistent security policy. For example, if a particular database on the network is used for contact management, and the sales department needs access to it, the administrator can create a group called Sales and allow anyone in Sales to access the database, without having to explicitly list each principal. Anyone looking at the security policy for the database would see immediately that Sales was allowed to use the database, no matter who happened to be in the Sales department on any given day.

Another type of authorization attribute is called a **privilege.** Whereas groups are used in access control decisions dealing with individual objects, privileges control security policy decisions in a more sweeping fashion, as will be demonstrated a bit later.

Groups

An administrator can configure a group account in the domain security database, containing all the SIDs that belong in the group. The idea is that if Alice is assigned to a group, her **security context** will include an authorization attribute (a group SID), and she can be granted (or denied) access on the basis of this SID just as easily as she can be granted or denied access on the basis of her unique principal SID. Alice's authority is responsible for storing her group assignments and making these authorization attributes (group SIDs) available to any servers that authenticate Alice.

Groups are typically used to model an organization; for instance, a set of groups such as foo\sales, foo\engineers, and foo\staff makes an administrator's job much easier when someone new joins the organization. Groups can be nested in Windows 2000.[1] (This wasn't possible in earlier versions of Windows.)

Aliases and Roles

To make the model more flexible, an extra level of indirection is possible via the use of an **alias** (these are exposed to administrators as "local groups"). Aliases

---

[1] This assumes your domain is in *native mode,* which implies that all your domain controllers are Windows 2000 machines. See the Appendix for more details on groups in Windows 2000.

are similar to groups in that they represent a categorization of principals, but there are some major differences. Like groups, Windows identifies aliases via SIDs. Unlike groups, however, aliases are managed by the local security authority; an alias may be defined on any machine. This means that aliases have limited scope; in other words, if machine A defines an alias and assigns it to Foo\Alice, machine B won't ever know about this assignment. (Imagine if it didn't work this way—machine B would have to communicate with machine A and every other machine on the network to discover the aliases assigned to Alice.) This level of indirection is important for a couple of reasons: It helps deal with large organizations that have multiple cooperating authorities, and it can be used to decouple development-time and deployment-time constraints.

Say, for example, that AlicesMachine exposes resources (databases, files, printers, etc.) that are used by Foo\Sales and Bar\Accounting. By creating an alias AlicesMachine\TrustedDepartments and including Foo\Sales and Bar\Accounting in that alias, it is easy to grant access to both groups simultaneously by simply granting access to the alias. Later, if Quux\Marketing needed to be granted access to the same set of resources, it could also be added to the TrustedDepartments alias.

Aliases can include principals or groups from any authority, but may not include other aliases (this limitation exists even on Windows 2000).[2] On Windows 2000, where groups can be nested, aliases are less critical than on Windows NT 4, where group nesting is not allowed.

Aliases were designed to help decouple design- and development-time decisions from deployment-time decisions. Developers understand how their application fits together, including which subsystems need to have access to other subsystems. At design and implementation time, certain logical **roles** are evident; for instance, Supervisors, Staff, and Customers might be the logical roles for an application that simulates a pet store. Customers are allowed to purchase and pet the animals, staff are allowed to feed the animals, and supervisors are allowed to give raises. These constraints are all known at design time. At deployment time, the store manager (Bob, say) installs the software, but

---

[2] Note that on Windows 2000, custom aliases cannot be created on machines that are domain controllers, so you may want to consider using nested groups where you would have used an alias on that platform. Domain local groups work well for this.

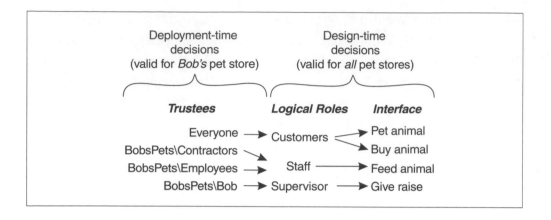

Figure 3.1.   Logical roles

doesn't know the details of the implementation (for instance, Bob doesn't know what access permissions need to be granted to various subsystems in the application). However, if the pet store software provides the list of logical roles, Bob can clearly provide concrete mappings for each logical role: For instance, BobsPets\Bob is the supervisor, BobsPets\Contractors and BobsPets\Employees are considered staff, and Everyone is considered a customer (Figure 3.1).

If the pet store software created three aliases when it was installed on Bob's machine, PS_Supervisors, PS_Staff, and PS_Customers, then all Bob has to do is add principals and groups to these aliases using the administrative tools built into Windows itself. Of course, the pet store application should describe the semantics of each of these roles in the documentation of the product. The developer can use these hardcoded aliases (discovering their actual SIDs dynamically via `LookupAccountName`) to make decisions at runtime, no matter where the product ships.

Another good example of logical roles (implemented using aliases) can be found by looking at Windows itself. Consider the Administrators alias on a machine: This acts as a logical role that defines who administers that machine. Any process running on that machine with a token containing the Administrators alias has administrative privileges there. The operating system often looks for this SID directly and grants or denies access based on its presence or absence; you can install services on a machine if you have this SID in your token. In a typical organization, how does a principal normally get included in this powerful role? The answer is that whenever you join a machine into a domain, the machine automatically bestows the Administrators role on the Foo\Domain Admins group (where *Foo* is the domain being joined). This shows how aliases and groups are designed to work together. The administrator of the Foo domain simply has to keep the Foo\Domain Admins group up to date, and all his or her administrative staff will have administrative privileges on all computers in the domain. The group is used to allow the administrator to model the organization, and the alias is used in an implementation-specific way in an application (in this case, the application is the operating system itself).

Using aliases this way is powerful but has a couple of drawbacks. First, all aliases on a machine live within the same namespace; note that in the pet store example I used a "PS_" prefix for each alias in a feeble attempt to avoid conflicts with other applications. Second, aliases are a machine-specific phenomenon, and there is no built-in infrastructure for pushing these definitions to a **server farm.** (The pet store example probably wouldn't require this, but many distributed applications care quite a lot about scalability.) Therefore, Microsoft Transaction Server (MTS) introduced (and COM+ carried forward) the notion of application-specific roles, and provided infrastructure for propagating them (along with other application and component attributes) to machines in a server farm. COM+ roles are discussed in more detail in Chapter 9, but if you understand the previous examples, COM+ roles are just another way to implement logical roles in an application.

Privileges

Imagine a directory structure as depicted in Figure 3.2, and imagine using the built-in Windows file system security editor to adjust the access control settings for directory A to deny all access to Alice. Then, on the file in directory C, grant Alice all access to that file. If Alice knows the full path to the file (`\A\B\C\C.TXT`), will Alice be granted or denied access when she attempts to open the file via `CreateFile`? Clearly, she has been granted access to the file, but should she even be able to *see* the file, considering that she's not allowed to see what's in directory A? Whenever I ask this question in a class or at a conference talk, about a fourth of the people think that she'll be

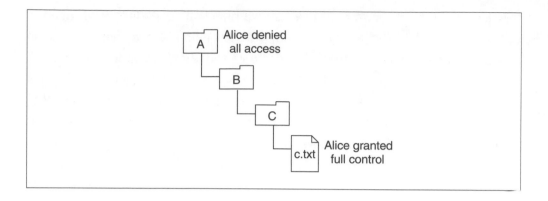

Figure 3.2.   An access control puzzle

granted access, and another fourth think that she'll be denied. The other half scratches their heads because they are surprised that they've never thought of this before.

The answer to the question is that it's up to the administrator of the machine to choose a policy, and the choice is determined via an authorization attribute known as a *privilege*. Privileges help administrators deal with global policy decisions like this one, and provide the flexibility to allow certain groups of users to be treated differently than others.

The privilege in this case is "Bypass traverse checking," and it's granted to Everyone by default. So it turns out that the answer to this question can be determined by the administrator of the machine, either on a global basis (by granting Everyone or no one the privilege) or on a per-principal, per-group, or per-alias basis. This is a particularly good example of one of the many privileges defined by the operating system. (See the appendix for a comprehensive list of privileges and what they mean.)

Privileges, like aliases, are local settings that apply to the machine where they are set, and to no other machines on the network.[3] The administrator of a machine may grant privileges to individual principals, groups, or aliases, and

---

[3] Domain controllers (DCs) in Windows NT 4 are an exception, in that all domain controllers for a particular domain share a common security database, including a common set of aliases and privileges; thus, any privilege assignments granted on the PDC percolate to all the BDCs in the domain.

when a principal establishes a logon session on that machine, he or she is granted the union of all privileges assigned to the principal's account directly or to any groups or aliases in which he or she is a member.

It seems as though system administrators of nontrivial enterprises must have a heck of a time making global security policy decisions, because privileges are local settings and are not global to the domain. To help the administrator provide a consistent security policy throughout the enterprise, Windows 2000 provides a group policy infrastructure (exposed via the directory service), which helps automate control over these per-machine settings. At runtime, Windows 2000 automatically applies these policies (which can control privilege assignments). The local policy object (managed by the LSA) allows localized customization of security settings, but only where the group policy doesn't provide a particular setting (group policy decisions by the domain administrator always take precedence over local policy decisions). In earlier versions of Windows NT, there was a separate tool called the Security Policy Editor, which was much more primitive but allowed an administrator to automate privilege assignment (as well as other registry settings) throughout the machines in the domain.

Discovering Authorization Attributes

Ultimately, the operating system and third-party applications need to be able to enumerate the authorization attributes (groups, aliases, and privileges) for each principal that requests service. For convenience and efficiency, this information is physically accessible via the token. Imagine that alice@foo.com establishes an interactive logon session on AlicesMachine. The Local Security Authority on AlicesMachine authenticates her (with some help from the foo.com authority), creates a logon session and a token, and populates the token with global authorization attributes (group SIDs) from Alice's authority, followed by local authorization attributes (aliases and privileges) from AlicesMachine (Figure 3.3).

If Alice then launches a monolithic application and starts requesting services by clicking buttons or typing commands, the application only has to look at its token to discover all Alice's authorization attributes. The application knows Alice's intentions based on the buttons she presses or the commands she types, and can therefore enforce an appropriate access control policy.

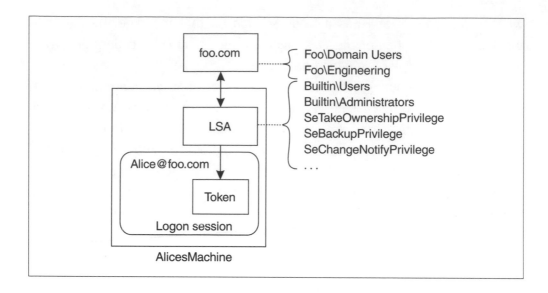

Figure 3.3.   Constructing a token

Distributed Applications

In a distributed application, things look much different. In this case, there are (at least) two processes involved, and they live on different machines: the client application (which may be a full-fledged native Windows application or simply a Web browser) and the server application. In this case, the server application is typically running long before any arbitrary client comes along, and will typically provide service to multiple clients simultaneously via the use of threads.

Because the server process must be launched before any client can make requests into it,[4] the server process itself must run under its own private logon session[5] and therefore will not be able to simply peek at its process token to discover an arbitrary client's authorization attributes. Instead, the server and client processes (and often the client's authority) will engage in a network authentication handshake (described in Chapter 7). Based on the results of this

---

[4] Even with a COM server, the server must be running (granted, server launch may be automated somewhat by the COM SCM, but nonetheless the server process must ultimately be running) before a client can successfully make a method call into the server.

[5] I've made a conscious choice here to ignore the Run As Activator feature in COM, which is virtually never used for distributed applications but is the most appropriate choice for nondistributed applications. This option is discussed in Chapter 9.

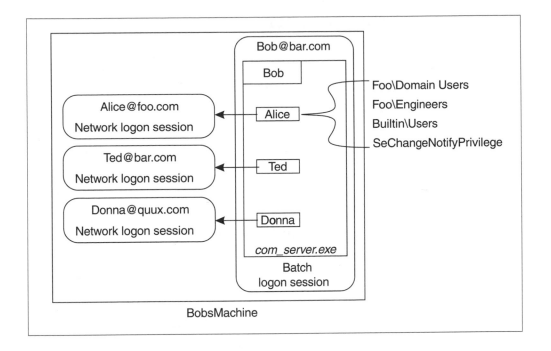

Figure 3.4 Server juggling client tokens

handshake, the LSA on the server machine constructs a **network logon session** to act as a badge for the client on the server machine, and produces a token for that session. This token can be thought of as a proxy (or stand-in) for the remote client, because it looks somewhat similar to a token that would have been produced for the client had the client logged in to the server box interactively. The authorization attributes in this new token contain the groups for the client (as specified by the client's authority), as well as the aliases and privileges that have been assigned to the client *on the server machine*. Figure 3.4 demonstrates this.

A distributed application will thus often need to juggle several tokens simultaneously: One token represents the logon session for the server process itself, and the other tokens represent the clients who are making various requests of the server. The server gleans the client's intentions via the COM method call or HTTP request, and just as in the monolithic application described earlier, it can now enforce an appropriate access control policy.

Objects and Security Descriptors

Windows provides built-in security for several different classes of objects, some of which include executive objects (processes, threads, semaphores, sections, etc.), file system objects (directories and files), registry keys, printers, and Windows 2000 directory service objects. Each of these objects provides fine-grained access control and auditing support for individual principals and groups of principals. Unlike traditional UNIX, for example, which has a very simple model for file system access control (an administrator can grant or deny read/write/execute permissions to three separate entities: the principal who owns the file, a single group, and everyone else), the model used in Windows is much more flexible (and considerably more complex as a result).

Each secure object in Windows carries a **security descriptor** (**SD**), which houses all the object's security settings, including the access control and auditing policies for the object. The security descriptor itself is a variable-length structure, primarily because the four data structures it contains are also variable length: an **owner,** a group, and two **access control lists** (Figure 3.5).

The group is technically called the **primary group**, and exists for compatibility with the (UNIX-like) POSIX subsystem, which requires that an owner and a group be designated for each object. This text generally ignores the primary group because it isn't important outside the scope of the seldom-used POSIX subsystem.

The owner of an object is generally the person who created the object in the first place, and is implicitly granted certain permissions. This method keeps peo-

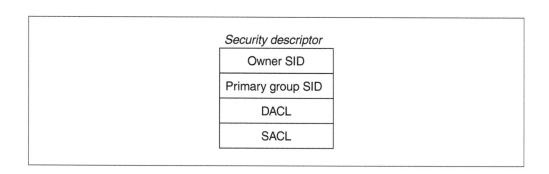

Figure 3.5.   Anatomy of a security descriptor

ple from accidentally locking down an object so that nobody at all has access to it (even to delete it). Ownership is covered in more depth in Chapter 6.

The access control lists consist of a **discretionary access control list (DACL)** and a **system access control list (SACL)**. The DACL (pronounced so that it rhymes with "jackal") is the list with which most Windows users are familiar— this list controls which principals, groups, and aliases are allowed to touch the object in various ways. A DACL can contain both positive and negative entries (positive entries grant access; negative entries deny access), thus allowing Alice to choose sophisticated access control policies. For instance, for a particular file, Alice can choose the following policy: "All Friends except Bob have read access." In this case, Alice grants read access to the Friends group via a positive entry in the DACL, and denies read access to Bob via a negative entry. The owner of an object controls the DACL, which is where the word *discretionary* comes in. Permissions on an object are granted at the owner's discretion.

The SACL controls auditing, and also can have positive and negative entries. In this case, however, a positive entry means "add an entry to the audit log if someone with this SID requests this type of access and it is *granted,*" whereas a negative entry means "add an entry to the audit log if someone with this SID requests this type of access and it is *denied.*"

Both access control lists employ an inheritance model, which is very simple in earlier versions of Windows NT but gets considerably more complex in Windows 2000. (Before you start to shiver, the Windows 2000 inheritance model is tremendously easier to administer and leads to more predictable behavior and a more maintainable system.) Inheritance simplifies the management of large object hierarchies, primarily in the file system, registry, and directory service, where it is not feasible for an administrator to manually specify an individual access control and audit policy for each object.

Regardless of the inheritance model in use, security descriptors are static containers; that is, to discover the security settings for an object, you can simply look at the security descriptor for *that object,* and ignore those of its parents. This model promotes efficiency at runtime, and the desire for efficiency also explains the reason why "Bypass traverse checking" is normally granted to Everyone. When this privilege is *not granted* to a principal, the file system must explicitly check each parent directory to discover whether traversal is allowed or denied, which reduces the performance of the system. Windows prefers to cache security settings for improved performance. Caching strategies are discussed later in this chapter.

Access Control Strategies

You've seen that tokens and logon sessions hold security-related information about principals, and that security descriptors hold security-related information about built-in secure objects in Windows. But how should one go about securing application-defined objects? First you need to consider the information that may or may not be at your disposal. In most secure systems, there are usually three pieces of information available to assist in access control decisions:

1. The authorization attributes for the principal requesting access

2. The intentions specified in the request

3. The security settings for the object to be accessed

Depending on how much of this information a server is able to discern at runtime, a more and more sophisticated access control policy emerges.

Impersonation Model

The impersonation model is the simplest because it only relies on the server being able to answer the first question. In other words, the server must be able to obtain a token for the client; in a distributed system, this means that the server must be able to authenticate the client (for example, they must share a common authority or have appropriate trust relationships). In this model, the server simply places the client's token on the thread that happens to be servicing the client, a technique known as **impersonation.**

Threads normally start life without any token, and thus, by default, they act on behalf of the logon session identified by the process token. However, in order to enable this simple model of access control, Windows allows each thread to temporarily take on an alternate identity. (The most direct approach is to simply call `SetThreadToken`, which is demonstrated in Chapter 4.) With the thread token in place, no matter what the client's request, the server will carry it out using the client's identity. Thus, the server doesn't have to worry about what the client is trying to do—it simply attempts to perform work on the client's behalf, and if it fails (perhaps a request to open a file will fail because the client hasn't been granted the appropriate access to that file), the server simply passes the failure code back to the client. I think of this as the *pass the buck* model, because the server is passing the responsibility to the underlying secure resource managers (such as the file system, registry, and kernel) to perform access control.

Impersonation is great for developing gateways such as a telnet application, where the client will start a remote session, and as the client types commands, the remote application will simply execute those commands and send the results back to the client. The telnet server has no idea what the client's intentions are, and it doesn't really care; as long as the client trusts the server to impersonate him or her, all is well. (The issue of trust as it relates to impersonation is discussed in Chapter 4.) If the client tries to do something he or she is not allowed to do, the server will fail on the client's behalf (since its thread is executing in the client's security context) and will inform the client of the failure.

Impersonation is also great for developing network file system redirectors as well as FTP and Web servers, where the client's intentions are known (the client wants to read or write a file), and the objects that the client is trying to access map *directly* to built-in objects that already have a sophisticated access control policy implemented by the operating system itself and administered directly via tools that ship with the operating system. In this case, when Alice requests the file \\bob\public\readme.txt, the file system redirector can simply impersonate Alice and open the file on her behalf. There is no need to build any further access control infrastructure, because the redirector simply passes the buck to the file system, which performs access control the same way it would for a local client.[6] See Figure 3.6 for an illustration.

This simple model begins to break down when the objects that a client is interested in are not easily mapped directly to single files or other objects that

---

[6] Technically, the file system redirector *does* add an extra level of access checks, because it must verify the client's access permissions to the file system share before attempting to do any work on the client's behalf. However, because the file system redirector impersonates Alice before accessing the file, this will never widen Alice's permission to the file—it will only serve to narrow those permissions. Alice must cross two hurdles as opposed to just one.

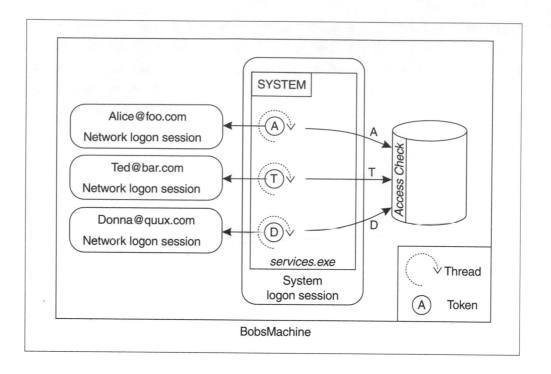

Figure 3.6   Impersonation model

already have built-in security. Imagine a server that manages text and image files for a document-imaging product. A client's request for a single logical document might be satisfied by opening *several* files, including text files and images that make up the logical document. In this case, a DACL needs to be applied to each of these files individually, which can get messy. A more difficult problem occurs if the system stores information about multiple logical documents in a single file (perhaps an index). What DACL should be placed on that index file? If the application simply impersonated its clients while it performed all its work, this DACL would need to include all possible clients. The whole point of using a simple impersonation scheme is to avoid having to deal with DACLs in your own application code. You get away with this by assuming that the system administrator will configure the DACLs using the administration tools built in to Windows. This sounds like a maintenance nightmare for the system administrator in this particular scenario.

This model simply melts in a three-tier system, however, because for one thing, prior to Windows 2000, the server could only get a token for a client (in other words, authenticate a client) that was at most a single network hop away. Having the middle tier simply impersonate and call into the back tier (typically a database) is conceptually reasonable, assuming the database provides built-in security, but it is not physically possible on Windows NT 4 because the client is two network hops away from the back tier, and authentication fails in this case.

Even in Windows 2000, where this single-hop authentication limit goes away in certain circumstances, there are other compelling arguments that suggest that access control should not simply be delegated from the second to the third tier via impersonation, including issues dealing with scalability and maintainability. This topic is covered in Chapter 9.

Role-Centric Model

If a server can glean not only the client's authorization attributes (via authentication) but also the client's intentions, it can implement an access control policy built around logical roles. For instance, in an RPC server that simulates a pet store, the server could glean the client's intentions based on the name of the function the client called (perhaps `FeedAnimals`) and could look in the client's token for an alias that the application had designated as being allowed to perform that action (in keeping with the earlier example, this would be PS_Staff). When the application is installed at Bob's Pet Emporium, the install program would set up these aliases, and Bob would be responsible for assigning these application-specific aliases to appropriate principals and groups in Bob's organization.

As mentioned earlier, support for this model is built in to COM+ in Windows 2000 (MTS in earlier versions of Windows). The reason is clear: COM+ was introduced to make it easier to build scalable three-tier **online transaction processing (OLTP)** applications, and the framers of COM+ knew that the classic impersonation model wasn't going to scale well. By providing automated role-based access checks via an interception layer (see Chapter 9), COM+ provides an easy-to-implement, easy-to-deploy security model that suffices for many applications.

When programming security, less application code is almost always better than more because it reduces the surface area that you expose to an attacker. (You must assume that the attacker knows every single bug in your code and is just waiting to exploit it.)

Object-Centric Model

Whereas the role-centric model depends exclusively on the authorization attributes and the intentions of a client (and often on the *class* of the target object), an object-centric model factors in the third question: Which particular object *instance* is the client after? This third model is the most powerful and flexible, and is the way the operating system itself works in most cases. Of the three models discussed so far, this model clearly requires the most blood, sweat, and tears to implement. However, more and more support is provided with each release of Windows to make it easier to transparently extend the security model used by the operating system to your own application-specific classes of objects.

The idea in this model is that each logical object in an application has an associated security descriptor, just like the secure objects in the operating system itself. One of the most challenging aspects of implementing this model used to be trying to duplicate the behavior of the security editors provided for the file system, the registry, and so forth. For instance, when you use REGEDT32.EXE and choose Security:Permissions to view or edit the DACL for a registry key, a nice little dialog pops up and allows you to add or remove a principal, group, or alias and to choose whether you want to grant or deny certain permissions to that entity. Prior to Windows 2000, this functionality was exposed via an undocumented interface housed in ACLEDIT.DLL (from what I've heard, it was an interface that only a mother could love), which didn't help independent software developers much.

To solve this problem on Windows NT 4, programmers often would create registry keys (or files) for each of their logical objects and have the administrator edit their DACLs via the built-in ACL editors in the operating system. Later, the application could extract the security descriptors for its own use or simply try to open the key or file corresponding to the logical object requested by the client and let the operating system perform the access checks. Besides feeling kludgy, the problem with this approach is that it only works if your logical object has permissions that map well onto the predefined permissions for files, registry keys, or whatever built-in class of object you happen to be using as a security proxy for your own internal objects.

Windows 2000 remedies this with a brand-new (and much more powerful) editor, which provides a user interface for editing the entire SD, and a well-documented programmatic interface.[7] Given this new editor, the major difficulty becomes managing the storage for the SD. In a three-tier system, where it's preferable to perform access checks as close to the client as possible for scalability reasons (see Chapter 9), the SD for the object must be available to the middle tier without much hassle. (It would be silly to make a round-trip to the third tier to scrape out the SD at each client request.) Clearly some sort of caching and replication strategy will help here.[8]

The final issue is that there is no automatic support in COM+ or MTS for implementing this model. You'll need to learn how to program security descriptors and perform your own access checking, auditing, and the like (this book will help with that).

A much simpler variation on this object-centric model may work if your objects don't require the sophisticated features that a full-blown security descriptor provides. Perhaps your object model is very simple in that there is only one principal (other than a system administrator) who can ever touch an object (perhaps the principal who created it in the first place). In this case, it's very easy to simply store the SID of the creator as a part of the object instead of a full-blown security descriptor. In this case, if an administrator wants to access the object, you can use a role-based decision to grant the administrator full control, and if a normal client wants to access the object, you could compare the client's SID with the SID that you stored with the object at creation time. It wouldn't kill your system to perform the comparison on the back tier, and COM+ propagates the SID of the original caller as out-of-band information with each method call. (This information is not limited to a single network hop,

---

[7] This tool can also be installed on Windows NT 4.0 Service Pack (SP) 4 (or greater), but it's not redistributable—it must be installed by the end user as part of the Security Configuration Editor add-on. See the SP4 readme file for more details.

[8] Of course, you should be very careful when sending this type of critical security policy information over the wire: It should at least be signed to protect it from external tampering.

and can be trusted as long as communication over each network hop—client tier to middle tier and middle tier to back tier—is individually authenticated.)

If you choose to implement a sophisticated object-centric access control model, be very careful to componentize your access checking logic so that you can rigorously test it with 100 percent code coverage. And, of course, rigorously verify that you are actually using it throughout your code. The more you can automate this, the better.

Choosing a Model

The first decision you should make is the easiest—whether to use impersonation as your primary mechanism for access control. Impersonation simply allows you to pass the buck to the next guy, and if the next guy is the file system or some other secure system whose granularity (and locality) matches that of your object model, then party on. However, in three-tier systems the middle tier can't simply pass the buck and expect to scale well, so you ought to choose a different mechanism.

If you can arrange the interfaces in the middle tier in such a way that you feel comfortable basing your access control policy solely on the interface or method being invoked[9] (coupled with knowledge of the caller's roles), then a role-centric model will make your life easy—incredibly easy if you happen to be writing COM components and can take advantage of COM+ or MTS.

For those of you who need a sophisticated object-centric model similar to the one that Windows exposes, obviously you're left writing code to manage security descriptors. However, the benefit you'll see is tremendous integration with Windows, both in terms of access control and auditing; this book will help you achieve your goal.

All three of these models leverage the notion of **single sign on,** which means that end users only have to know a single password to unlock not only Windows itself, but also your own application. By taking the time to learn the Windows security model and factor it into your designs, your applications will become more seamlessly integrated with Windows than ever before.

---

[9] Be aware that although COM+ supports method-level granularity for setting access control via roles, MTS only supports interface-level granularity.

What about Amazon.com?

If you are building a massively scalable Web application that will service millions of online users outside your enterprise, which of the models should you choose? Well, first you have to assume that you won't be able to authenticate 99.99 percent of your users, so the question is somewhat moot. Authentication requires a tightly administered environment; that is, there must be a path of trust from the server to the client's authority if the server is to have any chance of knowing who the client is. What if the server is running on Windows 2000, but the client is running on a Macintosh? Client-side certificates might eventually fill this gap, but public key infrastructures are still pretty new, and we are a long way from deploying this infrastructure to the masses in a standard way.

Ultimately, you'll have two types of users in this sort of system: authenticated users (typically administrators or other privileged individuals) and anonymous users. You'll have to treat the anonymous users all the same unless you build in your own application-specific authentication mechanism,[10] which is the model used by Web sites that require registration. (Most people despise having to register with a Web site, so this isn't a great solution for many .com companies.) As far as mapping anonymous users to accounts in your security database, your Web server of choice will do this for you. (For instance, Internet Information Server [IIS] will automatically map all anonymous HTTP or FTP requests to an account called IUSR_MACHINE,[11] where MACHINE is a placeholder for the NetBIOS host name of the machine.) Once this is done, you can choose any of the three models, but keep in mind that all anonymous users will be treated as a single well-known principal as far as the operating system is concerned.

Caching Mechanisms

Windows provides several caching mechanisms that significantly enhance runtime efficiency, and it's incredibly important for the designer of a system-level application to be aware of the ramifications of these mechanisms. Windows

---

[10] Some third-party middleware such as Site Server provides this functionality.

[11] When you install IIS, the setup program adds this account, but you can change the principal and credentials used on a per-resource basis.

security is very much session oriented, in that the runtime performs expensive security checks such as authentication and access control when a logical session is opened; as long as the session is in use, the cost of performing further security checks is negligible. I'll make this concrete by illustrating two of the most important types of sessions: logon sessions and handles.

Recall that when alice@foo.com establishes a logon session on AlicesMachine (perhaps by pressing Control-Alt-Delete and typing in her password), the LSA on AlicesMachine constructs a logon session and a token for Alice that contains all of Alice's authorization attributes. This includes groups from Alice's authority (foo.com), plus aliases and privileges from AlicesMachine. These attributes are cached and flattened in the token for efficiency, in three logical steps:

1. All groups in which Alice is a member are included in the token.

2. The union of all alias assignments on AlicesMachine that apply directly to Alice or to any of her groups is included in the token.

3. The union of all privilege assignments on AlicesMachine that apply directly to Alice, to any of her groups, or to any of the aliases (discovered in step 2) is included in the token.

The effect of this caching mechanism is twofold. First, whenever an access check needs to be performed, there is no need to look up any of Alice's authorization attributes by contacting her authority, because they are already cached in the token. Second, if anything changes after Alice has already established a logon session (for instance, if Alice is granted a new privilege), or if her group or alias assignments change in any way, the current logon session (and any tokens linked to that session) won't be affected by this change. This trade-off in cache coherency versus runtime efficiency is totally reasonable considering that these sorts of changes don't happen very often; even if they did, without the stable environment provided by a logon session, a developer would have to contend with lots of tricky failure modes and race conditions. When Alice closes her logon session and establishes a new session, any new settings will take effect at that point.

An interesting consequence of the distributed nature of Windows' authorization settings is that Alice's token will often look quite different depending

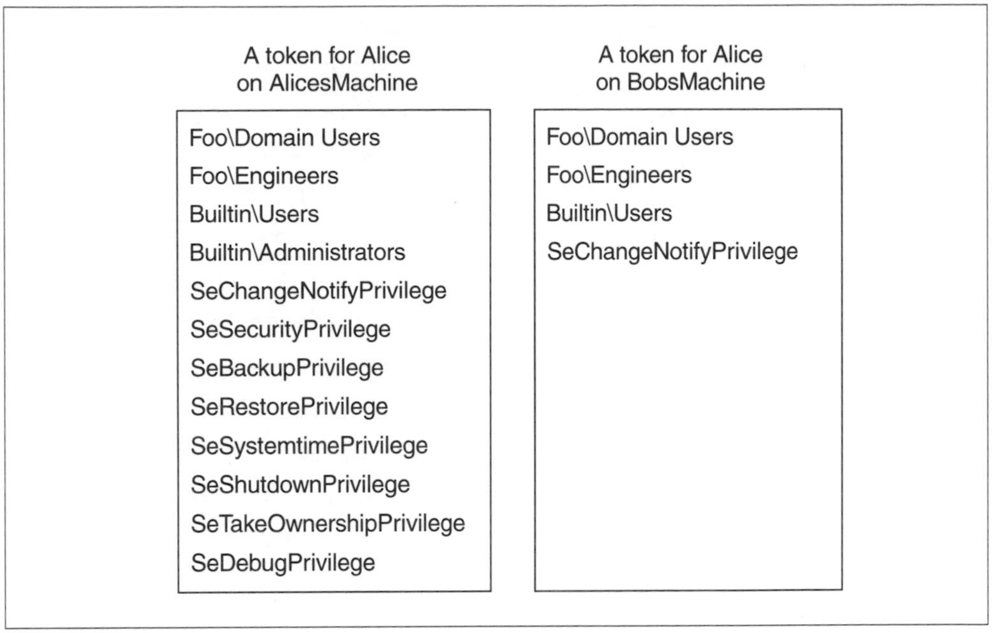

A token for Alice on AlicesMachine	A token for Alice on BobsMachine
Foo\Domain Users	Foo\Domain Users
Foo\Engineers	Foo\Engineers
Builtin\Users	Builtin\Users
Builtin\Administrators	SeChangeNotifyPrivilege
SeChangeNotifyPrivilege	
SeSecurityPrivilege	
SeBackupPrivilege	
SeRestorePrivilege	
SeSystemtimePrivilege	
SeShutdownPrivilege	
SeTakeOwnershipPrivilege	
SeDebugPrivilege	

Figure 3.7.   Peering into a token

on the machine on which she has established the logon session. Figure 3.7
shows an example of two tokens for Alice (abbreviated for brevity): one on
AlicesMachine and another on BobsMachine. Notice how in this case the
groups have remained the same, but alias and privilege assignments may vary
dramatically. The point is that tokens are machine relative. It doesn't make any
sense to try to send a token from one machine to another to propagate authorization attributes. The SIDs for custom aliases defined on one machine are
completely meaningless to any other machine. Windows also represents each
privilege in a fashion that is not guaranteed to have any meaning on another
machine (this is totally reasonable considering that tokens are not meant to be
shared across host boundaries).

The second type of session is inherent in the programming model exposed
by native Windows objects such as files, window stations, and so forth. To take
a concrete example, the normal life cycle for file I/O follows a well-known
sequence: Alice first opens a file handle (thus opening a logical session to the

file object), performs operations on the file, and then closes the handle (thus closing the session). When Alice opens the file handle, she must state her intentions up front, traditionally by specifying some combination of GENERIC_READ and GENERIC_WRITE bit flags in an **access mask.** The operating system will then use Alice's authorization attributes (by looking at her token), coupled with the security descriptor on the file and Alice's specified intentions, and return a valid file handle only if she is granted the requested permissions. In case Alice is successful, the file handle itself is annotated with the granted permissions so that future operations requested via the file handle can be satisfied or refused based on the cached permissions in the handle (Figure 3.8). No further verification of Alice's authorization attributes is required.

This mechanism tremendously reduces the overhead required for providing security. The permission annotation on the handle is managed in protected kernel memory that is not accessible to user-mode processes. The process can continue to use this open session throughout its lifetime, and because the process always runs with a snapshot of Alice's authorization attributes (maintained in the process token), further access checks aren't necessary.

As a result of this mechanism, changes to the object's security descriptor have no effect on outstanding handles. This is something you should consider in your designs. You can always force a new access check by closing the handle and reopening it, or (in certain cases described in Chapter 6), by calling DuplicateHandle.

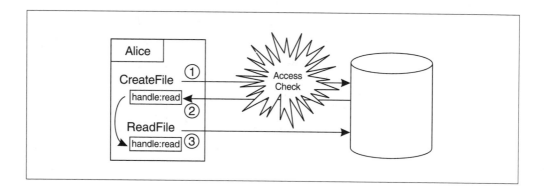

Figure 3.8. **Handles act as sessions**

Impersonation as a Workaround?

Throwing impersonation into the mix changes things significantly, however. Imagine that Alice impersonates Bob temporarily (by putting Bob's token on her thread) and opens a file handle while impersonating, thus acquiring a resource on Bob's behalf. Once this file handle is opened, the operating system doesn't care whether Bob or Alice (or anybody else in the process) uses that file handle, as long as he or she only exercises the permissions granted to Bob when he originally opened the handle. Access control and (generally) auditing are only performed when objects are *opened,* not when objects are *used*. Thus Alice can use a handle opened by Bob. The `DuplicateHandle` API even allows one process to hand an open handle to another process (potentially running in a different logon session), and as long as permissions are not expanded during the duplication, no access checks are performed during (or after) the handoff. So a process running as Bob can acquire and hand off resources to a process running as Alice.[12]

System developers sometimes use impersonation in an attempt to work around the session-oriented nature of Windows security. The classic example is when the developer would like an application to run 24×7 but allow various principals to "log in" to the process at various times during the day, either because the developer considers it too expensive to have someone log off the machine and log back on (recall that when the interactive user logs off, all applications running in the interactive logon session must shut down) or because the application running in the interactive logon session is monitoring or controlling external processes (hardware devices, for example) and thus must run constantly.

Whatever the case may be, what often ends up happening is that the developer attempts to collect credentials on the fly (by presenting the user with a dialog that collects an authority/principal/password tuple[13]), calls `LogonUser`[14] to

---

[12] See Chapter 6 for more details.

[13] This presents its own share of problems—recall that you want to avoid putting up dialog boxes that prompt the user for credentials because it makes It easier for a Trojan horse to mimic your dialog and steal passwords.

[14] As shown in Chapter 4, only very privileged principals can call this function; administrators don't even have this privilege by default. This in itself should be a warning sign.

obtain a logon session and a token for the user, sticks this token on the main application thread, and begins acquiring resources using these temporary credentials. Although a clever developer can make this work with some very careful programming (and a strong knowledge of Windows security), it becomes very difficult to ensure that the system is secure and is not leaking handles from one principal to the next. Imagine that Alice launches the application, and then Bob (the supervisor) comes along and wants to use it; he thus provides his credentials, and the application starts impersonating him, opening a file handle along with some other resources to do work for Bob. When Bob logs out of the program, the program stops impersonating him and Alice can now use the program again. However, what if the program forgot to close some of the resources that Bob opened? There is no guarantee by the operating system that this won't happen, and it's possible that Alice could end up being allowed to access resources that Bob acquired, with permissions that she would not normally be granted. To be completely safe, the process should close all outstanding handles acquired on behalf of the previous principal, and should reopen those resources on behalf of the new principal. Might as well shut down the process and restart it, eh?

To solve this classic problem, it is helpful to split the application into two separate processes, with some sort of secure interprocess communication between the two (COM is a very natural choice here). The core part of the application runs as a daemon process and will not be tied to the interactive logon session (in fact, it may even run in the System logon session if that is desirable). This daemon process can safely run 24×7, and is not affected by the coming and going of interactive users. The user interface can then be partitioned into a separate process running in the interactive logon session, and should be as lightweight as possible to facilitate a quick startup and shutdown. For vertical applications, it's often convenient to replace the shell itself (EXPLORER.EXE) with the user interface program to reduce login latency even further. This trick also makes it considerably more difficult for average users to install or run random software from the console. The daemon process can perform access checks on COM method calls using one of the three strategies outlined earlier, and can acquire resources using the daemon's credentials (as opposed to using the client's credentials) as necessary.

The moral of the story is that you should understand the session-oriented nature of Windows security and make it work *for* you, rather than *against* you. This sort of example also demonstrates how considering security in the design phase of any nontrivial project can be critical. Retrofitting security into an existing application is often a painful proposition; this may explain why so many developers are frustrated by security.

Summary

- If authentication answers the question "Who are you?" then authorization answers the question "What can you do?"

- Authorization attributes in Windows consist of groups, aliases, and privileges, and these attributes are generally assigned in a decentralized fashion.

- Privileges are assigned on a per-machine basis, but this can be automated with group policy objects in Windows 2000 or the Security Policy Editor in earlier versions of Windows.

- Aliases are assigned on a per-machine basis and are traditionally used to model logical roles.

- Group assignments are managed by an authority; thus, they have a wider scope than aliases and are traditionally used to model an organization (the Appendix has more details on groups in Windows 2000).

- When a logon session is established, the system takes the union of the authorization attributes from the relavent authorities (groups) and the local authorization attributes (aliases and privileges) and caches them in a token.

- Distributed applications can use network authentication to establish a network logon session on a server for each remote client. This allows the server to get a token for the client that contains the client's authorization attributes.

- A security descriptor is a data structure that contains all the security settings for an object (perhaps a file, registry key, process, or a custom class of object that you define). This includes an owner, discretionary access control list (DACL), and system access control list (SACL).

- The DACL is basically a list that says who can touch the object and in exactly what way. The DACL is specified at the owner's discretion (thus the word *discretionary*).

- The SACL is a list that says who will be audited if they succeed or fail while attempting to touch the object in a particular way. The SACL is nondiscretionary; the owner has no special permissions to the SACL.

- There are three idiomatic models for performing access control in Windows: the impersonation model, the role-centric model, and the object-centric model. (These are arranged in order of complexity.)

- The impersonation model works great if you can pass the buck directly to a local resource manager that performs its own access checks.

- The role-centric model focuses on the roles to which a principal has been assigned. The Administrators alias is a great example of a logical role upon which the operating system itself relies.

- The object-centric model is the most powerful and therefore the most complex to implement and administer. Each object maintains its own security settings (usually this takes the form of a security descriptor).

- Windows security is session oriented. Logon sessions and handles are two examples of sessions you'll encounter.

- Access checks on operating system objects are only performed when you open a handle. Giving the handle away (via impersonation or `DuplicateHandle`) has interesting security ramifications because no further access checks will be performed.

PART II

Mechanics

Chapter 4

Logon Sessions

Chapter 2 introduced the logon session and put some shape around it. Produced by the LSA, a logon session represents an instance of a particular principal on a particular machine, very much like the badge one obtains from a security guard when entering a secure building. The easiest type of logon session to imagine is an interactive logon session (in which Alice hits Control-Alt-Delete and logs in via the console), but there are other equally important types of logon sessions that are covered in this chapter. Recall that the motivation for using a logon session is to allow the operating system to perform work on behalf of the logged-on principal without constantly having to verify the principal's identity (by asking for a password, for example).

Each logon session is represented by a physical data structure managed by the operating system and identified by a locally unique identifer (**LUID),** which is simply a 64-bit integer whose uniqueness is bounded by the machine.[1] This allows us to distinguish one logon session from another on a particular machine.

Logon sessions never extend across machine boundaries, so in order for a process running under Alice's logon session on AlicesMachine to access secured resources on BobsMachine, some magic must occur. BobsMachine needs to ascertain the identity of the user represented by the logon session on AlicesMachine; in other words, BobsMachine needs to authenticate Alice. The logon session on AlicesMachine will normally cache Alice's credentials to streamline this procedure, which allows the system to do work for Alice (potentially over the network) without constantly having to prompt her for a password. To protect Alice, the logon session on BobsMachine won't normally have access to these cached credentials,[2] thus limiting the radius where Alice's credentials may be used to a single network hop. Figure 4.1 shows an example of logon sessions created on various machines, and their relation to one another.

You may be surprised at the number of logon sessions that exist at any given time on a typical machine, especially if that machine happens to provide services to other machines on the network. This chapter discusses these various logon sessions in chronological order so you can get a feel for the environment likely to be present on a machine at any given stage in its life cycle. Before beginning, take a look at the flowchart in Figure 4.2. The order in the figure shows a typical progression that emphasizes that a Windows machine is quite functional without an interactive user present at all.

The basic order of events is as follows. Taking AlicesMachine as an example, the System logon session is the first to appear; it is born early in the boot sequence as AlicesMachine comes to life. This logon session is designed to bootstrap the operating system. As part of this bootstrapping, a process running within this initial logon session creates new logon sessions for daemons (also known as services) configured to autostart as distinct principals. The entity that starts these daemons is known as the System Service Control Manager (SCM), and most system-level Windows developers are familiar with the basic services it provides.

---

[1] LUIDs may be recycled when the machine is rebooted, so technically they don't maintain their uniqueness across reboots, but logon sessions don't persist across reboots either. LUIDs are used in other places as well; see the `AllocateLocallyUniqueId` API for more detail.

[2] Under Windows 2000, in certain scenarios it is possible (but usually inadvisable) to change this behavior. The details are discussed in Chapter 7.

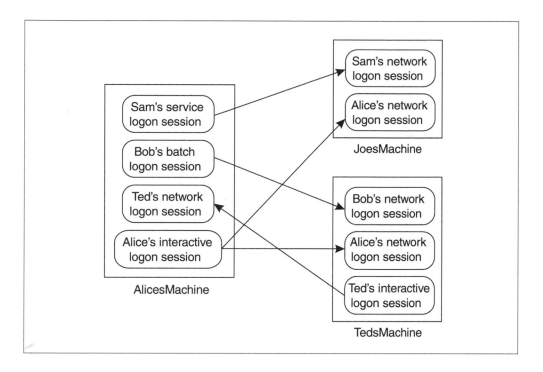

Figure 4.1. Logon sessions

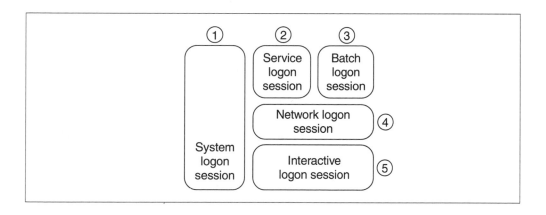

Figure 4.2. Sample logon session flowchart

After these logon sessions have been created and the daemons are happily running, one of two things may happen (in any order). An interactive user may happen to walk up to the console and establish an interactive logon session,[3] or a process on a remote machine may (via the network) request a secured resource from a daemon running on AlicesMachine (the file system redirector may receive a connection request, or the COM SCM may receive an activation request, or an RPC server may receive an authenticated remote procedure call, etc.). In all these cases, *the operating system needs to establish a logon session for the client on AlicesMachine* in order for that client to gain access to secured resources there.

Let's drill down into each of these logon sessions in turn, and see what role they play in the operating system and how they affect you as a systems developer.

Logon Session 999

The operating system establishes a special logon session at boot time, which has a hardcoded identifier: number 999, or 0x3E7 in hexadecimal (just search for SYSTEM_LUID in the winnt.h header file to find this identifier). This is the System logon session that was described briefly in Chapter 3, and (at least by default) it houses the entirety of the user-mode processes that make up the trusted computing base. This includes the Local Security Authority subsystem (LSASS.EXE), the logon process (WINLOGON.EXE), the RPC subsystem (RPCSS.EXE),[4] and the Win32 subsystem (CSRSS.EXE). The reason I chose to title this section Logon Session 999 was not because the number 999 is important (although it's an interesting choice), but because the fact that you can put your finger on the exact LUID for this logon session helps to emphasize that *on each machine there is only one System logon session*.

The System logon session is identified by a well-known SID (S-1-5-18) and a human-readable name, **SYSTEM.** You'll never see an account for SYSTEM

---

[3] Technically, with the advent of Terminal Services, this interactive user need not walk up to the machine; rather, he or she may connect via a remote terminal. However, the interactive logon session established by a remote terminal (via Terminal Services) looks and smells so similar to a normal interactive logon session that I don't see the need to distinguish between the two in this book.

[4] Although RPCSS.EXE is now technically hosted in a service surrogate (SVCHOST.EXE), I'll refer to it as RPCSS.EXE for clarity.

listed in User Manager, because it has no account in the security database; the groups and privileges assigned to the System logon session are fixed by the operating system, and I can't imagine choosing the hours in which it is allowed to log in to the machine. However, you *will* see SYSTEM listed in various **ACL editors** (the user interface you see when editing security settings on files, registry keys, shares, and so on). This means that you can grant access to the System logon session just as easily as any other real principal or group. Often I'm asked the question "What's the password for the SYSTEM account?" It should be clear by now that this question is moot. On any given machine, SYSTEM simply represents a single logon session (number 999); this session is established implicitly at boot time by the operating system, so a password is unnecessary. Just think of S-1-5-18 as specifically identifying the System logon session versus identifying a principal in the traditional sense.

As an intrinsic part of the operating system, the System logon session has tremendous power on the local machine. Its authorization attributes include the Administrators alias, and therefore all the privileges normally granted to that powerful alias, including the ability to read and write *any* file on any local NTFS partition, regardless of the security settings on the file, as well as the ability to *change* the security settings on those files. (These are simply the Backup, Restore, and Take Ownership privileges, by the way, but it gives you a feel for the awesome power that an Administrator wields.[5]) Beyond these privileges, the System logon session is also granted other privileges, the most important of which is the **TCB privilege** (better known to most administrators by its friendly name, "Act as part of the operating system"), which implies that code running under the System logon session acts on behalf of the operating system and therefore has the capacity to help enforce or to subvert the security policy of the machine. (A definition of TCB is provided in the glossary.)

Because of the power of the System logon session, it is often convenient to write code that executes in the warm sanctuary that it affords. However, code that runs in this logon session must be carefully written; bugs in code that runs

---

[5] Note that an administrator is subject to access checks just like any other principal, but given the privileges normally assigned her, she can get around any DACL that stands in her way. Even if she's not granted a necessary privilege, a clever administrator can ultimately obtain that privilege by changing the local security policy.

in the TCB are clearly more dangerous than bugs outside. My own personal preference is to avoid running my own code in the System logon session unless it is absolutely necessary, and even then I prefer to keep this to a minimum. One approach is to factor out the privileged code into a COM server (although any interprocess communication mechanism would do) and make calls into the server when you need privileged work done. This allows precise unit testing of the critical piece of code you'll be injecting into the TCB. You'd be surprised at how little code you *really* need to inject into the TCB to move really big mountains in Windows.

So how does one get code injected into the System logon session? How does one get code injected into *any* particular logon session? This is discussed in Chapter 2. You must have a process that's already running in that logon session either load your code directly via a DLL or launch a separate process by calling `CreateProcess`. Whenever you call `CreateProcess`, the new process *always* inherits the logon session of the creator's process. It turns out that the System SCM runs in the System logon session and is happy to call `CreateProcess` to inject a new process into the System logon session as a service. So the first option is to write a few extra lines of code to make your application into a service. (You'll need to call `StartServiceCtrlDispatcher` and friends to get along with the SCM, and your setup program will need to call `CreateService` to install your application into the service database.)

The second option is to leverage an existing process that is already running in the System logon session (one that's more forgiving). Simply ask it to call `CreateProcess` on your behalf. This second option is convenient because you don't need to code to the service APIs, but is problematic because there aren't many existing services that are willing to do this for you.[6] If you have several processes that need to run in the System logon session, you could potentially write a single bootstrapping service to be launched by the System SCM, which in turn would call `CreateProcess` to spawn other processes running in the

---

[6] A classic trick is to get the Task Scheduler service to start a process on your behalf. The schedule service runs in the System logon session by default, and will happily inject code into the TCB (check out the `AT` command if you want to play with this). This is a cool demo to show off to your friends, but not terribly useful for production code. Only administrators can run `AT.EXE`, by the way.

System logon session. I'm using this example to emphasize that the System logon session works just like any other logon session; it's not special other than its elevated level of privilege and the fact that it happens to be the bootstrapping logon session. I'd personally avoid dumping lots of processes into the TCB for the reasons mentioned earlier.

One strange thing about SYSTEM is that it appears as though it would have the same SID everywhere on the network. What happens when an application running under the System logon session on AlicesMachine tries to access a remote file (via a file share) on BobsMachine? If the SID for SYSTEM is S-1-5-18 on AlicesMachine as well as all other machines on the network, there is no way for Bob (the administrator on BobsMachine, say) to expose a file share (or any other secure resource) and grant or deny access to AlicesMachine versus SarahsMachine versus RonsMachine. Because of this and other issues, prior to Windows 2000 the SYSTEM account had no network credentials at all, and therefore couldn't be authenticated.[7] There was no way to tell one machine from another on the network, other than by looking at its network address (which is easily faked and therefore can't be used for securing resources[8]). Windows specifically provides a couple of back doors that allow you to satisfy unauthenticated requests for file shares and other secure resources, but this isn't a pretty solution. (These back doors—the NULL session and the Guest account—are discussed in Chapter 7.)

This problem does not exist for Windows 2000 machines running in a Windows 2000 domain. In this case, each machine is a first-class principal in the domain and has a dual identity. On the local machine, the System logon session is identified via our old friend, SYSTEM (S-1-5-18); this is good, because you wouldn't want existing code that relied on this identifier to break. However, things look different on the network. Here's a concrete example: Assume that AlicesMachine and BobsMachine (both Windows 2000 boxes) are members of Foo (a Windows 2000 domain), and that an application running in

---

[7] Technically, even on Windows NT 4, a machine can be authenticated by its primary domain (for the purpose of establishing a secure channel for pass-through authentication), but by no other entity on the network.

[8] I should mention that by using IP Security (which is implemented in Windows 2000), it is possible to authenticate a machine's network address; to make this work, however, some sort of security credentials are required for each machine being authenticated.

the System logon session on AlicesMachine contacts BobsMachine over the network. After authentication, BobsMachine will see the request as coming from a domain principal named Foo\AlicesMachine, with a unique SID scoped by Foo (as opposed to the well-known SID S-1-5-18). This would work even if BobsMachine was in a different domain, as long as the appropriate trust relationships were in place (which is pretty hard to screw up in Windows 2000, because all domains in a forest share transitive trust relationships, and typical organizations will likely have a single dominant forest).

This behavior makes it appear as if the System logon session develops a multiple personality disorder in Windows 2000, but it is clearly a very useful feature. In fact, machines are now listed alongside users as first-class principals in the domain, and can be assigned to groups (consider that AlicesMachine will be in a group named Foo\Domain Computers by default). So in Windows 2000, when you want to grant access to your local operating system (that is, the System logon session on your machine), you must grant access to SYSTEM. When you want to grant access to AlicesMachine (that is, the System logon session on AlicesMachine), you grant access to *XXXX*\AlicesMachine, where *XXXX* is the domain to which AlicesMachine belongs.

Daemon Logon Sessions

So far we've established that the first logon session to be created is the System logon session. But often other logon sessions are created as the operating system starts; in particular, the System SCM creates logon sessions for services that are configured to run as distinguished principals. For an example of how this works, take a look at the `CreateService` API that setup programs use to install applications as services:[9]

```
SC_HANDLE CreateService(
    SC_HANDLE hSCManager,        // in, indicates host
    LPCTSTR   lpServiceName,     // in, short name
    LPCTSTR   lpDisplayName,     // in, pretty name
    DWORD     dwDesiredAccess,   // in
```

---

[9] If you're looking for a reference on how to implement a service (that is, how to call `StartServiceCtrlDispatcher` and friends), see Richter (1999b).

```
    DWORD       dwServiceType,       // in, interactive/etc.
    DWORD       dwStartType,         // in, auto/manual/etc.
    DWORD       dwErrorControl,      // in
    LPCTSTR     pBinaryPathName,     // in, path to EXE
    LPCTSTR     lpLoadOrderGroup,    // in, optional, for drivers
    LPDWORD     lpdwTagID,           // in, optional, for drivers
    LPCTSTR     lpDependencies,      // in, optional, multisz
    LPCTSTR     lpServiceStartName,  // in, optional, principal
    LPCTSTR     lpPassword           // in, optional, password
);
```

This function simply takes the settings given it and updates the registry of the machine on which the service is being installed (the machine was indicated when the *hSCManager* handle was acquired via OpenSCManager). This provides the System SCM with all the information it needs to create an appropriate environment and allocate a process for your service either at boot time or in response to a call to the StartService API.

The *lpServiceName* and *lpDisplayName* parameters are the short and pretty names, respectively, of the service being installed. The *dwDesiredAccess* parameter is the access mask by which you specify exactly what you intend to do with the handle returned from the function. The *dwServiceType* parameter allows you to specify whether or not you plan on exposing multiple services from a single process; more important (for our purposes), this parameter allows you to choose the window station allocation policy that the System SCM will use when creating a process to host your service, specifically via the presence or absence of the SERVICE_INTERACTIVE_ PROCESS flag (see Chapter 5 for a thorough discussion of window stations). The *dwStartType* parameter allows you to specify whether the service starts at boot time (SERVICE_AUTO_START) or only when prompted via the StartService API (SERVICE_DEMAND_START). The *dwErrorControl* parameter allows you to choose how critical a startup failure really is to system startup, and the *lpBinaryPathName* and *lpDependencies* parameters allow you to specify the EXE image that holds your service code, and any dependencies your server may have (RPCSS is important to list if you're going to act as an RPC or COM server). The *lpLoadOrderGroup* and *lpdwTagID* parameters are only used for protected mode drivers, so you'll normally pass NULL for both of these.

Finally, *lpServiceStartName* and *lpPassword* allow you to specify on whose behalf the process should run. Pass NULL for both to run as SYSTEM. If you specify a distinguished authority and principal (Foo\Bob, say), `CreateService` will store "Foo\Bob" in the service database in the registry, but will tuck the password away in a local password stash maintained by the LSA to which only administrators (and therefore the System logon session) have access (see the appendix for details of programming against this stash). In this case the index into the password stash is based on the short name of the sevice (for example, a service with a short name of `MyService` would have its password stored at index `_SC_MyService`).

When the service needs to be started (either at boot time or via an explicit request initiated via a call to `StartService`), the System SCM looks up the authority and user name from the registry, and passes this information (along with an index into the password stash) to the LSA. The LSA attempts to authenticate the principal using the stashed password, and upon success, creates a brand-new logon session for Foo\Bob. The SCM takes this new logon session and launches the EXE that was specified as the image name for the service, attaching this new process to the new logon session.

If you install two separate services that are configured to run in separate processes, and both services use the same principal name (say, Foo\Bob), you might think that they would share the same logon session, but this is not the case (at least as of this writing). Once both processes are started they will run in distinct logon sessions from one another (even though both logon sessions will represent the same principal). It's as if there were two separate *instances* of the principal logged in to the machine. This may seem like a nitpicky point, but developing an intuition for logon session boundaries is important if you want to master Windows security programming. Figure 4.3 shows an example of logon session boundaries when several services are running.

Although I'll save the details for Chapter 9, I should mention that a COM server designed to run as a distinguished principal runs in a distinct daemon logon session just as a service would. The difference in this case is that the

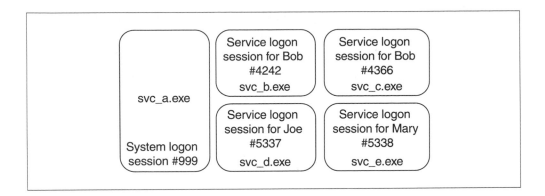

Figure 4.3. Service logon sessions

COM Service Control Manager (SCM) is the one that launches COM servers. Whereas the System SCM establishes a **service logon** for a service, the COM SCM establishes a **batch logon** for a COM server.[10] The minor differences between these two logon types are discussed later in this chapter, but from a practical standpoint, you can look at both of these logon types as simply vanilla daemon logon sessions, they are so similar. The fact that there are two types of daemon logon sessions is simply an unfortunate historical footnote in the evolution of Windows.

Network Logon Sessions

Now that AlicesMachine has booted, the System logon session is happily running, and some services and COM servers have started in service- and batch-style logon sessions, respectively, AlicesMachine is a fully functional node on the network.

Suppose that Sarah, the administrator of the Foo domain (where AlicesMachine is a member) wishes to update some software on AlicesMachine. Before the operating system on AlicesMachine will allow Sarah to do anything, Sarah must authenticate herself, thus establishing a logon session on AlicesMachine. The question is, Does Sarah have to physically walk over to

---

[10] This discussion assumes that the COM server in question is not packaged as a service (in that case, the COM SCM simply defers to the System SCM by calling StartService).

Alice's office to get the work done? Thankfully, the answer is no. Sarah can simply authenticate herself across the network to the file system redirector on AlicesMachine and connect to an administrative share (C$, say). Sarah can now simply copy the files to AlicesMachine without having to physically visit the machine. After authentication is complete, Sarah now has a logon session on AlicesMachine; the file system redirector (which runs in the System logon session) holds a token to this session, and can therefore verify that Sarah does indeed have permission to upload files via C$. Sarah has established what is known as a **network logon** on AlicesMachine.

What if Sarah wanted to make a secure RPC or COM call across the network to AlicesMachine? A similar procedure takes place in this case as well: Sarah authenticates herself across the network, thus establishing a network logon session on AlicesMachine. The COM or RPC server can discover Sarah's identity and authorization attributes by looking at the resulting token.

Interactive Logon Sessions

The System logon session hosts a process known as Winlogon (WINLOGON .EXE), which acts as the gateway for interactive users. When Alice walks up to AlicesMachine in the morning and presses Control-Alt-Delete, Winlogon displays a user interface to collect Alice's credentials. More specifically, a pluggable DLL known as the **GINA** (Graphical Identification and Authentication) hosts all the user interface components displayed from the Winlogon process. Take a peek at the resources inside MSGINA.DLL (this is the default GINA DLL that lives in the %SYSTEMROOT%\System32 directory) using Visual C++ (or whatever tool you prefer), and you'll see lots of familiar dialogs.

Just as the System SCM creates logon sessions for daemons, Winlogon creates logon sessions for humans. After Alice presents her credentials, the Winlogon process hands these credentials off to the LSA, which verifies Alice's identity and produces a logon session and a token for her. Winlogon then looks in the registry for a named value Shell under the following registry key:

```
HKLM\Software\Microsoft\Windows NT\CurrentVersion\Winlogon
  @Shell="explorer.exe"
```

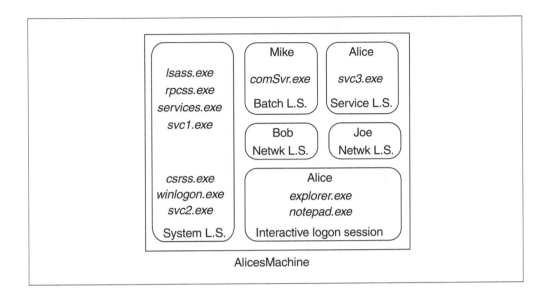

Figure 4.4. A typical collection of logon sessions

Winlogon launches this application, starting the process in Alice's new logon session.[11]

When Alice uses the Start menu to launch an application (or any of the myriad other ways she can launch applications via Explorer), the shell ultimately calls CreateProcess, which starts a new process running in the same logon session. Figure 4.4 shows an example of the logon sessions and a few processes to give you a feel for how the system looks at this point. When Alice chooses to log off, the operating system will tear down each process running in her interactive logon session, and then the logon session itself will be torn down.

So what happens if Alice chooses to configure a service to run using her own account (DOMA\Alice)? Recall what the System SCM does when it is asked to start a service running as a distinguished principal. It asks the LSA to

---

[11] Technically, at this point Winlogon executes a helper program known as USERINIT.EXE in the newly established logon session for the client, which sets up the client's environment, restores persistent network connections, runs logon scripts, and then starts the shell. See the MSDN documentation for WlxActivateUserShell for more information.

authenticate the principal (using a stashed password), which results in a brand-new logon session for Alice. This is a *different logon session* from the one hosting Explorer and all the other interactive processes that Alice has launched via Explorer. So what happens when Alice logs off, terminating her interactive logon session? The same thing as before—all processes running in the interactive logon session are shut down. This does not affect the service running as Alice; that service continues to run happily, even when no interactive user is present.

Network Credentials

Five different types of logon sessions have now been described: the System, service, batch, network, and interactive logon sessions. Which of these logon sessions have network credentials? Recall that a logon session with network credentials hosts processes whose outgoing network communications can be authenticated. The only sessions that might *not* have network credentials are the System logon session (as discussed earlier in this chapter) and virtually all network logon sessions.

Network logon sessions are designed to represent remote clients; to protect those clients, their credentials are not normally delegated to the servers with which they authenticate. It would be very dangerous indeed if Sarah (the domain administrator) were to allow her credentials to propagate to each server she contacted during the day, because if a bad guy compromised any of these servers, he or she could easily masquerade as Sarah on the network and do tons of damage throughout the domain. After reading Chapter 7, you'll have a much better understanding of how this works.[12]

Tokens

All this discussion of logon sessions is very important, but the majority of programmers will never get their hands on one directly. Instead, developers see logon sessions through a level of indirection known as a token. Chapter 2 introduced the relationship of tokens to logon sessions and postulated that a token was just part of the surface area of a logon session—a level of indirection that

---

[12] In Chapter 7 you'll also learn that with Kerberos, it is possible (but inadvisable) to delegate Sarah's credentials across multiple network hops; you'll also learn the hoops you have to jump through to enable this.

allows localized customization of the characteristics of a logon session on a per-process basis. I like this view of the world because it emphasizes the importance of thinking about the logon session behind the token.

Before moving on, I'd like to specifically define a term that I've been using rather loosely so far: **security context.** Security context is a collection of **out-of-band** settings that affect the security-related behavior of a process or thread. It's just a convenient name that encapsulates many of the concepts we've been talking about so far. One example is the cached network credentials that Alice's interactive logon session holds. Any process running within this logon session can access remote resources as Alice because its security context has network credentials. This particular part of the security context comes directly from the logon session, but tokens add a set of customizable attributes that a process can modify to suit its needs (the default security settings for new objects was an example used in Chapter 2). Therefore, the security context of a particular process is determined by the token associated with that process plus the logon session that the token represents. Security context is an abstract idea, and the term will be used when discussing security settings in a token or logon session in situations in which it's not important to distinguish exactly where the setting is stored.

Anatomy of a Token

Tokens contain several settings that are categorized in Figure 4.5. Each bit of information shown in the figure is accessible via a couple of APIs that are discussed shortly.

Identity and Authorization Attributes

The first category, identity and authorization attributes, constitutes the most influential characteristics of a security context. The *user SID* is the read-only SID of the principal whom the logon session represents. This is the principal whose name will show up in the audit log when code executing in this security context opens secure resources such as files and registry keys.[13]

---

[13] Assuming auditing has been enabled (Chapter 6 discusses auditing).

Identity and Authorization Attributes	
User SID User Name*	Group SIDs Privileges
Defaults for New Objects	*Miscellaneous Stuff*
Owner SID Group SID DACL	Logon session ID Token ID Modification ID Token type Expiration time Impersonation level

*Technically the user name is stored in the logon session

Figure 4.5. Anatomy of a token

The *user name* is a cached string representation of the principal's name. Although you can discover this name by brute force (just pass the user SID as input to the `LookupAccountSid` function), this may be quite expensive (think several network round-trips) if the account is managed on a remote domain controller. The `GetUserName(Ex)` function exists to extract the value that was cached when the logon session was created; therefore, it's preferable to use this function as opposed to mapping the SID to a name at runtime.[14]

The *group SID list* is a fixed collection of SIDs for all groups and aliases that have been assigned either directly or indirectly to the principal indicated by the user SID. Each group SID in the list is accompanied by a set of flags that determines how the group can be used and how it will affect the security context. (Each group SID can either represent a group or an alias, but the distinction is unimportant for this discussion.) Here's a description of what these flags mean.

SE_GROUP_ENABLED is a read-write flag indicating that the group should be considered when access checks are performed using this token. If this bit is cleared for a particular group, the security context would act as if it were not a member of that group. Because an object may not only *grant* access to a group SID but also *deny* access to a group SID, this isn't a terribly useful feature. As

---

[14] These functions are often used in conjunction with impersonation; their use (and a rather nasty trap to avoid) is discussed later in this chapter.

it stands, it would be a rather subtle security hole if groups in a token could be arbitrarily disabled. For instance, if Alice explicitly denies the Accountants group access to a file on AlicesMachine, a smart accountant with an interactive logon session on AlicesMachine could simply write code to disable this group SID in his or her token before accessing the file. This flag is set in all group SIDs that I've ever seen in a token.

SE_GROUP_ENABLED_BY_DEFAULT is a read-only flag that means just what it says. Once again, in all the tokens that I've ever looked at, I've never seen a group SID with this bit clear.

SE_GROUP_MANDATORY is a read-only flag indicating that the SE_GROUP _ENABLED flag may not be cleared. Virtually all groups in any token you'll ever see have this flag set, most likely because of the issue discussed earlier. The only scenario I've encountered in which this flag is cleared is on the Administrators alias in any token for the System logon session. This makes sense because code running in the System logon session is part of the TCB and can ultimately do whatever the heck it needs to do, regardless of security constraints. This flag seals the potential security hole exposed by SE_GROUP _ENABLED, and effectively renders that flag read-only for tokens other than those for the system logon session part of the TCB.

SE_GROUP_OWNER is a read-only flag indicating that this group can potentially act as the owner SID in an object's security descriptor (detailed discussion of this concept is deferred until Chapter 6). In practice, this flag is always clear, except in one notable case: The Administrator alias (if present) will have this flag set.

SE_GROUP_LOGON_ID is a read-only flag indicating that this group is actually not a group at all, but rather is a SID that identifies the logon session that this token represents. This allows a DACL to grant or deny access not only to a particular principal, but also to a particular *instance* of that principal.

SE_GROUP_USE_FOR_DENY_ONLY is a read-only flag indicating that this group SID will only be used for comparisons with negative DACL entries, not positive ones (see Chapter 6 for details). Having a group with this attribute set can never help you get access to an object; it can only be used to deny access. This is a Windows 2000 feature. Tokens that contain deny-only group SIDs are known as **restricted tokens** (I'll talk about these later in the chapter).

The *privilege list* is the collection of all privileges assigned to the principal represented by the user SID. These privileges may be assigned directly to the principal or indirectly via a group or alias; see Chapter 1 for a detailed discussion of how privileges are populated in the token.

Each privilege in the token is identified by a LUID as opposed to a string, and there are APIs (demonstrated shortly) to map the LUIDs in the privilege list to well-known privilege names and localized, administrator-friendly description strings. Having LUIDs in the token as opposed to strings is beneficial for a number of reasons:

1. Programming against fixed-length data structures is easier than dealing with variable-length strings.

2. Storing LUIDs in the token saves space.

3. The system caches the LUID mappings, and it's more time efficient to compare LUIDs with one another as opposed to comparing variable-length strings.

4. The added complexity helps us keep our high-paying jobs as security-savvy developers.

Just as each group SID is annotated with a set of flags, so each privilege in the token is annotated with a couple of flags.[15] SE_PRIVILEGE_ENABLED is a read-write flag that determines whether the privilege is in effect in this security context. Most privileges are disabled by default, so this bit will normally be clear except in a few rare cases that are enumerated later (see Figure 4.6).

SE_PRIVILEGE_ENABLED_BY_DEFAULT is a read-only flag that means just what it says. In the average token, this bit is clear in all privileges except SeChangeNotifyPrivilege ("Bypass traverse checking"), which is always enabled by default if it is present in the token. In any token for the System logon session, several privileges are enabled by default (see Figure 4.6 for an example).

---

[15] There is a third flag named SE_PRIVILEGE_USED_FOR_ACCESS that you will come across if you scout around in the documentation for using privileges. This flag is not maintained as part of the state of a privilege in a token; rather, it is used to communicate whether or not a particular privilege was used to grant access to a resource.

Defaults for New Objects

Chapter 3 introduced the notion of a security descriptor, a data structure that encapsulates the security settings for an individual object such as a mutex, file, or registry key. When you create a new mutex, for instance, you have the chance to specify exactly what you'd like its security descriptor to look like via the well-loved LPSECURITY_ATTRIBUTES parameter to CreateMutex. Even if you broke down and actually passed a security descriptor here, it'd be nice if you only had to populate that security descriptor with the information that you cared about. For instance, the main reason you'd bother passing something other than NULL is to provide a customized DACL that grants very particular access permissions to certain individuals and denies others. However, a security descriptor has much more in it than just a DACL. Do you also have to specify the owner and primary group and SACL? The answer is a resounding no. Any information you neglect to pass can simply be extracted from default values in your token.

The *default owner SID* is a read-write value that will be used to populate the owner SID in the security descriptors of new objects you create where you don't explicitly specify an owner SID.

Similarly, the *default primary group SID* is a read-write value that will be used to populate the primary group SID in those security descriptors. This is a godsend since few people care about the POSIX subsystem in Windows.

Finally, the *default DACL* is a read-write value that will be used in certain situations to generate a reasonable DACL for the security descriptors of new objects you create where you don't explicitly specify a DACL. This mechanism is discussed further in Chapter 6.

Note the distinct lack of a default SACL field. SACLs are applied at the system administrator's discretion; random principals are not allowed to determine the auditing policy on a given machine.

What's great about these default attributes is that if you pass NULL for the LPSECURITY_ATTRIBUTES parameter to CreateMutex and friends, the system will grab all this default information from your token and apply it automatically for you. This means you have one-stop shopping to adjust the DACL applied to objects you create[16] in a particular security context.

---

[16] This works a bit differently for objects arranged hierarchically (files, registry keys, desktops, etc.). See Chapter 6 for details.

Miscellaneous Stuff

The following attributes make up the rest of the documented token settings.

The *logon session LUID* is the read-only 64-bit identifier for the logon session that this token represents. Many tokens can be associated with a single logon session. (Remember that each process has its own distinct token, and many processes can run within the context of a single logon session.)

The *token LUID* is a read-only 64-bit identifier for the token object itself, and is simply a unique identifier that allows you to perform an identity test between two token handles.

The *modification LUID* is a read-only 64-bit identifier that changes whenever any information in the token is adjusted. (For example, if you call into a DLL and it enables and disables a privilege, you can detect it by tracking this value.) The token and modification LUIDs are designed to be used in concert when implementing a performance-tuned access control scheme: Prior to performing a full-blown access check, the server consults a cached dictionary to look for the token LUID for the client making the request. A cache hit results in a record containing a modification LUID and the resulting permissions granted from an earlier access check. Assuming that the modification LUID in the client's token still matches the one in the cache, and that the DACL on the object in question hasn't changed, the server can safely skip the access check because nothing has changed. A cache miss means the server would have to perform the access check, caching the results, of course.[17]

The *expiration time* field never has been (and probably never will be) used for anything. Tokens do not expire (even on Windows 2000).

The *token type* is a read-only value that indicates (for historical reasons) whether this is a **primary token** or an **impersonation token.**

The *impersonation level* is a read-only value that indicates the level of trust the system places in your usage of this token. More information is provided about this and the token type later in the chapter (in the discussion of impersonation).

---

[17] This feels very much like a microoptimization, but considering that someone on the Windows team took the time to implement this feature, perhaps one of the subsystems benefited from a caching scheme such as this. (As this book goes to press, I've heard rumors that COM in fact does use this technique internally.)

```
┌──────────────────────────────────────────────────────────────────────────────┐
│              SYSTEM                              Alice@foo.com                  │
│  ┌──────────────────────────────────────┐   ┌──────────────────────────────┐  │
│  │ Group SIDS:                          │   │ Group SIDs:                  │  │
│  │ Builtin\Administrators               │   │ Foo\Domain Users             │  │
│  │ Everyone                             │   │ Everyone                     │  │
│  │ Authenticated Users*                 │   │ Builtin\Users                │  │
│  │                                      │   │ S-1-5-5-0-96645 (logon session SID) │
│  │ Privileges:                          │   │ Local                        │  │
│  │ SeTcbPrivilege (enabled by default)  │   │ Interactive                  │  │
│  │ SeCreateTokenPrivilege (disabled)    │   │ Authenticated Users          │  │
│  │ SeTakeOwnershipPrivilege (disabled)  │   │                              │  │
│  │ SeCreatePagefilePrivilege (enabled by default) │ Privileges:            │  │
│  │ SeLockMemoryPrivilege (enabled by default) │ SeChangeNotifyPrivilege (enabled by default) │
│  │ SeAssignPrimaryTokenPrivilege (disabled) │ SeUndockPrivilege* (disabled) │  │
│  │ SeIncreaseQuotaPrivilege (disabled)  │   │                              │  │
│  │ SeIncreaseBasePriorityPrivilege (enabled by default) │ Defaults for New Objects: │
│  │ SeCreatePermanentPrivilege (enabled by default) │ Owner DIS: Foo\Alice  │  │
│  │ SeDebugPrivilege (enabled by default) │  │ Group SID: Foo\Domain Users  │  │
│  │ SeAuditPrivilege (enabled by default) │  │ Default DACL:                │  │
│  │ SeSecurityPrivilege (enabled by default) │ grant GENERIC_ALL to Foo\Alice │  │
│  │ SeSystemEnvironmentPrivilege (disabled) │ grant GENERIC_ALL to SYSTEM  │  │
│  │ SeChangeNotifyPrivilege (enabled by default) │                         │  │
│  │ SeBackupPrivilege (disabled)         │   │                              │  │
│  │ SeRestorePrivilege (disabled)        │   │                              │  │
│  │ SeShutdownPrivilege (disabled)       │   │                              │  │
│  │ SeLoadDriverPrivilege (enabled)      │   │                              │  │
│  │ SeProfileSingleProcessPrivilege (enabled by default) │                  │  │
│  │ SeSystemTimePrivilege (enabled)      │   │                              │  │
│  │ SeUndockPrivilege* (enabled)         │   │                              │  │
│  │                                      │   │                              │  │
│  │ Defaults for New Objects:            │   │                              │  │
│  │ Owner SID: Builtin\Administrators    │   │                              │  │
│  │ Group SID: SYSTEM                    │   │                              │  │
│  │ Default DACL:                        │   │                              │  │
│  │ grant GENERIC_ALL to SYSTEM          │   │                              │  │
│  │ grant 0xA0020000 to Builtin\Administrators │                            │  │
│  └──────────────────────────────────────┘   └──────────────────────────────┘  │
└──────────────────────────────────────────────────────────────────────────────┘
```

Figure 4.6.   Tokens for SYSTEM and Alice@foo.com

Peering into a Token

As an example, Figure 4.6 shows some of the more interesting contents of
a token for the System logon session on Windows 2000 (asterisks mark
the elements that are not present in earlier versions of Windows NT), placed
side by side with a token for Alice@foo.com, a normal, nonadministrative
principal.

Getting a Process Token

There are several ways to get a token. The simplest is to reach up into your process and take a peek at the token that attaches your process to its logon session. The `OpenProcessToken` API exists for exactly this purpose.

```
BOOL OpenProcessToken(
  HANDLE   ProcessHandle, // in, handle or pseudohandle
  DWORD    DesiredAccess, // in
  PHANDLE  TokenHandle    // out
);
```

As a first-class citizen of the Windows executive, a token is secured just like any other object (such as a process, thread, or semaphore), and the operating system will always perform an access check when you call `OpenProcessToken`. This isn't terribly interesting when you're getting *your own* process token, because by default you'll be granted virtually all access permissions to it.[18] However, it is possible to open *another process's* token, in which case this access check protects against external tampering. An example of a program that opens another process's token is the version of `PVIEW.EXE` that ships with the Resource Kit. (If you haven't installed the Resource Kit, you should stop reading this now and go install it—the utilities it contains are tremendously useful for developers.) Figure 4.7 shows a screenshot of `PVIEW.EXE` in which I've opened a random process's token to peer into it.[19]

If all you plan to do is peek into the token (perhaps to enumerate the group SIDs), you'll only need to ask for `TOKEN_QUERY` permissions, and here's the classic code you'll quickly get used to writing:

```
HANDLE htok;
OpenProcessToken(GetCurrentProcess(), TOKEN_QUERY,
                 &htok);
```

---

[18] Be careful not to blindly open the token asking for `TOKEN_ALL_ACCESS` permissions, because this macro includes the undocumented permission `TOKEN_ADJUST_SESSIONID`, which you are *not* granted. This shouldn't generally be a problem, because as explained in Chapter 6, you should avoid asking for *all* permissions to any object. Instead, only ask for the permissions you really need.

[19] `PVIEW.EXE` works best when run from the System logon session. I often use a tool called cmdasuser (downloadable from my Web site) that allows me to launch PVIEW (and other programs) in the System logon session. (Although useful for debugging and exploratory purposes, injecting random processes into the TCB isn't a good practice in a production system.)

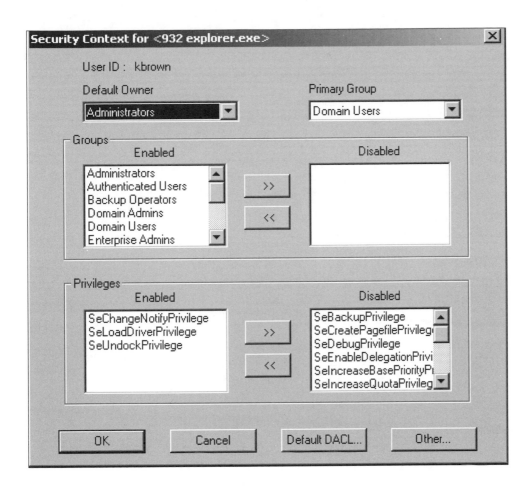

Figure 4.7. `PVIEW.EXE` from the Resource Kit

```
// do something with the token,
// then close it when you're done
CloseHandle(htok);
```

Creating New Logon Sessions

Another way to get a token is to create a new logon session. Later in this chapter (when I cover impersonation), I'll talk about how you can get a token by
authenticating a principal who has sent you a request over the network (examples of secure network protocols you might use to do this include named pipes,
RPC, and COM).

You can also choose to create a brand-new logon session on the fly (just like the way the System SCM does for daemon processes) via the `LogonUser` API, as long as the security context from which you make the call is part of the TCB. The `LogonUser` API is quite easy to use, allowing you to pass in an authority/principal/password tuple and get back a token representing a new logon session for that principal, assuming the LSA could successfully authenticate the principal using the specified password.

```
BOOL LogonUser(
    LPTSTR   lpszUsername,     // in, principal
    LPTSTR   lpszDomain,       // in, authority
    LPTSTR   lpszPassword,     // in
    DWORD    dwLogonType,      // in
    DWORD    dwLogonProvider,  // in, optional
    PHANDLE  phToken           // out
);
```

When you specify the authority via *lpszDomain*, you have three choices. The first choice is to explicitly provide an authority name; the second choice is to pass ".", which indicates that the system should use the local authority (if the machine is a domain controller, then this indicates that *lpszUsername* is a domain account; otherwise, `LogonUser` looks for a matching local account). Finally, if you pass NULL for *lpszDomain*, the system searches for the closest authority (including the local authority) with a matching account name. This is the *documented* behavior, but in earlier versions of Windows NT, passing NULL for *lpszDomain* erroneously results in an access violation, so you will probably want to avoid this third option unless you know for certain your code will only run on Windows 2000 or greater.

You should always pass 0 for the optional *dwLogonProvider* parameter so that your code won't be tied to a single version of Windows NT (there is one exception to this rule that I'll discuss later in the chapter). If successful, `LogonUser` drops a handle to the new token wherever you point *phToken*.

The *dwLogonType* parameter has been purposely left for last, because it's the most interesting of the bunch. You are allowed to create four fundamental types of logon sessions: interactive, batch, service, and network, each of which has different semantics. The first important point to note about each

Table 4.1. Fundamental logon types and rights

Manifest Constant	Value	Logon Rights
LOGON32_LOGON_INTERACTIVE	2	Log on locally
		Deny log on locally[20]
LOGON32_LOGON_BATCH	4	Log on as a batch job
		Deny log on as a batch job
LOGON32_LOGON_SERVICE	5	Log on as a service
		Deny log on as a service
LOGON32_LOGON_NETWORK	3	Access this computer from network
		Deny access this computer from network

of these logon types is that the principal you're attempting to log in must have a distinct logon right on the machine where you are establishing the logon session. Table 4.1 lists the manifest constants that indicate the type of logon you desire, the value of the constant, and the friendly names of the associated logon rights. If the subject hasn't been granted the corresponding logon right, the LSA will deny the logon request, and GetLastError will answer ERROR_LOGON_TYPE_NOT_GRANTED. The appendix shows how to grant these rights programmatically.

By far the best way to detect problems like this during development is to turn on auditing of logon and logoff events. You can do this via the Group Policy snap-in in Windows 2000, or via User Manager in earlier versions of Windows NT. Auditing is an important debugging tool for the traditional systems-level developer; the screenshots in Figure 4.8 show how to enable it in both versions of Windows.

Each time a new logon session is created or destroyed, an entry is placed in the security event log that shows the time, authority and principal name, and the type of login (via the corresponding number shown in Table 4.1). The beauty

---

[20] Windows 2000 introduced the negative flavor of logon rights. Earlier versions of Windows only have positive logon rights.

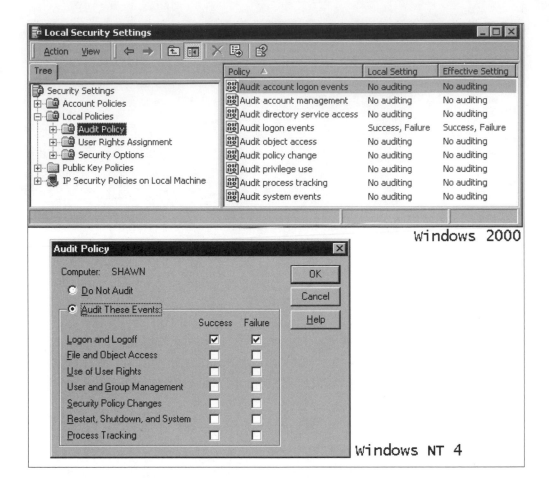

Figure 4.8. Enabling auditing of logon and logoff events

of auditing is that when a logon request fails, the entry in the log will usually tell you exactly what went wrong. Classic examples include the following:

- You forgot to turn off the "User Must Change Password at Next Logon" option when you added the account.

- The account may be disabled.

- The principal may not have the corresponding logon right on the machine where you're attempting to establish the logon session.

Go turn on the auditing feature on the machines you use for development if you haven't done it yet. As long as you're not calling `LogonUser` in a tight loop, or authenticating network clients right and left, it won't hurt your application's performance in any noticeable way, and in the lab, you'll benefit immensely during testing.

By default, all principals are granted the right to a network-style logon, but only specific principals designed to sponsor daemon processes are granted the right to establish a batch or service logon (recall that the COM SCM uses a batch-style logon, whereas the System SCM uses a service-style logon). If you call `CreateService` to install a service configured to run as a distinguished principal, the System SCM will eventually need to create a logon session for that principal. The `CreateService` API doesn't grant the service logon right automatically, so if you neglect to grant this right on the machine where the service is hosted, the SCM won't be able to establish the required logon session, and the service will fail to start.[21] Of course, if you use tools such as the Windows 2000 Services snap-in or the Services applet in the Windows NT Control Panel to configure a service to run as a distinguished principal, these tools will grant the service logon right automatically (and they'll tell you so with a dialog box). Regardless, a well-written install program should be coded to configure the services it installs automatically (see the appendix for a discussion of programmatically granting logon rights and privileges).

When you establish an interactive logon on a machine that is a member of a domain, once the LSA successfully authenticates the principal, it caches enough information on disk to allow local logon in case the machine becomes disconnected from the network (and thus cannot contact its authority for help authenticating domain principals). According to my own tests, `LogonUser` normally takes about 1 millisecond to authenticate a local account, and on the order of 10 milliseconds for a domain account (with a fast, lightly loaded network with a domain controller planted on the same subnet). `LogonUser` is,

---

[21] The same hiccup occurs for COM servers if the RunAs principal is not granted the right to a batch-style logon. If auditing has been enabled as suggested, debugging this problem is a cinch.

well, blazingly fast.[22] However, an interactive-style logon, likely due to the added disk activity, takes on the order of 600 milliseconds.[23] Among the types of logon sessions, the network-style logon stands out as unique in two ways. First, in this case `LogonUser` creates what is known as an **impersonation token,** as opposed to the **primary token** created for the other types of logon sessions. The distinction between these two types of tokens is a historical artifact that is discussed shortly. The second difference is much more important: The logon session produced by `LogonUser` for a network-style logon does not have network credentials (although Windows 2000 provides a variation on this theme as I'll discuss shortly).

Another logon type that was only recently documented for use with `LogonUser` is used by the GINA DLL to unlock the local workstation (this also generates an audit log entry if auditing of logon events is enabled): `LOGON32_LOGON_UNLOCK`. I mention this for completeness; outside of the GINA, I don't see a use for this type of logon.

Windows 2000 added a couple of other interesting logon types that are simply variations on the four fundamental logon types that I've already introduced. The first is a slight modification to the NETWORK logon session that causes it to cache the credentials specified to `LogonUser` (thus the resulting logon session *will* have network credentials); this is `LOGON32_LOGON_NET-WORK_CLEARTEXT`.

The other flag is really twisted and quite a bit of fun: `LOGON32_LOGON_NEW_CREDENTIALS`. This flag causes `LogonUser` to duplicate the token of the caller but give an alternate set of network credentials, specifically the credentials specified to `LogonUser`. Thus the new security context will be represented locally via the original token, but on the network, it'll be authenticated using the new credentials. As I'll discuss in Chapter 5, the RunAs service uses this trick in certain cases. In order to successfully use this logon type, you must

---

[22] If you're not getting similar results, be sure to turn off auditing of logon and logoff events on the machine where you're calling `LogonUser` before you do any performance tests. Also, please don't put too much stock in these actual numbers; your mileage will vary depending on many factors.

[23] If the machine isn't associated with a domain controller, there isn't any appreciable difference in performance between any of the four types of logins (according to my own tests), but this isn't a terribly interesting case for most people.

specify `LOGON32_PROVIDER_WINNT50` for the *dwLogonProvider* argument to `LogonUser`.

Identifying Logon Sessions at Runtime

It was mentioned earlier that logon sessions are identified by a 64-bit number (a LUID). This value can be discovered at runtime by calling `GetToken Information` and requesting the `TokenStatistics` class of information. Well, it turns out that you can also grant or deny access to logon sessions either individually or based on the type of logon session. Each token produced for a particular logon session generally has two special SIDs added to the list of group SIDs for exactly this purpose.

The first SID is a well-known SID that represents the type of logon session in use: INTERACTIVE, NETWORK, BATCH, or SERVICE. You've probably seen some of these in ACL editors. For instance, when you go to a file and grant access to INTERACTIVE, you are granting access to anyone who has established an interactive-style logon session on the machine. When you deny access to NETWORK, you are denying access to anyone who has established a network-style logon. Because all secure transports use network-style logons to represent remote principals making requests via the network, it's clear how useful these two SIDs can be. Distinguishing between interactive, batch, and service logons is less interesting, although Windows 2000 does list the batch and service SIDs in its ACL editors for completeness.

The other special group SID is created on the fly, and is denoted in the token with the `SE_GROUP_LOGON_ID` flag. This SID takes the form S-1-5-5-*X-Y*, where *X* and *Y* are the high- and low-order parts of a LUID that uniquely identifies the logon session.[24]

Why on earth would you want such a thing? It gives you a very fine-grained model of access control, because you can now grant access not just to Alice, say, but to a particular *instance* of Alice. This fine-grained model is used by con-

---

[24] This LUID looks a lot like the logon session identifier, but it's another LUID that's allocated when the logon session is created. It's not clear why there need to be two LUIDs for identifying each logon session, but this is the way it works. A logon session with ID 0x4242 will have an associated logon session SID that looks similar: S-1-5-5-0-0x4237, for instance.

vention with the interactive window station to grant or deny access to individual logon sessions, as you'll see later in Chapter 5.

The System logon session has neither of these two special SIDs. It is not an interactive-style logon. It is not a batch-, service-, or network-style logon either. It just exists implicitly whenever the operating system is alive. It has no logon session SID, because there will only ever be a single instance of the System logon session, and you can always identify it (to grant or deny access) via the SYSTEM SID, S-1-5-18.

Managing Tokens

Often you'll need to peer into a token at runtime. The `GetTokenInformation` API provides access to all the data stored in the token.

```
BOOL GetTokenInformation(
    HANDLE                   TokenHandle,           // in
    TOKEN_INFORMATION_CLASS  TokenInformationClass, // in
    LPVOID                   TokenInformation,      // out
    DWORD                    TokenInformationLength, // in
    PDWORD                   ReturnLength           // out
);
```

For instance, to retrieve the list of group SIDs along with their attributes, you'd allocate a block of memory, pass a pointer to that block via the `TokenInformation` parameter, specify the size of the memory block in bytes via the `TokenInformationLength` parameter, and specify `TokenGroups` for the `TokenInformationClass` parameter. As long as you guessed the buffer size correctly, the function will return a nonzero value indicating that it filled your buffer with a variable-length `TOKEN_GROUPS` data structure, whose format in memory is shown in Figure 4.9.

If you didn't guess the buffer size correctly (or if you passed 0 for the `TokenInformation` and `TokenInformationLength` parameters, indicating that you do not bend spoons with your mind for a living), the system will tell you how large a buffer you need via the `ReturnLength` parameter, and you then make a second call to this function passing a correctly sized buffer. As Figure 4.9 indicates, even though the `TOKEN_GROUPS` data structure contains pointers to SIDs that are variable length by nature, all this information is stuffed into that single block of memory that you allocated.

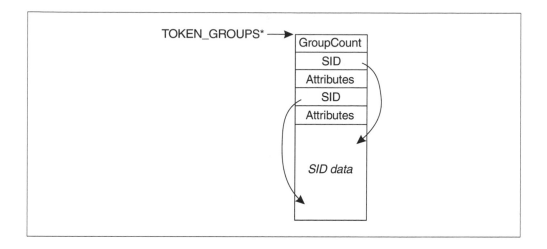

Figure 4.9. The TOKEN_GROUPS data structure

Generally speaking, you'll have no problem figuring out how to extract the information you need from a token via GetTokenInformation. The documentation for the API lists all the classes of information you can retrieve and the corresponding data structure that the function will return. For instance, to retrieve the user SID, you'd specify the TokenUser class of information, and the function would return a TOKEN_USER structure. It's pretty straightforward.

There are a few tricky points to note, however. Many of the elements I included in the Miscellaneous Stuff category (a few sections back) must be retrieved as a bundle via the TokenStatistics class of information. In the TOKEN_STATISTICS structure, there is a LUID with a somewhat confusing name: AuthenticationId. This is simply the logon session LUID. The DynamicCharged field in TOKEN_STATISTICS specifies how many bytes the system has reserved in the token for storing the default settings for new objects (the default owner and primary group SIDs and the default DACL). From what I can tell, this value is always fixed at 500 bytes. The DynamicAvailable field specifies how many of these bytes are free, with the majority of the space being occupied by the default DACL.[25]

---

[25] 500 bytes is room enough to store a default owner, primary group, and a DACL with approximately 12 plain-vanilla entries—plenty of space for most applications (if it's not, you should revisit your design and consider using group nesting or aliases). I know of no documented way to adjust this allocation size.

The following code fragment shows an example of using `GetToken Information` to print out the user SID for a given token.

```
void _printUserSid(HANDLE htok) {
  BYTE buf[sizeof(TOKEN_USER) + _maxSidSize];
  DWORD cb = sizeof buf;
  if (GetTokenInformation(htok, TokenUser,
                          buf, cb, &cb)) {
    TOKEN_USER* ptu = (TOKEN_USER*)buf;
    _printSid(ptu->User.Sid); // see appendix
  }
}
```

You can update the read-write settings in the token via three functions: `SetTokenInformation`, `AdjustTokenGroups`, and `AdjustToken Privileges`. The first of these functions is used to adjust the default settings for new objects:

```
BOOL SetTokenInformation(
  HANDLE                    TokenHandle,           // in
  TOKEN_INFORMATION_CLASS TokenInformationClass,  // in
  LPVOID                    TokenInformation,      // out
  DWORD                     TokenInformationLength, // out
);
```

The usage of this function is very straightforward. Just specify the class of information you want to update (`TokenOwner`, `TokenPrimaryGroup`, or `TokenDefaultDacl`), and pass in the corresponding data structure.

`AdjustTokenGroups` is useless in virtually all scenarios because groups normally cannot be enabled or disabled using this mechanism. (The one esoteric exception was mentioned earlier—a process running in the System logon session can adjust the groups in its token to disable the Administrators group SID.) Aside from `AdjustTokenPrivileges`, which is discussed shortly, this is the extent to which you can change the settings in a token. As you can see, the vast majority of information in a token is immutable.

Memory Allocation and Error Handling Strategies

Let's take a short interlude and talk about how the Windows security APIs deal with memory management and error handling. They generally follow one of two models. The approach taken by `GetTokenInformation` is consistent throughout most of the pre-Windows NT 4.0 security APIs. The caller is responsible for allocating memory, which means the caller always makes two calls to functions that return variable-length data. The first call retrieves the length of the buffer, and the second call actually gets the data. A typical optimization would be to allocate a small block of memory on the stack via an automatic variable and to pass that in on the first try, just in case the data returned is small.

When Windows NT 4.0 was released, a whole new set of APIs was documented that, for better or worse, used a completely reversed scheme for memory management. Rather than forcing the caller to guess the buffer size, these functions allocate memory via `LocalAlloc`, so you are responsible for freeing it via `LocalFree`. This is similar to the model that COM programmers are familiar with, and it's convenient because you only need to make a single call to the API. The compiler can easily enforce the differences between these two models, because in the first model, you must pass a pointer to a block of memory, whereas in the second model, you must pass a pointer to a pointer variable. The error handling story isn't quite so pretty, though.

The earlier APIs use the traditional mechanism of error handling by which each function returns a `BOOL` to indicate success or failure, and by calling `GetLastError` you can retrieve more details. This means you look for a *nonzero value to indicate success*.

The APIs introduced in Windows NT 4.0 use the same style of error handling popularized by COM and the registry APIs (the registry was originally introduced in Windows 3.1 to support COM). These newer APIs return an error code directly, as opposed to a `BOOL`. This means you don't have to call `GetLastError` because the function has already handed you all the information you need via the return value. In this case, you look for a *zero value to indicate success*. Every programmer working with the security APIs gets bitten by this little gotcha eventually, because he or she ends up using the older APIs in concert with the newer ones at some point.

Just to mix things up a bit, Microsoft added some new APIs in Windows 2000 (`ConvertSidToStringSid` is one example) that use the old-style error handling model and the new-style memory allocation model. I once postulated that the Windows API is not inconsistent; rather, it's built from islands of consistency. These are just particularly small islands.

Using Privileges

Privileges are interesting beasts.[26] Not only are they cached in a token using a LUID mapping that isn't guaranteed to be unique across machine reboots,[27] but they are also almost invariably disabled by default; to use a privilege you must first enable it.

Let's stop and review the big picture. When an administrator grants Alice a privilege on AlicesMachine, all new logon sessions she establishes there will include this privilege as an authorization attribute, and all (nonrestricted) tokens will hold this privilege. This generally does *not* mean that a process running in Alice's logon session can use this privilege accidentally. Programs usually need to be deliberate about their use of privileges, manually enabling them and disabling them as appropriate. For instance, as an administrator, by default you are granted `SeDebugPrivilege`, which means that code running in your logon session is allowed to open up *any* process on the machine for all permissions. (This is convenient if you want to kill a daemon that has hung; in this case you must open the process handle for `PROCESS_TERMINATE` access in order to call `TerminateProcess`.) However, lots of folks have discovered that Task Manager often reports `ERROR_ACCESS_DENIED` when asked to kill a daemon process, even when running with administrative privileges. When run by an administrator, Task Manager's token includes `SeDebugPrivilege`, but *it's not enabled*, and Task Manager doesn't enable it (to try to keep you from hurting yourself). If you want Task Manager to be able to kill any process on your machine, you can use a tool such as `PVIEW.EXE` to enable `SeDebug`

---

[26] I dedicated a column to this topic in the August 1999 issue of *Microsoft Systems Journal*. See http://www.develop.com/books/pws for links to all my *MSJ* articles.

[27] The use of LUIDs was introduced as a level of indirection to allow the future addition of user-defined privileges. This feature is not currently available, however, even in Windows 2000. Perhaps someday...

`Privilege` in its process token. `KILL.EXE`, as an example, enables this privilege to perform its work (both `KILL.EXE` and `PVIEW.EXE` ship with the Resource Kit).

Many developers have actually exercised privileges without explicitly writing code to enable them. Sometimes a function exposed by the Windows API will temporarily enable a privilege in order to perform its job (and then will restore it to its previous value). Microsoft is really good about documenting the privileges on which any given API relies, and whether or not it'll automatically enable the privilege for you, but you have to be aware that if one of the required privileges isn't even present in your token to begin with, the function is going to fail when it attempts to enable that privilege.

Recall how privileges get injected into a token in the first place. At authentication time, the LSA constructs a token, populates the user and group SIDs, and then takes the union of all privileges assigned to any of these SIDs and dumps those privileges into the token. That's it. You cannot later inject additional privileges into an existing token. To grant a privilege, you must add a privilege assignment either directly to the principal's account or to a group or alias that you can then assign to the principal.

Once a logon session is created, any (nonrestricted) tokens it exposes contain a snapshot of the authorization attributes for the principal that were captured at the beginning of the session (in other words, at authentication time). This implies that granting a privilege (or a group membership, for that matter) to a principal has *absolutely no effect* on existing logon sessions. After granting a privilege, you may want to "refresh" by reauthenticating and creating a new logon session. The token you get back from this new logon session will have the updated information.

Refreshing means closing all processes currently running within the stale logon session, and restarting them in the new logon session. For an interactive logon session, this can be accomplished by logging out and logging back in (this *does not* mean rebooting Windows, of course). For a daemon process managed by the System or COM SCM, this means shutting down and reactivating the service or COM server.

Each privilege is uniquely identified by a short string (the *programmatic name*), such as `SeTcbPrivilege` and `SeBackupPrivilege`. These names are defined via manifest constants (such as SE_TCB_NAME, SE_BACKUP_NAME, etc.) in the winnt.h header file. Each privilege also has a slightly longer (and localized) *display name* that administrators are familiar with, such as "Act as part of the operating system," "Back up files and directories," and so forth. Sometimes the display names don't look much like the programmatic names (the classic example is SeChangeNotifyPrivilege, whose display name is "Bypass traverse checking"); Table A.4 in the appendix will help you find your way through the jungle.

As mentioned earlier, many functions automatically enable privileges. Here are a few examples: LogonUser requires SeTcbPrivilege. Create ProcessAsUser requires two privileges: SeIncreaseQuotaPrivilege and SeAssignPrimaryTokenPrivilege. GetSecurityInfo requires the SeSecurityPrivilege, but only if you request the SACL of an object.

There are other scenarios in which you will need to manually enable a privilege in order to use it. One classic example is backing up a set of files to which you have not been explicitly granted access. The SeBackupPrivilege exists to grant overarching backup rights to trusted accounts that are normally used for running backup software. This allows an administrator to make a global policy decision as opposed to having to muck with the DACLs of each individual file that needs to be backed up. To exercise the SeBackupPrivilege (assuming it's already in your token), you need to adjust your token to enable the privilege; when you open the file, you specify a special flag that indicates to the file system that your intention is to perform a backup operation. The key function you'll call is AdjustTokenPrivileges:

```
BOOL AdjustTokenPrivileges(
  HANDLE             TokenHandle,         // in
  BOOL               DisableAllPrivileges, // in
  PTOKEN_PRIVILEGES  NewState,            // in, optional
  DWORD              BufferLength,        // in, optional
  PTOKEN_PRIVILEGES  PreviousState,       // out, optional
  PDWORD             ReturnLength         // out, optional
);
```

The *TokenHandle* parameter specifies a token that has been opened for at least TOKEN_ADJUST_PRIVILEGES permissions. If you want to use the

PreviousState parameter to retrieve the old state of whatever privileges you're modifying, *TokenHandle* will also require TOKEN_QUERY permissions. Passing TRUE for *DisableAllPrivileges* causes the function to ignore the *NewState* and *BufferLength* parameters entirely; this disables *all* privileges in the token, including ones that are enabled by default, such as SeChangeNotifyPrivilege.

The *NewState* parameter (and its corresponding byte-length indicator, *BufferLength*) is the core of this API. The TOKEN_PRIVILEGES structure is simply a counted array of pairs; each pair contains a LUID representing the privilege you'd like to tweak and the flags you want to change in the token (the only flag you're allowed to adjust is SE_PRIVILEGE_ENABLED). Because this is a variable-length data structure, if you want to enable more than one privilege in a single shot, you have to do some dynamic memory allocation and some nasty casts. In practice, however, you'll usually only be adjusting a single privilege at a time, which is quite straightforward because the data structure is already declared with one entry in the array.

A convenient way to approach error handling is to simply attempt to enable the privilege you require via AdjustTokenPrivileges, and check to see if it worked. If the token doesn't have the privilege cached inside it, AdjustTokenPrivileges will indicate this, but not by returning FALSE; you must instead call GetLastError and look for the distinguished error code ERROR_NOT_ALL_ASSIGNED. This subtlety is a nasty one because it'll trip you up only in failure conditions.

Given a privilege's programmatic name (such as SeBackupPrivilege), you'll need to look up its local LUID mapping. (The mappings can change across reboots, so don't hardcode these values into your application.) To do this, you'll need to use the LookupPrivilegeValue API:

```
BOOL LookupPrivilegeValue(
  LPCTSTR lpSystemName, // in, optional, machine name
  LPCTSTR lpName,       // in, programmatic name
  PLUID   lpLuid        // out, the LUID mapping
);
```

If for some esoteric reason you needed to obtain the LUID mapping for a privilege on another machine, this function would theoretically be able to obtain it for you if you pass a non-NULL *lpSystemName*, although I can't think of any reason for needing this functionality. In practice, you'll pass NULL for this first parameter and pass the programmatic name via *lpName*, and the function will look up the LUID mapping and dump it wherever you point *lpLuid*. Generally you'll drop this mapping either into a global variable for later use or directly into a TOKEN_PRIVILEGES structure, as in the following code. The following code snippets demonstrate a very common set of helper functions for enabling and restoring privileges that every Windows security developer ends up writing eventually.

```
bool _enablePrivilege(HANDLE htok,
                      const wchar_t* pszPriv,
                      bool bEnable,
                      TOKEN_PRIVILEGES& tpOld) {
    // fill out the request form :-)
    TOKEN_PRIVILEGES tp;
    tp.PrivilegeCount = 1;
    tp.Privileges[0].Attributes =
                      bEnable ? SE_PRIVILEGE_ENABLED : 0;
    if (!LookupPrivilegeValue(0, pszPriv,
                              &tp.Privileges[0].Luid))
        return false;

    // htok must have been opened with these permissions:
    // TOKEN_QUERY (to get the old privileges setting)
    // TOKEN_ADJUST_PRIVILEGES (to adjust the privileges)
    DWORD cbOld = sizeof tpOld;
    if (!AdjustTokenPrivileges(htok, FALSE, &tp,
                               cbOld, &tpOld, &cbOld))
        return false;

    // Check GetLastError() to see if the privilege was
    // successfully adjusted - don't forget this step!
    return (ERROR_NOT_ALL_ASSIGNED != GetLastError());
}

void _restorePrivilege(HANDLE htok,
                       TOKEN_PRIVILEGES& tpOld) {
    AdjustTokenPrivileges(htok, FALSE, &tpOld, 0, 0, 0);
}
```

The following code snippet shows how to use the helper functions from the previous code to exercise `SeBackupPrivilege` in order to dump the contents of any local file, regardless of its DACL.

```
void _backupFile(const wchar_t* pszFile) {
  // open token with permissions needed to adjust privs
  HANDLE htok;
  OpenProcessToken(GetCurrentProcess(),
          TOKEN_QUERY | TOKEN_ADJUST_PRIVILEGES,
          &htok);

  // enable SeBackupPrivilege
  TOKEN_PRIVILEGES tpOld;
  if (_enablePrivilege(htok, SE_BACKUP_NAME,
                       true, tpOld)) {

    // open the file with the intention of backing it up
    HANDLE hfile = CreateFile(pszFile, GENERIC_READ,
                     0, 0,
                     OPEN_EXISTING,
                     FILE_FLAG_BACKUP_SEMANTICS, 0);
    if (INVALID_HANDLE_VALUE != hfile) {
      _dumpFile(hfile);
      CloseHandle(hfile);
    }

    // clean up when we're done
    _restorePrivilege(htok, tpOld);
  }
  else wprintf(L"Failed to enable SeBackupPrivilege"
            L" - do you have this privilege?\n");
  CloseHandle(htok);
}
```

Another classic example in which you'll need to enable a privilege is when you call `ExitWindowsEx` requesting that the operating system shut down or reboot. In this case, you'll exercise `SeShutdownPrivilege`.

There are a couple of other functions related to privileges that bear mentioning. The `LookupPrivilegeName` function performs the reverse mapping (from LUID to programmatic name) and comes in handy when you're dumping the contents of a token and want to list the privileges cached there. `LookupPrivilegeDisplayName` maps from the programmatic name to the localized human-readable name that administrators know and love. These functions are similar in usage to `LookupPrivilegeValue`.

Impersonation

If there were no adjustable settings in a security context (such as privileges and the default DACL), there would be no reason to have tokens; rather, each process could simply have a handle to a logon session where *all* the data in the security context (groups, etc.) would be stored. But because each process needs to have the capacity to make localized changes to settings in its security context without stepping on other processes in the same logon session, the token was introduced as a level of indirection to solve race conditions between processes. But even with a token per process, isn't there still the potential for race conditions within a single process?

Think about what happens when one thread disables a privilege in the token attached to its process. Doesn't this affect all other threads in the same process, all of which are sharing the single security context afforded by the process token? The answer is most clearly yes. If you are writing a multithreaded application, threads can't just start enabling and disabling privileges willy-nilly or changing the default DACL in your token at uncontrolled times. The most common way of dealing with this issue is to simply punt, and set up your token exactly the way you need it for the duration of the process's life, before you start spawning other threads. This is fine as long as all threads need to run in the same security context. But what if one thread needs something a little different?

When you call `CreateThread`, or its little brother in the C runtime, `_beginthreadex`, you've simply created a new schedulable thread of execution within the security context of the process. By default, all threads in a process run within the same security context, specifically, that dictated by the process token. However, there is a function called `SetThreadToken` that allows a thread to slip into a different security context. This feature is known as **impersonation,** which is really just a big word for a very simple mechanical feature of the Windows operating system. By giving a thread its own private token, that thread has complete freedom to adjust privileges, the default DACL, and so

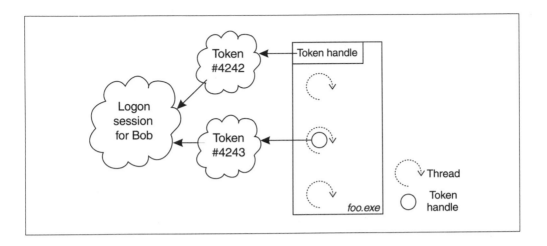

Figure 4.10. Thread tokens solve race conditions

on, without fear of causing race conditions in other parts of the application. Figure 4.10 shows how this works.

The API for `SetThreadToken` is quite straightforward:

```
BOOL SetThreadToken(
  PHANDLE Thread,   // in, optional (NULL implies this thread)
  HANDLE  Token     // in, new security context
};
```

The following code snippet shows an example of a naïve approach to solving a race condition by attempting to give a single thread its own token:

```
DWORD WINAPI _threadProc1(void*) {
  HANDLE htok;
  OpenProcessToken(GetCurrentProcess(),
                   TOKEN_IMPERSONATE, &htok);
  // the goal is to give this thread its own token
  // but does this really do the job?
  SetThreadToken(0, htok);

  // do work (adjust privileges, etc.)

  // by removing the thread token, we revert
```

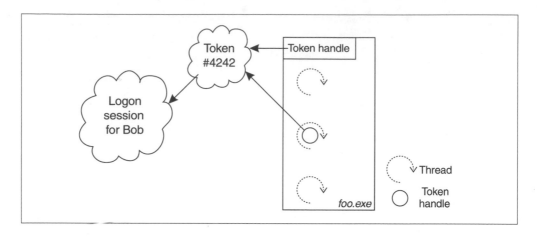

Figure 4.11.   A nonsolution

```
// back to the process's security context
SetThreadToken(0, 0);
return 0;
}
```

As you probably guessed, this code doesn't really do what you want (disregarding the fact that a historical feature of the operating system will cause the first call to SetThreadToken to fail). Figure 4.11 shows what would happen if this code actually ran without errors. In this case, the process and the thread refer to the same physical token object. Duplicating the handle wouldn't help either, because DuplicateHandle doesn't make a copy of the underlying object, which is what you really need here.

Instead, you need to physically duplicate the token so the thread will have its own copy of all the privilege settings, the default DACL, and so on. A function exists to provide this service:

```
BOOL DuplicateTokenEx(
    HANDLE                        ExistingToken, // in
    DWORD                         DesiredAccess, // in
    LPSECURITY_ATTRIBUTES         Attributes,    // in, optional
    SECURITY_IMPERSONATION_LEVEL  ImpLevel,      // in
    TOKEN_TYPE                    Type,          // in
    PHANDLE                       NewToken       // out
);
```

As mentioned earlier, tokens are first-class executive objects, as the *Attributes* parameter indicates. The *ImpLevel* parameter specifies the quality of service the new security context will be allowed to provide (more on this later), and *NewToken* points to the memory location where the function will drop a handle to the new token object.

The *Type* parameter is a historical artifact. If you look at the definition of the TOKEN_TYPE enumeration, you'll find that tokens have been taxonomized into two categories: impersonation versus primary tokens. Don't get hung up on this nomenclature; the meaning is actually much simpler than it sounds. Impersonation tokens can only be attached to threads, and primary tokens can only be attached to processes. That's all it means. The process token obtained earlier via OpenProcessToken was therefore a primary token.

In very early versions of Windows NT (3.x), there were much more severe restrictions on what you could do with a token, depending on where you originally got it from, and hence the token type was introduced to track the intended usage of the token. Because this text assumes you're using Windows NT 4.0 or greater, just think of an impersonation token as a "thread token," and a primary token as a "process token," and use DuplicateTokenEx to convert between the two whenever necessary. Windows NT 4.0 tore down the boundaries between the two by introducing DuplicateTokenEx; the Windows NT 3.x version of this function, DuplicateToken, was hardcoded to only produce impersonation tokens. In fact, now you should be able to see the silly bug that causes the first call to SetThreadToken to fail: The code is attempting to attach a primary token (the one obtained from the process) to a thread (which requires an impersonation token). That's a no-no.

To fix both the logical problem and the silly historical problem, here's the corrected code:

```
DWORD WINAPI _threadProc2(void*) {
  HANDLE htok;
  OpenProcessToken(GetCurrentProcess(),
                   TOKEN_DUPLICATE, &htok);
  // the goal is to give this thread its own token
  // so let's duplicate the object and make it happen
  HANDLE htokForMyThread;
  DuplicateTokenEx(htok, TOKEN_ALL_ACCESS, 0,
```

```
        DEFAULT_IMPERSONATION_LEVEL,
        TokenImpersonation, // ask for a thread token
        &htokForMyThread);

    SetThreadToken(0, htokForMyThread);

    // do work (adjust privileges, etc.)

    // when finished messing with the token handle, we can
    // close it anytime; the thread still references it
    CloseHandle(htokForMyThread);

    // by removing the thread token, we revert
    // back to the process's security context;
    // note that this also destroys the token we created
    // because the thread no longer references its handle
    SetThreadToken(0, 0);
    return 0;
}
```

Note that in order to place a token on a thread, you must have a handle to the token opened with at least TOKEN_IMPERSONATE permissions, and in order to duplicate a token, you must have a handle to the token opened with at least TOKEN_DUPLICATE permissions.

Because giving a thread its own security context to avoid race conditions is such a common practice, a shortcut API performs the duplication and impersonation automatically:

```
BOOL ImpersonateSelf(
    SECURITY_IMPERSONATION_LEVEL ImpLevel, // in
);
```

The single parameter *ImpLevel* sets the impersonation level for the new token (I'll talk about what this means in the upcoming section on trust). Using this API can simplify the code tremendously:

```
DWORD WINAPI _threadProc3(void*) {
  ImpersonateSelf(DEFAULT_IMPERSONATION_LEVEL);
```

```
    // do work (adjust privileges, etc.)

    RevertToSelf();
    return 0;
}
```

Note the usage of `RevertToSelf`, which is effectively the same as a call to `SetThreadToken(0,0)`.

```
BOOL RevertToSelf();
```

This is the preferred function to call to remove the thread token when you're done impersonating.

Impersonating Other Logon Sessions

So far the coverage of impersonation has dealt with race conditions, but this usage is rather pedestrian. What gets really interesting is when you take a token from a foreign logon session and attach it to a thread. Now you can have one thread in a security context for Alice and another thread in a security context for Bob, all hosted in a process whose default security context is that of Charlie. One classic example of this technique is in the System logon session on Windows NT 4.0 and earlier, which didn't have network credentials. Suppose you host a process there, but you need it to be able to make authenticated requests on the network (perhaps you need authenticated access to a remote file system). Here's some code that attempts to achieve this feat:

```
HANDLE _openFileAsUser1(wchar_t* pszAuthority,
                        wchar_t* pszPrincipal,
                        wchar_t* pszPassword,
                        wchar_t* pszFile,
                        DWORD dwDesiredAccess) {
  // attempt to establish a batch-style logon session
  // for the specified principal
  HANDLE htok;
  if (!LogonUser(pszPrincipal, pszAuthority,
                 pszPassword,
                 LOGON32_LOGON_BATCH, 0, &htok))
    return INVALID_HANDLE_VALUE;
```

```
// put the token on our thread (does this work?)
if (!SetThreadToken(0, htok))
  return INVALID_HANDLE_VALUE;

// open the remote file
HANDLE hfile = CreateFile(pszFile, dwDesiredAccess,
                          0, 0, OPEN_EXISTING, 0, 0);

// remove the token from our thread
SetThreadToken(0, 0);

CloseHandle(htok);
return hfile;
}
```

This code is fine, from a logical standpoint, except for that little gotcha about token types. `LogonUser` returns a primary token in most cases. (The network-style logon is the exception; in this case, `LogonUser` returns an impersonation token.) Because the goal here is to obtain a logon session with network credentials, I've chosen to use a batch-style logon, which means I'll get back a primary token, which is not suitable for placing on a thread; `SetThreadToken` is going to fail in this case. This is annoying at best. So what you need to do is duplicate the token, creating an impersonation token suitable for placing on the thread. This is such a common practice that a helper function, `ImpersonateLoggedOnUser`, is provided specifically for this purpose, and makes the code rather trivial.

```
BOOL ImpersonateLoggedOnUser(
  HANDLE Token, // in, impersonation or primary token
);
```

This function takes either type of token (primary or impersonation), performs the conversion to an impersonation token if necessary, and drops the resulting token on the current thread.

The following code snippet shows how to use this shortcut function, and has the added benefit that it actually works, regardless of the type of logon session that you acquire (assuming that the principal being logged in has the corresponding logon right).

```
HANDLE _openFileAsUser2(wchar_t* pszAuthority,
                        wchar_t* pszPrincipal,
                        wchar_t* pszPassword,
                        wchar_t* pszFile,
                        DWORD dwDesiredAccess) {
    // attempt to establish a batch logon session
    // for the specified principal
    HANDLE htok;
    if (!LogonUser(pszPrincipal, pszAuthority,
                    pszPassword,
                    LOGON32_LOGON_BATCH, 0, &htok))
        return INVALID_HANDLE_VALUE;

    // put the token on our thread (this works!)
    ImpersonateLoggedOnUser(htok);

    // open the remote file
    HANDLE hfile = CreateFile(pszFile, dwDesiredAccess,
                        0, 0, OPEN_EXISTING, 0, 0);

    // stop impersonating
    RevertToSelf();

    CloseHandle(htok);
    return hfile;
}
```

Here's a usage example from within a daemon process running in the System logon session, using the _readSecret helper function developed in the appendix.[28]

---

[28] This technique is not necessary in Windows 2000 domains because, as mentioned earlier, the System logon session *does* have network credentials in this case.

```
wchar_t szPassword[80];
_readSecret(L"MyDaemonSecret", szPassword,
            sizeof szPassword / sizeof *szPassword);
HANDLE hfile = _openFileAsUser2(L"MyDomain",
                    L"MyDaemonAccount",
                    szPassword,
                    L"\\\\machine\\share\\foo.txt",
                    GENERIC_READ);
ZeroMemory(szPassword, sizeof szPassword);
```

The assumption is that the install program for this application has created an account in MyDomain known as MyDaemonAccount, and stuffed the password for this account into the password stash in the LSA for later use by this piece of trusted code that runs in the TCB. Also, the install program should have granted the batch logon right to MyDaemonAccount; otherwise, the call to LogonUser will fail.

Although this is an interesting example of manipulating logon sessions, you should think long and hard about storing passwords (especially for domain accounts) on random machines on the network, because the local administrator of the machine can read those passwords. Managing secrets is just plain hard.

One final thing should be clarified regarding impersonating another logon session. When a process running as Alice has a thread that impersonates Bob, that thread is running in Bob's security context, not some random security context created by mixing Bob's and Alice's authorization attributes. In fact, often you might want to write code that looks at the current effective token: If there's a thread token, you'll want that; but if not, you'll settle for the process token. Here's a helper function that I've found quite useful in the past.

```
HANDLE _getEffectiveToken(DWORD dwDesiredAccess,
                          BOOL  bWantImpToken,
    SECURITY_IMPERSONATION_LEVEL impLevel) {
  HANDLE htok;
  if (OpenThreadToken(GetCurrentThread(),
                      dwDesiredAccess, TRUE, &htok)) {
    return htok;
  }
  else if (ERROR_NO_TOKEN == GetLastError()) {
```

```
    DWORD grfAccess = bWantImpToken ? TOKEN_DUPLICATE :
                                      dwDesiredAccess;
    if (OpenProcessToken(GetCurrentProcess(),
                         grfAccess, &htok)) {
        if (bWantImpToken) {
            // convert primary to impersonation token
            HANDLE htokImp;
            if (!DuplicateTokenEx(htok, dwDesiredAccess, 0,
                    impLevel, TokenImpersonation, &htokImp)) {
                htokImp = 0;
            }
            CloseHandle(htok);
            return htokImp;
        }
        else return htok;
    }
    return 0;
}
```

Note the careful consideration given to the type of token returned. It can be quite annoying, but some functions (such as `AccessCheck`, `CheckToken Membership`, etc.) expect you to pass an impersonation token as opposed to a primary token. This helper function optionally transforms the process token into an impersonation token before handing it back; thus, you'll always get an impersonation token even if your thread is not currently impersonating.

Impersonating Remote Clients

What this chapter has been leading up to is the traditional use of impersonation in a classic client/server distributed system. The runtime components of most sophisticated communication subsystems exposed on Windows (named pipes, RPC, and COM, for example) automatically establish a network-style logon session once a client (Alice, say) is authenticated, keeping the security context alive in case the server (Bob, say) needs it. The named pipes subsystem (technically, this is just the file system redirector) stores the security context so that it is accessible via the pipe handle. MSRPC stores it so it's accessible via the binding handle. COM (which sits on top of RPC) allows access to this information via an implicit mechanism using thread local storage. The important point is that the logon session is established whether or not you decide to impersonate, and the cost of impersonation is really just a switch to protected mode to access a security context that's already there (*establishing* the logon session in the first place is the expensive part).

Assuming the client is successfully authenticated, the server can impersonate the client by making a single function call:

```
BOOL ImpersonateNamedPipeClient(HANDLE NamedPipe);
BOOL RpcImpersonateClient(RPC_BINDING_HANDLE h);
HRESULT CoImpersonateClient();
```

These functions cause the underlying security infrastructure to look at the client's security context (which was already established after authentication) and drop a corresponding token on the caller's thread to cause the thread to run in that security context.

To stop impersonating, there's a matching set of functions:

```
BOOL RevertToSelf();
BOOL RpcRevertToSelf();
HRESULT CoRevertToSelf();
```

The beauty of this model is that it insulates the developer from having to write custom access checks (bugs in access-checking code can be devastating in a sensitive secure application). While impersonating, any local executive objects opened by the thread will be opened on the client's behalf, and the operating system will perform all the necessary access checks and audits using the client's security context. You might want to review the benefits and limitations of this model in Chapter 3.

If you plan on using a more sophisticated access control strategy, you'll need direct access to the client's token. Ultimately what you want is a function named `GetClientToken`. Unfortunately, this function doesn't exist, but it is trivial to implement by hand. To do this, temporarily impersonate the client just long enough to reach up and get a handle to the client's token by calling `OpenThreadToken`, and then stop impersonating *immediately*.

```
BOOL OpenThreadToken(
    HANDLE  ThreadHandle,  // in
    DWORD   DesiredAccess, // in
    BOOL    OpenAsSelf,    // in
    PHANDLE TokenHandle    // out
);
```

To use this function, pass the handle of a thread (or the pseudohandle returned by `GetCurrentThread`) for the first parameter, pass the access permissions you need via *DesiredAccess*, and pass TRUE for *OpenAsSelf* (more on this later). The function will drop the token handle wherever you point via *Token Handle*.

At this point you've obtained your own reference to the client's token, and as long as you hold the handle open, you can safely stop impersonating (which causes the thread to close its own reference to the token). You can continue to use the token until you're done with it, at which time you should naturally call `CloseHandle`.

Here's the function (using COM as a concrete example):

```
HANDLE _getClientToken() {
  CoImpersonateClient();
  HANDLE htok;
  OpenThreadToken(GetCurrentThread(), TOKEN_QUERY,
                  TRUE, &htok);
  CoRevertToSelf();
  return htok;
}
```

Trust

Figure 4.12 shows an example of a COM server (running as Bob) using the classic impersonation model, impersonating each client (Alice and Ted, say) and performing work from within the confines of the client's security context. How do Alice and Ted feel about this? Perhaps Alice trusts Bob to impersonate her, but Ted might not feel the same way. We need some way of limiting the scope of what Bob can do with a client's token, in order to provide some form of protection for clients. In all the communication services discussed so far there is such a mechanism; it is specified as a fixed enumeration known as the

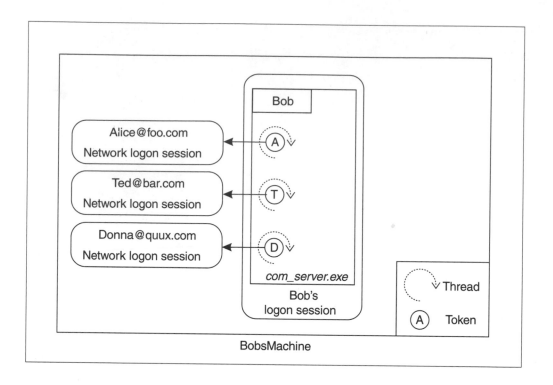

Figure 4.12. The classic impersonation model

impersonation level. Each token has an impersonation level that indicates how the security context may be used, and there are four levels to choose from:

```
typedef enum _SECURITY_IMPERSONATION_LEVEL {
    SecurityAnonymous,
    SecurityIdentification,
    SecurityImpersonation,
    SecurityDelegation
} SECURITY_IMPERSONATION_LEVEL;
```

The loosest setting is `SecurityDelegation`, which indicates that the security context doesn't have any restrictions on its use. If Alice grants this level of impersonation, Bob can happily use her security context to acquire local resources, and (assuming the authentication protocol supports it and the security gods are smiling on him[29]) Bob can use Alice's security context to make authenticated calls on the network, acquiring network resources on Alice's behalf. If Bob makes an authenticated call to Shannon using Alice's security context, Shannon will think the call came from Alice. She'll have no idea that it's really Bob masquerading as Alice.[30]

What's really interesting, though, is that Shannon can now use Alice's security context to talk to Juan, and so on. The only limit on this chain of delegation of Alice's network credentials is that they will expire after a certain amount of time (less than ten hours by default; see Chapter 7 for details). This shouldn't give you a warm fuzzy feeling, though; a bad guy can do a lot of damage in one hour, let alone ten. My own recommendation is to avoid relying on delegation if at all possible. This impersonation level is implemented on Windows 2000, but isn't supported by earlier versions of Windows NT.

A much tighter setting is `SecurityImpersonation`, whose name is somewhat misleading. Regardless of what impersonation level a token has, you can always take that token and drop it on your thread (thus impersonating). What the impersonation level controls is what sort of things you can do while you're running in the client's security context. If Bob gets a token from Alice at the `SecurityImpersonation` level, he'll be able to acquire *local* resources using Alice's security context, but he is not allowed to make authenticated network hops under this guise. This is a requirement for file and Web servers that use authentication and impersonation to stream back requested files to a client. (The file and Web server that ships with Windows requires this, so when you open a remote file, you're implicitly granting this level of trust.) Named pipes, RPC, and COM allow the client to choose the impersonation level programmatically, as demonstrated later.

The preferred setting for applications that shun the impersonation access control model in preference to a role- or object-centric model is `Security Identification`, because it keeps honest servers honest. A token with this

---

[29] This is a cute way of saying that there's some configuration you need to tweak to make delegation really work, even in Windows 2000 with Kerberos. See Chapter 7 for the details.

[30] This is the behavior of the Windows 2000 implementation of Kerberos. Other implementations (DCE is the classic example) provide more details on the impersonation chain, but are necessarily much more complex.

level of impersonation may not be used to acquire *any* resources on the client's behalf, not even local resources. As soon as Bob puts a token of this class on his thread, his thread runs in a severely weakened security context. The thread is not allowed to open even local executive objects such as files, processes, and semaphores, because that would violate the trust granted by the client. If Bob tries to call `CreateFile`, for instance, to open a local file while impersonating, `CreateFile` will fail and `GetLastError` will return `ERROR_ACCESS _DENIED`, which makes sense—the client is denying Bob the right to use his or her security context in this fashion. This impersonation level appears to put the client in control.

So what use is a token in this state? It's of absolutely no use for impersonation, but it has all the client's identity and authorization attributes tucked neatly inside and can therefore be used for performing access checks. Once Bob has Alice's token, he can call `GetTokenInformation` to see if she's a member of a particular group or alias (this is a form of role-centric access control). He can also call the `AccessCheck` function (which is discussed in Chapter 6) to perform object-centric access checks.

So, assuming that Bob wants to use one of these more sophisticated access control models, and that Alice can therefore make calls to him granting only `SecurityIdentification` trust without breaking his code, Bob is now in an interesting conundrum. Remember that the only way Bob can get his hands on Alice's token is to impersonate via `CoImpersonateClient` (or one of its siblings listed earlier). Recall the code suggested earlier for acquiring the client's token:

```
HANDLE _getClientToken() {
  CoImpersonateClient();
  HANDLE htok;
  OpenThreadToken(GetCurrentThread(), TOKEN_QUERY,
                  TRUE, &htok);
  CoRevertToSelf();
  return htok;
}
```

Let's say Bob uses this function to get a handle to Alice's token. When the call to `OpenThreadToken` executes, whose security context is the thread running in? It's running in Alice's context because Bob has impersonated Alice. But because Alice has limited her security context to `SecurityIdentification`, Bob isn't allowed to open executive objects while impersonating Alice, and a token is a first-class executive object. Well, to get Bob out of this pinch, `OpenThreadToken` takes a third parameter, `OpenAsSelf`, that can be used to indicate that the system should ignore the fact that the thread is impersonating Alice and should use the process's security context (Bob's token) to do the work. If you forget this and pass `FALSE`, `OpenThreadToken` will fail with `ACCESS_DENIED` in this case. Chant with me now: I've got job security...I've got job security...

The last setting, `SecurityAnonymous`, is rather odd, and as far as I can tell, it's only actually implemented for local communication. It also appears to work on the wire with named pipes, but is silently promoted to `SecurityIdentification` for remote calls using RPC and COM. In any case, this type of token cannot be opened *at all*. Calls to `OpenThreadToken` will fail, and `GetLastError` will return `ERROR_CANT_OPEN_ANONYMOUS`. This allows a client to prove to the server that she can be authenticated, but she doesn't want to disclose her identity (whether this is useful is another question entirely).

One very common trap related to trust levels manifests itself via an undocumented feature (or a bug—it's your call) in `GetUserName(Ex)`. This function fails if called from within a security context whose impersonation level is less than `SecurityImpersonation`.

Before leaving this topic, here's a word of advice. Take the guarantees provided by `SecurityIdentification` and `SecurityImpersonation` with a grain of salt. First of all, Alice must trust the remote operating system to not allow Bob (the server principal) to misuse Alice's token. If Bob's system is compromised, `SecurityIdentification` clearly can be upgraded to `SecurityImpersonation` without Alice's consent. What's critical is that Alice doesn't send her *network* credentials to Bob, because then the damage wouldn't be limited to the already compromised machine. Another issue arises with local communication specifically when using NTLM authentication (which is what COM uses by default for all local communications as of this writing). NTLM simply copies around tokens when you authenticate with local servers.

This means that a local server will have a token to the same physical logon session as the client, and even if the client specifies `SecurityImpersonation`, *local servers will have full access to the client's network credentials*. On the other hand, `SecurityDelegation` means something real: This is a client-controlled limit (among other system controlled limits that I discussed earlier) that helps determine whether her network credentials are sent to remote servers. A bad guy cannot force a client to give up her network credentials without compromising the client's machine.

Restricting Authorization Attributes

Consider a process token. In it are SIDs and privileges, which I refer to generically as authorization attributes. What would happen if you were to remove some of these attributes from the token? Let's consider privileges first. Would the token confer more or less access to the process if it had half as many privileges? Privileges are always used to *grant* some particular type of access, so it's quite simple: If you remove a privilege from a process's token, you always lower its level of access.

What about a group, though? As mentioned earlier in this chapter, because it's possible to grant access *and* to deny access to groups, it's not safe to say that removing a group from a process's token would reduce its access. (In practice, it almost always will, but security isn't about saying *almost*.)

The only way to safely eliminate access from being granted via a particular group SID is to annotate it with the `SE_GROUP_USE_FOR_DENY_ONLY` flag in the token. If this sounds interesting, you'll like the following function, which was introduced in Windows 2000:

```
BOOL CreateRestrictedToken(
    HANDLE   ExistingTokenHandle,              // in
    DWORD    Flags,                            // in
    DWORD    DisableSidCount,                  // in
    PSID_AND_ATTRIBUTES  SidsToDisable,        // in, optional
    DWORD    DeletePrivilegeCount,             // in
    PLUID_AND_ATTRIBUTES PrivilegesToDelete,   // in, optional
    DWORD    RestrictedSidCount,               // in
    PSID_AND_ATTRIBUTES  SidsToRestrict,       // in
    PHANDLE NewTokenHandle                     // out
    );
```

Given an existing token object opened for TOKEN_DUPLICATE permissions, you can call this function to create a new token with restricted authorization attributes. It's pretty clear-cut how to restrict privileges: Simply remove them from the new token. The privileges you'd like to remove are represented by *DeletePrivilegeCount* and *PrivilegesToDelete*, and the *Flags* parameter (whose only valid nonzero value is DISABLE_MAX_PRIVILEGE) can be used to indicate that the new token should have no privileges whatsoever.

When dealing with restricting SIDs, if you have a particular SID in mind that you want stripped from the token (at least for the purposes of granting access), the easiest thing to do is to annotate that SID in the new token with the SE_GROUP_USE_FOR_DENY_ONLY flag. CreateRestrictedToken takes the intersection of the SIDs in the token and the SIDs you specify via the counted array *DisableSidCount* and *SidsToDisable*, and sets the deny-only flag for those SIDs (note that you can even restrict the user SID in this fashion).

If you don't know ahead of time which SIDs will need to be disabled in this fashion, but you know which SIDs you're willing to *allow* the token to use in order to gain access, you can specify them via the counted array *Restricted SidCount* and *SidsToRestrict*. Thus the resulting token will have not only a user SID and a list of group SIDs, but also the list of restricting SIDs that you specified.

Remember how access checks work: The system simply compares a list of SIDs in a token with a list of SIDs in a DACL and grants or denies access appropriately (see Chapter 6 for a more detailed description). When a list of restricting SIDs is present, the system will perform the access check *twice,* using first the normal list of SIDs (the user SID plus the group SIDs) and then, if that succeeds, making a second check with the list of restricting SIDs. Access is granted only if *both* these access checks succeed.

With the introduction of restricted tokens in Windows 2000, you need to be very careful about writing code that looks for a particular SID by traversing the user and group SIDs. If the token you're looking at has a list of restricting SIDs, you need to take that into consideration. Windows 2000 will tell you whether or not there is a list of restricting SIDs via the following function:

```
BOOL IsTokenRestricted(
    HANDLE TokenHandle  // in
);
```

Practically speaking, however, if you need to check for the logical presence of a SID in a token, the safest and easiest way is to simply call `CheckToken Membership`:

```
BOOL CheckTokenMembership(
    HANDLE TokenHandle, // in, optional
    PSID   SidToCheck,  // in
    PBOOL  IsMember     // out
);
```

This function takes a token and a SID, and tells you whether an access check would actually use that SID to grant access, and thus whether or not you should consider that SID as being an enabled authorization attribute in the token.

This function doesn't exist in Windows NT 4, but neither do tokens with lists of restricting SIDs. The function is quite easy to implement by hand on both platforms in case you need portable code. An implementation is included here for your convenience; if some of it looks foreign at this point, hang in there—`AccessCheck` and friends are discussed in Chapter 6.

```
#if _WIN32_WINNT < 0x500
BOOL WINAPI CheckTokenMembership(HANDLE TokenHandle,
                                 PSID    SidToCheck,
                                 PBOOL   IsMember) {
  // if no token was passed, CTM uses the effective
  // security context (the thread or process token)
  if (!TokenHandle)
    TokenHandle = _getEffectiveToken(TOKEN_QUERY, TRUE,
                            SecurityIdentification);
  if (!TokenHandle)
    return FALSE;

  // create a security descriptor that grants a
  // specific permission only to the specified SID
  BYTE dacl[sizeof ACL + _maxVersion2AceSize];
  ACL* pdacl = (ACL*)dacl;
```

```
        InitializeAcl(pdacl, sizeof dacl, ACL_REVISION);
        AddAccessAllowedAce(pdacl, ACL_REVISION, 1,
                            SidToCheck);
        SECURITY_DESCRIPTOR sd;
        InitializeSecurityDescriptor(&sd,
          SECURITY_DESCRIPTOR_REVISION);
        SID world = { SID_REVISION, 1,
                      SECURITY_WORLD_SID_AUTHORITY,
                      SECURITY_WORLD_RID };
        SetSecurityDescriptorOwner(&sd, &world, FALSE);
        SetSecurityDescriptorGroup(&sd, &world, FALSE);
        SetSecurityDescriptorDacl(&sd, TRUE, pdacl, FALSE);

        // Now let AccessCheck do all the hard work
        GENERIC_MAPPING gm = { 0, 0, 0, 1 };
        PRIVILEGE_SET ps;
        DWORD cb = sizeof ps;
        DWORD ga;
        return AccessCheck(&sd, TokenHandle, 1, &gm,
                           &ps, &cb, &ga, IsMember);
    }
#endif
```

This code implements the documented semantics of `CheckToken Membership`, and it works on both Windows 2000 and Windows NT 4 (although for Windows 2000, you'll notice that my implementation is removed by the preprocessor in favor of the implementation provided by the OS).

Restricting Authorization Attributes Using Jobs

If you think that `CreateRestrictedToken` is neat, just wait until you see what you can do with a job object. Job objects are new to Windows 2000. (If you're not familiar with them, there are existing texts that can give you an introduction.)[31] This section focuses on how to use a job to restrict the authorization attributes of all the processes (and even the threads) in the job. As you'll see, this is really quite a powerful sandboxing mechanism.

A job is a lot like a strip of flypaper. Once you attach a process to a job, you can never remove it (if you try, you'll get `ERROR_ACCESS_DENIED`). The main

---

[31] See, for example, Richter (1999a).

goal of the job object is to assign quotas and other types of restrictions on a set of processes, and it's important that a process can't decide to remove those restrictions. In fact, a process can't even get "unstuck" by launching another copy of itself (or of any other program, for that matter); by default, jobs are configured so that all child processes are also associated with the same job, which closes this loophole.

With this in mind, take a look at the security limits that you can place on a job:

```
typedef struct _JOBOBJECT_SECURITY_LIMIT_INFORMATION {
    DWORD               SecurityLimitFlags;
    HANDLE              JobToken;
    PTOKEN_GROUPS       SidsToDisable;
    PTOKEN_PRIVILEGES   PrivilegesToDelete;
    PTOKEN_GROUPS       RestrictedSids;
} JOBOBJECT_SECURITY_LIMIT_INFORMATION;
#define JOB_OBJECT_SECURITY_NO_ADMIN         0x00000001
#define JOB_OBJECT_SECURITY_RESTRICTED_TOKEN 0x00000002
#define JOB_OBJECT_SECURITY_ONLY_TOKEN       0x00000004
#define JOB_OBJECT_SECURITY_FILTER_TOKENS    0x00000008
```

The first field is a set of flags that indicate what sort of security limits you'd like to set. The first two flags are pretty straightforward. The first flag (NO_ADMIN) blocks processes whose tokens contain the Administrators alias (in the CheckTokenMembership sense) from joining the job. The second flag (RESTRICTED_TOKEN) blocks processes running without a restricted token from joining the job.

The third flag (ONLY_TOKEN) indicates that as each process is added to the job, the system should replace that process's token with the one you specify via *JobToken*. Normally this will happen automatically as processes that are already in the job create new child processes. In order to make this safe, the process must not have done any work by the time it's added to the job; thus, to add a new process (one that was created outside the job) you need to create the new process in a suspended state, add it to the job, and then call ResumeThread to let it run. AssignProcessToJobObject will fail if you forget to do this.

The last flag (`FILTER_TOKENS`) is the most mind-twisting and cool one of the bunch. This flag indicates that if a thread in a job attempts to impersonate some arbitrary token (even by calling `SetThreadToken`), the system will take that token and create a new restricted token using the last three counted arrays in the data structure just shown: *SidsToDisable*, *PrivilegesToDelete*, and *RestrictedSids*. The restricted token is what will end up on the thread.

Terminating a Logon Session

Think about what it would take to completely terminate a logon session. The operating system would have to terminate all processes using the logon session, and would have to deal with any threads in other processes that are running in the security context of that logon session (via impersonation). What should the operating system do with a thread that's impersonating? Terminate it? Silently stop it from impersonating? Let it keep impersonating but invalidate its token so that each new resource it attempts to acquire fails? It's a hard problem. `ExitWindowsEx` provides a simple enough solution that works pretty well in most cases.

```
BOOL ExitWindowsEx(
    UINT Flags,      // in
    DWORD Reserved   // in, ignored
);
```

The older sibling, `ExitWindows`, is simply a macro that expands to a call to `ExitWindowsEx(EWX_LOGOFF, 0xFFFFFFFF)`. What's interesting about the documentation for `EWX_LOGOFF` is that it seems to imply that it terminates a logon session, when in actuality it's much simpler-minded: It simply shuts down all processes whose tokens refer to the logon session of whoever called `ExitWindowsEx`. As long as no other processes hold open handles to tokens from that logon session, this will naturally terminate the logon session. There are no guarantees, though. This function is sensitive to impersonation, so if a process running as Bob has a thread that is currently impersonating Alice and that thread calls `ExitWindowsEx`, it will affect processes in *Alice's* logon session, not Bob's.

One rather bizarre limitation of this function is that it may only be called from a process attached to the interactive window station. (This restriction is discussed further in Chapter 5.)

Summary

- There are several types of logon sessions: the System logon session as well as service, batch, network, and interactive logon sessions.

- The System logon session always exists, and there is only one of these per machine.

- A service is configured by default to run in the System logon session, but can also be configured to run as a distinguished principal, in which case the System SCM will start a new service logon session for the process.

- Another type of daemon logon session is the batch logon, used by the COM SCM. It is virtually indistinguishable (from a practical perspective) from a service logon.

- A network logon session is initiated whenever a remote client is successfully authenticated. Network logon sessions do not normally have network credentials, which is done to protect the clients that they represent.

- Interactive logon sessions are normally produced via Winlogon.

- `LogonUser` can be used to create new logon sessions, but may only be called from the TCB.

- Tokens represent the surface area of a logon session. The token contains a snapshot of the authorization attributes discovered at authentication time, as well as other settings that affect the security context. Most of these settings are immutable.

- Each process has a token that attaches it to a logon session.

- A thread can override the default security context of the process by impersonating.

- Often impersonation is used simply to eliminate race conditions in a multithreaded program. In this case, `ImpersonateSelf` is a useful shortcut.

- For historical reasons, there are two types of tokens: primary and impersonation tokens. The only difference is that a primary token can be associated with a process (not a thread), and an impersonation token can be associated with a thread (not a process). Use `DuplicateTokenEx` if you need to convert between the two types.

- When making an authenticated request via named pipes, RPC, or COM, a client can programmatically specify the level of trust he or she has in the server. This is known as the impersonation level.

- The impersonation level controls how strong or weak a security context the server gets when it impersonates the client. The two most common impersonation levels used in distributed Windows applications are `SecurityIdentification` and `Security Impersonation`. The former only allows the server to perform access checks and obtain information about the client. The latter allows the server to also obtain local resources (and call `GetUserName`) while impersonating the client. Prefer `SecurityIdentification` to protect your clients unless you are using the impersonation model for access control.

- Restricted tokens can be used (on Windows 2000) to limit the authorization attributes in a security context. In the presence of restricted tokens, one must be careful about enumerating SIDs in a token. Prefer to use `CheckTokenMembership` to check for SIDs in a token, even if you have to roll your own implementation in Windows NT 4 for portability.

- Jobs can be used to automatically apply a policy of restricting tokens in all processes attached to the job.

- `ExitWindowsEx` can be used to simulate a logoff. This function closes (with optional forcefulness) all processes in the caller's logon session.

Chapter 5

Window Stations and Profiles

Lots of developers are surprised to find that window stations even exist. Most folks think that window handles are valid anywhere on a machine, and that as long as you don't try to send them across the wire, you can call `SendMessage` to perform interprocess communication. This works pretty well in 16-bit Windows, up to and including Windows 9x, but often fails miserably in Windows NT and Windows 2000, where security is taken seriously.

This chapter is useful for people developing services and COM servers that are activated by the System or COM SCM, because these SCMs decide in which window station your code will run, which can make a tremendous difference in how your server behaves in production, as well as in the lab. The chapter is even more useful for people who want to *emulate* the services of the System and COM SCMs.

What Is a Window Station?

The user interface (UI) in Windows has classically been one of the most fine-tuned and well-oiled pieces of machinery on the platform. Back in the early 1990s, shortly before Windows 3.1 shipped, reasonably fast and affordable video hardware was becoming widely available, and consumers began to expect a smooth and responsive user interface. Windows user interface developers quickly became adept at harvesting every ounce of performance from the Graphical Device Interface (GDI) and USER, sometimes even at the expense of program readability and maintainability. But programs that consistently provided a snappy, responsive UI were well regarded in those early days. With today's faster processors and advanced video hardware, developers don't have to work nearly as hard as they used to in order to achieve this, but consumers still place a high value on a responsive UI.

Just as Windows takes a session-oriented approach to authentication via the logon session, so too it takes a session-oriented approach to its user interface, via the **window station.** Rather than shackling each and every GDI and USER object with individual security settings, Windows simply provides a protected world within which these objects can take a laissez-faire view of security. This approach provides a reasonable security model for user interface components without affecting their performance in any noticeable way. It also keeps user interface programmers happy—they generally don't have to think much about security.

A window station is a secure executive object that encapsulates an entire USER environment, complete with a clipboard, an atom table, and a set of one or more desktops. The security descriptor associated with the window station allows its owner to control access to several aspects of the environment, including which principals are allowed to create windows, menus, and desktops or to view the clipboard contents. Generally the system grants these permissions as a group, and there is no documentation as to how individual permissions are applied in the face of impersonation.[1]

As discussed in Chapter 2, each process is associated with a single logon session and a single window station, and normally window station and logon

---

[1] Because each process implicitly opens handles to its window station and desktop early during process initialization (these are the handles returned from GetProcessWindowStation and GetThreadDesktop), figuring out which handles are used to grant or deny access during the process's lifetime can be tricky. If a thread in Bob's process suddenly starts impersonating Alice and then creates a menu, will the system attempt to open a new handle to the desktop or simply use the handle acquired earlier on Bob's behalf? Because this behavior is not documented and could therefore potentially change from service pack to service pack, I simply mention this as a caveat to those who would try to use a finer-grained model of window station security, especially in concert with impersonation.

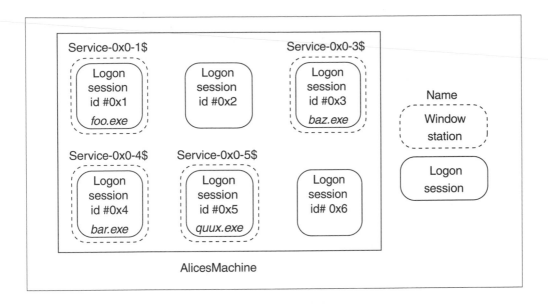

Figure 5.1. Natural window station boundaries

session boundaries coincide, as shown in Figure 5.1. (I'll talk about the strange-looking window station names shortly.) Also note that a window station is naturally created on demand, that is, when the first process in the logon session starts. (If no processes live in a particular logon session, there's no reason to have a window station, as Figure 5.1 demonstrates.)

A window station is truly a private container of windows. Whenever a thread creates a window, that window is forever bound to the window station where it was created. Threads running in processes attached to *other* window stations cannot see or touch that window. Recall that pointers are *process relative,* making it meaningless for a thread in process A to share pointers with process B unless B agrees to expose a section of shared memory explicitly (even then, the physical pointer values won't normally coincide). Similarly, window handles are *window station relative,* making it impossible for threads in process A to touch the windows in process B if A and B live in different window stations; there is no mechanism for sharing window handles across window station boundaries. If a thread in process A wants to talk to windows that live in process B (perhaps via `SendMessage` or `PostMessage`), it must temporarily attach process A to

B's window station. (Even this back door generally won't work without manipulating window station DACLs, as discussed shortly.) From a practical perspective, one implication of this feature is that you cannot use window messages as an interprocess communication mechanism across window station boundaries.

There are two functions that can be used within a process to get or set its corresponding window station, which means that *theoretically* a process can migrate from one window station to any another during its lifetime. (Practically speaking, this is more difficult than it sounds because access permissions need to be addressed, but those details will be discussed later.) The functions are as follows:

```
HWINSTA GetProcessWindowStation();
BOOL SetProcessWindowStation(HWINSTA hWinSta);
```

Window Station Permissions

Given that a window station protects a USER environment, just what sort of permissions can you control with it? The set of window station permissions is documented sparsely, but by doing lots of searches and lots of experiments, I've figured out how most of these permissions affect your life.[2]

- **WINSTA_ENUMDESKTOPS** A window station handle open with this permission may be passed to the EnumDesktops function.

- **WINSTA_ACCESSCLIPBOARD** If a process is granted this permission,[3] all threads in that process can call OpenClipboard; otherwise, OpenClipboard will fail with ERROR_ACCESS_DENIED.

- **WINSTA_ACCESSGLOBALATOMS** If a process is granted this permission, all threads in that process can call GlobalAddAtom (and friends); otherwise, these functions fail with ERROR_ACCESS_DENIED. These APIs were classically used with DDE (Dynamic Data Exchange).

---

[2] Because the documentation is so vague, you should take these details with a grain of salt, since they could potentially change across service packs. My goal here is to give you a feel for how these permissions affect your programs. I find it especially interesting that some permissions consider the thread token (if present), whereas others ignore it completely.

[3] In other words, if the calling thread happens to be impersonating, the impersonation token is ignored and the process token is used to determine whether or not to grant the request.

- **WINSTA_CREATEDESKTOP** If a thread is granted this permission[4] to the window station, then it may call CreateDesktop. Otherwise, CreateDesktop will fail with ERROR_ACCESS_DENIED.

- **WINSTA_WRITEATTRIBUTES** If a process is granted this permission, all threads in that process can call SystemParametersInfo to *update* system parameters. This permission also controls access to ClipCursor and SetCursorPos.

- **WINSTA_READATTRIBUTES** This permission works similarly to WINSTA_WRITEATTRIBUTES, controlling who can *read* system parameters or call GetClipCursor and GetCursorPos.

- **WINSTA_EXITWINDOWS** If a process is granted this permission, any threads within that process are allowed to call ExitWindows(Ex) to shut down the logon session associated with the currently executing thread. (In other words, if the thread is currently impersonating, the thread token determines the logon session whose processes should be shut down, while the process token determines whether that thread is allowed to call ExitWindows(Ex) in the first place.) As if this combination weren't mind-twisting enough, for some odd (probably historical) reason, ExitWindows(Ex) can only be called from Winsta0 (the function fails if you call it from any other window station), which implies that this particular permission is only meaningful when applied to Winsta0.

- **WINSTA_ENUMERATE** A thread that calls EnumWindowStations will only see window stations that have granted this permission to the thread.

- **WINSTA_READSCREEN** If a thread is not granted this permission, it may not call BitBlt to read the screen.[5]

---

[4] In other words, the impersonation token (if any) is tested for access permissions. If no thread token exists (that is, the thread isn't currently impersonating), the process token is used as you'd expect.

[5] Thanks to a friend at Microsoft for this tidbit, which wasn't documented in MSDN at the time of this writing.

Natural Window Station Allocation

Most applications don't create window stations explicitly; rather, the operating system creates them whenever they are required. The basic allocation strategy is simply based on creating one window station per logon session. Each window station has a name, which is normally constructed in the following manner:

```
Service-0xHIGH-LOW$
```

where *HIGH* and *LOW* represent the high and low 32-bit hexadecimal values of the logon session identifier. It seems to me that it would have made more sense to prefix these names with "Daemon" instead of "Service," but Microsoft seems to prefer the latter term to describe applications designed to run in the background.[6] In any case, the concrete examples that follow will help drive this allocation strategy home as we reexamine the events that occur during system startup.

Daemon Window Stations

As you'll recall from Chapter 4, the first logon session that comes into being is the System logon session. To host processes that live there, the system creates a window station named in the natural way (recall that the System logon session is numbered `0x3e7`):

```
Service-0x0-3e7$
```

Any process created in the System logon session will naturally be directed into this window station unless the creator explicitly specifies another window station (I'll show how this is done later in the chapter).

During startup, the System SCM launches processes to host services configured to autostart. If one of these services is configured to run as a distinguished principal, the SCM creates a new logon session and then creates a

---

[6] Perhaps this was an attempt to help distinguish the Windows operating system from UNIX: *Service* sounds so much more light and happy than *Daemon*. In any case, the "Service" naming convention is somewhat misleading, because not just services run in noninteractive window stations (COM servers are the classic example of nonservice processes that often run in noninteractive window stations).

process to host the service, attaching it to the new logon session (see Chapter 4). For the sake of argument, let's say the new logon session ID is `0x4242`; in this case the system checks to see if a corresponding window station named `Service-0x0-4242$` already exists. If it doesn't already exist (it shouldn't at this point—this is a brand-new logon session), the system creates a new window station with this name and directs the process into it. If the service later calls `CreateProcess` to start a new process running in the same logon session (`0x4242`), the system will naturally direct that new process into the same window station.

If two separate services (configured to run in separate processes) both run as the same distinguished principal (Bob, say), then because the System SCM still creates two separate logon sessions (as described in Chapter 4), they will be hosted in separate window stations as well. As will be shown later, this can chew up limited resources pretty quickly on early versions of Windows unless something is done to alleviate the problem.

Most daemon processes are designed to be completely void of user interface components, and this is generally a good strategy. Why then does the system bother giving daemon processes a private USER environment? My best stab at an answer is that sometimes it's impossible to run a daemon without a user interface. For instance, your daemon may rely on some critical third-party component that (to your utter dismay) insists on displaying dialog boxes occasionally. If the system simply failed this request, those components would break. (Perhaps this would be a good thing in the long run, but senior management isn't often as concerned with purity when it comes to shipping a product.) The workaround, however hideous it may be, is to send a message manually to that dialog to dismiss it. Because this all happens in a noninteractive window station, the interactive user (if any) will be unaware that any of this magic is happening.

Ultimately, however, the main reason why window stations exist is to protect the interactive logon session from attacks that leverage USER objects. Imagine that Bob has decided to sandbox a daemon (FOOBAR.EXE) by running it as a distinguished principal with very few privileges (it's generally a good practice to run programs at the lowest level of privilege that they require). If that daemon is running on BobsMachine, and Bob decides to log on to the same machine interactively, it would clearly be a breach of security if the daemon could suddenly start running as Bob. The attack is quite simple; the daemon waits for an interactive user to log on, and then sends keystrokes into the input queue (the VBScript function `SendKeys` works quite nicely):

```
<Control><Escape>
"r"
"c:\pathtofoobar\foobar.exe"
<Enter>
```

As long as Bob is using Explorer as his shell (a reasonable assumption), the previous sequence of keystrokes will cause Explorer to call `CreateProcess` on `foobar.exe`, thus starting a copy of the daemon process outside the sandbox, running as Bob. This isn't much of a sandbox—it's more like a sieve. The natural window station allocation strategy guarantees that this cannot happen. Daemons cannot send messages into a window station without first being granted access to enter that window station.[7]

Winsta0

There is only one window station that is allowed to receive input from the keyboard, mouse, and other interactive devices and to produce output that actually gets sent to the screen.[8] Having only a single window station with this special status really simplifies the model. However, consider that between system restarts, many interactive users may log in and out at various times, creating several different logon sessions. The system cannot name the interactive window station after each of these logon sessions, because even after an interactive user logs out and his or her logon session is destroyed, the interactive

---

[7] As this manuscript was being prepared to be sent to the publisher, Windows 2000 had been released for a little over a month. In this very first release, an attack similar to the one just described actually works because there is a bug in the enforcement of window station security as new processes are created. I discovered this bug while doing some final research on the newly released operating system and informed Microsoft; as a result they plan to release a hotfix for the problem (the fix should be included in the first service pack for Windows 2000). If you're interested in learning more about this vulnerability, go to the archives of www.ntbugtraq.com and search for "Potential bug in window station/desktop security."

[8] For servers running Terminal Services, there will be one of these window stations per session, but within any given session, all the names, mechanisms, and rules discussed in this chapter still apply.

window station must live on, if only to host Winlogon's user interface that collects the next potential interactive user's credentials. Therefore, the interactive window station is named Winsta0, and it is always present, even when no interactive user happens to be logged on.[9]

Winlogon is the first process I've mentioned that flouts the natural window station assignment strategy. Winlogon is hosted in the System logon session and would therefore normally be assigned to the window station named `Service-0x0-3e7$`, and yet it lives in Winsta0 because it needs to interact with humans. Other daemons also choose to live in the System logon session but prefer to be attached to the interactive window station; the Messenger service[10] is a good example—this is the service that displays a window when someone sends a message via `net send`, or when a printer sends a notification that a print job has finished.

To direct a service into Winsta0, specify the `SERVICE_INTERACTIVE_PROCESS` flag via the *dwServiceType* parameter to `CreateService` (when installing the service programmatically), or use the Windows administration tools and check the "Allow Service to Interact with Desktop" box. The next time the process hosting the service starts, it'll be directed into Winsta0.

A potential issue with the approach just described is that Winsta0 has an extremely limiting DACL; only the System and interactive logon sessions are granted access to Winsta0. This means that the only daemons the System SCM will be able to start in Winsta0 are those that run in the System logon session. You don't even have the option of running in Winsta0 if your service runs as a distinguished principal. You can verify this by calling `CreateService` specifying a distinguished principal along with the `SERVICE_INTERACTIVE_PROCESS` flag (the function fails, as expected).

Here's an interesting caveat. Keep in mind that it is possible to package multiple services into one process. (You indicate this when calling `CreateService` by setting the `SERVICE_WIN32_SHARE_PROCESS` flag in the *dwServiceType* parameter, and specifying the same EXE image via the *lpBinaryPathName* parameter.) If you have services built in this fashion,

---

[9] `WINLOGON.EXE` creates Winsta0 when it initializes.

[10] Technically, this is bundled in a single process with several other services, and the entire bundle has opted to run in Winsta0.

always be consistent about your usage of SERVICE_INTERACTIVE_PROCESS to avoid the following silly race condition: Imagine service A and B are both packaged in MYSERVICES.EXE and are configured to share the same process via the SERVICE_WIN32_SHARE_PROCESS flag. Service A specifies SERVICE _INTERACTIVE_PROCESS, whereas service B does not. If A is started first, the process runs in WinstaO; otherwise, the process runs in Service-0x0-3e7$. Most developers would prefer to live without these sorts of surprises.

See Figure 2.5 in Chapter 2 for a diagram of a typical set of window stations, including WinstaO.

Daemons in the Lab

Chapter 2 noted that even applications designed to run as daemons typically have a user interface in debug builds: the friendly ASSERT dialog. For daemons running outside WinstaO, it seems as though the ASSERT macro should be avoided. It turns out that this is not the case; with a little planning, you can still use ASSERT (or at least something like it) from any window station you like.

Assertions are typically implemented by calling MessageBox, and the MessageBox API has a special flag (MB_SERVICE_NOTIFICATION) you can pass via the fourth parameter that does exactly what you want—it injects a single message box on your behalf into WinstaO, so that even if there is no interactive user present, you'll see the message pop up on top of Winlogon's user interface.[11] As of this writing, the implementation of ASSERT provided by the compiler I happen to be using (Visual C++) does not use this flag, which makes this implementation of ASSERT unsafe for use in daemon processes. However, there is a way to hook into the Visual C++ ASSERT implementation, and since many folks reading this book will also be using Visual C++, I thought it would be a useful piece of code to include here.[12] Call the _makeAssertSafeForDaemons helper function when your daemon process

---

[11] This doesn't mean your process temporarily attaches to WinstaO; rather, the Win32 subsystem (CSRSS.EXE) running in the System logon session (and WinstaO) does this on your behalf. One other tidbit you should be aware of is that calls to MessageBox using this flag are queued by CSRSS.EXE; thus, only one of these message boxes will ever be active at any given time on a particular machine.

[12] If you can't figure out how to apply this technique to your own compiler's implementation, consider hacking up your own custom ASSERT macro that uses MB_SERVICE_NOTIFICATION.

first starts up, and from then on, ASSERT will do the right thing. I'll leave it to you to read up on this vendor-specific feature (search the Visual C++ docs for _CrtSetReportHook for more info).

```
void _makeAssertSafeForDaemons() {
  _CrtSetReportHook(_crtDbgReportHook);
}

// discussed in the documentation for _CrtSetReportHook,
// this function is called whenever an assertion fires
int _crtDbgReportHook(int    reportType,
                      char*  message,
                      int*   returnValue) {
  if (_CRT_ASSERT == reportType) {
    // here is the key piece of code
    switch (MessageBoxA(0, message, "SafeAssert",
                        MB_SERVICE_NOTIFICATION |
                        MB_ABORTRETRYIGNORE |
                        MB_ICONSTOP))
    {
      case IDABORT:
        ExitProcess(1);
        break;
      case IDRETRY:
        *returnValue = 1; // start debugger
        break;
      case IDIGNORE:
        *returnValue = 0; // continue execution
        break;
    }
    return 1; // no further reporting necessary
  }
  return 0;
}
```

Other Window Stations

Although the natural window station allocation scheme works well, you might want to explicitly provide a window station and direct several processes to run in that window station. There are a couple of reasons you might want to do this. First, you might be starting several daemon processes running in distinct logon sessions, and to conserve resources you'd like to force all these processes to share the same window station, as opposed to letting the operating system create private window stations for each individual logon session. Second, you might have a couple of older daemon processes that expect to be able to use window handles to perform interprocess communication (perhaps via the WM_COPYDATA message), and if they run in different window stations this breaks.

Whatever the reason, there is a function that can be used to create a window station on the fly: CreateWindowStation.

```
HWINSTA CreateWindowStation(
    LPTSTR                Name,           // in, optional
    DWORD                 Reserved,       // must be zero
    DWORD                 DesiredAccess,  // in
    LPSECURITY_ATTRIBUTES Attr            // in
);
```

Only members of the Administrators alias are allowed to specify names for window stations (thus, if you're running in the System logon session you can do this). All others must specify NULL for the first parameter, which indicates that the system should automatically come up with a name; in this case, the natural name (based on the logon session identifier) is used.

The following code creates two distinct window stations, returning a handle to each:

```
HWINSTA h1, h2;
h1 = CreateWindowStation(L"Foo", 0, READ_CONTROL, 0);
h2 = CreateWindowStation(L"Bar", 0, READ_CONTROL, 0);
```

If the Foo window station already existed prior to the call to CreateWindow Station, h1 would refer to the existing window station Foo, somewhat similar to the way the CreateXXXX functions in KERNEL32 (CreateMutex, etc.) work.[13]

---

[13] The difference is that if you call CreateMutex, CreateFile, and so on, GetLastError will inform you if the named object already exists (the error code is ERROR_ALREADY_EXISTS). Unfortunately, as of this writing, CreateWindowStation doesn't follow this rule.

The following code creates two handles to the same window station, whose name is based on the logon session identifier:

```
HWINSTA h1, h2;
h1 = CreateWindowStation(0, 0, READ_CONTROL, 0);
h2 = CreateWindowStation(0, 0, READ_CONTROL, 0);
```

Just for kicks, I ran this code snippet from a process in Winsta0, and the resulting window station was named `Service-0x0-4916$` (after my logon session LUID). Since only administrators can create named window stations, this effectively means that unless you're an administrator, you'll only be able to access the natural window station named after your logon session, although as you can see from this example, Winsta0 is a special case.

To discover the name of a window station, call the helpful function `GetUserObjectInformation`.

```
BOOL GetUserObjectInformation(
  HANDLE  Object,        // in, handle to winsta/desktop
  int     Index,         // in, type of info you want
  PVOID   pInfo,         // out, pointer to buffer
  DWORD   Length,        // in, buffer size in bytes
  LPDWORD pLengthNeeded  // out, buffer size required
);
```

The `Object` parameter can either be a window station or desktop (I'll discuss desktops shortly), and the index refers to one of four possible pieces of information:

- **UOI_NAME** Indicates the name of the window station.

- **UOI_TYPE** For window stations, indicates `WindowStation`; for desktops, indicates `Desktop`.

- **UOI_FLAGS** For window stations, this indicates whether this is an interactive or a noninteractive window station; for desktops, this indicates whether or not alternate principals can install hooks. In both cases, the function indicates whether the handle specified is inheritable (this second piece of information can also be retrieved by calling `GetHandleInformation`).

- **UOI_USER_SID** For the interactive window station and any of its desktops, this request returns the text form of the logon session SID for the interactive user. If there is no current interactive user, or if you make this request of a noninteractive window station or desktop, GetUserObjectSecurity will succeed, but the length specifier (*pLengthNeeded*) will be set to 0 to indicate that no SID is associated with the object. This gives daemons a quick (if a bit kludgy) way to determine whether anyone is currently logged on interactively (although by the time you're ready to process this information, the user could already be logging off).

GetUserObjectInformation normally writes a null-terminated string to the buffer specified by *pInfo*, except in the case of UOI_FLAGS, in which case it writes a data structure of type USEROBJECTFLAGS.

Exploring Window Stations

One of the best ways to learn about window stations is to write a program that enumerates them and dumps out interesting information about them. You can do this via the EnumWindowStations function.

```
typedef BOOL (CALLBACK* WINSTAENUMPROC)(LPTSTR, LPARAM);
BOOL EnumWindowStations(
  WINSTAENUMPROC EnumProc, // in, ptr to callback function
  LPARAM         lParam    // in, user-defined parameter
);
```

EnumWindowStations follows the long-standing tradition of Windows enumeration functions, in which you write a callback function that is called once for each object being enumerated. The second parameter is typically used to pass a pointer to a user-defined data structure to give your callback function some extra information that it needs in order to do its work. The callback function must be declared following the signature shown earlier for WINSTAENUMPROC.

Here's an example that illustrates how you can enumerate all the window stations on your machine (at least those that grant you access to enumerate them; if you have been assigned the Administrators alias, then you'll normally be able to see all of them):

```
BOOL CALLBACK _myWinstaEnumProc(wchar_t* pszName,
                                LPARAM lp) {
  // just append the name (and a newline) to the output
  wchar_t* pszOutput = (wchar_t*)lp;
  lstrcat(pszOutput, pszName);
  lstrcat(pszOutput, L"\n");

  return TRUE; // continue enumerating
}

void _listWindowStations() {

  // I'm punting on buffer management for simplicity
  wchar_t szOutput[4096];
  szOutput[0] = L'\0';

  // tell the system to call _myWinstaEnumProc once
  // for each window station that we are allowed to see
  EnumWindowStations(_myWinstaEnumProc,
                     (LPARAM)szOutput);

  MessageBox(0, szOutput, L"Window Station List",
             MB_SETFOREGROUND | MB_ICONINFORMATION);
}
```

On a Windows 2000 machine (as well as a Windows NT 4 machine with the Option Pack), the previous code results in the following output:

```
WinSta0
Service-0x0-3e7$
__X78B95_89_IW
```

The window station with the custom name appears to be used by Internet Information Server (IIS), at least based on my probing.

Closing Window Station Handles

Because window stations are executive objects, handles to window stations are stored in the same per-process handle table as other executive object handles and can be duplicated using `DuplicateHandle`, even though they have their own typedef (`HWINSTA`). The only oddity about window station handles is that there is a special function provided for closing them:

```
BOOL CloseWindowStation(HWINSTA Winsta);
```

This function works just like `CloseHandle`, but it keeps you from accidentally closing the window station handle associated with the current process. Before calling `CloseHandle`, `CloseWindowStation` checks to see if the handle specified by `Winsta` is safe to be closed, and if not, simply returns `FALSE`.

The following code results in a runtime exception:

```
CloseHandle(GetProcessWindowStation()); // whoops!
```

The exception thrown is $0xC0000235$, which indicates that this handle has been protected from closure.[14] The moral of the story is to use `CloseWindowStation` instead of `CloseHandle` to close arbitrary handles to window stations, because `GetProcessWindowStation` will typically give you a protected handle that the system is using internally as well.[15]

```
// safe, actually does nothing
CloseWindowStation(GetProcessWindowStation());
```

---

[14] `SetHandleInformation` allows you to protect handles in this fashion. In fact, you can unprotect your process's window station and desktop handles by calling `SetHandle Information`; by calling `CloseHandle`, you can force them closed (this isn't a terribly good idea unless you've already switched to another window station or desktop). Using Mark Russinovich's cool Handleex tool (www.sysinternals.com), I verified this and also discovered that the process actually caches *two* handles to its window station during initialization; therefore, it's not practical to detach a process from its original window station *entirely* without shutting that process down (there's no documented way of reading or writing this second handle).

[15] I don't see why `GetProcessWindowStation` doesn't simply duplicate the handle so that you can safely close it via `CloseHandle` when you're done, just like you do with any other handle. It's odd.

Window Stations and Access Control

Of all the window stations that need protection, Winsta0 is critical, because this is where all visible USER objects in the system will live. An example of a typical attack was provided earlier, in which a daemon was able to hijack the interactive user's logon session. Thus you can expect to see very tight security on Winsta0 to protect against these kinds of shenanigans.

When no interactive user exists, Winsta0 has a DACL that looks *something* like this (a bit more detail will be provided later once desktops have been discussed):

grant 0x000F037F to SYSTEM

grant 0x00020166 to Administrators

The hexadecimal numbers shown here are a bitwise combination of the permissions being granted or denied. Without going into too much detail, this implies that the System logon session has all possible access to Winsta0 (0xF037F is the combination of all the possible permissions for a window station), and that anyone with the Administrators alias in his or her token is granted the ability to do most things in the window station except read the contents of the screen.

When an interactive user logs in via Winlogon, the system completely reconstructs the DACL on Winsta0 (from the ground up) to allow the new interactive logon session to have all possible access permissions to Winsta0. Note that it's the *logon session* that's granted these permissions, as opposed to the principal who is logged in. For instance, if Alice logs in (via Winlogon) to AlicesMachine, AlicesMachine establishes a new logon session for Alice; for kicks, let's say the logon session SID is S-1-5-5-0-0x4242. The new DACL on Winsta0 will look something like this:

grant 0x000F037F to SYSTEM

grant 0x00020166 to Administrators

grant 0x000F037F to S-1-5-5-0-0x4242

grant 0x00000024 to Alice

As you can see, although very limited permissions are granted to Alice the principal (access to the clipboard and global atoms), Alice's *logon session* is granted full permission to Winsta0. This implies that just because Alice is logged on interactively, daemon processes that also happen to be running as Alice—but in alternate logon sessions—won't necessarily be able to have their way with Winsta0. The operating system has granted access to a specific *instance* of Alice on AlicesMachine—to be precise, the instance authenticated by Winlogon.

Noninteractive window stations generally don't follow this ultra-fine-grained convention; for instance, a window station created by the System SCM to host a daemon process running as Alice will have a DACL that looks something like this:

```
grant 0x000F006E to Alice
grant 0x00000100 to Administrators
```

This DACL allows Administrators to enumerate the window station (in other words, an administrator can discover its presence by calling `EnumWindow Stations`), and Alice (the principal) is granted a slightly restricted set of access permissions; she can do pretty much anything she'll ever need to do in a noninteractive window station.

It's important to note that the example just discussed was contrived to drive home the unique convention used in constructing the Winsta0 DACL. Generally speaking, daemon processes run in distinguished accounts that are not normally used by interactive users (that is, Alice the human won't typically run daemon processes under her own personal account). This policy is often enforced by revoking the "Log on locally" right for daemon accounts, and instead granting those accounts the right to alternate types of logon sessions, "Log on as a service" or "Log on as a batch job," depending on whether you plan on having the System SCM or the COM SCM start the process.

Desktops

A window station is an executive object associated with a process. It provides a secure USER environment, and each executing process must be attached to exactly one window station. A desktop, on the other hand, is an executive object that is associated not with a process, but with a thread. Each window station can have any number of desktops, but using multiple desktops is only interesting in Winsta0. (Thus, unless explicitly noted, assume that all processes and desktops discussed in this section are hosted in Winsta0.)

When a process is launched (via `CreateProcess` and friends), the system chooses a window station and desktop (based on a documented algorithm that is discussed later in this chapter). The primary thread of the process starts life on this predetermined desktop, and all new threads created in the process (via `CreateThread`) will also start life on that same desktop. Threads can dynamically migrate between desktops by calling `SetThreadDesktop`, but this is the exception to the rule—normally a thread lives a full and productive life attached to a single desktop. To get the current desktop associated with a thread, call `GetThreadDesktop`; to close a desktop handle, call `CloseDesktop` (this function behaves similarly to `CloseWindowStation`, discussed earlier).

```
BOOL   SetThreadDesktop(HDESK Desktop);
HDESK GetThreadDesktop(DWORD ThreadId);
BOOL   CloseDesktop      (HDESK Desktop);
```

Here's what makes desktops interesting from a security standpoint: Windows created on a particular desktop are only visible (and can only receive messages from input peripherals such as the keyboard and mouse) when that particular desktop is *active*. You can determine the currently active desktop by calling `OpenInputDesktop` (this function only works if called from Winsta0, because only desktops in Winsta0 can ever be active):

```
HDESK OpenInputDesktop(
  DWORD Flags,          // in
  BOOL  Inherit,        // in, governs handle inheritance
  DWORD DesiredAccess   // in, desired access mask
);
```

The first parameter, `Flags`, is normally 0; the only valid flag is DF_ALLOWOTHERACCOUNTHOOK (which I must admit I've not found a use for in this context). The `Inherit` parameter determines whether the resulting handle will be inheritable, and finally, *DesiredAccess* allows you to state your intentions (how you intend to use the handle). Because a desktop is a secure executive object, this function first performs an access check, comparing the active desktop's DACL with the security context of the thread making the call; it will fail if the access permissions requested aren't granted.

So what does all this mean? With an understanding of window stations and desktops, you are now poised to create a hidden user interface that can only be accessed by principals of your choosing (note that a desktop isn't nearly as strong a sandbox as a window station, as window messages may be sent across desktop boundaries within the same window station, but desktops do allow you to restrict hooks). By creating a private desktop in Winsta0, secured with a restrictive DACL, and by choosing that desktop when creating the process hosting your user interface, you create a private environment that only certain users can see. Of course you'll need to provide a mechanism to allow a user to attempt to switch from the normal desktop (Default) to your private desktop. The function you'll need to call to activate your desktop is SwitchDesktop, and it's also very straightforward:

```
BOOL SwitchDesktop(HDESK Desk);
```

One of the permissions a desktop DACL can grant or deny is DESKTOP _SWITCHDESKTOP, and whoever wants to call SwitchDesktop must have been able to acquire a handle with these permissions (either via OpenDesktop, OpenInputDesktop, or CreateDesktop). If, for instance, you want to switch to an existing desktop whose name you know, you'll need to call OpenDesktop to acquire a handle to the desktop, specifying DESKTOP_SWITCHDESKTOP permissions.

```
HDESK OpenDesktop(
  LPTSTR Desktop,        // in, desktop name
  DWORD  Flags,          // in
  BOOL   Inherit,        // in, governs inheritance
  DWORD  DesiredAccess   // in, desired access mask
);
```

This function works like `OpenInputDesktop`, except that the first parameter allows you to choose any desktop you like. Bear in mind that desktop names are scoped by window stations, and so the name of the desktop is evaluated based on the window station to which the calling process is attached at the time the call is made. What this means is that if you'd like to get a handle to the desktop `Winsta0\Foo`, you'd better first make sure your process is attached to Winsta0. (A daemon process running in a noninteractive window station can temporarily migrate to Winsta0—assuming it has access permissions to do so—before making the call to `OpenDesktop`.)

Here's an example of a helper function that activates a desktop by name:

```
bool _switchToDesktop(const wchar_t* pszDesk) {
  // open the specified desktop
  // with the intention of switching
  bool bSucceeded = false;
  HDESK hd = OpenDesktop(pszDesk, 0, 0,
                         DESKTOP_SWITCHDESKTOP);
  // make the switch
  if (hd) {
    if (SwitchDesktop(hd))
      bSucceeded = true;

    CloseDesktop(hd);
  }
  return bSucceeded;
}
```

Except for a couple of reserved parameters, the function for creating desktops is similar to the `CreateWindowStation` function described earlier.

```
HDESK CreateDesktop(
  LPCTSTR              Desktop,        // in, name
  LPVOID               Device,         // reserved
  LPVOID               DevMode,        // reserved
  DWORD                Flags,          // in
  DWORD                DesiredAccess,  // in
  LPSECURITY_ATTRIBUTES Attr           // in
);
```

The most notorious (and somewhat annoying) requirement of this function is that you must ask for *at least* DESKTOP_CREATEWINDOW access permissions, because the operating system creates at least one window in the process of creating a desktop. Forget this and you'll be scratching your head wondering why the function fails with ERROR_ACCESS_DENIED.

The following function creates a new desktop, switches to it, and then displays a message box on the blank desktop before switching back.

```
void _baitAndSwitchDesktop() {

  // first remember the old desktop
  // so we can switch back
  HDESK hdOld =
    GetThreadDesktop(GetCurrentThreadId());

  // create a desktop (assuming it doesn't already
  // exist), with the intention of switching to it
  const DWORD grfAccess = DESKTOP_CREATEWINDOW |
                          DESKTOP_SWITCHDESKTOP;
  HDESK hdNew = CreateDesktop(L"Foo", 0, 0, 0,
                              grfAccess, 0);
  if (hdNew) {

    // migrate our thread to the Foo desktop
    // and make it the active desktop
    SetThreadDesktop(hdNew);
    SwitchDesktop    (hdNew);

    // display a stunning user interface
    MessageBox(0, L"Hello World!", L"Foo Desktop", 0);

    // switch back
    SwitchDesktop    (hdOld);
    SetThreadDesktop(hdOld);

    // because this is the last reference to the
    // desktop Foo, the operating system destroys it
    CloseDesktop(hdNew);
  }
  CloseDesktop(hdOld);
}
```

Daemon processes running in the System logon session are normally granted full access permissions to the interactive window station (recall the DACL shown earlier), so by simply adding a few function calls to the previous code, you can first migrate the daemon process into Winsta0 and then switch to the desktop you want. This is sometimes used as a brute-force approach for piercing into Winsta0 and displaying a user interface on the interactive desktop. Because the code is so similar to the previous code, I won't repeat it here, but I will demonstrate how you must always migrate the process into the target window station *first* if you want `OpenDesktop` and friends to have any meaning there:

```
HWINSTA hwsOld    = GetProcessWindowStation();
HWINSTA hwsTarget = OpenWindowStation(L"Winsta0",
                               FALSE, READ_CONTROL);
SetProcessWindowStation(hwsTarget); // do this first!
HDESK hdTarget = OpenDesktop(L"Default", 0, FALSE,
                         DESKTOP_SWITCHDESKTOP);
```

This technique is mentioned for completeness; most experienced developers generally avoid writing daemons that directly host a user interface (even though the code to make it work is obscure enough to confer a large dose of job security). If a daemon needs to grow a user interface, it's usually best to split the user interface into a separate program that a human can simply launch at will; this naturally places it in the interactive window station on the active desktop, leaving the daemon in a noninteractive window station where it belongs. Of course, in this case some form of interprocess communication will be necessary between the two processes (COM is great for this).

Although window handles can be used across desktop boundaries (within the same window station, of course), functions such as `EnumWindows` called from desktop A won't see windows living on desktop B. Pressing Alt-Tab from desktop A lists top-level windows running on A. Pressing Alt-Tab from desktop B lists top-level windows running on B, and so forth. The human sitting behind the console really can't tell the difference (especially if his or her shell, typically `EXPLORER.EXE`, is running).

Winlogon is a great example of an application that uses private desktops to secure access to its user interface. At system startup, Winsta0 has two desktops: Default and Winlogon. The Winlogon desktop is what Alice sees before she logs in to her computer in the morning. Once Alice is authenticated, the system rebuilds the DACL on Winsta0 and the Default desktop (granting Alice's logon session full access), and then switches to the Default desktop, directing the shell process onto that desktop. If Alice later presses Control-Alt-Delete, the system switches back to the Winlogon desktop, thus hiding all Alice's work in progress and allowing Alice to log out, shut down the machine, or lock her workstation. In Windows 2000 the workstation can be locked programmatically via a call to `LockWorkstation`.[16]

```
BOOL LockWorkstation();
```

The system creates a third desktop with the name `Screen-saver` whenever a screen saver starts running[17] (and destroys this desktop when the screen saver is deactivated). This leads us to a somewhat subtle point about the Winsta0 DACL, which is discussed in the next section.

Winsta0 and ACL Inheritance

Chapter 6 discusses the details of ACL inheritance, so without going into detail about how ACL inheritance works, let me point out a subtle but critical issue for those considering modifying the DACL on Winsta0. The system-provided DACL on Winsta0 normally contains several inherit-only entries that are used to construct the default DACL for new child desktops (to keep things simple, these were omitted earlier). The critical issue is that if you clobber these entries, the resulting DACL on the screen-saver desktop will be *empty,* thus denying access to the screen-saver program (and everyone else, for that matter). This opens a subtle security hole: When the human using the terminal goes to lunch, he or she may rely on a password-protected screen saver to protect his or her desk-

---

[16] I found it interesting that although the MSDN documentation for this function seems to imply that it will only work from Winsta0, I've called it successfully from noninteractive window stations, even when running in a logon session for a normal (non-TCB, nonadministrative) principal. This seems to me to be a bug in the implementation, because it appears to violate the protection and privacy that Winsta0 affords the interactive user.

[17] On Windows NT, this is always the case. On Windows 2000, screen savers normally run on the Default desktop unless they are password protected, in which case they run on this special desktop.

Figure 5.2. Access denied!

top. However, when the screen saver's process starts on its newly created desktop, the process will immediately abort with a rather nasty dialog (see Figure 5.2 for an example).

Here's what the DACL on Winsta0 looks like, including the inheritable entries:

grant `0x000F037F` to SYSTEM

grant `0xF0000000` to SYSTEM, inherit only

grant `0x00020166` to Administrators

grant `0x200000C7` to Administrators, inherit only

grant `0x000F037F` to S-1-5-5-0-0x4242

grant `0xF0000000` to S-1-5-5-0-0x4242, inherit only

grant `0x00000024` to Alice

The entries for SYSTEM, Administrators, and Alice's logon session SID now grant access not only to Winsta0, but also to any desktops that might be created there. The inherit-only entries do not apply to Winsta0; instead, they are stored until a new desktop is created as a child of Winsta0, at which point these entries are used to build the default DACL for the new desktop. Be careful to preserve these inherit-only entries if you modify the DACL on Winsta0, as mentioned earlier. Chapter 6 discusses a nasty bug in the `SetEntriesInAcl` API that can bite you on Windows NT 4.

Desktop Permissions

As with the window station access permissions, I've provided a list of desktop access permissions, along with any extra insight that I can offer.

- **DESKTOP_CREATEWINDOW** If a process is granted this permission, all threads in that process can call `CreateWindow(Ex)`; otherwise, these calls will fail with `ERROR_ACCESS_DENIED`.

- **DESKTOP_CREATEMENU** If a process is granted this permission, all threads in that process can call `CreateMenu` or `LoadMenu`; otherwise, these calls will fail with `ERROR_ACCESS_DENIED`.

- **DESKTOP_HOOKCONTROL** If a process is granted this permission, all threads in that process can call `SetWindowsHookEx` to install all types of hooks (local or global) except journal hooks, which are explicitly controlled by the next two permissions.

- **DESKTOP_JOURNALRECORD** If a process is granted this permission, all threads in that process can call `SetWindowsHookEx` to install a `WH_JOURNALRECORD` hook. Note that the process does *not* need the `DESKTOP_HOOKCONTROL` permission in this case.

- **DESKTOP_JOURNALPLAYBACK** If a process is granted this permission, all threads in that process can call `SetWindowsHookEx` to install a `WH_JOURNALPLAYBACK` hook. Note that the process does *not* need the `DESKTOP_HOOKCONTROL` permission in this case.

- **DESKTOP_ENUMERATE** If a thread is granted this permission on desktop X, the thread can discover desktop X when enumerating via `EnumDesktops`.

- **DESKTOP_SWITCHDESKTOP** This one is pretty clear: If you can successfully open a desktop handle with this permission, you'll be able to call `SwitchDesktop` to switch to it. Because this permission must be acquired when the handle is opened, it is sensitive to whether you are impersonating when you open the handle.

- **DESKTOP_READOBJECTS and DESKTOP_WRITEOBJECTS** These permissions control access to USER objects on the desktop. As with `WINSTA_READSCREEN`, there is very little documentation on what these permissions really control. In my own tests, I discovered that without these permissions, it's impossible to initialize `USER32.DLL`, and thus the host process would fail to start.[18]

Desktop Limitations

In Windows NT 4, there is a nasty configuration problem that limits the number of desktops that can exist on a given machine to 48/3 = 16 desktops. The arithmetic comes from a Knowledge Base article (Q169321) that discusses a 48MB shared memory section managed by USER that is divided among all the desktops on a machine. By default, each desktop, regardless of whether it lives in Winsta0 or not (in other words, regardless of whether it will host interactive applications), reserves a 3MB chunk of linear address space from that shared section.

Why does this matter? Consider that each service process that runs as a distinct principal gets its own private logon session (even two service processes that run as the *same principal* get distinct logon sessions). Because window station boundaries normally parallel logon session boundaries, each of these processes ends up in a distinct window station. Each of these window stations will have a distinct desktop. In practice, this generally means that you can run about 12 service processes or COM server processes (as distinguished principals) on a single Windows NT4 machine.

Both the Option Pack and Service Pack 4 sought to address these problems in different ways. The Option Pack, when it is installed, automatically applies the fix suggested by the Knowledge Base article mentioned earlier (the fix is to adjust a registry setting that reduces each noninteractive desktop's consumption of the shared linear address space by a factor of six). Service Pack 4 added an interesting twist to the COM SCM. When two COM servers run as the same distinguished principal, as long as they are started (by the COM SCM) within a few minutes of one another, the SCM will use the same logon session (it basically caches tokens for a short period), and thus the two processes will share

---

[18] I ran a process under my own interactive logon session (which of course has this permission), and then impersonated a user who had no permissions to my desktop whatsoever. While impersonating, I was able to call `FindWindow` and `SendMessage` to find and close another application on my desktop. This tells me one of two things: Either impersonation tokens are ignored by this permission, or the permission controls access to objects other than window handles.

a single window station and desktop. Both these fixes are present in Windows 2000 at the time of this writing, and make this problem pretty much a non-issue.

Jobs, Revisited

The use of job objects to limit authorization attributes was discussed in Chapter 4, but there's another category of limitations that looks and smells very much like those provided by window stations. Here's the data structure you must fill out in order to configure a job's UI-related limitations, along with the documented restriction flags:

```
typedef struct _JOBOBJECT_BASIC_UI_RESTRICTIONS {
    DWORD UIRestrictionsClass;
} JOBOBJECT_BASIC_UI_RESTRICTIONS;
#define JOB_OBJECT_UILIMIT_HANDLES          0x00000001
#define JOB_OBJECT_UILIMIT_READCLIPBOARD    0x00000002
#define JOB_OBJECT_UILIMIT_WRITECLIPBOARD   0x00000004
#define JOB_OBJECT_UILIMIT_SYSTEMPARAMETERS 0x00000008
#define JOB_OBJECT_UILIMIT_DISPLAYSETTINGS  0x00000010
#define JOB_OBJECT_UILIMIT_GLOBALATOMS      0x00000020
#define JOB_OBJECT_UILIMIT_DESKTOP          0x00000040
#define JOB_OBJECT_UILIMIT_EXITWINDOWS      0x00000080
```

The HANDLES limitation indicates that processes inside the job will be blind to any USER objects created by processes outside the job. Unlike a window station, though, this job limit only restricts processes inside a job from seeing out. Processes outside the restricted job (assuming they share a window station) can see USER objects created by processes inside the job. Also, unlike a window station, it's possible for a process to "brighten" an individual USER object so that a particular job can see it, even if that job has been blinded with the HANDLES limitation. This can be done via the UserHandleGrantAccess function, introduced in Windows 2000:

```
BOOL UserHandleGrantAccess(
    HANDLE hUserHandle, // in
    HANDLE hJob,        // in
    BOOL   bGrant       // in
);
```

The READCLIPBOARD, WRITECLIPBOARD, GLOBALATOMS, DESKTOP, and EXITWINDOWS job limitations control access to the same types of objects as the permissions already described for window stations. The SYSTEMPARAMETERS and DISPLAYSETTINGS limitations specifically protect calls to System ParametersInfo and ChangeDisplaySettings, preventing processes in a job from making sweeping changes to the system.

You might be wondering what the difference is between jobs and window stations, since they seem to overlap somewhat (at least with respect to UI limitations). Jobs can be used to create sandboxes smaller than even a window station.[19] In contrast with a window station, the limitations a job imposes are principal agnostic: If you specify a limitation on a job, all processes in that job will be controlled by that limitation, regardless of the security context, unless of course the job is still accessible and a principal who has access permissions to do so changes the job's configuration. You can easily eliminate this loophole by closing all handles to the job object; once the last handle to a particular job is closed, the job can never be opened again (named jobs lose their name after being closed). Even after a job becomes inaccessible for reconfiguration, its limitations continue to be enforced, even as new child processes enter the job.

Processes

I assume any systems programmer reading this book will likely have called CreateProcess once or twice in his or her career. However, there is a much more powerful function called CreateProcessAsUser that takes a single extra parameter: a handle to a token. This allows you to inject a new process into the logon session of your choice, enabling you to create what I like to call a *logon session broker,*[20] kind of like the System SCM and COM SCM, both of which launch processes upon request in the logon session of their choice. You will need a couple of privileges in order to call this function, namely, SeIncreaseQuotaPrivilege and SeAssignPrimaryTokenPrivilege.[21]

---

[19] In fact, nothing stops you from creating jobs that include processes in different window stations.

[20] See Brown (2000b) for more details on building logon session brokers.

[21] Technically, you don't need this latter privilege if all you are doing is making a restricted token from your own token and creating a process with restricted authorization attributes.

The System logon session has both these privileges, and code that calls `CreateProcessAsUser` normally runs there.

```
BOOL CreateProcessAsUser(
  HANDLE Token,                            // in
  LPCTSTR ApplicationName,                 // in, optional
  LPTSTR CommandLine,                      // in, optional
  LPSECURITY_ATTRIBUTES ProcessAttrs,      // in, optional
  LPSECURITY_ATTRIBUTES ThreadAttrs,       // in, optional
  BOOL InheritHandles,                     // in
  DWORD CreationFlags,                     // in
  LPVOID Environment,                      // in, optional
  LPCTSTR CurrentDirectory,                // in, optional
  LPSTARTUPINFO StartupInfo,               // in
  LPPROCESS_INFORMATION ProcessInfo        // out
);
```

Assuming that you already have a token from somewhere (perhaps you called `LogonUser` or one of the various impersonation functions to impersonate a client), the trickiest decision you have to make when calling this function is which window station should host the process. If you call this function the same way most folks call `CreateProcess`—that is, by passing a `START UPINFO` structure that's been completely zeroed out—you'll almost always run into trouble. The third parameter of `STARTUPINFO` is *lpDesktop*, which has four (somewhat subtle) possible settings:

- **"*bar*"** This setting implies that the new process should be placed in the caller's window station, and the primary thread should start life on the desktop named *bar* in that window station.

- **"*foo\bar*"** This setting implies that the new process should be placed in the window station named *foo*, and the primary thread should start life on the desktop named *bar* in the window station named *foo*.

- **NULL (a null pointer)** This setting implies that the new process should be placed in the caller's window station.

- **"" (an empty string)** This setting implies that the system should use the natural window station allocation policy, creating a new window station for this logon session if it doesn't already exist (plus a default desktop).

If you really know what you're doing, it's possible that one of the first three options will work, but you may very well need to change the DACL of the target window station (and desktop) to make this work. The classic case in which this occurs is when you'd like to start an interactive process (which implies "Winsta0\Default"). Remember how tight the DACLs on these objects can be. You'll usually need to modify these DACLs somewhat to allow this, and the conventional way to do this is to grant access to the logon session SID for the logon session hosting the new process.

If you are simply launching a noninteractive daemon, you should use the fourth option (passing an empty string) to allow the system to follow the natural window station allocation scheme. If the system needs to construct a new window station and desktop pair for the logon session you are using, it will set up the DACLs on these objects correctly.

What happens if you call `CreateProcessAsUser` and direct the process into a window station or desktop (or both) that doesn't grant permissions to the logon session/principal represented by the token? You'll see a variant of the nasty dialog mentioned earlier (see Figure 5.2).

Here is some code that demonstrates launching a daemon in a new logon session and window station without running into window station headaches:

```
bool _startDaemonAsUser(
    wchar_t* pszAuthority,
    wchar_t* pszPrincipal,
    wchar_t* pszPassword,
    wchar_t* pszCommandLine) {

    HANDLE htok;
    BOOL bOk = LogonUser(pszPrincipal,
                         pszAuthority,
                         pszPassword,
                         LOGON32_LOGON_BATCH, 0,
                         &htok);
    if (bOk) {
      STARTUPINFO si = { sizeof si, 0, L"" };
```

```
        PROCESS_INFORMATION pi;
        wchar_t szCmd[MAX_PATH];
        lstrcpy(szCmd, pszCommandLine);
        bOk = CreateProcessAsUser(htok,
                                  0, szCmd,
                                  0, 0,
                                  FALSE, 0, 0, 0,
                                  &si, &pi);
    if (bOk) {
      CloseHandle(pi.hThread);
      CloseHandle(pi.hProcess);
    }
  }
  return bOk ? true : false;
}
```

The STARTUPINFO initialization code is a simple shortcut that I've gotten used to typing over and over. It simply leverages the fact that the structure size is the first data member, that the *lpDesktop* parameter is the third, and that I want everything else to be set to 0. Also note that I explicitly make a copy of the command line onto the stack. CreateProcessW and CreateProcessAsUserW both touch the memory pointed to by the command-line parameter and expect it to be writable; this produces an access violation unless you provide a writable pointer (this is why these functions take an LPTSTR as opposed to an LPCTSTR for their command-line argument). The "A" versions of these functions already make copies of all string arguments (in the process of converting them to Unicode strings), so you won't run into this little gotcha unless you're making a Unicode build. Watch out.

Here's a sample code snippet that calls this function to start MYDAEMON.EXE in a batch logon session for Alice. Figure 5.3 shows the results; note that the caller is running in the System logon session, and thus has all the privileges required to call LogonUser and CreateProcessAsUser.

```
_startDaemonAsUser(L"foo",
                   L"alice",
                   L"password",
                   L"mydaemon");
```

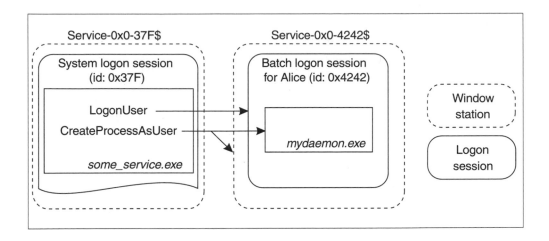

Figure 5.3. Leveraging natural window station allocation

All of this is well and good, and since most daemon processes aren't designed to run on behalf of various interactive users and therefore don't look at things such as `HKEY_CURRENT_USER` or per-user environment variables, `CreateProcessAsUser` doesn't deal with setting these things up; you have to do this manually if it's really necessary. But how?

The User Profile
The first thing you have to understand is that each principal *has the potential* to have an associated user profile on any machine where that principal can log in. If you're curious what makes up a user profile, simply peek into the following directory:

Windows 2000: `%SYSTEMROOT%\..\Documents and Settings`

Windows NT 4: `%SYSTEMROOT%\Profiles`

On Windows 2000, some of the most interesting files and folders are hidden, so if you're using Explorer to poke around, you should temporarily enable viewing of system and hidden files (being an administrator helps as well).

Each subdirectory represents a user profile; Winlogon normally creates one of these subdirectories and initializes it when a human logs on to the machine for the very first time (creating the profile can take a while, as you probably know from experience). Directly under each profile's root directory, you'll find a file called NTUSER.DAT. This is the HKEY_USERS hive for the user; normally, when a thread opens a registry key under HKEY_CURRENT_USERS, the hive it is reaching into is determined by the user SID in the thread's security context.

Now run REGEDT32.EXE and look at HKEY_USERS. Note that it is possible to have multiple hives loaded simultaneously under this key. (In fact, it's common practice for administrators to load hives for individual users in order to manually tweak per-user settings.)[22] Each time Alice logs in via Winlogon, the system loads Alice's hive; when Alice logs out, the system unloads her hive. If Alice's hive were not loaded and a thread running in her security context tried to open a registry key under HKEY_CURRENT_USERS, it would be shunted into the hive loaded under HKEY_USERS\.DEFAULT, which by default is readable by all authenticated users but only writable by administrators. This is the hive that daemon processes will often see if they go snooping under HKEY_CURRENT_USER, because the COM SCM doesn't bother loading profiles for daemons—it would be a waste of time because daemons don't normally store per-user state via profiles.[23] Profiles were designed for interactive users (humans), not daemons (although the system SCM does load profiles for services that run as distinguished principals; go figure).

Note that each user hive loaded under HKEY_USERS is named based on the text form of the user's SID (this is a quick way to see the SID for your account). Drill down into your profile (it's most likely the only one loaded) and look for a subkey called Environment. Here you'll find all your per-user environment variables. Clearly, there's lots of important information in this hive!

If for some reason you need to start a process running in a distinct logon session (perhaps one that you established via LogonUser), and you'd like to ensure that this process has a fully functional environment, you can't simply call CreateProcessAsUser and be done with it. You'll need to load the user's

---

[22] If you've never tried this before, from REGEDT32, highlight HKEY_USERS and choose the menu item Registry:Load Hive, and go find a copy of NTUSER.DAT that you'd like to peek at. (You'll need to be a member of the Administrators alias to look at other users' hives.)

[23] I can't tell you how many times I've heard people complain about this on the DCOM listserver (http://discuss.microsoft.com): "Why doesn't my COM server have the correct environment?" The answer is to not rely on per-user-profile information.

hive. But what if the hive hasn't even been created yet? Well, unlike many developers before you, you're in luck. Windows 2000 documents some new APIs for dealing with user profiles, and these functions are also supported on earlier versions of Windows.[24]

The core profile-related APIs that you'll want to know about are as follows:

```
typedef struct _PROFILEINFO {
    DWORD    dwSize;
    DWORD    dwFlags;
    LPTSTR   lpUserName;
    LPTSTR   lpProfilePath;
    LPTSTR   lpDefaultPath;
    LPTSTR   lpServerName;
    LPTSTR   lpPolicyPath;
    HANDLE   hProfile;
} PROFILEINFO;

BOOL LoadUserProfile(
    HANDLE Token,
    LPPROFILEINFO ProfileInfo
);

BOOL UnloadUserProfile(
    HANDLE Token,
    HANDLE Profile
);
```

The documentation for these functions is pretty spotty, but I've gotten them to work robustly on Windows 2000, plus virtually all service packs of Windows NT 4, so I feel pretty comfortable recommending them. What else are you going to do if you need to create a profile from scratch?

The first function, LoadUserProfile, loads the HKEY_USERS hive for the specified user. You must provide not only a token for the user, but also the user's

---

[24] The story behind this is rather interesting. After publishing Brown (2000b) (which documented the fact that these functions appeared to be fully operational on Windows NT 4), I noticed that (quite by coincidence, I'm sure) a brand-new Knowledge Base (KB) article had been published, and that the editors at *Microsoft Systems Journal* had updated my article to refer to this KB article as if I had simply overlooked it (I hate that!). This Knowledge Base article basically confirms that these functions are in fact supported on Windows NT 4.

name (the reason for this isn't clear, since the user's name can be garnered from the token by calling `GetUserName` while impersonating). The beauty of this function is that if the user hasn't yet physically logged in to the machine via Winlogon, `LoadUserProfile` happily constructs a brand-new profile by copying the default profile and then customizing it (changing the DACLs, for instance) for the new user.

Here's some code that loads the user profile, given a token:

```
bool _loadUserProfile(HANDLE htok, HANDLE& hprof) {
  if (!ImpersonateLoggedOnUser(htok))
    return false;
  wchar_t szUserName[256];
  DWORD cch = sizeof szUserName / sizeof *szUserName;
  bool bOk = false;
  if (GetUserName(szUserName, &cch)) {
    RevertToSelf();
    PROFILEINFO pi = { sizeof pi, 0, szUserName };
    bOk = LoadUserProfile(htok, &pi) ? true : false;
    if (bOk)
      hprof = pi.hProfile;
  } else RevertToSelf ();
  return bOk;
}
```

The handle `hprof` refers to HKEY_CURRENT_USER for the newly loaded hive. Unloading the profile is straightforward: Just call `UnloadUserProfile`, passing the token and the handle returned from `LoadUserProfile`.

The header file you'll need to include is `userenv.h`, and the import library is `userenv.lib`. These files ship with versions of the Platform SDK that support Windows 2000.

Even after loading the user's profile, you're still not quite finished, however. In order to make the process feel warm and cozy inside its logon session, you'll want to create an appropriate environment block.

Environment Block

Try the following experiment: Bring up a command prompt and type `set u`. Here's what I get on my Windows 2000 machine:

MECHANICS

```
USERDNSDOMAIN=foo.com
USERDOMAIN=FOO
USERNAME=kbrown
USERPROFILE=C:\Documents and Settings\kbrown
```

This is clearly customized on a per-principal basis. The problem is that `CreateProcessAsUser` simply makes a copy of the environment block of the parent process unless you pass something other than NULL for the *Environment* parameter. Once again, `userenv.h` comes to the rescue:

```
BOOL CreateEnvironmentBlock(
  LPVOID* Environment,    // out
  HANDLE  Token,          // in, optional
  BOOL    Inherit         // in
);
BOOL DestroyEnvironmentBlock(LPVOID Environment);
```

The optional *Token* argument allows you to create an environment for a particular user, or an environment for a daemon (in which only the system environment variables are used, as opposed to per-user variables). The system allocates memory and drops a pointer to the new environment block wherever you aim the *Environment* argument; to free this memory, call `DestroyEnvironmentBlock`.

The trick to using these functions is to make sure that the user's profile is loaded *before* calling `CreateEnvironmentBlock`. If you forget this step, the system will end up getting environment variables from `HKEY_USERS/.Default`, which isn't what you want. You should also note that `CreateEnvironmentBlock` always returns a Unicode string, so you should pass the `CREATE_UNICODE_ENVIRONMENT` flag to `CreateProcessAsUser` to indicate that you are specifying an environment using Unicode characters.

Here's some code that pulls all this together, loading a user profile, creating an appropriate environment block, and launching a new process:

```
bool _runAsUser(
    wchar_t* pszAuthority,
    wchar_t* pszPrincipal,
    wchar_t* pszPassword,
```

```
        wchar_t* pszCommandLine) {

    HANDLE htok;
    BOOL bOk = LogonUser(pszPrincipal,
                         pszAuthority,
                         pszPassword,
                         LOGON32_LOGON_BATCH, 0,
                         &htok);
    if (bOk) {
      HANDLE hprof = 0;
      bOk = _loadUserProfile(htok, hprof);
    }
    void* pEnv = 0;
    if (bOk) {
      bOk = CreateEnvironmentBlock(&pEnv, htok, FALSE);
      if (!bOk)
        pEnv = 0;
    }
    if (bOk) {
      STARTUPINFO si = { sizeof si, 0, L"" };
      PROCESS_INFORMATION pi;
      wchar_t szCmd[MAX_PATH];
      lstrcpy(szCmd, pszCommandLine);
      bOk = CreateProcessAsUser(htok,
              0, szCmd,
              0, 0,
              FALSE,
              CREATE_UNICODE_ENVIRONMENT, pEnv,
              0,
              &si, &pi);
      if (bOk) {
        CloseHandle(pi.hThread);
        CloseHandle(pi.hProcess);
      }
    }
    if (pEnv)
      DestroyEnvironmentBlock(pEnv);
    return bOk ? true : false;
}
```

There is a glaring problem with this code. Who unloads the user profile after it's been loaded? It won't be safe to unload the profile at least until the launched process exits, but that means the code would need to keep a thread alive waiting for this to happen. Windows 2000 introduced a solution to this problem: It's called the RunAs service, and it solves lots of headaches by acting as a built-in logon session broker.

The Windows 2000 RunAs Service

The RunAs service is a daemon that runs in the System logon session; therefore, it is allowed to call `LogonUser` and `CreateProcessAsUser` at will. It normally runs all the time; it autostarts at boot time by default, and won't accept a stop request until all processes it's managing have exited. You can access this service programmatically by calling a function that was also introduced in Windows 2000:

```
BOOL CreateProcessWithLogonW(
    LPCWSTR           lpUsername,           // in
    LPCWSTR           lpDomain,             // in
    LPCWSTR           lpPassword,           // in
    DWORD             dwLogonFlags,         // in
    LPCWSTR           lpApplicationName,    // in, optional
    LPWSTR            lpCommandLine,        // in, optional
    DWORD             dwCreationFlags,      // in
    LPVOID            lpEnvironment,        // in, optional
    LPCWSTR           lpCurrentDirectory,   // in, optional
    LPSTARTUPINFOW    lpStartupInfo,        // in
    LPPROCESS_INFORMATION lpProcessInfo // out
);
```

Note that you lose some of the flexibility of `CreateProcess` when you call this function. You can no longer specify security attributes for the process and thread (this isn't such a bad thing; the system uses the default security settings from the target user's token). You also cannot use this function to pass inheritable handles to the target process. The reason is that you are asking another process (the RunAs daemon) to create the process on your behalf, rather than creating the process directly.[25] The other parameters are the same (except, of course, that you can specify a set of alternate credentials).

The parameter *dwLogonFlags* allows you to use the RunAs service in three different ways. By passing 0 for this parameter (as of this writing, it's not clear from the documentation whether this is supported, but it works, so I'll mention it), the system simply starts the process in a new interactive logon session without loading the user's profile. This works for most generic daemon processes because they generally should not rely on user profiles. If you want the RunAs daemon to load the profile and set up the environment (just like the example code earlier), pass LOGON_WITH_PROFILE for this parameter. The RunAs daemon places each new process it creates into a job, and monitors that job (via a completion port) to track when the process and any child or grand-child processes have shut down; only then does it unload the profile.[26]

There is one other value you can pass for *dwLogonFlags*, LOGON _NETCREDENTIALS_ONLY. This flag causes the RunAs daemon to specify the LOGON32_LOGON_NEW_CREDENTIALS flag in its call to LogonUser (discussed in Chapter 4) so that the new process runs with the caller's token, but has the network credentials that were specified via the first three parameters to CreateProcessWithLogonW.

One thing you should be aware of is that the RunAs service was designed to be used by the interactive user as well as daemon processes. In fact, in case you haven't already discovered this, on Windows 2000, use the Start menu (or any Explorer window) to find an application you'd like to start. Instead of left-clicking to activate the program, right-click while holding down the Shift key. You should get a popup menu (as you'd expect), but because you held the Shift key down, you'll see an extra entry: "Run as...". Select this entry, type in the

---

[25] Technically, since the RunAs service is really part of the operating system, I'd imagine that it would have been possible (given internal knowledge of the way handles work) to pass through inherited handles to the child process.

[26] According to my experiments, the child processes are confined to the job. I verified this by calling CreateProcess specifying the CREATE_BREAKAWAY_FROM_JOB flag from a process spawned by the RunAs daemon, which failed with ERROR_ACCESS_DENIED. This means that if you start a process by calling CreateProcessWithLogonW, you won't be able to assign it to a job of your own.

authority/principal/password tuple, and Explorer will happily call `Create
ProcessWithLogonW` on your behalf.[27]

Although this UI feature is pretty convenient, the reason I'm going down
this path is to point out an interesting undocumented feature that kicks in
when you invoke this function from the interactive logon session (specifically,
the one started via Winlogon) as opposed to a daemon logon session. In the
former case, the job created by the RunAs daemon has a lifetime limited to
that of the interactive logon session; when the interactive user logs out, the
RunAs daemon shuts down any processes started by that user (even though
they are in separate logon sessions). This feature was added to satisfy the principal of least surprise (most end users are accustomed to having all processes
they've launched from the shell shut down when they log off). When calling
`CreateProcessWithLogonW` from a logon session *not* created by Winlogon
(for instance, a daemon logon session or an interactive logon session created
by manually calling `LogonUser`), the process's lifetime isn't limited in this
fashion.

Summary

- A window station is an encapsulated USER environment that is
  normally created on an as-needed basis to host processes. Window
  stations are naturally allocated by the system on a per-logon session
  basis.

- Each process is always associated with a single window station,
  although processes may migrate between window stations.

- By placing a DACL on a window station and making all USER handles relative to that window station, Windows avoids the overhead
  of having DACLs on every single USER object.

- The interactive window station, Winsta0, is the only place where
  windows are visible and can receive device input. This window
  station is the most heavily guarded in the operating system.

---

[27] There is also a `runas.exe` utility that you can use from the command line. Type `runas` at a
Windows 2000 command prompt to get a list of options.

- Beware of the ASSERT macro in noninteractive (daemon) window stations.

- Each window station can have several desktops, although this is only really interesting in Winsta0.

- Each thread is always associated with a single desktop.

- Each desktop also has a DACL that gives highly secure processes such as Winlogon more control over the Windows user interface.

- Be aware of inheritable ACLs in the DACL for Winsta0, in case you feel the need to modify it.

- A job can provide many of the same protections as a window station, and can be used within or across window station boundaries.

- Avoid relying on per-user state stored in profiles when writing daemons. Profiles are designed for humans, not daemons. Creating and loading profiles is not cheap.

- If you'd like to run an interactive process under alternate credentials, either use the Windows 2000 RunAs daemon or be prepared to write a lot of code to deal with loading profiles and modifying window station DACLs.

Chapter 6

Access Control and Accountability

Of the three access control strategies described in Chapter 3, object-centric access control is the most flexible, and correspondingly the most daunting option. Since I've already discussed the simplicity of the impersonation model in Chapters 3 and 4, and since I'll cover COM+ role-centric access control in Chapter 9, this chapter is dedicated to object-centric access control, the traditional form of access control provided by the Windows kernel.

I left this chapter until the very end of the Mechanics section for a reason. Before I started my journey into the world of security, I believed (like a lot of Windows developers) that security was all about calling AddAce and friends, and that it wasn't terribly glamorous. However, what I found was that access control (ACL maintenance and the like) was really just one part of a more interesting picture. Authentication is where security becomes interesting (in my opinion), whereas access control is pretty much just bookkeeping; as a security programmer, fortunately you get to do both.

This chapter is all about bookkeeping: how to keep your DACLs ordered correctly (this is a bit trickier in Windows 2000 than it used to be), how ACL inheritance really works and how to use it correctly, and so forth. I didn't think I'd enjoy writing this chapter, but it turned out to be a lot of fun, given all the cool new stuff that Windows 2000 brought to the table, and I think you'll enjoy this chapter as well.

Permissions

What do `OpenProcess`, `OpenService`, `RegOpenKeyEx`, and `OpenWindow Station` all have in common? Each of these functions requires you to specify your intentions before it will issue a handle. Your intentions take the form of a bitmask (32 bits wide), with each bit representing a particular permission that you desire. This is a very simple mechanism, and it makes it tremendously easy to program, but how is it possible to scrunch all the possible permissions for all possible classes of objects into a namespace that has only 32 slots?

Well, a couple of solutions come to mind. The first and simplest solution is to give each class of object its own namespace. When you call `OpenProcess`, you'll specify the permissions that make sense for a process. When you call `OpenService`, you'll specify permissions that make sense for a service. In fact, the header files in Windows provide manifest constants for these various permissions; for instance, here are the first two permissions defined for the types of objects mentioned earlier:

```
// from winnt.h
#define  PROCESS_TERMINATE          (0x0001)
#define  PROCESS_CREATE_THREAD      (0x0002)

// from winsvc.h
#define  SERVICE_QUERY_CONFIG       0x0001
#define  SERVICE_CHANGE_CONFIG      0x0002

// from winnt.h
#define  KEY_QUERY_VALUE            (0x0001)
#define  KEY_SET_VALUE              (0x0002)

// from winuser.h
#define  WINSTA_ENUMDESKTOPS        0x0001L
#define  WINSTA_READATTRIBUTES      0x0002L
```

Specific Permissions

What you are looking at in the list just given are known as **specific permissions;** they really only make sense when applied to a known class of object. For instance, no developer would ever try to open a registry key for PROCESS

_TERMINATE permission—this wouldn't have any meaning—so, assuming we always work with distinct classes of objects, there is no problem sharing a common physical namespace and having every class of object use the same set of bits (assigning local semantics to each bit), as shown earlier. Note that each permission is defined as a 16-bit mask; this is because the 32-bit mask representing access permissions is actually split into four parts, with 16 bits reserved for specific permissions (Figure 6.1).

Standard Permissions

There are several permissions that virtually all objects have in common, especially when it comes to access control and auditing. It would be silly to have each object define its own permission for DELETE, for instance: FILE_DELETE, KEY_DELETE, SERVICE_DELETE, and so on. So instead, everyone simply agrees that there is a standard permission called DELETE (with a common physical bitmask), and we get on with it.

Recognizing the need for permissions that were polymorphic across all different classes of objects, 8 of the 32 bits were carved out and called **standard permissions,** and 5 of them are in use today (3 are presumably reserved for future use):

```
// from winnt.h
#define DELETE              (0x00010000L)
#define READ_CONTROL        (0x00020000L)
#define WRITE_DAC           (0x00040000L)
#define WRITE_OWNER         (0x00080000L)
#define SYNCHRONIZE         (0x00100000L)
```

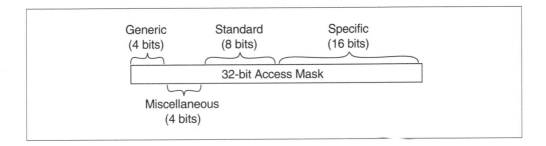

Figure 6.1 Anatomy of the access mask

Besides DELETE, which is obvious, the standard permissions and what they control are as follows:

READ_CONTROL	Read access to the owner, group, and DACL
WRITE_DAC	Write access to the DACL
WRITE_OWNER	Write access to the owner SID
SYNCHRONIZE	Ability to wait on the handle[1]

Although I'll describe these bits later, I should mention up front that the "miscellaneous" bit positions in the access mask are used in a way that may seem a bit strange. For example, the two bits that are currently defined,

```
// from winnt.h
#define ACCESS_SYSTEM_SECURITY  (0x01000000L)
#define MAXIMUM_ALLOWED         (0x02000000L)
```

will never be found in a DACL. The other two miscellaneous bits are reserved for future use.

Having a set of standard permissions is a really good thing because it allows us to treat objects polymorphically, which is important in a couple of scenarios having to do with the creation of new objects. Being able to assign permissions polymorphically enables a basic form of ACL inheritance, but more important, it enables us to have a single default DACL that can apply to all objects—or does it? What about specific permissions? How does the system allow you to assign specific permissions in a polymorphic way?

Generic Permissions

The most significant four bits in the mask provide a reasonable and simple solution to the problem. Using the universal hammer of computer science, the Windows security team added a level of indirection that allows you to choose an access mask (some combination of standard and specific permissions) in a polymorphic way. There are four **generic permissions** that can be used to accomplish this:

---

[1] Via WaitForMultipleObjects and friends.

```
#define GENERIC_READ                        (0x80000000L)
#define GENERIC_WRITE                       (0x40000000L)
#define GENERIC_EXECUTE                     (0x20000000L)
#define GENERIC_ALL                         (0x10000000L)
```

Each class of object internally has a mapping of the four generic permissions onto real permissions (standard and specific), which is represented by the GENERIC_MAPPING data structure:

```
typedef struct _GENERIC_MAPPING {
    ACCESS_MASK GenericRead;
    ACCESS_MASK GenericWrite;
    ACCESS_MASK GenericExecute;
    ACCESS_MASK GenericAll;
} GENERIC_MAPPING;
```

Thus, GENERIC_READ will map onto files and registry keys in different ways, but it's pretty predictable. GENERIC_READ for a file includes the following bits that logically grant all possible read permissions:

READ_CONTROL

SYNCHRONIZE

FILE_READ_DATA

FILE_READ_ATTRIBUTES

FILE_READ_EA

GENERIC_READ for a registry key includes the following bits that grant all possible read permissions:

READ_CONTROL

KEY_QUERY_VALUE

KEY_ENUMERATE_SUB_KEYS

KEY_NOTIFY

As will be shown later, you can make GENERIC_READ (and friends) mean whatever you like for your own private objects as well.

Anatomy of a Security Descriptor

A security descriptor does just that—it describes the security settings for an object. Security descriptors are associated with all intrinsically secured objects provided by Windows. Executive objects such as processes, threads, semaphores, sections, waitable timers, and window stations, as well as other objects such as files (NTFS), registry keys, and services, are all examples of objects whose security is enforced intrinsically by the operating system; thus, each of these objects has an associated security descriptor.

As shown in Figure 6.2, each security descriptor contains a revision number and control word, plus four pointers (or offsets, depending on the flavor) to the variable-length guts of the descriptor: the owner SID, primary group SID, DACL, and SACL. These settings are squashed into a semi-opaque data structure (SECURITY_DESCRIPTOR) that is usually stored as a contiguous variable-length blob of bits alongside the object with which it is associated.

There is no central store of security descriptors in Windows; rather, each subsystem that exposes secure objects must manage security descriptors individually (fortunately, the good folks at Microsoft have already implemented most of the secure subsystems that you care about). For instance, the NTFS file system manages security descriptors for files and directories, and the System Service Control Manager manages security descriptors for service objects. The latter you can actually see—just poke around in the service database at HKLM\SYSTEM\CurrentControlSet\Services and look for a subkey called

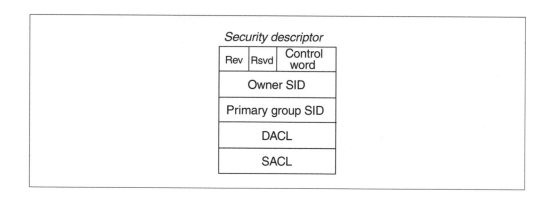

Figure 6.2 Anatomy of a security descriptor

`Security` under each user-mode service. You'll never read or modify this value directly, but this is where the System SCM stores the security descriptor for a service.

The Owner

Each security descriptor has a SID that indicates the owner of the object; this may be an individual principal, but it also may be a group or alias. In fact, when an administrator of a domain creates new objects, either the Administrators alias or the Domain Admins group is assigned as the owner, depending on the type of object being created.[2]

Ownership implies the most basic permissions on an object: `READ_CON-TROL` and `WRITE_DAC`. The owner is *always* granted the permission to read and change the DACL, so that even if she accidentally denies all access to everyone (including herself), she will have the implicit permission to fix the problem.

If Alice is the owner of an object (a file, for example), she can delegate the authority to manage the security on that file to Bob by granting Bob `WRITE_DAC` permissions. Bob can now change the DACL in any way he likes. In fact, because Bob is not the owner of the object, Bob can accidentally lock himself out by denying himself permission to access the file. But because Alice is the owner, he can't accidentally (or maliciously) lock her out of the file.

From a completely practical perspective, what this means is that if you are trying to get access to an object, you will always be able to open the object for at least `READ_CONTROL` and `WRITE_DAC` permission if the object's owner SID is present in your token, regardless of the state of the object's DACL. But what if you're not the owner?

Imagine that Alice created lots of files (some very large) on your file server and was subsequently abducted by aliens. If Alice was an administrator of the file server, those files would naturally be owned by the Administrators alias, and therefore you (being an administrator) could easily grant yourself `DELETE`

---

[2] As a concrete example, in Windows 2000, while running as a member of the Domain Admins group (and also the local Administrators alias) on a domain controller, I created a new file on an NTFS partition, a new registry key, and a new object (a user) in the Active Directory. For the file and registry key, the system assigned ownership to the Administrators alias, whereas for the directory object, the system assigned ownership to Domain Admins.

permissions and clean them up. However, let's say that Alice is just a normal user, not an administrator of the file server. In this case, Alice (as an individual) will be the owner of each file, so unless Alice had set up the DACLs to grant you some permissions, you'll be completely locked out of these files.

Windows provides a solution for this via `SeTakeOwnershipPrivilege` (apparently some Microsoft employees were in fact abducted by aliens, making the problem apparent). If you enable this privilege in your token, you can open virtually any object[3] in the system for `WRITE_OWNER` permission. With `WRITE_OWNER`, you can change the owner SID to one of the SIDs in your token. (Technically this is limited to either your user SID or any group/alias that is marked as having the potential for being an owner, the Administrators alias being the canonical alternative.) Once the owner has been changed to one of the SIDs in your token, you can now reopen the handle for `READ_CONTROL` and `WRITE_DAC` permissions and change the DACL to grant yourself `DELETE` permission. You can then open yet a third handle to the object asking for `DELETE` permission and delete the object (in this case you'd just call `DeleteFile`).

`SeTakeOwnershipPrivilege` is granted to the Administrators alias by default. Note that this privilege does *not* confer the right to give ownership *back*. This makes it harder for an administrator to casually take ownership of a file (owned by Alice, say), silently modify the DACL, and then give ownership back to Alice without her knowledge.

The Primary Group

The primary group SID is present in each security descriptor for compatibility with the POSIX subsystem. Because this is not a terribly popular subsystem, I won't be spending much time talking about this setting (it has virtually no meaning at all in the Win32 subsystem).

Any developer who has worked on a vanilla UNIX platform is familiar with the simple access control model present there. Each file has a matrix of nine attributes, grouped into three sets of read, write, and execute permissions. The

---

[3] I use *virtually* as a weasel word for two reasons: First, it would be impossible for me to verify that this *always* works; second, I've actually found a case where it *doesn't* work. I failed to take ownership of the Winlogon desktop (both in Windows NT 4 and Windows 2000). This particular limitation appears to be hardwired into the system.

I'm an administrator, so I've also included the default DACL for a sample principal named Alice (who is not an administrator):

grant `0x10000000` to Alice

grant `0x10000000` to SYSTEM

The access mask being granted in each of these cases is `GENERIC_ALL`. When an administrator creates new objects and this default DACL is applied, those objects are usable by any other local administrator, which makes it easier to share administration duties. When a random user (not an administrator) creates new objects, they are usable by that particular user. No matter what, the System logon session has access permissions by default.[7] Note the use of generic permissions; the system maps these automatically based on the class of object being created.

For example, if Alice created a named mutex (passing NULL for `SECURITY_ATTRIBUTES`) while she was running in a security context with a default DACL as shown previously, the resulting mutex would have the following DACL:

grant `0x001F0001` to Alice

grant `0x001F0001` to SYSTEM

how the generic permissions were mapped automatically based on the of object (mutex in this case) that Alice created. In this case, the high (`0x001F`) represents all standard permissions (including `SYNCHRONIZE`), the low word (`0x0001`) represents all specific permissions for a mutex (`MUTANT_QUERY_STATE`).

you want to change this default behavior for your process, at process initialization time create a custom DACL (be sure to stick with generic permissions this DACL will likely be used to create lots of different types of objects). this DACL into your process token by calling `SetTokenInformation` (Chapter 4), and pass NULL to your heart's content.

---

ranting access to SYSTEM is purely a convenience; sophisticated code running in the System on session can ultimately construct a token with any authorization attributes needed to access objects on the machine. That's what it means to be part of the TCB.

first set applies to the owner of the file, the second applies to the group associated with the file, and the third applies to everyone else (world). For instance, the following set of permission attributes, `rwxr-xr--`, grants the owner full control, the group read and execute access, and everyone else read access. The UNIX utility `chmod` is used to adjust these settings.

It's clear based on the way security in UNIX works that each object needs to provide storage for an owner SID and a group SID, and although the owner has very well-defined semantics in the Win32 subsystem, the group SID effectively languishes as a historical footnote.

The DACL

DACL stands for discretionary access control list, and based on the previous discussion of ownership, it may already be clear what is implied by *discretionary*. The access control policy for any given object is specified at the owner's discretion (the owner of an object is implicitly granted `READ_CONTROL` and `WRITE_DAC` permissions to that object). This is very different from the mandatory access controls used in military systems.[4]

Conceptually, the DACL is simply a list of principals, groups, and aliases that are allowed to touch an object in certain ways.

The SACL

SACL stands for System access control list, and unlike the DACL, the SACL is nondiscretionary; it has no relationship whatsoever to the owner of the object. So far the only use Windows has found for the SACL is for audits and alarms, and as of this writing, alarms are not supported (even on Windows 2000).

The audit entries in the SACL provide a list of principals, groups, and aliases that are to be audited when attempting to touch an object in certain ways. I'll drill down into both the DACL and SACL a bit later in this chapter.

The Control Word

The control word group of bitflags houses several different configuration options, most of which are simply used to communicate extra semantic information

---

[4] See Kaufman (1995).

between you and the system when getting or setting security information on an object (although some of these settings are also directly maintained as part of the state of the security descriptor of an object). These flags are covered in this chapter as appropriate.

Where Do Security Descriptors Come From?

Let's take a very simple example, the lowly mutex:

```
HANDLE CreateMutex(
    LPSECURITY_ATTRIBUTES MutexAttrs, // in, optional
    BOOL InitialOwner,                // in
    LPCTSTR Name                      // in, optional
);
```

When giving talks on Windows security, I often jokingly ask the crowd the following question: "Who in this room has ever passed anything other than NULL?" Most people in the room snicker, while a few proud souls raise their hands in earnest. Most Windows developers are trained from birth to pass NULL whenever they see the dreaded LPSECURITY_ATTRIBUTES parameter, so let's quickly dispel the fear behind it.

```
struct SECURITY_ATTRIBUTES {
    DWORD  nLength,      // sizeof SECURITY_ATTRIBUTES
    LPVOID psd,          // optional pointer to SD
    BOOL   bInheritHandle // is handle inheritable?
};
```

By passing an explicit security descriptor wrapped in a SECURITY _ATTRIBUTES structure, you can inject custom security settings for the new mutex. If you provide a fully formed security descriptor, complete with owner, group, DACL, and SACL, you'll have complete control over the security settings for the mutex. However, the code you'd have to write to make this work would be somewhat drawn out, and generally speaking, the more custom security-related code you write, the more chances you have for accidentally opening up a security hole in your application.

Instead of providing *all* the settings (assuming you don't jus nine times out of ten you'll only provide the DACL. Any elements descriptor that you don't provide will be supplied by the syste scrapes the owner and group SIDs from the default owner ar your token, and then constructs a default SACL based on th SACL. (In the case of a mutex, there is no parent, so the default.) If you don't specify a DACL, the system construct the parent object or, as in the case with a mutex where the applying the default DACL in your token to the class of obj token has a DACL with generic permissions; these gen mapped to specific and standard permissions to produce the specific class of object you are creating.)

How to Pass NULL and Lead a Happy Life

As mentioned earlier, the less security-related code yo there are for you to accidentally goof up and leave a g application. By passing NULL for LPSECURITY_ NULL for the security descriptor pointer contained consistent policy for security on all the objects tha simply look into your token if it needs help with ing security descriptors for new objects. The tri default DACL that reflects the overall policy you

Although this is not documented anywhere here's what the default DACL looks like in a system (it looks the same on both my Wind machines, by the way):

grant 0x10000000 to Administrators

grant 0x10000000 to SYSTEM

---

[5] I'm purposely deferring the details of how cussion of ACL inheritance later in the cha

[6] ACL inheritance has not yet been discu object will completely determine the DAC itly. Still, the owner and primary group w

190

MECHANICS

Security Descriptor Usage Patterns

Because each piece of information stored in a security descriptor is variable length (SIDs and ACLs), for convenience security descriptors come in two flavors: self-relative (serialized) and absolute. All this means is that when you have a pointer to a security descriptor, your pointer may simply reference a contiguous block of memory that contains all the information in the descriptor (this is the self-relative flavor), or it may point to a fixed-length data structure that holds four pointers, one to each element of the descriptor, each of which could potentially be in a separately allocated block of memory (this is the absolute flavor). Generally the security descriptors that you provide to the system programmatically tend to be in absolute format, and the security descriptors that you retrieve from the system are self-relative, as demonstrated in the following code fragments:

```
//////////////////////////////////////////////////
// here we use a SECURITY_DESCRIPTOR to communicate
// security information *to* the system
SECURITY_DESCRIPTOR sd; // absolute SD
InitializeSecurityDescriptor(&sd,
    SECURITY_DESCRIPTOR_REVISION);
SetSecurityDescriptorOwner(&sd, g_pOwner, FALSE);
SetSecurityDescriptorDacl (&sd, TRUE, g_pDacl, FALSE);

SECURITY_ATTRIBUTES sa = {sizeof sa, &sd, FALSE};
HANDLE hMutex = CreateMutex(&sa, FALSE, L"MyMutex");
// ...
CloseHandle(hMutex);

//////////////////////////////////////////////////
// here we use a SECURITY_DESCRIPTOR to retrieve
// security information *from* the system
void* psd = 0; // self-relative SD
if (GetNamedSecurityInfo(L"c:\\foo.txt",
    SE_FILE_OBJECT, OWNER_SECURITY_INFORMATION,
    0, 0, 0, 0, &psd)) {
    // do something with the information...
    LocalFree(psd); // one call frees the SD
}
```

Self-relative security descriptors are easy to free (as the previous code demonstrates); they are also easy to drop into persistent storage (for instance, as values in registry keys for securing services), but they are very difficult to modify in place. When you need to construct (or modify) a security descriptor on the fly, you'll usually prefer the absolute form because it's more convenient. The system provides a set of accessor functions for retrieving the contents of a security descriptor, so it really doesn't matter (in most cases[8]) what form you present to the system. Here are two of the prototypical accessors:

```
BOOL GetSecurityDescriptorOwner(
    PSECURITY_DESCRIPTOR psd,   // in
    PSID* pOwner,               // out
    LPBOOL OwnerDefaulted       // out
);

BOOL GetSecurityDescriptorDacl(
    PSECURITY_DESCRIPTOR psd,   // in
    LPBOOL DaclPresent,         // out
    PACL* pDacl,                // out
    LPBOOL DaclDefaulted        // out
);
```

When *retrieving* information from a security descriptor associated with an object in the system (for instance, a file, a registry key, a thread, or even a custom object under your control), the boolean flags in these APIs should generally be ignored (in fact, having them present in the functions just given is rarely useful, and typically leads to confusion). When *building* a security descriptor for an object, these flags are very useful indeed, because they convey extra (sometimes subtle) semantics for the operation. How these flags are used is discussed later in the chapter.

There are eight functions overall for getting and setting the four parts of a security descriptor, and they are very straightforward to use:

`Get/SetSecurityDescriptorOwner`

`Get/SetSecurityDescriptorGroup`

---

[8] `CoInitializeSecurity` is a notable exception—it assumes the caller will pass an absolute security descriptor. Whoops.

```
Get/SetSecurityDescriptorDacl

Get/SetSecurityDescriptorSacl
```

A self-relative security descriptor contains *offsets* as opposed to *pointers* to its elements, so avoid relying on the SECURITY_DESCRIPTOR structure definition in winnt.h and instead treat security descriptors as opaque and use the programmatic API (described earlier) for accessing the contents of any security descriptor. This way your code won't break when it is handed an unexpected flavor of descriptor. The PSECURITY_DESCRIPTOR typedef, for instance, simply evaluates to void* (thus the use of void* for brevity in the code snippet given earlier).

Note that in the code snippet, I created a security descriptor that was only partially filled. The call to InitializeSecurityDescriptor simply set the revision number, initialized the owner and group to NULL (indicating that they are not specified), and reset the flags in the descriptor to indicate that the DACL and SACL were not specified. I then explicitly attached an owner SID and DACL that I had previously constructed (you'll have to use your imagination here) to the security descriptor before calling CreateMutex. Recall that this *doesn't mean* that the resulting mutex will have no primary group or SACL in its security descriptor. The other elements will be provided automatically by the system, as explained earlier.

The point that I'm trying to make here is that the SECURITY_DESCRIPTOR structure is generally used as a communication vehicle for transporting security information about an object between you and the system, and nine times out of ten, it will not contain all four elements. To reinforce this, note the second example, in which I called GetNamedSecurityInfo to retrieve a security descriptor from a file. In this case, I only asked for the owner SID, so the resulting security descriptor will only contain this single element. If I were to call Get SecurityDescriptorDacl, the function would indicate (via the Dacl Present flag) that no information about the object's DACL is present in the descriptor. If I were to call GetSecurityDescriptorGroup, the function would indicate (by returning a null pointer) that the primary group is not present. This doesn't mean that the file doesn't have a DACL or group; it just means that I didn't ask for that information.

Occasionally at runtime it's useful to discover whether a particular security descriptor is self-relative as opposed to absolute. To do this, call GetSecurity DescriptorControl and check for the SE_SELF_RELATIVE flag:

```
BOOL GetSecurityDescriptorControl(
    PSECURITY_DESCRIPTOR SecurityDescriptor, // in
    PSECURITY_DESCRIPTOR_CONTROL Control,    // out
    LPDWORD Revision                         // out
);
```

Here's a helper function that I've often found useful:

```
bool _isSelfRelativeSD(void* psd) {
  // SECURITY_DESCRIPTOR_CONTROL == WORD
  SECURITY_DESCRIPTOR_CONTROL control;
  DWORD rev;
  if (!GetSecurityDescriptorControl(psd, &control, &rev))
    throw "whoops, you passed a malformed SD";
  return (control & SE_SELF_RELATIVE) ? true : false;
}
```

How ACLs Work

Access control lists are flexible but complex beasts, and even more so in Windows 2000—and dramatically so in the Active Directory. This section starts by looking at the basics of how ACLs work, and then discusses the model of ACL inheritance used in Windows NT 4 and the new model introduced in Windows 2000. It also includes a primer on ACL programming for those just getting started.

How the DACL Works

The DACL is the heart of any security descriptor. It consists of a list of **access control entries** (**ACEs**) that say who is allowed to touch an object in various ways. Think of it as a set of records with the following columns: ACE type (positive or negative), who, and what (Figure 6.3).

The first column in an ACE determines whether the ACE adds or subtracts permissions. The second column indicates the target **trustee**, and is physically represented by a SID. The trustee can be either an individual principal or (more

+/-	Trustee	Mask
−	Alice	Read
+	Friends	Read

Figure 6.3   Simplified view of a DACL

commonly) an alias or group SID. The third column is a fixed-width bitmask (32 bits wide) that specifies the set of permissions in question (any combination of generic, standard, or specific permissions).

Here's a set of rules that will help you understand the semantics of a DACL:

1. Positive entries in the DACL add permissions; negative entries subtract permissions.

2. Whenever there is a conflict between a positive and negative ACE, the negative ACE always prevails. Thus, if you are explicitly denied access via a negative ACE, you cannot counteract this by adding an opposing positive ACE. There is a very specific exception to this rule that has to do with ACL inheritance in Windows 2000, but I'll defer discussing this until later in the chapter.

3. Unless you are explicitly granted a permission (directly via your user SID or indirectly via a group or alias), you are implicitly denied. Thus an **empty DACL** doesn't grant anyone any permissions at all.

4. If no DACL at all is provided for an object (not even an empty one), everyone is granted all access. This degenerate case is often referred to as having a **NULL DACL.**

Assuming Alice is a member of the Friends group, the example in Figure 6.3 can be read as follows: "All Friends except Alice are granted read permissions."

Note that because negative entries always prevail over positive entries, it wouldn't make much sense to reverse the sense of the ACEs in Figure 6.3 to try to achieve the following: "All Friends are denied read access, except Alice— she's OK." If Alice is a member of the Friends group, she will be denied.

Negative entries are designed to surgically deny access to small groups or individuals.

Empty DACLs versus NULL DACLs

One of the degenerate cases mentioned earlier is a DACL with no entries at all. DACLs work on an additive basis, so if none of the SIDs in your token is listed in a DACL, that DACL implicitly denies you all access. (There are exceptions to this rule; for instance, recall that the owner of the object still has READ _CONTROL and WRITE_DAC implicitly, regardless of the state of the DACL.)

Here is a code fragment that creates a mutex[9] with an empty DACL:

```
// construct an empty DACL
ACL acl;
InitializeAcl(&acl, sizeof acl, ACL_REVISION);

// here we use a SECURITY_DESCRIPTOR to communicate
// the DACL to the system
SECURITY_DESCRIPTOR sd;
InitializeSecurityDescriptor(&sd,
    SECURITY_DESCRIPTOR_REVISION);
SetSecurityDescriptorDacl(&sd, TRUE, &acl, FALSE);

SECURITY_ATTRIBUTES sa = {sizeof sa, &sd, FALSE};
HANDLE hMutex = CreateMutex(&sa, FALSE, L"MyMutex");
// ...
CloseHandle(hMutex);
```

Although it may seem strange to create an object whose DACL denies everyone all access, I present this code to demonstrate the difference between an empty DACL and a NULL DACL. (Incidentally, this turns out to be rather useful when used in conjunction with the DuplicateHandle API, as discussed later in the chapter.)

The other interesting degenerate case is the NULL DACL. A security descriptor can be given a NULL DACL explicitly, which indicates that the owner (or

---

[9] I chose a mutex for simplicity—you could use this code to create any executive object, file, or registry key, as long as the create function takes an LPSECURITY_ATTRIBUTES parameter.

someone else with WRITE_DAC permission) simply doesn't care about access control on this object, and therefore the security descriptor for the object doesn't need a DACL at all. Having no DACL at all is very different from having a DACL that happens to be empty. An object with a NULL DACL is effectively the same as an object with a DACL that grants everyone all access; it's just more efficient in this case to leave the DACL out altogether.[10]

Here's a code fragment that demonstrates creating a mutex with a NULL DACL:

```
// here we use a SECURITY_DESCRIPTOR to communicate
// that we don't want *any DACL at all*
SECURITY_DESCRIPTOR sd;
InitializeSecurityDescriptor(&sd,
    SECURITY_DESCRIPTOR_REVISION);
SetSecurityDescriptorDacl(&sd, TRUE, 0, FALSE);

SECURITY_ATTRIBUTES sa = {sizeof sa, &sd, FALSE};
HANDLE hMutex = CreateMutex(&sa, FALSE, L"MyMutex");
// ...
CloseHandle(hMutex);
```

The key distinction here is in the second and third parameters to Set SecurityDescriptorDacl, which say there is a DACL, and the DACL pointer should be NULL. If you set a NULL DACL on a file or registry key and later look at the DACL via the built-in ACL editor, you'll see that Everyone is granted all permissions. (Depending on which version of the operating system you are using, there may not be a clear distinction in the user interface between a NULL DACL and a DACL that grants everyone all access.)

DACL Evaluation

Recall from Chapter 3 that the operating system looks at three pieces of information in order to perform an access check:

---

[10] Watch out for this if you are writing code to retrieve the DACL from an object! Many programmers forget that a NULL DACL is a perfectly valid state in a security descriptor, and functions such as GetSecurityInfo may very well give you a null pointer for the DACL, indicating that the object has a NULL access control policy (thus, everyone has all access).

1. The authorization attributes for the principal requesting access

2. The intentions specified in the request

3. The security settings for the object to be accessed

The authorization attributes are cached in the token. The intentions are stated programmatically (either via an explicit access mask passed as a parameter, or via the intrinsic semantics of the API being used to access the object). The security settings for the object are stored in the security descriptor. The `AccessCheck` API pretty much sums up these ideas:

```
BOOL AccessCheck(
    PSECURITY_DESCRIPTOR psd,    // in
    HANDLE ClientToken,          // in
    DWORD DesiredAccess,         // in
    PGENERIC_MAPPING pgm,        // in
    PPRIVILEGE_SET pps,          // out
    LPDWORD PrivilegeSetLen,     // in, out
    LPDWORD GrantedAccess,       // out
    LPBOOL AccessStatus          // out
);
```

Note that the first three parameters to this function correspond to the three elements mentioned earlier. The generic mapping structure allows any generic permissions in the DACL to be mapped correctly based on the class of object being accessed, and the privilege set indicates whether a privilege was used to effectively override the security settings for the object (`SeTakeOwnership Privilege` comes to mind). Those details aside, you are basically passing in the three core pieces of information (the token, security descriptor, and requested access mask) and getting back a boolean result (`AccessStatus`) that says whether or not the requested access was granted (`GrantedAccess` will be covered later).

Many systems programmers will never need to call `AccessCheck`, but under the covers, a check like this is being performed each time you open a handle to a secure executive object. Regardless of who initiates it, the access check is performed in a very well defined way (the description following may not reflect the actual physical implementation, but it does accurately describe

MECHANICS

the documented and observed behavior of the system). First the system creates an accumulator (a bitmask, 32 bits wide) to represent the set of permissions collected while traversing the DACL, and initializes all the bits to 0. Then the system looks at the mask requested by the client and determines whether to grant any of the permissions implicitly (for instance, if requested, READ_CONTROL and WRITE_DAC are granted intrinsically if the owner SID in the security descriptor is present in the client's token). Some permissions might also be granted based on enabled privileges in the token (if requested, WRITE _OWNER will be granted as long as SeTakeOwnershipPrivilege is enabled, for instance). Any permissions granted based on these implicit rules are reflected by latching the appropriate bits in the accumulator.

If the permissions accumulated so far don't satisfy the client's requested access mask, the system begins to traverse the DACL from top to bottom, trying to satisfy the client's request (if a NULL DACL is present, we're done; the system simply grants the requested access). The system checks each ACE it encounters for relevance to the current client request. Relevance means two things: The SID in the ACE must be present and enabled in the client's token, and the mask in the ACE must relate to permissions the client is requesting that have not yet been collected in the accumulator. In mathematical terms:

```
DWORD _relevantPermissionsInAceMask(DWORD accumulator,
                                    DWORD desiredAccess,
                                    DWORD aceMask) {
    return (desiredAccess & ~accumulator) & aceMask;
}
```

If this function returns 0 for any given ACE, that ACE is not relevant, and the system skips it and moves on to the next one. If, on the other hand, the ACE is relevant and is positive (and the SID in the ACE is present and enabled in the client's token), the system latches the corresponding bits in the accumulator.

This process continues until one of three things happens: If all requested permissions have been accumulated, access is granted, and the traversal ends immediately. If a relevant negative ACE is found, access is denied, and the traversal ends immediately. If the traversal exhausts all the ACEs in the DACL without accumulating the requested permissions, access is denied.

If access is granted at this point and a *restricted token* is in use (see Chapter 4), the system repeats this algorithm a second time using the list of restricting SIDs in the token. Only if *both passes* say it's OK will access be granted. The list of restricting SIDs is just that: restricting. It can only be used to restrict access, not to expand access.[11]

The handling of negative ACEs brings up an important point about DACL ordering. Negative ACEs must always be traversed first in order to guarantee the expected semantics of a DACL (if you explicitly deny someone access, they are guaranteed to be denied); thus, they must be at the top of the DACL.[12] The platform SDK documentation states that this is the *recommended order* for DACLs, but if you violate this ordering, you'll be doing yourself and your customers a vast disservice because the DACLs that you create will behave very differently from the DACLs created by the operating system (and other third-party vendors). Don't do this. Also note that the exact ordering of ACEs gets a bit trickier in Windows 2000 with its more complex inheritance model. These differences are discussed later in the chapter.

A Note on Correctness and Efficiency

As DACLs get longer (more ACEs) and tokens get fatter (more groups and aliases), evaluation obviously becomes more expensive.[13] A great way to help reduce the overhead of an access check (and improve the security and robustness of your application) is to *only ask for the permissions you really need*. Many programmers have gotten into the habit of opening objects and requesting all possible permissions (PROCESS_ALL_ACCESS, KEY_ALL_ACCESS, etc.), often because they are too lazy to look up the more specific access masks

---

[11] Recall that another way to restrict use of authorization attributes is to use group SIDs marked with SE_GROUP_USE_FOR_DENY_ONLY. In this case, the algorithm simply ignores any positive ACEs that apply to group SIDs marked deny-only.

[12] If I had to guess, I'd say that a lot of the confusion over how ACLs work comes from the way the old Windows NT 4 ACL editor (ACLEDIT.DLL) used to display DACLs. Entries were listed in alphabetical order, without regard to whether they were positive or negative. The Windows 2000 ACL editor (at least in Advanced mode) shows the ACEs in their correct order.

[13] A friend of mine at DevelopMentor once sent me a token dump from a company at which he was consulting. The token had 73 groups and aliases packed into it. This also happened to be one of the few companies where the software development team members were not allowed to be members of the Administrators alias on their own machines.

that they really should be using.[14] This generally sacrifices correctness and efficiency at runtime for efficiency at development time, which is rarely good. Most developers debug and test their code while running under their own administrative accounts (I know of very few developers who are not administrators on their own development machines). Code written this way will often break when run in less privileged security contexts, and these sorts of bugs are often difficult to root out. Code written this way will also chew up more CPU cycles because the DACL needs to be traversed further to grant the requested permissions.

With this in mind, there are occasions when you really *need* the system to traverse the entire DACL. An example is when you want to determine the full range of possible permissions that could be granted, given a particular security descriptor. This is where the MAXIMUM_ALLOWED access mask (which won't ever be found in a DACL) comes in. If you pass this flag to AccessCheck (via the *DesiredAccess* parameter), the entire DACL will be traversed and the result of the traversal will be placed into the 32-bit mask pointed to by the *GrantedAccess* parameter. (I used to wonder what *GrantedAccess* was for until I discovered this feature.)

How the SACL Works

The SACL physically looks just like the DACL, but the +/– column means something totally different. Rather than granting or denying a permission, a positive ACE in the SACL says that the system should audit a *successful* acquisition of a permission, and a negative ACE says that the system should audit a *failed* acquisition of a permission (where success and failure are determined based on access checks alone). Note that for efficiency, an ACE in the SACL can be both positive and negative (in other words, a single ACE can audit both success or failure).

When I say *acquisition,* I am implying that auditing takes place at the same time as access control. Interestingly enough, calling AccessCheck *does not* cause the SACL to be evaluated (and thus no audits are generated by this API). Rather, another family of functions exists for performing SACL traversal and req-

---

[14] Hey, I'm not exempt from this either. As a professional software developer, many of my own programs suffered from this flaw before I came to grips with security.

uisite audit generation. Here are two of the most commonly used auditing functions:

```
BOOL ObjectOpenAuditAlarm(
    LPCTSTR SubsystemName,       // in
    LPVOID HandleId,             // in
    LPTSTR ObjectTypeName,       // in
    LPTSTR ObjectName,           // in
    PSECURITY_DESCRIPTOR psd,    // in
    HANDLE ClientToken,          // in
    DWORD DesiredAccess,         // in
    DWORD GrantedAccess,         // in
    PPRIVILEGE_SET pps,          // in
    BOOL ObjectCreation,         // in
    BOOL AccessGranted,          // in
    LPBOOL pfGenerateOnClose,    // out
);
BOOL ObjectCloseAuditAlarm(
    LPCTSTR SubsystemName,       // in
    LPVOID HandleId,             // in
    BOOL GenerateOnClose         // in
);
```

The idea is that any subsystem that exposes auditable objects will call the first function immediately after one of the objects is opened (or fails to be opened because of access checks) and when the object is closed. Events will be added to the audit log only if the local security policy indicates that object access (or "file and object access" in Windows NT 4.0) should be audited.

In the first function, if you get past the first four parameters (which are purely informational for recording in the audit log), you'll see that most of the remaining parameters are similar to those passed to AccessCheck. In fact, some of these parameters you'll retrieve from AccessCheck and simply pass through to this function, the most important being *AccessGranted*, which indicates whether the client's request was successful or not. This maps directly to the *AccessStatus* out parameter generated by a call to AccessCheck. The output parameter, *pfGenerateOnClose*, is a flag that you should pass through to ObjectCloseAuditAlarm that indicates whether or not an audit should be generated (if object access auditing is disabled in the local security policy, no audits should be generated at all). This allows you to call these functions all the time, regardless of whether auditing is enabled or disabled, thus allowing the system to transparently add alarms at some future date. (I won't even speculate as to what shape this will take, or what future version of the operating system will support them.)

When you call these auditing functions, you are adding events to a very tightly controlled log—the security event log. As such, your process must indicate its trustworthiness to the system by enabling `SeAuditPrivilege` ("Generate security audits"), which is not granted to any principals or groups by default. The System logon session has this privilege, which makes sense because processes running in this logon session are trusted to help enforce the security policy of the system (they are part of the TCB). If your server runs under a distinguished account, that account will need to be granted this privilege, and you'll need to enable it manually (if you run in the System logon session, this privilege is enabled by default).

Here's a code fragment that performs access control and auditing for a fictitious user-defined class of object called a Widgit:

```
// imagine we were storing our widgit's security
// descriptors in a database somewhere...
extern void* _getWidgitSD(DWORD widgitId);
extern Widgit* _getWidgit(DWORD widgitId, DWORD access);


// from Chapter 4
HANDLE _getEffectiveToken(DWORD dwDesiredAccess,
                           BOOL  bWantImpToken = FALSE,
    SECURITY_IMPERSONATION_LEVEL impLevel =
                                 SecurityImpersonation);


Widgit* _tryToOpenWidgit(DWORD widgitId,
                         DWORD dwDesiredAccess) {
    // to keep this short, I skip obvious error checks
    void* psd = _getWidgitSD(widgitId);
    HANDLE htok = _getEffectiveToken(TOKEN_QUERY);
```

```
        // perform the access check
        PRIVILEGE_SET privSet;
        DWORD cbprivSet = sizeof privSet;
        DWORD dwGrantedAccess;
        BOOL bAccessGranted;
        if (!AccessCheck(psd, htok, dwDesiredAccess,
            &g_widgitGenericMapping, &privSet, &cbprivSet,
            &dwGrantedAccess, &bAccessGranted)
            || !bAccessGranted) {
            SetLastError(ERROR_ACCESS_DENIED);
            return 0;
        }

        // open the object
        Widgit* pWidgit = _getWidgit(widgitId, dwGrantedAccess);

        // perform the audit
        if (!ObjectOpenAuditAlarm(L"WidgitSubsystem",
            pWidgit, L"Widgit", L"",
            psd, htok, dwDesiredAccess,
            dwGrantedAccess, &privSet,
            FALSE, bAccessGranted,
            &pWidgit->m_bGenerateAuditOnClose)) {
            delete pWidgit;
        }
        return pWidgit;
    }

    void _closeWidgit(Widgit* pWidgit) {
        ObjectCloseAuditAlarm(L"WidgitSubsystem",
            pWidgit, pWidgit->m_bGenerateAuditOnClose);
        delete pWidgit;
    }
```

Managing SACLs

There is no particular required order for ACEs in a SACL, because negative entries don't cancel positive entries as they do in a DACL. In order to view or change the SACL on an object, however, you must open the object using a special permission: ACCESS_SYSTEM_SECURITY. This permission won't be found in any DACL;[15] rather, it is a special permission that is granted purely based on whether a certain privilege has been enabled in your token: `SeSecurity Privilege`. Administrators are granted this privilege by default, although you'll have to enable it manually because it is not enabled by default.

Whereas DACLs are discretionary, and the `READ_CONTROL` and `WRITE _DAC` permissions are granted implicitly to the owner (and can be delegated by the owner to others), SACLs are nondiscretionary. The owner of an object has no special permissions with regard to the SACL. This often surprises developers who are new to security. Just keep in mind what auditing is all about; an administrator needs the ability to transparently apply audits to the system without anyone being able to subvert or remove the audit settings, or even detect that they are being audited. Using privileges helps enforce these global policies.

Here's an example of applying a SACL to the current thread,[16] using `SetSecurityInfo` (which is discussed shortly):

```
// first enable SeSecurityPrivilege
HANDLE htok;
OpenProcessToken(GetCurrentProcess(),
                 TOKEN_QUERY | TOKEN_ADJUST_PRIVILEGES,
                 &htok);
TOKEN_PRIVILEGES tpOld;
if (!_enablePrivilege(htok, SE_SECURITY_NAME,
                      true, tpOld))
    throw "You do not have SeSecurityPrivilege!";

// open a session to the current thread,
// requesting read/write access to its SACL
HANDLE hThread = OpenThread(ACCESS_SYSTEM_SECURITY,
                            FALSE,
                            GetCurrentThreadId());
// don't need that privilege anymore
_restorePrivilege(htok, tpOld);
```

---

[15] Although putting it in the SACL causes the system to audit the usage of the privilege.

[16] This code uses the `OpenThread` function introduced in Windows 2000, but `Duplicate Handle` works just as well in earlier versions of Windows; I just haven't had a chance to discuss how `DuplicateHandle` works security-wise, so I've refrained from using it here.

```
// set the SACL
SetSecurityInfo(hThread, SE_KERNEL_OBJECT,
                SACL_SECURITY_INFORMATION,
                0, 0, 0, g_psacl);

CloseHandle(hThread);
```

And here's a somewhat simpler example of doing the same to a file, using SetNamedSecurityInfo:

```
// first enable SeSecurityPrivilege
HANDLE htok;
OpenProcessToken(GetCurrentProcess(),
                 TOKEN_QUERY | TOKEN_ADJUST_PRIVILEGES,
                 &htok);
TOKEN_PRIVILEGES tpOld;
if (!_enablePrivilege(htok, SE_SECURITY_NAME,
                      true, tpOld))
    throw "You need to have SeSecurityPrivilege!";


// set the SACL
SetNamedSecurityInfo(L"c:\\foo.txt", SE_FILE_OBJECT,
                     SACL_SECURITY_INFORMATION,
                     0, 0, 0, g_psacl);

// don't need that privilege anymore
_restorePrivilege(htok, tpOld);
```

Security Descriptors and Built-in Objects

For built-in objects, four functions exist that allow you to easily retrieve and adjust security descriptor settings:

```
GetSecurityInfo

GetNamedSecurityInfo

SetSecurityInfo

SetNamedSecurityInfo
```

Here's the first function for retrieving a security descriptor:

```
#include <aclapi.h>
DWORD GetSecurityInfo(
    HANDLE Handle,                    // in
    SE_OBJECT_TYPE ObjectType,        // in
    SECURITY_INFORMATION Info,        // in
    PSID* ppsidOwner,                 // out, optional
    PSID* ppsidGroup,                 // out, optional
    PACL* ppDacl,                     // out, optional
    PACL* ppSacl,                     // out, optional
    PSECURITY_DESCRIPTOR* ppsd        // out
);
```

Handle is virtually any type of handle that the system exposes (file, registry key, service, mutex, process—you name it). A handle to a service object, a handle to a registry key, and a handle to a thread are not polymorphic with each other—they are implemented by different parts of the system—and thus *ObjectType* is a required hint to the system indicating the type of handle you are passing. *Info* is a bitmask that indicates which elements of the object's security descriptor you want to see, and *ppsd* points to where the system should drop a pointer to the information you requested. (This function allocates memory and fills it with a self-relative security descriptor, and you should call `LocalFree` to free the memory when you're done.)

Because you'll likely want to access individual elements of the security descriptor, the API provides four optional parameters to save you the work of calling `GetSecurityDescriptorXXXX` yourself, but don't free these pointers; they point into the self-relative security descriptor that you'll free with a single call to `LocalFree`.

`GetNamedSecurityInfo` looks and acts similarly, except you don't have to provide a handle to the object; the first parameter is instead a string specifying the name of the object. In the case of a named mutex, a file, or a service, it's pretty obvious what the name should be, but in the case of something like a registry key, there are special strings that indicate which hive you want to drill into (see the documentation for `SE_OBJECT_TYPE` for the details). This function won't work with objects that aren't named with strings (such as processes, threads, and tokens).

Here's the corresponding function to *change* the security descriptor on a built-in object:

```
#include <aclapi.h>
DWORD SetSecurityInfo(
    HANDLE Handle,                 // in
    SE_OBJECT_TYPE ObjectType,     // in
    SECURITY_INFORMATION Info,     // in
    PSID psidOwner,                // in, optional
    PSID psidGroup,                // in, optional
    PACL pDacl,                    // in, optional
    PACL pSacl                     // in, optional
);
```

The first three parameters are used in the same way as the previous function, and the four optional parameters are somewhat less optional now—if `Info` indicates that you are providing a DACL, say, then this function uses `pDacl` to figure out what sort of DACL should be applied. The code snippets provided earlier in this chapter demonstrate a couple of usage patterns of these functions, including how to set a NULL DACL. Those snippets use `SetNamedSecurity Info`, which takes a string as opposed to a handle, but otherwise the usage pattern is exactly the same.

A caveat is worth mentioning since I've already talked about SACLs: Don't ask to read or change the SACL unless you have successfully enabled `SeSecurityPrivilege` (see the code snippets in the previous section).

Security Descriptors and Private Objects

Prior to Windows NT 4.0, the four security descriptor functions described previously were not available. Rather, each subsystem exposed a different function to get and set security settings. This makes sense (although it tends to enlarge the surface area of the API) because as I mentioned earlier, there is no central repository for security descriptors; rather, each subsystem manages them separately. (The system doesn't mandate any particular persistent storage format; for

`AccessCheck` to work, the system simply needs to provide an in-memory representation of the security descriptor.)

A valid implementation of `GetSecurityInfo` (and friends) would be one that consists (at least partly) of a massive switch statement that delegates to the individual subsystems (the subsystem is determined based on the `ObjectType` parameter). Clearly this won't work for arbitrary third-party objects like the Widgit example given earlier. However, there is enough support provided by the Windows API to make it relatively easy to seamlessly extend this model to your own private classes such as the Widgit. I've already demonstrated the code for performing access checks for Widgits, but what I didn't show was how the security descriptor for each Widgit was created in the first place, and how to expose a user interface to an administrator to view or edit the security descriptor.

Creating your own security descriptors is trivial, given the `Create PrivateObjectSecurity` API:

```
BOOL CreatePrivateObjectSecurity(
    PSECURITY_DESCRIPTOR ParentDescriptor,   // in, optional
    PSECURITY_DESCRIPTOR CreatorDescriptor,  // in, optional
    PSECURITY_DESCRIPTOR* ppNewDescriptor,   // out
    BOOL IsContainer,                        // in
    HANDLE hToken,                           // in
    PGENERIC_MAPPING GenericMapping          // in
);
```

Recall from earlier in the chapter the way `CreateMutex` works with regard to security. The system looks in three places to discover the security settings for a new object being created: the security descriptor provided by the creator via `LPSECURITY_ATTRIBUTES`, the parent object's DACL, and finally, the creator's token, where a default owner, group, and DACL are stored. When the system uses the default DACL in the creator's token, it converts the generic permissions in the default DACL into the specific and standard permissions that are meaningful for the class of object being created. Given this, and ignoring the `IsContainer` parameter that is described later, can you guess how `Create PrivateObjectSecurity` works?

This API provides all the core functionality that Windows uses internally when creating security descriptors for built-in objects. The system will use any elements specified by the creator via the `CreatorDescriptor` parameter as the preferred choice. If an element is missing from `CreatorDescriptor` (or if this parameter is NULL), the system will follow the same algorithm described earlier for built-in objects, looking in the specified parent's security descriptor (if present) and the specified token to discover appropriate default values.

`CreatePrivateObjectSecurity` returns a security descriptor that is fully formed[17] and that can be passed as a parameter to `AccessCheck` and friends. Your job is to manage the resulting security descriptor (this often means storing it somewhere in persistent storage). During the design phase of your project, you'll need to figure out when it makes sense to perform access checks and audits. You'll also need to provide either a programmatic or GUI-based editing mechanism to allow an administrator to adjust these DACLs. In Windows 2000, the system exposes a powerful access control editor that you can include in your own applications.[18]

Hierarchical Object Models and ACL Inheritance

In the beginning, there was the file system. The file system consisted of a hierarchy of directories and files, and it was good. The design of the registry was similar in many respects, and it was also good. To allow these systems to support thousands of files and keys, it was necessary to provide some help to administrators for managing the security descriptors associated with each of these objects, and thus the notion of ACL inheritance was born.

A strategy of ACL inheritance leverages the natural hierarchy of a system in order to administer security. This directly opposes the laissez-faire approach of having each process choose its own default DACL for new objects, and instead prefers to assign default DACLs to new objects by propagating entries in the parent's DACL. This tends to provide a more consistent flow of permissions across a hierarchy of objects.

---

[17] A SACL will not necessarily be present, but this is not a problem.
[18] See Brown (1999a).

For instance, looking at the root of my NTFS partition, I can see that everyone is granted all permissions. However, as soon as I dip down into the profiles directory (\Documents and Settings on Windows 2000, %SYSTEMROOT%\ Profiles on Windows NT 4), I start to see tighter control being applied (I've simplified these DACLs a bit for brevity):

grant full control to Administrators

grant read control to Everyone

If I drill down even further into Alice's profile directory, I see tighter control still:

grant full control to Administrators

grant full control to Alice

Because of the effects of ACL inheritance, files and directories created in the root of this NTFS partition inherit the one entry from the DACL on the root directory that grants everyone all access. Files and directories created in the profile directory inherit entries from the profile directory's DACL, and thus grant read-write access to Administrators, while everyone else gets read access. And finally, files created in Alice's profile directory are only accessible by Alice or by an administrator. ACL inheritance makes this flow of permissions very natural.

ACL inheritance matured quite a lot in Windows 2000, but it makes sense to first look at the Windows NT 4 model to understand the changes made in Windows 2000.

ACL Inheritance in Windows NT 4

Let's take file system DACLs as a concrete example. ACL inheritance comes into play whenever you create a new file or directory without specifying a custom DACL via the LPSECURITY_ATTRIBUTES parameter to CreateFile. The system looks at the parent directory where you are creating the new object and copies **inheritable ACEs** to form the new DACL. For the sake of simplicity, I didn't mention this before, but each ACE actually has an extra bitmask containing instructions that indicate whether the ACE should be inherited at all, and some semantics controlling when and how the inheritance should occur.

A very simple inheritance scheme would be to simply have a boolean value indicate whether the inheritable ACE should propagate to child objects, but this breaks down in the file system because there are *two* types of objects that can be created there: files and directories. Consider the following inheritable ACE:

grant 0x00000020 to Bob, and inherit for all new children

Here's the mapping of permission 0x00000020 for files and directories (from winnt.h):

```
#define FILE_EXECUTE        ( 0x0020 )      // file
#define FILE_TRAVERSE       ( 0x0020 )      // directory
```

These permissions have very little to do with one another. So it turns out that it's not enough to simply say that you want an ACE to be inherited by children; you also need to be able to say what class of child object should inherit the ACE. Because the file system only has two classes of objects, the inheritance scheme in Windows NT 4 was designed to accommodate two classes of objects: containers (directories) and objects (files).

Here are the various inheritance flags that can be present in an ACE (from winnt.h):[19]

```
#define OBJECT_INHERIT_ACE          (0x1)
#define CONTAINER_INHERIT_ACE       (0x2)
#define NO_PROPAGATE_INHERIT_ACE    (0x4)
#define INHERIT_ONLY_ACE            (0x8)
```

To grant FILE_EXECUTE permissions to Bob via ACL inheritance when new files are created, you could give the parent directory the following ACE:

grant 0x00000020 to Bob, inheritance: 0x01

When new subdirectories are created, this ACE will be ignored because it's only designed to be propagated to files, so child directories won't accidentally be granted FILE_TRAVERSE. However, remember that to enable the ACL inheri-

---

[19] Windows 2000 added a fifth inheritance flag that I'd prefer to leave shrouded in mystery until I discuss the new inheritance model.

tance mechanism, you had to modify the DACL on the parent directory, and in doing so, you have inadvertently granted Bob FILE_TRAVERSE permission on the parent directory itself, which was not the intention at all. To really clarify things, you can do the following instead:

grant 0x00000020 to Bob, inheritance: 0x01 | 0x08

By adding in the INHERIT_ONLY_ACE flag, this ACE now has no effect at all on the parent directory, and is only stored in the parent's DACL so that it can be propagated to children via ACL inheritance.

I picked the FILE_EXECUTE/FILE_TRAVERSE bit for these examples because it has such different meaning depending on whether it is applied to a file or a directory, and it therefore illustrates the point that inheritable ACEs need to have a permission mask that makes sense for child objects. The safest way to go is to simply keep inheritable ACEs separate from noninheritable ACEs by always using the INHERIT_ONLY_ACE flag in any inheritable ACEs.

To simplify administration (and save space in ACLs), most of the file system permissions were designed to have similar meanings when smeared across both files and directories (the following was excerpted and simplified from winnt.h):

```
#define FILE_READ_DATA          ( 0x0001 )   // file
#define FILE_LIST_DIRECTORY     ( 0x0001 )   // directory

#define FILE_WRITE_DATA         ( 0x0002 )   // file
#define FILE_ADD_FILE           ( 0x0002 )   // directory

#define FILE_APPEND_DATA        ( 0x0004 )   // file
#define FILE_ADD_SUBDIRECTORY   ( 0x0004 )   // directory

#define FILE_READ_EA            ( 0x0008 )   // file & dir
#define FILE_WRITE_EA           ( 0x0010 )   // file & dir

#define FILE_EXECUTE            ( 0x0020 )   // file
#define FILE_TRAVERSE           ( 0x0020 )   // directory

#define FILE_DELETE_CHILD       ( 0x0040 )   // directory
```

```
#define FILE_READ_ATTRIBUTES  ( 0x0080 )  // file & dir //

#define FILE_WRITE_ATTRIBUTES ( 0x0100 )  // file & dir //
```

Thus it is common in file system ACLs to have inheritable ACEs that also apply directly to the container object itself. A great example of this is FILE_READ _DATA/FILE_LIST_DIRECTORY, which has a very nice symmetry: Granting read access to the directory and all its children can be done with a single ACE marked with an inheritance mask of 0x03. This doesn't work so well with FILE_EXECUTE and FILE_TRAVERSE.

The only flag that still needs explaining is the somewhat esoteric INHERIT _NO_PROPAGATE, which indicates that during ACL inheritance, the inherited ACE in the child should have *its* inheritance mask cleared. This allows you to create inheritable ACEs that only affect direct children, as opposed to grand-children. I was curious to see if this flag was actually used by the operating system, so I hacked up a quick program to scan my NTFS partition for directories with ACEs having this flag. I didn't find any directories using this flag on either Windows 2000 or Windows NT 4.

After this discussion, you should be able to see one reason why the *IsContainer* parameter of CreatePrivateObjectSecurity exists. You need to indicate to the system which types of inheritable ACEs you want to flow from the parent: ones marked with the CONTAINER_INHERIT_ACE flag, or ones marked with the OBJECT_INHERIT_ACE flag. A second reason for having this parameter is one of efficiency: By knowing that a leaf object is being created, the system can avoid adding ACEs designed solely for propagating inheritable permissions to children (by definition, leaf objects will never have children).

Maintaining Consistency

Don't confuse ACL inheritance with runtime access control. Inheritance is used to help an administrator maintain a consistent security policy in a large hierarchy of objects without too much micromanagement of individual objects. However, at runtime, when access checks are performed, the system does not search up the hierarchy looking for inheritable ACEs. All ACEs are assumed to be statically assigned to each object, either manually or via inheritance. This makes the system perform well.

What this means is that at object creation time, the system provides a convenient ACL inheritance service, giving the new object a default DACL consistent with where it lives in the hierarchy. But once the object has been created, it is possible to modify the DACL and either remove or augment the ACEs that were initially provided via inheritance. In other words, it is possible for an administrator to individually modify the DACL on each file and directory in the system so that there is no indication that there was ever any consistent flow of permissions at all. (Obviously, doing this is chaotic and would not be very desirable, but nothing inhibits it.)

Windows NT 4 provides a rather crude way of reducing the chaos: Anytime an administrator makes a change to the DACL of an existing directory via the file system ACL editor, the ACL editor provides an option to recursively overwrite the DACLs of all the children (simply copying the parent DACL to child directories or files or both). This brute-force approach works reasonably well for simple systems, but makes it impossible to protect small, critical sections of the file system (where micromanagement is desirable) from sweeping changes initiated closer to the root of the tree.

ACL Inheritance in Windows 2000

This problem is addressed violently (and effectively) in Windows 2000, and the semantics of the way inheritance works are quite different from Windows NT 4 as a result. In Windows 2000, by default, inheritable entries flow to child objects not only when the child is first created, but at any time thereafter when the parent or child's DACL changes. The system maintains consistency (of inherited ACEs) at all times throughout the tree, avoiding the chaos that often develops in Windows NT 4. As an important bookkeeping measure, ACEs inherited from a parent object are distinguished in the child with the following inheritance flag (introduced in Windows 2000):

```
#define INHERITED_ACE          (0x10)
```

The access control editor GUI protects ACEs marked with this flag from modification, directing the user to traverse up the hierarchy to the parent if those permissions need to be changed. In fact, if you use the Advanced dialog box to edit an ACL, you'll see that the icons for inherited entries are shown slightly dimmed.

The automatic synchronization of inherited entries is very powerful, especially when used in concert with a couple of security descriptor flags introduced in Windows 2000:

```
#define SE_DACL_PROTECTED                    (0x1000)
#define SE_SACL_PROTECTED                    (0x2000)
```

These flags, when present in a security descriptor, cause the inheritance flow (in the DACL and SACL, respectively) to be interrupted at that point, starting a new root from which inheritable entries can flow once again (see Figure 6.4).

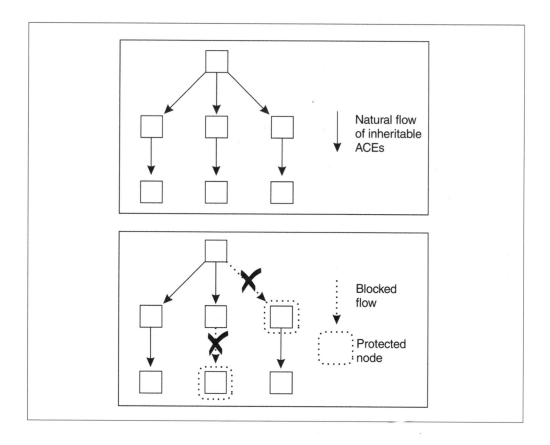

Figure 6.4   Blocking the inheritance flow by protecting a node

MECHANICS

This allows various regions in a large hierarchical system to be controlled independently, without being affected by inheritable ACEs higher in the tree.

Let's make this concrete by building a sample hierarchy of objects. I'll start with the root object (say this is a mount-point in the file system represented by a drive letter). This root object (C) has a DACL with two ACEs:

grant Bob FILE_LIST_DIRECTORY, inheritance: 0x00

grant Friends FILE_ALL_ACCESS, inheritance: 0x03

The first ACE applies directly to C, whereas the second ACE applies to C and will be inherited by any children created under C. Figure 6.5 shows the results. Now let's create some child objects (directories and files). Figure 6.6 shows the new picture, with a few subdirectories and files created as children of C. All the new directory objects start life with the following default DACL simply by applying the rules of ACL inheritance at creation time:

grant Friends FILE_ALL_ACCESS, inheritance: 0x13

The new files (foo.txt and bar.txt), being leaf objects and therefore without the potential to have children, start life with a similar DACL:

grant Friends FILE_ALL_ACCESS, inheritance: 0x10

Note that the ACE propagated to each child is marked with the INHERITED _ACE flag (0x10) to keep it distinct from any direct permissions that may be defined directly on the child later on.

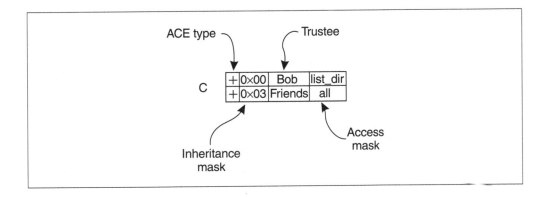

Figure 6.5 Applying a DACL to an object

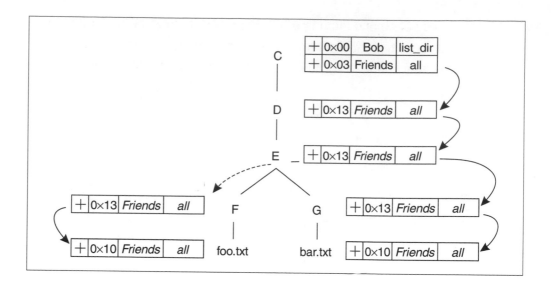

Figure 6.6   New children inherit ACEs from parent

Now let's change the DACL on directory E with the following code:

```
// form the SID for BUILTIN\Administrators
SIDWithTwoSubauthorities sid = {
    SID_REVISION, 2,
    SECURITY_NT_AUTHORITY,
    SECURITY_BUILTIN_DOMAIN_RID,
    DOMAIN_ALIAS_RID_ADMINS
};
DWORD cb = sizeof(ACL) + _maxVersion2AceSize;
ACL* pdacl = (ACL*)malloc(cb);
InitializeAcl(pdacl, cb, ACL_REVISION);
AddAccessAllowedAceEx(pdacl, ACL_REVISION, 0,
                      FILE_LIST_DIRECTORY, &sid);

SetNamedSecurityInfo(L"c:\\d\\e", SE_FILE_OBJECT,
                     DACL_SECURITY_INFORMATION,
                     0, 0, pdacl, 0);
free(pdacl);
```

The first few lines of code build a DACL (this procedure is discussed later in this chapter) with a single ACE that grants `FILE_LIST_DIRECTORY` to Administrators. The DACL applied to E will actually end up with two entries:

grant Administrators `FILE_LIST_DIRECTORY`, inheritance: `0x00`

grant Friends `FILE_ALL_ACCESS`, inheritance: `0x13`

`SetNamedSecurityInfo` first applies the DACL to the object, then checks the security descriptor to see if the `SE_DACL_PROTECTED` flag is set (it's not, by default), so the function flows the inheritable ACEs from D to E once again, ensuring consistency.

Figure 6.7 shows the new system. Note that the new permission that was added does not flow to children, because the ACE specified didn't have any inheritance flags set.

Check out this next block of code, and try to figure out what the system will look like after it is executed:

```
// form the SID for BUILTIN\Guests
SIDWithTwoSubauthorities sid = {
    SID_REVISION, 2,
```

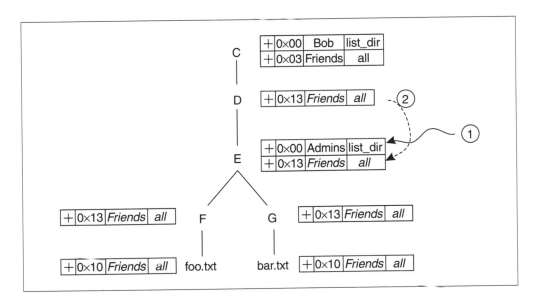

Figure 6.7   Maintaining consistency of inherited ACEs

```
        SECURITY_NT_AUTHORITY,
        SECURITY_BUILTIN_DOMAIN_RID,
        DOMAIN_ALIAS_RID_GUESTS
};
DWORD cb = sizeof(ACL) + _maxVersion2AceSize;
ACL* pdacl = (ACL*)malloc(cb);
InitializeAcl(pdacl, cb, ACL_REVISION);
AddAccessDeniedAceEx(pdacl, ACL_REVISION,
        CONTAINER_INHERIT_ACE | OBJECT_INHERIT_ACE,
        FILE_ALL_ACCESS, &sid);

SetNamedSecurityInfo(L"c:\\d", SE_FILE_OBJECT,
                    DACL_SECURITY_INFORMATION,
                    0, 0, pdacl, 0);
free(pdacl);
```

This code applies a DACL with a single *inheritable* ACE, and so the system will first compute the full DACL on directory D by combining the specified ACEs with the parent's inheritable ACEs, resulting in the following DACL for D:

deny Guests FILE_ALL_ACCESS, inheritance: 0x03

grant Friends FILE_ALL_ACCESS, inheritance: 0x13

Once the system has calculated the resulting DACL for D, it then updates the inheritance flow down the tree, so the DACL on directory E now looks like this (see Figure 6.8):

grant Administrators FILE_LIST_DIRECTORY, inheritance: 0x00

deny Guests FILE_ALL_ACCESS, inheritance: 0x13

grant Friends FILE_ALL_ACCESS, inheritance: 0x13

The reason why the denied entry isn't at the top of the DACL is discussed in the next section.

Let's say that deep down in the file system (at directory G, perhaps) you needed to apply a totally different security policy (for instance, everyone has all access below a certain point). You'd need to interrupt the flow of inheritance by adding the SE_DACL_PROTECTED flag to the security descriptor of G. Windows 2000 provides two bitmasks that you can pass to Set(Named)Security

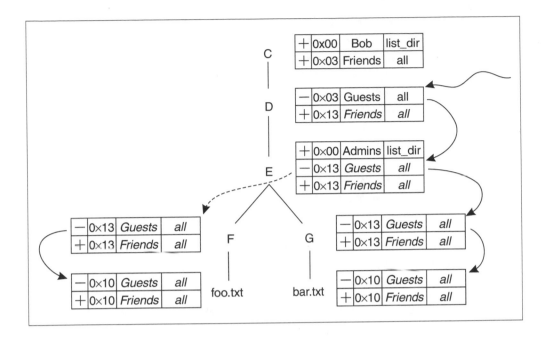

Figure 6.8 Reflowing inheritable ACEs throughout an entire subtree

`Info` to either set or clear this flag, plus two more to control a similar flag for the SACL:

```
#define PROTECTED_DACL_SECURITY_INFORMATION   0x80000000
#define PROTECTED_SACL_SECURITY_INFORMATION   0x40000000
#define UNPROTECTED_DACL_SECURITY_INFORMATION 0x20000000
#define UNPROTECTED_SACL_SECURITY_INFORMATION 0x10000000
```

Here's a code snippet that interrupts the flow of inheritance at directory G:

```
// form the SID for Everyone
SID sid = {SID_REVISION, 1,
           SECURITY_WORLD_SID_AUTHORITY,
           SECURITY_WORLD_RID};
DWORD cb = sizeof(ACL) + _maxVersion2AceSize;
ACL* pdacl = (ACL*)malloc(cb);
InitializeAcl(pdacl, cb, ACL_REVISION);
AddAccessAllowedAceEx(pdacl, ACL_REVISION,
```

```
                CONTAINER_INHERIT_ACE | OBJECT_INHERIT_ACE,
                FILE_ALL_ACCESS, &sid);

        SetNamedSecurityInfo(L"c:\\d\\e\\g", SE_FILE_OBJECT,
                    DACL_SECURITY_INFORMATION |
                    PROTECTED_DACL_SECURITY_INFORMATION,
                    0, 0, pdacl, 0);
        free(pdacl);
```

The results are shown in Figure 6.9. Now, even if you were to make changes to the inheritable ACEs of C, D, or E, directory G will not be affected by these changes because the flow is interrupted at G. I should note that the built-in access control editor UI does provide an option (hidden in the Advanced dialog) so that an administrator can sweep an entire hierarchy of objects from any node, forcefully restoring the flow of inheritance from that node down. Figures 6.10 to 6.12 show various dialogs provided by the Windows 2000 access control editor, with annotations that show which options affect which flags in the security descriptor and DACL.

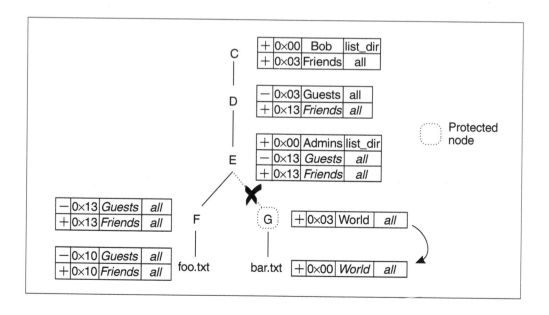

Figure 6.9   Flow of inheritance blocked at directory G

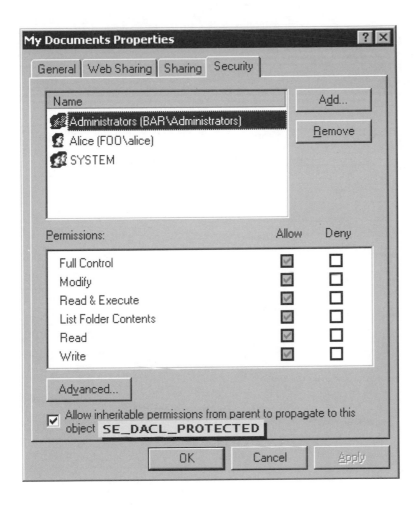

Figure 6.10   Windows 2000 access control editor property page

Order of ACEs in Windows 2000 ACLs

Windows 2000 ACLs are managed much differently than their older cousins.
Each inherited ACE is tracked (via the INHERITED_ACE flag mentioned earlier)
and is effectively kept read-only to maintain a consistent flow of permissions
throughout the hierarchy. Still more flexibility can be gained from this model,
though. If an administrator has a large hierarchy of objects, and one object
requires micromanagement, the administrator has two options: either block the
flow of inheritance completely with SE_*XXXX*_PROTECTED and take over management of that object *and all its children* as if it were disconnected from the

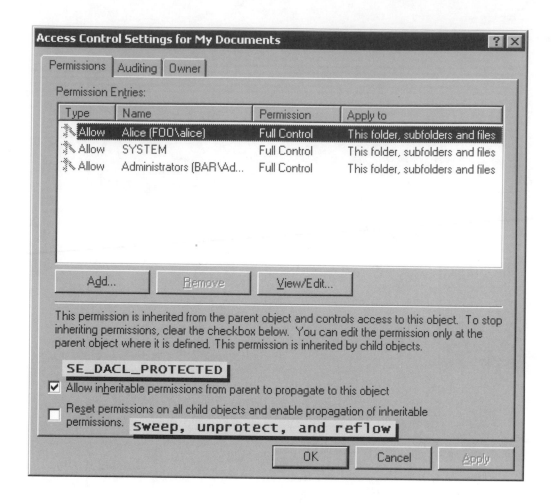

Figure 6.11   The Advanced dialog of the access control editor

rest of the hierarchy, or apply direct ACEs to that object and hope for the best. Overuse of the first option can lead to chaos, because each node that blocks inherited permissions basically becomes a new subtree that must be managed independently. The second option is problematic unless the order of ACEs is addressed.

Imagine that throughout a hierarchy, you wanted to grant DELETE access to everyone but Bob. This is easy—just apply the following ACEs to the root object:

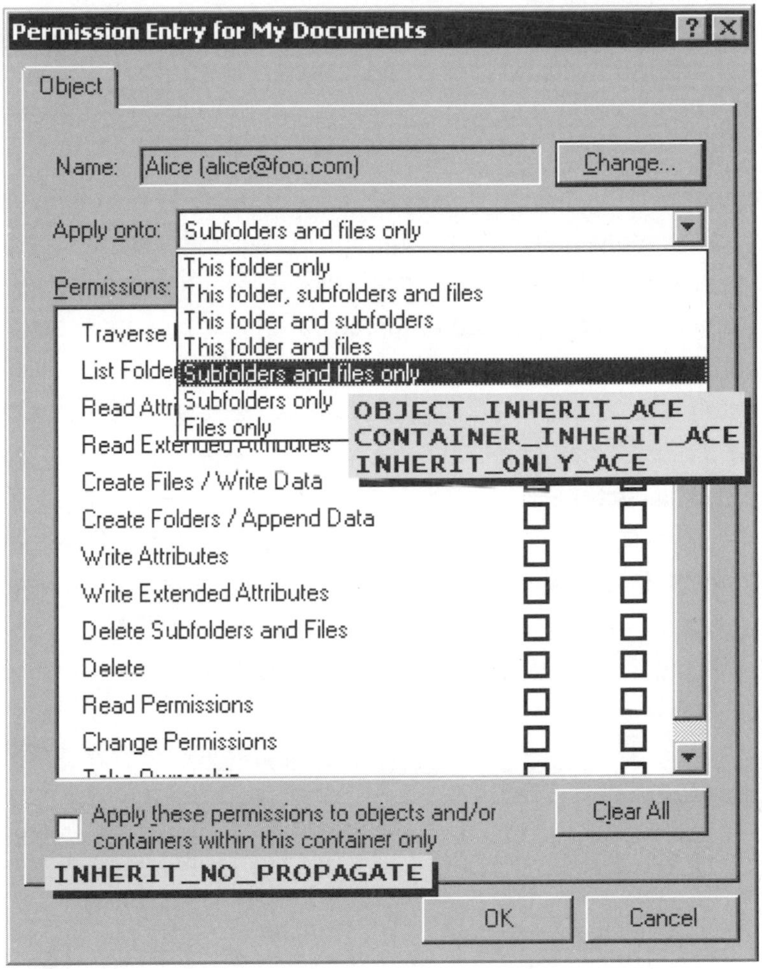

Figure 6.12   Editing an individual ACE in the Advanced dialog

deny DELETE to Bob, inheritance: 0x03

grant DELETE to Everyone, inheritance: 0x03

Now, somewhere deep in the hierarchy, you decide that there is one particular object that Bob needs to be able to delete, so you add an ACE directly to that object that explicitly grants him permission:

deny DELETE to Bob, inheritance: 0x13

grant DELETE to Everyone, inheritance: 0x13

grant DELETE to Bob, inheritance: 0x00

See the problem? If the system managed ACLs in this way, you wouldn't be able to micromanage individual objects without cutting off the flow of inheritable ACEs, be-cause denied entries would *always* be evaluated first, regardless of whether or not they were inherited or directly applied to the object in an attempt at micromanagement.

Fortunately this is not the case. In Windows 2000–style ACLs, *ACEs that are applied directly to an object always take precedence over those that were inherited*. This allows the administrator to micromanage an object in the hier-archy while still keeping a consistent flow of permissions. (The potential for chaos still exists, because each object could be micromanaged in this way, but it would take a lot more dedicated effort!) Thus the actual ACL ordering in the previous example is as follows (also see Figure 6.13):

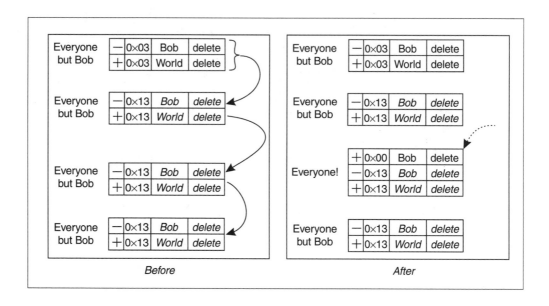

Figure 6.13 Micromanaging a single node without blocking the flow

grant DELETE to Bob, inheritance: 0x00

deny DELETE to Bob, inheritance: 0x13

grant DELETE to Everyone, inheritance: 0x13

Note that the DACL evaluation algorithm discussed earlier works even in this scenario. Once DELETE permission has been granted in this case, even if the traversal continues in order to authorize other permissions, the algorithm will treat the second (negative) ACE as irrelevant because the DELETE access bit has been latched in the permissions accumulator.

The order of ACEs in Windows 2000–style DACLs is as follows:

1. Direct negative ACEs

2. Direct positive ACEs

3. Inherited negative ACEs

4. Inherited postive ACEs

If you'd like to create Windows 2000–style ACLs for your own custom hierarchy of objects, use CreatePrivateObjectSecurityEx (this function is discussed in detail shortly). If you have an existing hierarchy of objects using the older inheritance mechanism and want to upgrade, take a look at the ConvertToAutoInheritPrivateObjectSecurity API. This function is smart enough to compare the parent and child security descriptors, factor out what's common, and automatically create a flow of inherited entries. (This is akin to what happens to Windows NT 4 file system DACLs when an administrator installs the Security Configuration Editor, which upgrades the file system ACLs to use this new inheritance model.)

ACLs that take advantage of this new mechanism for inheritance are not distinguished by a new version number; they often will have the same version as their older cousins—version 2 ACLs. If you want to determine whether a particular ACL is participating in a Windows 2000–style automatic inheritance synchronization scheme, look for the following bits in the control word of the security descriptor by calling GetSecurityDescriptorControl:

SE_DACL_AUTO_INHERITED

SE_SACL_AUTO_INHERITED

If you're writing code that runs on Windows NT 4 Service Pack 4 or greater, be aware that the file system may be using either the old or the new model, so be careful to take this into consideration when writing ACL manipulation code. The ACL programming section in this chapter provides examples demonstrating that this is possible (and not terribly difficult either).

Inheritance Using Generic Permissions

Imagine an industrial automation application for a candy factory modeled in a hierarchical fashion. The root object is the factory, with child objects representing gumball machines, chocolate bar machines, time clocks, security doors, and folders to organize these objects. These are all very different types of objects, and while the gumball and chocolate bar machines will likely define similar specific permissions, the time clocks and security doors will have very different specific permissions. In this system you can't play the bit-mapping game that the file system developers did and come up with a single set of specific permissions that works for all objects somewhat transparently. So how can you employ ACL inheritance in this scenario?

One answer is to use generic permissions to give yourself an extra level of indirection. On the factory and any folders, set up inheritable ACEs that grant only generic permissions as opposed to specific permissions. Generic permissions are meaningful across different classes of objects, because each class provides its own mapping via the GENERIC_MAPPING structure that was introduced earlier in the chapter. You'll fill out one of these structures for each class of object you need to secure, and pass it any time you call Create PrivateObjectSecurity(Ex) so the system can provide an appropriate mapping of each inherited ACE.[20]

---

[20] When defining the GENERIC_MAPPING structure for any class of object, be careful to always be brutally honest when specifying the mask for GenericAll. When you call Create PrivateObjectSecurity(Ex), any ACEs that apply directly to the object (in other words, ACEs that aren't flagged with INHERIT_ONLY_ACE) will be "strained" through GenericAll (a bitwise AND is performed) so that you can't accidentally apply permissions that don't make sense for an object. If, for instance, you completely ignore generic permissions and specify a GENERIC_MAPPING of {0, 0, 0, 0}, CreatePrivateObjectSecurity will create ACLs full of ACEs that have access masks with 0x00000000 in them. Not very useful!

An Example

When building a system around Windows-based ACLs, you'll almost always start by discovering the classes of objects in the system along with their specific permissions; for each class, you'll need to figure out how to map generic permissions. Look at the following sample definition for a FOLDER (a class of object designed to organize other objects in the factory). Notice the traditional progression from defining specific permissions, to grouping them into the four generic categories, to creating a GENERIC_MAPPING structure:

```
// excerpt from FOLDER.H
// first define the specific permissions for folders
#define FOLDER_LIST_CONTENTS 0x00000001
#define FOLDER_ADD_ITEM       0x00000002
#define FOLDER_DELETE_ITEM    0x00000003

// group standard and specific permissions into the four
// categories of generic permissions (this is useful for
// documentation purposes so people know what they are
// getting when they use generic permissions)
#define FOLDER_READ       (STANDARD_RIGHTS_READ      |\
                            FOLDER_LIST_CONTENTS)

#define FOLDER_WRITE      (STANDARD_RIGHTS_WRITE     |\
                            FOLDER_ADD_ITEM          |\
                            FOLDER_DELETE_ITEM)

#define FOLDER_EXECUTE    (STANDARD_RIGHTS_EXECUTE)

#define FOLDER_ALL        (STANDARD_RIGHTS_REQUIRED  |\
                            FOLDER_READ              |\
                            FOLDER_WRITE             |\
                            FOLDER_EXECUTE)

// excerpt from FOLDER.CPP
GENERIC_MAPPING g_gmFolder = {
  FOLDER_READ,      // GenericRead
  FOLDER_WRITE,     // GenericWrite
  FOLDER_EXECUTE,   // GenericExecute
  FOLDER_ALL        // GenericAll
};
```

Note how careful I was in these definitions to include standard permissions in my calculations (the STANDARD_RIGHTS_*XXXX* macros are just system-provided mappings onto READ_CONTROL, DELETE, etc.). Also note how one can easily look at the definitions for FOLDER_READ, FOLDER_WRITE, and so forth and discover how generic permissions map for this class of object. This is important because the actual GENERIC_MAPPING definition will not be included in the header file for your clients to see. For a real-world example, browse through winnt.h and search for KEY_READ, TOKEN_READ, and FILE_GENERIC_READ. This style is a good one to adopt.

Given these definitions, imagine that the root (factory) object had a DACL with the following inherit-only ACEs:

grant Employees GENERIC_READ, inheritance: 0x3 | 0x8

grant Supervisors GENERIC_ALL, inheritance: 0x3 | 0x8

If you were now to create a folder object as a child of the factory, you'd call CreatePrivateObjectSecurity to get a security descriptor for that object, passing the factory's security descriptor as the first parameter, NULL for the second parameter (indicating that you'll be satisfied with the DACL and SACL that results from propagating inherited entries), and finally the creator's token and the GENERIC_MAPPING structure for the folder. The owner and group for the new security descriptor will be culled from the creator's token (recall that each token has a default owner and group for exactly this purpose). Since the folder is logically a container, you'd indicate this as well by passing TRUE for *IsContainer*. Here's the code for creating the folder's security descriptor:

```
// imagine that we've previously constructed a security
// descriptor for the factory...
void* psdParent = _getFactoryObjectSD();

// retrieve the current security context
// (this was discussed in Chapter 4)
HANDLE htok = _getEffectiveToken(TOKEN_QUERY);

void* psdFolder = 0;
CreatePrivateObjectSecurity(psdParent, 0, &psdFolder,
                            TRUE, htok, &g_gmFolder);
```

```
// if everything went OK, psdFolder should now point to
// a fully formed security descriptor for the folder
```

The resulting DACL for the folder in this case will have *four* ACEs:

grant Employees GENERIC_READ, inheritance: 0x3 | 0x8

grant Employees FOLDER_READ, inheritance: 0x00

grant Supervisors GENERIC_ALL, inheritance: 0x03 | 0x08

grant Supervisors FOLDER_ALL, inheritance: 0x00

This results in Employees being able to *enumerate* the contents of the folder, but only Supervisors can *manipulate* those contents. Because TRUE was specified for *IsContainer*, the system is aware that it needs to continue the flow of inheritance; thus, in addition to applying the generic permissions (transforming them into specific and standard permissions in ACEs that apply directly to the object), it copies the inherit-only ACEs and (this is important) leaves these inherit-only ACEs in their generic form so that they can be later applied polymorphically to grandchildren of the factory.

In this example, I passed a null pointer for the *CreatorDescriptor* parameter, indicating that I didn't want to customize the child's DACL; instead, I wanted the system to use inheritance to form the new DACL. Had I instead passed a security descriptor for *CreatorDescriptor*, I could have provided some hints to the system. If *CreatorDescriptor* contains the SE_DACL _DEFAULTED flag, this indicates that the security descriptor provided by the creator should be used only in the case where the parent has no inheritable entries to contribute.[21] If this flag is not present, this indicates that I want to completely override the inheritance mechanism and use the DACL in *Creator Descriptor* instead. As you can see, SE_DACL_DEFAULTED is a temporary flag used to convey extra semantics during the construction of a new security descriptor.

---

[21] When *CreatorDescriptor* is NULL and the parent has no inheritable entries to contribute, CreatePrivateObjectSecurity turns to the default DACL in the token as opposed to simply creating an empty DACL for the object.

Maintaining the Flow in Private Objects

If you pass a nondefault DACL or SACL (or both) to `CreatePrivate ObjectSecurity` via *CreatorDescriptor*, you'll hide the parent's inheritable ACEs from the new child. This function follows the Windows NT 4 model of ACL inheritance, and does not attempt to maintain a consistent flow of inherited ACEs as is natural in Windows 2000. To flow inheritable ACEs *always*, you must use a function introduced in Windows 2000.

```
BOOL CreatePrivateObjectSecurityEx(
  PSECURITY_DESCRIPTOR ParentDescriptor,    // in, optional
  PSECURITY_DESCRIPTOR CreatorDescriptor,   // in, optional
  PSECURITY_DESCRIPTOR *NewDescriptor,      // out
  GUID *ObjectType,                         // in, optional
  BOOL IsContainerObject,                   // in
  ULONG AutoInheritFlags,                   // in
  HANDLE Token,                             // in
  PGENERIC_MAPPING GenericMapping           // in
);
```

Because this is a Windows 2000 API, it knows that inheritable ACEs from the parent are not just a suggested default, but *must* flow to children and be distinguished there via the `INHERITED_ACE` flag. So, unlike `CreatePrivate ObjectSecurity`, this function merges the ACEs you specify via the *CreatorDescriptor* parameter with the inheritable ACEs from *Parent Descriptor*. (The result is then placed in *NewDescriptor*, as with `Create PrivateObjectSecurity`.) You should think of *CreatorDescriptor* as a container for the *proposed* DACL (and SACL) that you would like to place on the new object, with the awareness that you'll also get some ACEs from the parent to maintain a consistent flow throughout the hierarchy. In fact, if any inheritable entries in the parent's DACL or SACL change at some later time, you'll need to call this function for all the child objects to synchronize the inheritable ACEs. In this case, *CreatorDescriptor* would be the existing security descriptor on the child, and any ACEs found there that are flagged with `INHERITED_ACE` would be completely replaced based on the current inheritable entries in *ParentDescriptor*.

`CreatePrivateObjectSecurityEx` is designed to automatically maintain the flow between a parent and a child, but you still need to actually call it when an administrator makes changes so that it can do its work. The system doesn't know what your hierarchy of objects looks like, so it's your job to traverse the hierarchy and keep the inheritable ACEs consistent by calling this function for each child object as ACLs change.

If the administrator makes a change to the root of the hierarchy, it can be rather expensive to traverse the entire tree synchronizing the inheritable entries, but it must be done to maintain consistency. To reduce the overhead of synchronizing inherited ACEs in child objects, there are several flags (specified via *AutoInheritFlags*) that you should use carefully:

`SEF_DACL_AUTO_INHERIT`

`SEF_SACL_AUTO_INHERIT`

These flags indicate whether the DACL or SACL (or both) need to be synchronized, so you should always specify both of these flags when creating *new* child objects. When synchronizing existing children, however, use only the flags you need. For instance, if the DACL on an existing node changes, its children can be synchronized without modifying their SACLs.

Normally the system checks for the presence (and enabled state) of `SeSecurityPrivilege` before allowing modifications to a SACL. Once you've done this check once (at the node where a change was actually initiated), performing this check again is redundant when propagating inheritable SACL entries to children. The following flag disables this check:

`SEF_AVOID_PRIVILEGE_CHECK`

Normally, `CreatePrivateObjectSecurityEx` assumes that you are creating a security descriptor for a new object, and so it validates the resulting owner SID (which may be explicitly specified or defaulted in various ways) to make sure that it is a legal owner SID for the client. (Legal owner SIDs are verified in *Token* as being either the user SID or any group SIDs that are annotated with the `SE_GROUP_OWNER` flag.) When synchronizing ACLs in child objects, you're not changing the owner, and this check is inappropriate (it's not just wasting cycles, it's semantically inappropriate). You should use the following flag to disable it:

```
SEF_AVOID_OWNER_CHECK
```

In fact, if you specify both of the SEF_AVOID_*XXXX* flags described previously, you can pass NULL for the *Token* parameter, because it's not needed anymore.

There are a few more parameters to this function:

```
SEF_DEFAULT_OWNER_FROM_PARENT

SEF_DEFAULT_GROUP_FROM_PARENT

SEF_DEFAULT_DESCRIPTOR_FOR_OBJECT
```

The first two flags simply indicate where the system should look for a default owner or primary group for the new object. If you specify these flags, the system will obtain the corresponding SID from *ParentDescriptor*; otherwise, the defaults in *Token* are used. The last flag is ignored completely unless you're working with version 4 ACLs.

Finally, pass NULL for *ObjectType* unless you're working with version 4 ACLs.

Maintaining the Flow in System Objects

Prefer to use the Set(Named)SecurityInfo functions when you're programmatically making changes to ACLs, especially if your code will run on Windows 2000. The older functions (SetFileSecurity, RegSetKeySecurity, etc.) do not automatically propagate inherited ACEs by default, unless the SE_*XXXX*_AUTO_INHERIT_REQ (where XXXX is DACL or SACL) is set in the security descriptor control word.

Version 4 ACLs and the Directory Service

As of this writing, the operating system uses version 2 ACLs (which have the semantics described earlier, including the automatic flow of inherited ACEs) pretty much everywhere except the directory service. The directory is a very sophisticated beast that uses a new type of ACL (version 4) that provides an incredibly fine-grained approach to access control.[22]

Version 4 ACLs look and act similar to the version 2 ACLs that you know and love, except that each ACE can apply not only to the object as a whole but also to individual properties (or sets of properties) on the object. The inheritance story also changes, because instead of using generic permissions, each class of object is identified with a GUID, and parent ACLs can have class-specific inherit-only ACEs that are inherited only by objects of the matching class.

Because `CreatePrivateObjectSecurityEx` is designed to work with both version 2 and version 4 ACLs, you can specify a GUID via the *Object Type* parameter in order to determine which ACEs should be inherited. Recall that in version 2 ACLs, there are only two "classes" of objects: containers and noncontainers. Version 4 ACLs allow as many classes of objects as you like; the main drawback is that each ACE is larger, and because of the high granularity of the access control model, there tend to be many more ACEs in each ACL.[23]

ACL Programming

I've managed to get through this entire chapter so far without showing you how to create a nontrivial ACL. Well, there are basically two ways of doing this: the easy way and the robust way. Back when Windows NT 4.0 was first released, it came with a couple of functions that were documented as being "high level" and "recommended," and until I personally experienced the nasty bugs in their implementation and the limitations in their design, I was a believer.

These two functions are known as `SetEntriesInAcl` and `GetExplicit EntriesFromAcl` and are deceptively easy to use. Both are designed to work

---

[22] In case you were wondering, version 3 appears to have been skipped for some unknown reason. My guess is that it had something to do with the (now obsolete) security model introduced during the early Windows NT 5.0 beta.

[23] Without having seen the source code for Active Directory, it's impossible to say whether it has some alternate scheme for implementing ACL inheritance. Because inheritable ACEs are now flowed automatically, technically a given implementation doesn't need to have each node in the hierarchy contain inheritable entries *all the time*. It's possible to generate those entries on an as-needed basis (a simple speed versus space trade off), but this would be pretty tricky to implement. In any case, there is no escaping the extra overhead introduced by this auto-synchronize model. Object-specific ACEs only exacerbate the overhead. Don't get me wrong—I wish I'd had auto-synchronizing ACLs much earlier in the history of Windows NT, but before you decide to start using object-specific ACEs in your own private ACLs, beware the complexity.

with a data type known as EXPLICIT_ACCESS. This structure contains a TRUSTEE (basically this is just a principal, group, or alias specified by name or SID) as well as an access mask and a set of flags. The idea is that you, the developer, simply fill out a counted array of EXPLICIT_ACCESS records, specifying strings for principals and groups, and the system will automatically form an ACL for you when you call SetEntriesInAcl. This involves mapping names to SIDs, making incremental changes to existing ACLs, and making sure ACEs are ordered correctly in DACLs. Going the other way, GetExplicit EntriesFromAcl maps SIDs back to names.

On Windows NT 4, these two APIs are virtually unusable. On Windows 2000 some of the bugs are fixed, but I still cannot recommend their use in systems that you care about. The most hideous bug is that SetEntriesInAcl discards all inheritable ACEs completely. This is clearly unacceptable when working with ACLs in any hierarchical system: the file system, the registry, window stations, and so on. GetExplicitEntriesFromAcl worked pretty well until it started ignoring generic permissions completely in Service Pack 4 of Windows NT 4.

Regardless of whether the implementation bugs are fixed, these APIs harbor two design problems. The most glaring problem is that because all the name-to-SID (and back) mapping is done behind the scenes, if one of these mapping operations fails, the entire operation fails with no indication of which name failed to be mapped. (You can avoid this in SetEntriesInAcl by always using SIDs in your TRUSTEE data structures to begin with; however, GetExplicitEntriesFromAcl *always* maps SIDs to names—you don't have a choice.) A more subtle problem is that it's unclear how to take an existing ACL and adjust the inheritable permissions in it in a predictable way (assuming you're not using a version of Windows where SetEntriesInAcl simply ignores them anyway).

Now that I've finished ranting, here's my recommendation. If you plan on programming ACLs yourself, you're going to need to use the "low-level" API in MSDN. Don't let the documentation fool you—these APIs are not in any way obsolete. Even though these functions might feel a bit grungy, they are actually very straightforward to use. If you can possibly avoid it, don't write your own user interface for editing ACLs; rather, rely on the built-in security descriptor editor that ships with Windows 2000. For Windows NT 4, this component is installed as a side effect of installing the Security Configuration Editor (this became available as of Service Pack 4). Using this component will usually eliminate most of the ACL manipulation code from your program. For those rare occasions where you do need to manipulate ACLs yourself, here's a modern primer on programming ACLs, specifically DACLs. (Once you know how to manipulate a DACL, working with a SACL is similar.)

First, be aware that an ACL consists of a contiguous buffer of memory that is populated with a header followed by zero or more ACEs. Each ACE is a variable-length data structure (the very last component of each ACE is a SID, which makes even version 2 ACEs variable length). The ACL header is defined as follows:

```
typedef struct _ACL {
  BYTE AclRevision;
  BYTE Sbz1;              // Should be zero
  WORD AclSize;
  WORD AceCount;
  WORD Sbz2;              // Should be zero
} ACL;
```

The revision numbers currently in use are 2 and 4; the latter can be found in the directory service, where object-specific ACEs roost. *AclSize* indicates the total number of bytes in the ACL, and *AceCount* indicates the number of ACEs that follow the header. You are required to treat ACLs as opaque, so a function you're likely to use often is GetAclInformation:

```
typedef enum _ACL_INFORMATION_CLASS {
  AclRevisionInformation = 1,
  AclSizeInformation
} ACL_INFORMATION_CLASS;

typedef struct _ACL_SIZE_INFORMATION {
    DWORD AceCount;
    DWORD AclBytesInUse;
    DWORD AclBytesFree;
} ACL_SIZE_INFORMATION;
```

```
BOOL GetAclInformation(
  PACL   Acl,                   // in
  LPVOID AclInformation,        // out, your buffer
  DWORD  AclInformationLength,  // in, buffer size in bytes
  ACL_INFORMATION_CLASS Class   // in
}
```

Once you've asked for `AclSizeInformation`, it's pretty easy to enumerate the entries in a version 2 ACL.

The next function you'll need to know about is `GetAce`:

```
BOOL GetAce(
  PACL    Acl,      // in
  DWORD   AceIndex, // in, zero based
  LPVOID* Ace       // out
);
```

This function gives you a pointer to the *N*th ACE, where *N* is the zero-based index passed via *AceIndex*.

All ACEs have a few fields in common that are represented by the ACE _HEADER structure:

```
typedef struct _ACE_HEADER {
    BYTE   AceType;
    BYTE   AceFlags;
    WORD   AceSize;
} ACE_HEADER;
```

The ACE size in bytes is provided via *AceSize*, the inheritance flags are housed in *AceFlags*, and the actual type of ACE is housed in *AceType:*

```
#define ACCESS_ALLOWED_ACE_TYPE            (0x0)
#define ACCESS_DENIED_ACE_TYPE             (0x1)
#define SYSTEM_AUDIT_ACE_TYPE              (0x2)
```

Note that positive and negative entries in the DACL are represented by two distinct types of ACEs (physically these ACEs look exactly the same, however). Things are different in the SACL, however, because it is possible for a single ACE to represent both a success and failure audit. In the SACL, two special flags (non-inheritance related) indicate whether to audit success, failure, or both:

```
#define SUCCESSFUL_ACCESS_ACE_FLAG      (0x40)
#define FAILED_ACCESS_ACE_FLAG          (0x80)
```

Here's what an ACE in a version 2 DACL looks like:

```
typedef struct _ACCESS_ALLOWED_ACE {
    ACE_HEADER Header;
    ACCESS_MASK Mask;
    DWORD SidStart;
} ACCESS_ALLOWED_ACE;
```

There is a similar declaration of type ACCESS_DENIED_ACE, but it looks exactly the same. As you can see, this structure simply adds a 32-bit access mask and a variable-length SID to the ACE_HEADER. Because it's impossible to declare a variable-length field in a C structure, *SidStart* represents a placeholder that contains the first 32 bits of the SID; take its address to get a pointer to the SID in the ACE.

The following code pulls all these ideas together, enumerating the contents of a version 2 DACL:

```
void _dumpDacl(ACL* pdacl) {
  ACL_SIZE_INFORMATION sizeInfo;
  GetAclInformation(pdacl,
                    &sizeInfo, sizeof sizeInfo,
                    AclSizeInformation);

  for (DWORD i = 0; i < sizeInfo.AceCount; ++i) {
    // allow/deny ACEs have exactly the same shape
    ACCESS_ALLOWED_ACE* pace;
    GetAce(pdacl, i, (void**)&pace);

    const wchar_t* pszGrantOrDeny;
    switch (pace->Header.AceType) {
    case ACCESS_ALLOWED_ACE_TYPE:
      pszGrantOrDeny = L"grant";
      break;
```

```
      case ACCESS_DENIED_ACE_TYPE:
        pszGrantOrDeny = L"deny";
        break;
    default:
        pszGrantOrDeny = L"<<unexpected ace type>>";
        break;
    }
    wprintf(L"%s 0x%08X (inh: %X) to ",
        pszGrantOrDeny,
        pace->Mask,
        pace->Header.AceFlags);

    _printSid(&pace->SidStart);
    wprintf(L"\n");
  }
}
```

If you're creating a DACL from scratch, just allocate enough memory to hold the number of ACEs you plan on using. Don't worry about getting the amount of memory exactly right, because if you're planning on calling Set(Named) SecurityInfo or CreatePrivateObjectSecurity(Ex) to apply your DACL to a security descriptor, the system won't use your DACL anyway; rather, it'll make a new one using your DACL as a starting point.

```
const DWORD _maxSidSize = GetSidLength Required (
    SID_MAX_SUB_AUTHORITIES);
const DWORD _maxVersion2AceSize =
    sizeof(ACCESS_ALLOWED_ACE) - sizeof(DWORD)
                                + _maxSidSize;
```

Given this, you can simply allocate some memory (using your favorite memory allocator) and start adding ACEs.

Before you add your first ACE, though, you'll need to initialize the ACL header:

```
BOOL InitializeAcl(
    PACL  Acl,           // out
    DWORD AclLength,     // in, size of memory block in bytes
```

```
   DWORD AclRevision   // in
);
```

To add each ACE, use one of the following two functions:

```
BOOL AddAccessAllowedAceEx(
   PACL  Acl,            // in, out
   DWORD AceRevision,    // in
   DWORD AceFlags,       // in
   DWORD AccessMask,     // in
   PSID  Sid             // in
);

BOOL AddAccessDeniedAceEx(
   PACL  Acl,            // in, out
   DWORD AceRevision,    // in
   DWORD AceFlags,       // in
   DWORD AccessMask,     // in
   PSID  Sid             // in
);
```

These two functions (introduced in Windows 2000) give you complete control over the new ACE; their older cousins (the non-Ex versions) omit the *AceFlags* mask, and thus you cannot control inheritance flags without writing some extra code. The parameters should be self-explanatory. *AceRevision* should be ACL_REVISION (or ACL_REVISION_DS if you're working with directory service DACLs).

Fortunately it's quite easy to implement these newer functions in terms of their older cousins if your code needs to be portable to Windows NT 4. For example:

```
#if _WIN32_WINNT < 0x500
BOOL AddAccessAllowedAceEx(PACL pAcl,
                           DWORD dwAceRevision,
                           DWORD AceFlags,
                           DWORD AccessMask,
                           PSID pSid) {
   if (!AddAccessAllowedAce(pAcl, dwAceRevision,
                            AccessMask, pSid))
```

```
    return FALSE;
  ACL_SIZE_INFORMATION info;
  if (!GetAclInformation(pAcl, &info, sizeof info,
                         AclSizeInformation))
    return FALSE;
  ACE_HEADER* pace = 0;
  if (!GetAce(pAcl, info.AceCount - 1, (void**)&pace))
    return FALSE;
  pace->AceFlags = (BYTE)AceFlags;
  return TRUE;
}
#endif
```

Here's an example that creates a DACL from scratch:

```
// grant GENERIC_ALL to Everyone
// except network logon sessions,
// making these ACEs inheritable
SID sidEveryone = {SID_REVISION, 1,
                   SECURITY_WORLD_SID_AUTHORITY,
                   SECURITY_WORLD_RID};
SID sidNetwork  = {SID_REVISION, 1,
                   SECURITY_NT_AUTHORITY,
                   SECURITY_NETWORK_RID};
DWORD cb = 2 * _maxVersion2AceSize;
ACL* pdacl = (ACL*)LocalAlloc(GPTR, cb);

InitializeAcl(pdacl, cb, ACL_REVISION);

DWORD grfInherit = OBJECT_INHERIT_ACE |
                   CONTAINER_INHERIT_ACE;
AddAccessDeniedAceEx( pdacl, ACL_REVISION,
                      grfInherit, GENERIC_ALL,
                      &sidNetwork);
AddAccessAllowedAceEx(pdacl, ACL_REVISION,
                      grfInherit, GENERIC_ALL,
                      &sidEveryone);

// call to Set(Named)SecurityInfo or
// CreatePrivateObjectSecurity(Ex) omitted
```

```
// now our (overly fat) DACL is no longer needed
LocalFree(pdacl);
```

Note in this example how careful I was to place the negative ACE before the positive ACE. This is because even though they are clearly aware of the type of ACE being added, *these functions do not make any attempt to maintain the correct order of the DACL on your behalf*. `AddAccessDeniedAceEx` (for instance) simply appends a new ACE to the end of an existing DACL, even though this may create a DACL that is out of order. This means that insertion of new ACEs into existing DACLs becomes nontrivial, because you have to insert them in the correct order.

Considering that you'll never be manually adding an ACE with the `INHERITED_ACE` flag set—recall that the flow of inherited ACEs is handled by the system via calls to `Set(Named)SecurityInfo` or `CreatePrivate ObjectSecurityEx`—all the ACEs you'll be adding will be direct ACEs. With this in mind, when adding a negative ACE, insert it as the very first ACE, before any of the existing ACEs. This is where the direct negative ACEs belong. When adding a positive ACE, insert it right before you see any ACEs marked with the `INHERITED_ACE` flag. If you don't see any ACEs marked this way, just add it to the end. Using these rules will allow you to write code that works with older Windows NT 4–style DACLs (which don't use `INHERITED_ACE`) as well as modern Windows 2000 ACLs.[24]

With these rules of thumb in mind, I wrote a couple of very simple functions that demonstrate how to safely insert positive and negative ACEs into a DACL.

```
ACL* _insertAccessAllowedAce(ACL* pdaclOld,
                             DWORD grfMask,
                             DWORD grfInherit,
                             PSID psid) {
  ACL_SIZE_INFORMATION si;
  GetAclInformation(pdaclOld, &si, sizeof si,
                    AclSizeInformation);
```

---

[24] Note that I'm specifically not addressing directory service ACLs (version 4), which use an even more complex model for ACL ordering.

```
// allocate a DACL with room for one additional ACE
DWORD cb = si.AclBytesInUse + _maxVersion2AceSize;
ACL* pdaclNew = (ACL*)LocalAlloc(GPTR, cb);

InitializeAcl(pdaclNew, cb, ACL_REVISION);

// a safe way to add a direct positive ACE is to
// add it right before the inherited ACEs begin
bool bInserted = false;
for (DWORD i = 0; i < si.AceCount; ++i) {
  ACE_HEADER* pace;
  GetAce(pdaclOld, i, (void**)&pace);
  if (!bInserted && pace->AceFlags & INHERITED_ACE) {
    AddAccessAllowedAceEx(pdaclNew, ACL_REVISION,
                          grfInherit, grfMask, psid);
    bInserted = true;
  }
  AddAce(pdaclNew, ACL_REVISION, MAXDWORD,
         pace, pace->AceSize);
}
if (!bInserted)
    AddAccessAllowedAceEx(pdaclNew, ACL_REVISION,
                          grfInherit, grfMask, psid);
return pdaclNew;
}

ACL* _insertAccessDeniedAce(ACL* pdaclOld,
                            DWORD grfMask,
                            DWORD grfInherit,
                            PSID psid) {
  ACL_SIZE_INFORMATION si;
  GetAclInformation(pdaclOld, &si, sizeof si,
                    AclSizeInformation);

  // allocate a DACL with room for one additional ACE
  DWORD cb = si.AclBytesInUse + _maxVersion2AceSize;
  ACL* pdaclNew = (ACL*)LocalAlloc(GPTR, cb);

  InitializeAcl(pdaclNew, cb, ACL_REVISION);

  // a safe way to add a direct negative ACE is to
  // add it at the very beginning of the ACL
```

```
    AddAccessDeniedAceEx(pdaclNew, ACL_REVISION,
                         grfInherit, grfMask, psid);
    for (DWORD i = 0; i < si.AceCount; ++i) {
      ACE_HEADER* pace;
      GetAce(pdaclOld, i, (void**)&pace);
      AddAce(pdaclNew, ACL_REVISION, MAXDWORD,
             pace, pace->AceSize);
    }
    return pdaclNew;
}
```

Of course, you should add in whatever error checking code makes sense for your project and to use your favorite memory allocator; I chose `LocalAlloc` in this example to stay consistent with `Get(Named)SecurityInfo` and friends.

Here's an example that uses these helper functions to add a denied ACE to a fictitious registry key:

```
// deny GENERIC_ALL to network logon sessions
SID sidNetwork  = {SID_REVISION, 1,
                   SECURITY_NT_AUTHORITY,
                   SECURITY_NETWORK_RID};
void* psd;
ACL* pdaclOld;
GetNamedSecurityInfo(L"MACHINE\\Software\\Test",
                     SE_REGISTRY_KEY,
                     DACL_SECURITY_INFORMATION,
                     0, 0, &pdaclOld, 0, &psd);

ACL* pdaclNew = _insertAccessDeniedAce(pdaclOld,
                        DELETE,
                        CONTAINER_INHERIT_ACE,
                        &sidNetwork);
SetNamedSecurityInfo(L"MACHINE\\Software\\Test",
                     SE_REGISTRY_KEY,
                     DACL_SECURITY_INFORMATION,
                     0, 0, pdaclNew, 0);
LocalFree(pdaclNew);
LocalFree(psd);
```

The bad news here is that ACL programming is pretty hard to get right, but the good news is that the main reason you used to get stuck doing it was in conjunction with a user interface. (Note that in these examples I've been using hardcoded SIDs; in a user interface, you'd also be stuck trying to look up account names over the network while trying to keep your user interface responsive.) The built-in access control editor should help significantly in this regard. (It's very sophisticated; it even performs its name-to-SID mappings on a separate thread to avoid locking up the user interface.) Check my Web site for examples of its use.

A Note on Negative ACEs and Windows NT 4

In the last example, I added a negative ACE to a registry key. This works fine in Windows 2000, but introduces some issues in Windows NT 4. From a security standpoint, things work the way you expect: Network logon sessions are denied access to the registry key. However, if an administrator tries to edit the DACL on that registry key, he or she will be greeted with a very nasty dialog box that indicates that the ACL editor on Windows NT 4 *doesn't know how to deal with negative ACEs*.[25] The administrator will have two choices: either stop editing the DACL immediately, or edit the DACL and have the ACL editor remove every single ACE from that DACL. Neither of these choices is good. If it was your program that added that negative entry, the administrator isn't going to like you much.

The moral of the story is that you should avoid using negative ACEs in Windows NT 4 anywhere an administrator is likely to edit them using the built-in ACL editor. This includes the file system,[26] registry, network shares, and COM server access and launch permissions. Executive objects (threads, window stations, semaphores, sections, etc.) and services are examples of objects for which the system doesn't provide an ACL editor, so you don't have to worry about this little problem here.

---

[25] My understanding is that it actually can deal with one very special type of negative ACE: a negative ACE that denies GENERIC_ALL.

[26] Technically, if the Security Configuration Editor has been installed, the file system won't have this problem, because it'll be using the Windows 2000 ACL editor.

Lots of people have asked me why Microsoft never documented the interface to the Windows NT 4 ACL editor (ACLEDIT.DLL). If I had to guess, I'd say this particular limitation was one of the motivating factors.

Handles

In a chapter on access control, I thought I'd share some insight that I've had regarding how access control works with handles in Windows. When you call CreateMutex to create a named mutex, the system gives you back a 32-bit handle that you can think of as representing a *session* to the mutex. If you were the actual creator of the mutex (in other words, you didn't end up opening somebody else's mutex), you'll get back a session that has full access permissions to the mutex (even if you specified a DACL via the *Security Attributes* parameter that denies yourself all access; the creator *always* gets a valid handle to the mutex, which is reasonable).

I often used to wonder what would happen if you were to call Duplicate Handle to give your handle to some other process (particularly one that was running in a different security context). For that matter, what would happen in a process running as Bob if a thread impersonating Alice opened a handle to a mutex? (Perhaps Alice has been granted access to the mutex, but Bob has not.) What would happen in this case if the thread stopped impersonating Alice and reverted to Bob? Or what if the thread then started impersonating Mary? Would the system track who had originally acquired the resource and complain if somebody else tried to use it?

It turns out that the model is quite simple. When you open up a session to an object, an access check occurs to make sure you're allowed to open the session in the first place, and the system annotates the resulting session (by dereferencing the appropriate entry in the process's handle table) with the access permissions you were granted. (This information is stored in protected kernel memory, so malicious user-mode code cannot adjust these annotations.) From then on, no security checks are performed when you use that session, regardless of what security context it is used from (other than verifying that the session isn't misused; for instance, you can't open a session for read-only access and then try to write using that same session). So Bob, while impersonating Alice, can acquire a mutex that only Alice has access to, and he can later use the handle as Bob, or Mary, or anybody else he can impersonate. (Technically, the security context he's using doesn't really matter, because he's still using a session opened by Alice.) The handle table in a process is not sensitive to security contexts; if you can impersonate someone, you can acquire a resource on his or her behalf and use it in your process (assuming, of course, the security context you impersonate is strong enough to allow you to open executive objects while impersonating; see Chapter 4 for a discussion of impersonation levels).

What about auditing? Well, because audits generally occur only when an object is opened or closed, as long as Alice opens and closes the object, any other principal who uses her session won't be recorded in the audit log; the system doesn't audit each time you *use* an existing session. "Audit object access" doesn't necessarily mean that the system will audit each usage of a session (which would be expensive and would bloat the audit log).

What happens when you share a mutex by giving it a name? Any thread that opens a handle to the mutex (by calling `OpenMutex` or `CreateMutex`) is opening a new session, and so the system performs an access check based on the calling thread's security context.

Correspondingly, what happens if you share a mutex by calling `Duplicate Handle`, or via handle inheritance to a child process? You are probably already familiar with `DuplicateHandle`,[27] but I'll repeat its signature here so I can refer to it when necessary:

```
BOOL DuplicateHandle(
    HANDLE    SourceProcessHandle,    // in
    HANDLE    SourceHandle,           // in
    HANDLE    TargetProcessHandle,    // in
    LPHANDLE  TargetHandle,           // out
    DWORD     DesiredAccess,          // in
    BOOL      InheritHandle,          // in
    DWORD     Options                 // in
);
```

From a security perspective, calling `DuplicateHandle` or using handle inheritance to give someone else a reference to an object is very different from hav-

---

[27] See Richter (1999a).

ing that person open the object by name. From a security perspective, you are giving someone else access to a session that you've already established. No additional access checks will be performed, with one exception. If you call `DuplicateHandle` and ask for at least one permission that you didn't have in your original session, the system detects this and does one of two things: It either blindly fails the call with `ERROR_ACCESS_DENIED` (the file system and registry work this way), or it performs an access check using the security context of the target process (represented via `TargetProcessHandle`) to decide whether to grant or deny the request.

Recall the definition of the `SECURITY_ATTRIBUTES` structure:

```
struct SECURITY_ATTRIBUTES {
    DWORD   nLength,        // sizeof SECURITY_ATTRIBUTES
    LPVOID  psd,            // optional pointer to SD
    BOOL    bInheritHandle  // is handle inheritable?
};
```

I used to wonder why `bInheritHandle` was a member of this structure, but when you consider that you will be giving away your handle to the child process with no access checks performed, it's pretty clear that this parameter is security related. Even if the child will run in a different logon session (via `CreateProcessAsUser`), that open session will still be shared with the child process without any further access checks.

In summary, if you care about security, treat handles as sessions to objects and be aware that access checks and audits are normally performed only upon opening the session. Handle inheritance and `DuplicateHandle` are ways of giving your session away to someone else without any access checks being performed. If you're interested in more information on this topic, see Brown (2000a).

Summary

- The 32-bit access mask includes three types of permissions: specific, standard, and generic. Specific permissions are defined for each class of object individually. Standard permissions have the same values for all objects in order to provide a limited amount of polymorphism.

- Generic permissions map to standard and specific permissions and allow an additional level of polymorphism across different classes of objects. The default DACL in your token is a great example of the use of generic permissions.

- Security descriptors are associated with objects, and contain an owner, primary group, DACL, and SACL.

- The owner is always implicitly granted READ_CONTROL and WRITE_DAC, regardless of what the DACL says.

- A trustee is either a principal or a group listed in an ACL.

- The DACL says which trustees are allowed to touch the object in certain ways; it is discretionary, which means that access policy is determined at the owner's discretion.

- The SACL is nondiscretionary. It can be viewed or manipulated only from security contexts that have SeSecurityPrivilege enabled (Administrators are granted this privilege by default).

- When creating new objects, use the SECURITY_ATTRIBUTES structure to customize various aspects (typically the DACL) of the new object's security descriptor. If you find yourself doing this a lot, consider changing the default DACL in your token to automate this.

- Security descriptors can be absolute or self-relative. The former is typically used to provide information to the operating system, and the latter is typically used when retrieving information from the operating system.

- Each access check takes as input three things: a token, a security descriptor, and a requested access mask. The AccessCheck API sums up this model quite nicely.

- During an access check, the DACL is traversed from top to bottom, and as permissions are granted, their corresponding bits are latched in an accumulator until either all requested access permission bits have been granted or any one of them has been denied. Thus the order of the DACL is significant.

- Negative ACEs in a DACL take precedence over positive ACEs, and are therefore listed first. If the Windows 2000 inheritance scheme is in use, direct (noninherited) ACEs are listed first (negative followed by positive), followed by inherited ACEs (negative followed by positive). This allows a direct positive ACE to override an inherited negative ACE.

- ACL inheritance in Windows NT 4 leads to chaos in nontrivial systems because inheritance is only honored at object creation time and the system provides no reasonable means for maintaining consistency.

- ACL inheritance in Windows 2000 tracks each inherited ACE in an ACL, which allows them to be resynchronized whenever a change occurs. This keeps hierarchical systems consistent, while providing a way to block the flow at distinguished nodes in the hierarchy.

- You can use security descriptors in your own private objects, and you can also leverage inheritance if you have a hierarchical system. Use `CreatePrivateObjectSecurity` if you buy into the Windows NT 4 model of ACL inheritance; use `CreatePrivateObject SecurityEx` if you buy into the Windows 2000 model. Call `AccessCheck` as appropriate to verify access.

- When constructing or parsing ACLs, consider using the "low-level" APIs, which are robust and flexible, as opposed to the "high-level" APIs, which have traditionally been horribly bug-ridden.

- Avoid programming ACLs if you can. Prefer to leverage the Windows 2000 access control editor user interface, which deals with ACL ordering automatically.

- Be aware that handles to operating system objects behave like sessions. Once you open a session, no further access checks are performed, so don't give away your sessions willy-nilly.

PART III

Distribution

Chapter 7

Network Authentication

Bob just received a TCP packet from someone on the wire. Who did it come from, friend or foe? Does the source IP address assure him of the origin of the message, or could a bad guy have sent the packet, hiding behind an IP address that Bob believes is within his security perimeter? Maybe Bob doesn't even care about the IP address; rather, he wants to know *on whose behalf* the packet was sent. Was it Alice (a valid client) or a bad guy? The only way to tell is to have the sender of the packet *prove* his or her identity. The way to do this electronically is via careful use of encryption algorithms.

But even before Alice can send Bob an encrypted packet, the two of them have to agree on a key with which to encrypt that packet, and exchanging that initial key without any bad guy seeing you do it is tricky. This is what network authentication protocols are all about: proving (electronically) to the server the identity of the client (and often the other way around), as well as exchanging encryption keys in a protected fashion.

I've found that having a good conceptual grasp of network authentication can help instill a better intuition for developing and debugging secure distributed systems, so this chapter is all about what happens when a client and server authenticate with one another. There's not going to be much code; rather, I want to help you develop a more intuitive feel for the sort of work that's going on underneath the hood of the secure network communication subsystems covered in this book. This chapter first talks about NTLM (because it's so simple), then discusses Kerberos v5, and finally covers SPNEGO, a metaprotocol for negotiating the real protocol that a client and server will use. It also talks about the role of GSSAPI and SSPI in secure systems. If you've never been introduced to network authentication before, I hope you'll find this to be a fun (and challenging) chapter.

The NTLM Authentication Protocol

NTLM is the native authentication protocol on Windows NT 4, and is also supported on Windows 2000 for backward compatibility. NTLM stands for NT/LAN Manager because it is an extension of the protocol that was developed for Microsoft's LAN Manager product. It is a simple protocol, and a virtually undocumented one (although much work has been done to reverse engineer it).[1] I will share what I know about it based on looking at the Common Internet File System (CIFS) documentation and by performing my own network traces while debugging COM servers over the last few years.

Basic Challenge/Response Using Local Accounts

To understand client/server authentication using NTLM, it's best to start simple. Let's say that there is no centralized authority (in Windows parlance, no domain controllers) and that Alice is logged in to AlicesMachine using a local account defined there. Alice wants to access a secured resource on BobsMachine, and that resource is managed by a daemon process (the server application) running as Bob, perhaps in the form of an RPC or COM server. Alice is interactively logged on to AlicesMachine, and a process (the client application) running in her interactive logon session will physically make the request on her behalf. For this to work, Alice must first establish a logon session on BobsMachine, which means she must be authenticated across the network. In order for Alice to be authenticated on BobsMachine using a *local account,* the security database

---

[1] Leighton (2000) has some interesting insights.

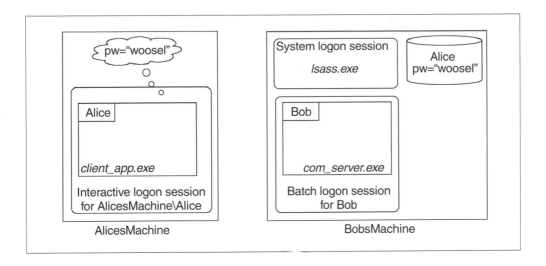

Figure 7.1. Ready for NTLM authentication using local accounts

there must also contain an account named Alice with a matching password. Figure 7.1 shows the system prior to authentication.

Alice sends an initial message to Bob to get things going. This is known as the Negotiate message. (Alice is allowed to help negotiate a session key as well as other low-level details of the protocol, hence the name of the message.) When Bob receives this message, he's not sure who sent it, but whoever it was wants to initiate an authentication exchange, so Bob generates a 64-bit **nonce** and sends it back as the reply; this is known as the Challenge message. (*Nonce* is pronounced such that it rhymes with "once" and is simply a number that will be used only once; in this case, Bob won't ever use that same challenge nonce again.)

Alice now needs to take this nonce and use it to help prove her identity to Bob. She takes a one-way hash of her password[2] and uses it as a cryptographic key to encrypt the nonce sent by Bob.[3] (I'll refer to the result of this encryption

---

[2] Technically, the system has cached the password hash down in her logon session, and thus Alice doesn't need to provide her password again (see Chapter 4).

3 This is very much a simplification of the actual algorithm, but it is detailed enough for my purposes in this book. For those who care, in NTLM v1 the hash algorithm used is MD4, and the encryption algorithm used is DES. See Leighton (2000) for more of the grungy details, including the few known details of NTLM v2, a newer version of the protocol introduced in Windows NT 4 Service Pack 4.

as R.) She then sends her authority name, principal name, and R back to Bob. Known as the Authenticate message, this is the final message in the exchange between Alice and Bob.

Bob forwards this information (plus the nonce that he generated for Alice earlier) to the Local Security Authority, expecting upon success to receive back a token referencing a new logon session for Alice. The LSA on BobsMachine, when it receives this information, looks at who Alice claims to be, and looks for a corresponding account in the local security database on BobsMachine. It then takes the password it has for Alice, computes R independently (using the nonce specified by Bob), and compares its result with what Alice computed. If these match, Alice is authenticated and the LSA establishes a network logon session[4] for her, and hands Bob back a token.

I'll mention right up front that if you're using COM or RPC (or even named pipes), you don't have to worry about performing this handshake—it's done under the covers by the corresponding communication subsystem. Even if you're programming simple sockets, although you'll have to be deliberate about shuttling the Negotiate, Challenge, and Authenticate messages back and forth, you won't have to worry about forming their contents; rather, you'll just delegate (as the other communication subsystems do) to a security service provider. This mechanism is discussed more in the section on SSPI.

Note that Alice's password was not sent across the wire. Thus the new logon session for Alice has no network credentials. Alice has now spent the single network hop allotted to her by the NTLM protocol, and although her logon session is valid on BobsMachine, it can go no further. If Bob impersonates Alice by putting her token on his thread and tries to contact JoesMachine, he won't be able to use Alice's credentials (this protects Alice, by the way).

Note also that Alice's *token* was not sent across the wire. Many developers I've spoken to have the impression that this is how authentication works. What would sending the contents of Alice's token prove? Anyone could replay those bits, and if that was all Bob relied on to prove her identity, he'd be in trouble.

---

[4] Note that this step will fail if Alice has not been granted the right to establish a network logon session on BobsMachine (recall the "Access this computer from network" logon right discussed in Chapter 4).

Also, does Alice's token that was established on AlicesMachine make any sense whatsoever on BobsMachine? Remember that many of the authorization attributes in a security context are local to a particular machine (think aliases and privileges). So when the LSA builds a token on BobsMachine, it builds one that has meaning there. Because there are no domain controllers involved, the resulting token will be populated with any aliases and privileges assigned to the Alice local account on BobsMachine.

Figure 7.2 illustrates the handshake just described. Notice that there are ultimately *three* logon sessions involved: Alice's interactive logon session, where her request originated; Bob's daemon logon session (to make this concrete, I used a batch logon, but a service logon is also common); and finally, Alice's network logon session on BobsMachine, which acts as a sort of proxy for her interactive logon session back on AlicesMachine. Bob must juggle his own security context and those of any clients making authenticated requests (Alice, in this case) via selective use of impersonation, as discussed in Chapter 4.

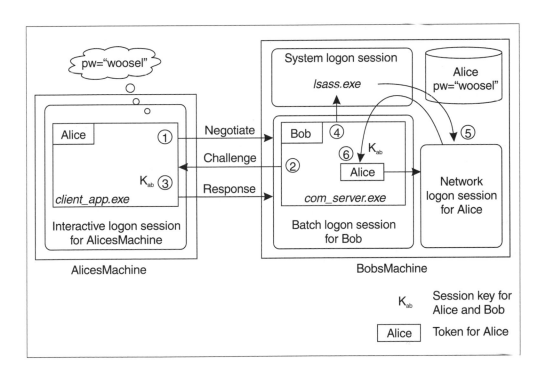

Figure 7.2.   Basic NTLM handshake (using local accounts)

If you've enabled auditing of logon and logoff events on BobsMachine, and if you look in the event viewer, you'll notice a new *success* audit indicating that Alice was just authenticated and has established a network logon session.

Session Key Discovery

So Alice has proved her identity to Bob. What now? The whole reason she went through all that hassle was to make authenticated requests to Bob (perhaps for sensitive data to which only she has access). Now that Alice and Bob are connected, and Alice has a logon session on BobsMachine, how does Alice continue to assure Bob that she is still the same principal? How does Bob discern that a given network packet really came from Alice, as opposed to some malicious router on the network that wants to hijack Alice's logon session on Bob's machine? The solution, once again, lies in selective use of cryptography.

Originally, Alice used her **master key** to prove her identity to Bob; this is her password hash. After the authentication handshake, Alice and Bob both discover a **session key**—technically, the **security service provider** (**SSP**) on either side manages this key (more details later)—which Alice can optionally use to authenticate data that she sends to Bob. Just as the response is a one-way function of Alice's password and Bob's challenge, so too the session key is discovered via a different one-way function with the same input: Alice's password and the challenge. Whoever knows Alice's password and the challenge can determine the session key. Thus, Alice discovers the session key when she receives the Challenge message from Bob. Bob discovers the session key when he contacts the Local Security Authority to verify Alice's response.

Using the Session Key

Once Alice and Bob have exchanged a session key, they can use it in two basic ways: to sign or seal messages sent between them. *Sealing* a message means encrypting it with the session key. *Signing* a message means sending the message in the clear, followed by a **message authentication code** (**MAC**). You can think of a MAC as a one-way hash of the payload in which the resulting hash value has been encrypted with the session key. Who can form the MAC for a given message? Only someone who knows the session key. Who can modify a MAC-protected payload? Only someone who knows the session key (because the MAC would need to be regenerated based on a hash of the new payload).

When Bob receives a message (including its MAC) that comes in over Alice's network connection, he can verify that Alice was the one who generated the message by independently calculating the MAC and comparing it with the one sent with the message. After this, Bob knows two things: Alice sent the message, and the message wasn't tampered with on the wire.[5] Usually the message header includes a sequence number (the header is protected by the MAC as well), so Bob can also discover if Alice's messages have been reordered on the wire.[6] Note that sealing can be much more expensive than signing, at least in terms of CPU cycles; the network packets aren't noticeably larger after encryption.

Each communication subsystem provides its own options for leveraging the session key. RPC and COM, for instance, allow the client to choose (programmatically, at each method call) how much to leverage the session key, whereas there is no such programmatic control over a named pipe.

Pass-Through Authentication Using Domain Accounts

So far we've seen that using a local account, Alice can prove her identity to Bob and establish a network logon session on BobsMachine. We've also seen that during the authentication exchange, Alice and Bob both independently discover a session key that can be used to authenticate (via signing or sealing) the actual data they send to one another. Now let's introduce a centralized authority.

Let's say Alice and BobsMachine are both principals in the Foo domain. BobsMachine is *not* a domain controller; it's just a normal machine whose primary domain is Foo. Alice's password is only known by Alice and the security database for Foo, so how can the LSA on BobsMachine authenticate her? The answer is that it cannot. Only Alice's authority can authenticate her, and BobsMachine must trust what her authority says (by virtue of being a member of the Foo domain, this implies that BobsMachine trusts Foo).

---

[5] The obvious assumption is that Alice hasn't given away her session key. But this isn't much different from saying that Alice shouldn't give away her password to begin with; if Alice gives away her password, she is basically giving away her network identity. There's not much that a software-based system can do to prevent this.

[6] If you're wondering why we don't just rely on TCP (for instance) to make sure packets arrive in order, be aware that TCP isn't designed to do this securely; a bad guy who compromises a router could easily forge TCP sequence numbers.

Physically, the handshake looks exactly the same as it did before: Negotiate, Challenge, Authenticate. However, when Bob's SSP calls into the LSA on BobsMachine, passing it the nonce plus Alice's name and her response, the LSA simply passes this information up to one of the domain controllers in its primary domain (Foo). Foo notes that the client has purported that her authority is Foo and her principal name is Alice, and thus looks up Alice's account, calculates R independently based on the password material stored in the security database, and verifies Alice's identity. It then sends confirmation, plus a list of global authorization attributes (groups) for Alice back to the LSA on BobsMachine, which takes those authorization attributes, combines them with local authorization attributes (aliases and privileges), and establishes a network logon session plus a token to hand back to Bob's SSP. The obvious question is: How does Bob's SSP discover the session key, which is essentially `OWF(password, challenge)`? Alice discovers the session key (as before) during the Challenge leg, and Foo discovers it by combining the nonce from Bob with the password material stored in the security database. Foo must somehow communicate this session key to BobsMachine without it being discovered by a bad guy, which means that it needs to be encrypted.

Chapter 1 made a really big deal of pointing out that machines in a domain are principals in that domain. This is where that relationship is really important. Because BobsMachine is a principal in the Foo domain, it has a machine account in that domain *with a password*. When BobsMachine boots, one of the system's duties on startup is to perform an authentication handshake with a domain controller in its primary domain. (Although the physical mechanism is a bit different, conceptually the handshake between BobsMachine and Foo is similar to the three-way handshake shown earlier using local accounts.) So by the time Alice comes along, BobsMachine has already exchanged a session key with Foo and thus has the potential to send and receive signed and sealed messages from Foo. The session key for Alice and Bob is therefore sent encrypted with the session key established earlier between BobsMachine and Foo.[7] So

---

[7] In classic NTLM, the session key is encrypted, but the global authorization attributes are neither encrypted nor protected with a MAC. This opens a rather nasty vulnerability because it offers the potential for a bad guy to insert extra authorization attributes into the data stream (Domain Admins being the classic example). NTLM v2 (introduced in Windows NT 4 Service Pack 4) solved this by sealing the entire payload during pass-through authentication.

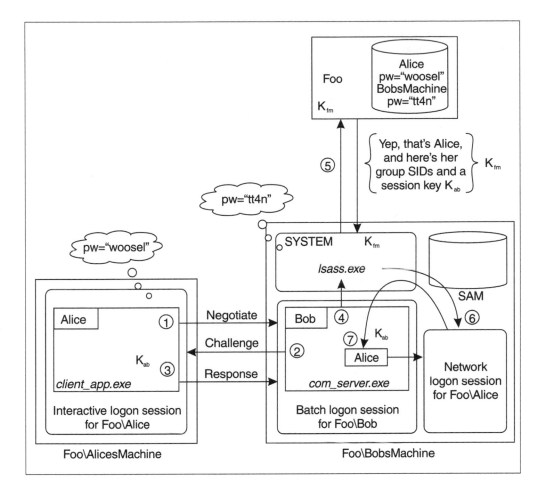

Figure 7.3. NTLM pass-through authentication

even in this case, Bob's SSP receives not only Alice's token from the LSA, but also a session key used to authenticate data sent to and from Alice. Figure 7.3 demonstrates this mechanism.

Cross-Domain Authentication

What happens if Alice and BobsMachine are in different domains? You can probably see where this is leading. Let's say that Alice is a principal in Quux, and BobsMachine is a principal in Foo. Alice wants to access a secured resource on BobsMachine and thus must establish a logon session there. To do this, she must be authenticated, and so once again she and Bob exchange the Negotiate,

Challenge, and Authenticate messages as before. Bob hands the results of the Authenticate message along with the nonce to the LSA on BobsMachine, which forwards the information to a domain controller for Foo (the primary domain for BobsMachine). Foo looks at the message, notes that Alice purports to have an authority called Quux, and knows that this authentication request cannot be satisfied without contacting Quux. So Foo looks in its list of trusted domains, and if it trusts Quux, it then forwards the request to Quux (similar to the way BobsMachine forwarded the request to Foo because of the implicit trust it has with Foo). Quux looks up Alice's record in the security database, calculates R and a session key, and sends an affirmation along with Alice's global authorization attributes (groups) back to Foo. Foo sends this information back to BobsMachine, and the LSA on BobsMachine establishes a network logon session and a token that contains the authorization attributes for Alice (from Quux) plus any local attributes (aliases and privileges).

In this case, Foo and Quux must share a session key of their own to protect the new session key (and authorization attributes) being sent across the wire. This is one reason that trust accounts must exist. If Foo trusts Quux, Foo in essence becomes a special kind of principal in the Quux domain and has a password that Quux can use to verify Foo's identity and establish a shared session key (see Figure 7.4).

The Path of Trust

Note that in all three of these scenarios, in order for Alice to establish a logon session on BobsMachine there has to be a path of trust directed from BobsMachine (the target machine) to the authority for Alice (the client). In the first case, the trust path was short: BobsMachine trusts its own LSA by definition (the LSA is part of the trusted computing base), and with a local account, the local authority *is* the authority that vouches for the principal. In the second case, BobsMachine trusts its primary domain (Foo). In the third case, BobsMachine trusts Foo, and Foo trusts Quux.

It's interesting to note that whereas BobsMachine sports a *transitive* trust relationship with Foo (that is, BobsMachine trusts Foo and all the domains that Foo trusts—Quux was one example), Foo's trust relationship with Quux is *not* transitive. Cross-domain trusts are never transitive under NT 4; because so

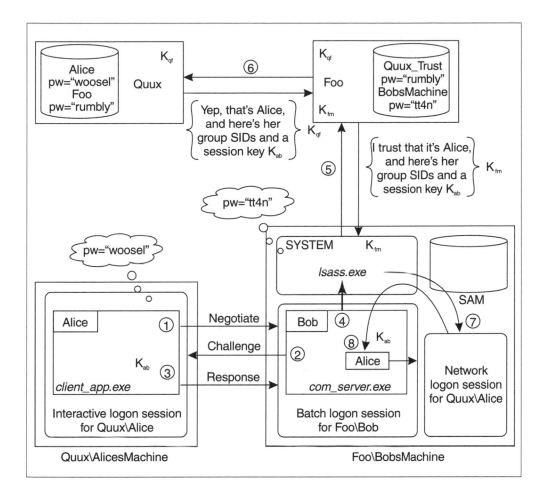

Figure 7.4. Cross-domain NTLM authentication

much of NTLM is undocumented, it's not clear whether this is a limitation of the protocol or simply a built-in throttle to avoid network congestion and brittleness.[8] So for a Windows NT 4–based system with four domains that all trust one another, there must be 12 trust relationships (see Figure 1.4 in Chapter 1).

---

[8] For an extreme example, imagine what would happen if Alice was a principal in the Z domain, and BobsMachine was a principal in the A domain. A trusts B, who trusts C, who trusts D, and so on all the way to Z. That's 25 network hops for authenticating Alice on BobsMachine (it's time-consuming and causes lots of extra network traffic). It also implies that 25 network connections must be alive and well in order for Alice to be authenticated on BobsMachine (this is very brittle). And each of these network connections would be used at *every single* network authentication between Alice and BobsMachine throughout the day!

Remember, if Foo and Quux trust each other, that's two trust relationships: one from Foo to Quux, and one from Quux to Foo. The administrator sets these relationships up manually, specifying a password for each individual trust account.

What can you do if Alice cannot be authenticated because the trust path is not complete? The simple answer is that you cannot authenticate as Alice. Either turn off authentication completely (depending on which communication subsystem you are using this can be done in a variety of ways, which will be demonstrated in upcoming chapters), or have Alice specify a different set of credentials. It's best to do the former if you don't need authentication, because it's usually best to avoid asking the user for credentials (or, heaven forbid, hard-coding account names and passwords into your programs).

Delegation of Credentials (or the Lack Thereof)

Because the response R in NTLM is a function of the challenge nonce and the client's password, it's clear that to represent a client (Alice, say) on the network, her password must be available. Technically, only a hash of her password is required, but think what would happen if even this hash was stolen by a bad guy: That bad guy would own Alice's network credentials and could masquerade as Alice anywhere on the network until she changes her password. (Be honest, when was the last time *you* changed *your* password?)

If Alice (on AlicesMachine) performs a network authentication with BobsMachine, thus establishing a network logon session there, that network logon session does not possess Alice's network credentials. Therefore, the daemon process on BobsMachine servicing her request has no possible way to masquerade as Alice on the network, even if Alice wanted to allow that. If Alice wants to delegate her credentials to the daemon on BobsMachine, she'd have to communicate her password hash to him. Imagine the implications of this! It's as if she had given her password away; there is no limit in time or space on what that daemon can do with Alice's credentials. Thus NTLM *does not support* delegation of credentials. The protocol just wasn't designed with this in mind. If the daemon attempts to use Alice's logon session to make NTLM-authenticated network requests, it'll end up using a NULL session instead. Speaking of NULL sessions . . .

NULL Sessions and Anonymity

Imagine that you wanted to have a system in which some clients were authenticated and others were not. To perform role- or object-centric access control, you'd have to have security contexts for both types of clients, plus a way of distinguishing the difference between the two that you could leverage directly in your access control scheme.

A security context implies a token, and a token implies a logon session. So in order to represent authenticated and anonymous clients polymorphically, you need to be able to establish a logon session for an anonymous client. That may sound bizarre, but it is possible on Windows and is actually very convenient for application developers. With that said, it's critically important that you know what the anonymous logon session looks like and how to control access to it.

The anonymous logon session is often referred to as a *NULL session* (the anonymous network connection is also sometimes referred to as a NULL session, which can cause some confusion), and the NTLM authentication protocol is one way of setting this up. If you look at a packet trace for the NTLM exchange between the client and server during NULL session establishment, you'll still see the Negotiate, Challenge, and Response messages, although they'll be quite empty of most content. If it seems strange to bother with a three-leg handshake even though we aren't truly authenticating, well, you aren't the only one who finds this strange. My guess is that it has to do with NTLM's early ties to the Server Message Block (SMB) protocol, which is the protocol that the Windows file system redirector uses. If you compare this with DCE RPC (and therefore COM, whose foundations lie on DCE RPC), DCE RPC has a provision for unauthenticated clients; it simply doesn't bother with the authentication handshake at all if the client doesn't want to be authenticated.

If you aren't using NTLM (perhaps you're using Kerberos), the way you represent an unauthenticated client is by not sending any authentication information to the server at all. In this case, no logon session will be established at all, which means you can't use your normal access-checking code paths because you won't have a token for the client. Windows 2000 provides a function that can help if you find this to be a problem:

```
BOOL ImpersonateAnonymousToken(
  HANDLE ThreadHandle    // in
);
```

This function is exported from ADVAPI32.DLL and is declared in winbase.h, but for some reason (perhaps an oversight), this useful function is not documented on MSDN as of this writing, so caveat emptor. The idea here is that if you don't have a security context for the client at all, you can use this special anonymous security context instead.[9]

Calling this function produces a token that references a hardwired logon session known as the *anonymous logon session* (like the System logon session, it also has a hardcoded identifier defined as ANONYMOUS_LOGON_LUID in winnt.h). The resulting token[10] after calling this function is shown in Figure 7.5. Using an NTLM exchange to produce a NULL logon session results in a token that looks similar, with the addition of the Network SID indicating that this is a network logon session (thus the asterisk next to it in the figure).

So how does one control access to the anonymous logon session? It includes the Everyone SID (as *all* tokens do); thus, if you grant access to Everyone, this clearly includes the anonymous logon session. (Please note that distributed systems will often provide special additional access checks for anonymous users; for instance, in the file system, just granting access to Everyone on a network share isn't quite sufficient to allow NULL sessions to access them. Discussions of how various communication subsystems deal with this are provided in the following chapters.) If you're using an object-centric access control model, one way of protecting yourself is to explicitly deny the anonymous logon SID (S-1-5-7). But in Windows 2000 (and most versions of Windows NT 4) there is an easier way. Read on.

---

[9] Note that some servers simply reject all requests from anonymous clients. In this case, you wouldn't bother creating a security context for an anonymous client; you'd just fail the request and move on.

[10] If the default DACL looks strange, that's because it's granting specific permissions, not generic permissions (interestingly enough, 0x01FF is equivalent to TOKEN_ALL_ACCESS). This is a rather nasty state of affairs for a default DACL, and thus I'd recommend that if you use ImpersonateAnonymousToken at all, you only use it to obtain a token temporarily for the purpose of performing access checks. (One hopes that Microsoft will clean up this implementation and document it at some point; it's quite useful.)

```
                    NULL session token
         ┌──────────────────────────────────────┐
         │ User Name: ANONYMOUS LOGON            │
         │ User SID: S-1-5-7                     │
         │                                       │
         │ Group SIDs:                           │
         │ Everyone                              │
         │ Network*                              │
         │                                       │
         │ Privileges: (none)                    │
         │                                       │
         │ Defaults for New Objects:             │
         │ Owner SID: Anonymous Logon            │
         │ Group SID: Anonymous Logon            │
         │ Default DACL:                         │
         │ grant 0x000F01FF to Everyone          │
         └──────────────────────────────────────┘
```

Figure 7.5. A token for the NULL session

Because the Windows NT 4 ACL editor really couldn't deal with negative ACEs in any reasonable fashion, in Service Pack 3 Microsoft added a new well-known SID called *Authenticated Users* (S-1-5-11). This SID is present as an authorization attribute in all tokens except those for the anonymous logon session, and allows you to control anonymous access with purely positive ACEs. To do this, instead of granting access to Everyone, grant access only to Authenticated Users.[11]

So far, this chapter has discussed at length the way NULL sessions work, the resulting anonymous logon session, and how to perform access control with NULL sessions in mind. What has not been discussed is how a client chooses to use a NULL session in the first place.

You won't normally see an NTLM NULL session exchange unless the client actually has *no network credentials at all*. My rule of thumb is that the system

---

[11] In Windows NT 4, this SID is *not present* in tokens for the System logon session. This oversight was corrected in Windows 2000. The upshot is that on Windows NT 4, if you want to grant access to all authenticated users and simply want to filter out the anonymous logon session, you should grant access not only to the Authenticated Users SID, but also to SYSTEM (which is technically an authenticated user; it's the operating system, for heaven's sake).

will attempt to use a NULL session if the client has NULL network credentials. When do you have NULL network credentials? The obvious case is when your security context is that of the anonymous logon session. A less obvious case is the SYSTEM logon session in Windows NT 4, where machines are not truly first-class principals. If you're running as SYSTEM and you attempt to perform NTLM authentication, you'll end up with a NULL session every time. On Windows 2000, if the machine is a principal in a Kerberos domain, it can be represented with its Kerberos credentials.

Another case in which you have NULL network credentials is an NTLM network logon session. If, for instance, in the middle tier of a three-tier system, you impersonate a remote client, your thread will enter a security context with NULL network credentials (the client already spent his or her one network hop getting to the middle tier). If you try to use the client's logon session to communicate with the back tier, the best you'll do is establish a NULL session.

Guests and Anonymity

NULL sessions are only used when the client is using a logon session with NULL network credentials. What if the client actually has credentials on his or her system, but the server has no trust path to the client's authority? Or what if the client is using some local account that the server has never heard of before? In this case, even using NTLM, a NULL session will not be established; rather, authentication will simply fail.

In order to group all these "unknown clients with credentials" into a common category and treat them polymorphically, each Windows machine has a well-known account named Guest. The SID is composed of the machine/domain identifier followed by a well-known RID:

```
DOMAIN_USER_RID_GUEST
```

The Guest account is normally disabled by default, but by enabling it and setting the password to an empty string (the default value), all clients with unknown authorities (or local accounts with no match on the server) will obtain a logon session under the guise of Guest on that machine. Note that this is a per-machine setting. (Enabling the Guest account on a domain controller only affects the domain controller; it doesn't have any special affect on the

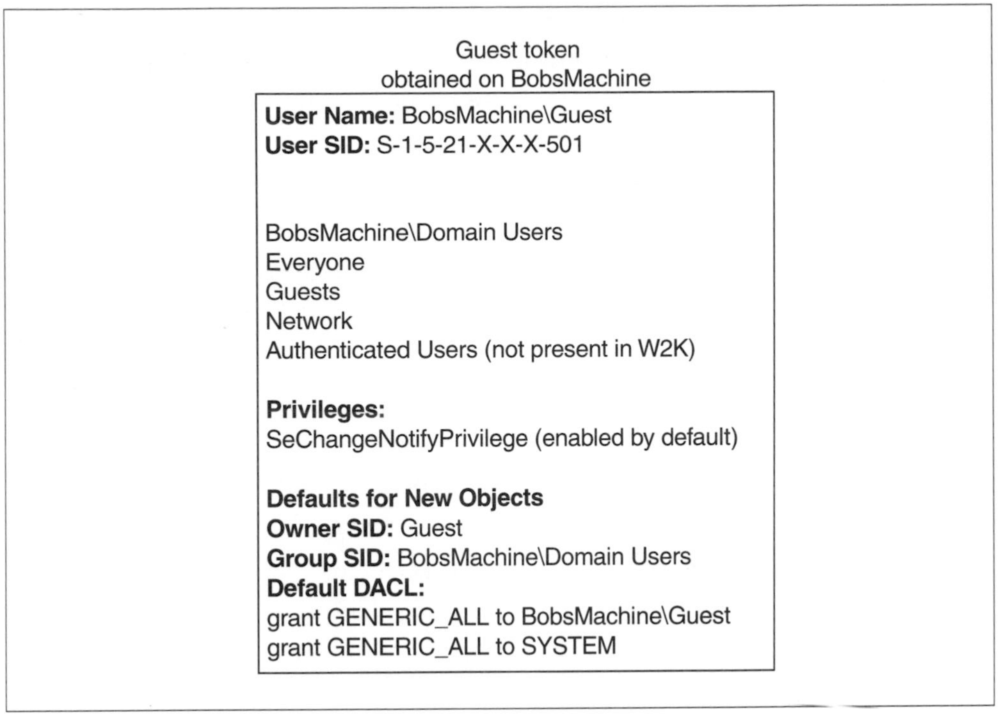

```
                    Guest token
               obtained on BobsMachine

    User Name: BobsMachine\Guest
    User SID: S-1-5-21-X-X-X-501


    BobsMachine\Domain Users
    Everyone
    Guests
    Network
    Authenticated Users (not present in W2K)

    Privileges:
    SeChangeNotifyPrivilege (enabled by default)

    Defaults for New Objects
    Owner SID: Guest
    Group SID: BobsMachine\Domain Users
    Default DACL:
    grant GENERIC_ALL to BobsMachine\Guest
    grant GENERIC_ALL to SYSTEM
```

Figure 7.6.   A token for a guest

machines in the domain.) Figure 7.6 shows the resulting token that the server obtains.[12]

Note that I've included the Authenticated Users SID with a note in Figure 7.6. In Windows NT 4, for some reason guests had this SID in their token.[13] Thus, if the Guest account was enabled, in order to correctly block access to *all* anonymous users (including guests), an administrator couldn't simply eschew the Everyone SID in favor of Authenticated Users because this would still allow

---

[12] On Windows 2000, `GetUserName` (while impersonating a guest logon session) returns the name "Guest," but on earlier versions of Windows, it used to return the name of the principal (or at least who that principal purported to be). Also note that the token shown here is just an example; since you can physically control the groups and privileges assigned to Guest (as opposed to the anonymous logon), a Guest token might look different on your system.

[13] This shocked the heck out me the first time I discovered this subtlety (and it always shocked students who attended my security classes at DevelopMentor). It also probably shocked a lot of administrators.

guests to leak through. The administrator had to explicitly add a negative ACE to deny access to guests. (Of course, disabling the Guest account blocks all guest logons, but administrators often need more fine-grained control.)

In Windows 2000, the Authenticated Users SID is *not present* in a Guest token. The other correction introduced in Windows 2000 (mentioned in footnote 11) is that tokens for the System logon session now include the Authenticated Users SID. So finally, three years after the Authenticated Users SID was originally introduced (Windows NT Service Pack 3), it actually works the way you would expect it to work!

It is possible to place a non-empty password on the Guest account for a particular machine. In this case, the client's password must match the one you've chosen (although this isn't documented, it appears to be verified via the NTLM challenge/response mechanism). Setting an empty password on the Guest account (which is the default state of affairs) indicates that you don't care what the client's password is.

If you choose to enable the Guest account, be aware that it may not work as smoothly as you might think. For instance, if an unknown client (Alice) happens to be using an account whose name matches that of a local account on your machine ("Alice"), the system will attempt to authenticate that user using the local account (not Guest), and if the passwords don't match, authentication will fail. One way of getting around this is to have the client specifically use the user name "Guest" when authenticating, which avoids this problem but requires a bit of extra work in the client application (it's doubtful that the client is actually logged in as "Guest" on the client machine, so the client-side application code needs to specify alternate credentials programmatically in most cases). Different ways of providing alternate credentials to various communication subsystems are described in the following chapters.

Benefits and Drawbacks of NTLM
NTLM has the following benefits:

- It is built in to Windows 2000 *and* earlier versions of Windows NT.
- It is simple to understand (at least conceptually).
- Authentication results in the exchange of a session key.

- It supports the use of centralized authorities.

- It supports cross-domain authentication.

NTLM has the following drawbacks:

- It is mostly undocumented; this can't be good.

- It can be expensive, especially with cross-domain authentication.

- It uses one-way authentication; the client proves his or her identity to the server, but never receives confirmation of the server's identity.

- The client and server must be connected to each other (thus, the protocol does not support disconnected operation such as authentication of MSMQ messages).

- Trust links must be operational for each client/server authentication handshake to succeed.

- The operating system must constantly cache a hash of the client's password in order to authenticate; if this hash is discovered by evil code lurking in the TCB, the client's network credentials have effectively been stolen.

- NTLM does not support cross-domain transitive trust relationships, making administration difficult.

- It does not support delegation of credentials.

The Kerberos v5 Authentication Protocol

Kerberos was originally introduced by the folks working on Project Athena at MIT back in the 1980s. Since then, Kerberos has undergone lots of revisions, but version 4 was the first version that was really fit for public consumption. The most recent version (v5) is documented in RFC 1510 and is the version of Kerberos that is implemented in Windows 2000. Compared with NTLM, Kerberos is much more sophisticated (and much more secure). It's also quite refreshing to study because it is fully documented; unlike the previous description of NTLM, there's no guesswork here.

The Three Subprotocols

Kerberos is named after the mythical three-headed dog that guards the entrance to Hell. I like to think of the three heads as representing the three subprotocols of Kerberos.[14] One of the beauties of this protocol is that the cost of authentication is effectively amortized across these three subprotocols, and each subprotocol is lazily performed on an as-needed basis.

Unlike NTLM, Kerberos *requires* a centralized authority (traditionally known as a **KDC** or **Key Distribution Center**). Each principal in a Kerberos **realm** has a master key, and the KDC itself also has a master key. A realm represents the scope of one authority (just like a domain does in Windows). Each master key is derived from a password.

Figure 7.7 shows the three subprotocols, their names, and the order in which they are executed. In the figure, Alice is the client, Bob is the server with whom she is authenticating, and Foo is Alice and Bob's authority, implemented by a Windows 2000 domain controller, which acts as a Kerberos KDC. In between the subprotocols, the client caches state that helps avoid unnecessary network round-trips; each entry in the cache consists of a Kerberos **ticket** plus a session key for use with that ticket.

Kerberos Tickets

For the last couple of years around Halloween, my wife and I have been taking our kids to a little pumpkin patch down on the corner close to our home. It's obligatory that my sons get to ride the ponies, jump in the bounce house, and ride on the kiddy Ferris wheel. The way this particular amusement park works is that you have to buy different colored tickets for each ride. If you don't have the right ticket, you don't get to ride.

Tickets in Kerberos are much like this; they are labeled with a target principal, and they can only be used to help you authenticate with that one particular principal. If Alice (a principal in the Foo realm) wants to authenticate with Bob and Mary (also principals in Foo), she'll actually need *three* tickets, not just two, because she'll first need to get a ticket for Foo before Foo will be willing to

---

[14] As I understand it, prior to Kerb 4 there were only two subprotocols, so my analogy doesn't hold much water from a technical standpoint, although I still like it. A third subprotocol was added in version 4 to allow implementations to avoid caching client passwords.

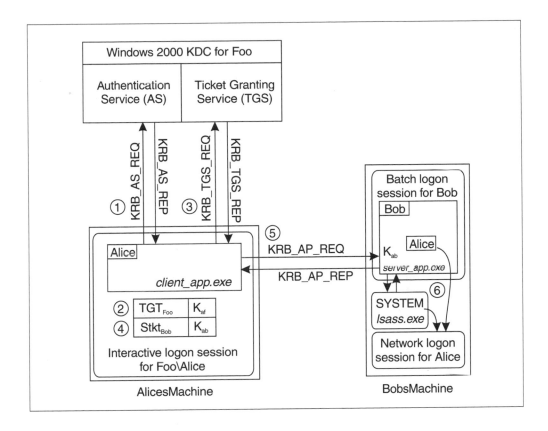

Figure 7.7. The three subprotocols of Kerberos v5

give her tickets for Bob and Mary. Foo is playing two roles here: It provides the Kerberos **Authentication Service** (AS) and the Kerberos **Ticket Granting Service** (TGS). The former is where Alice goes to get her very first ticket (the ticket for Foo), and the latter is where Alice goes to get tickets for Bob and Mary. These services are both provided by the KDC.[15] What's nice about a ticket is that once you have one, you can continue to use it to establish new authenticated connections until the ticket expires (expiration times are usually eight to ten hours, the duration of a typical workday).

---

[15] In Windows 2000, the AS and TGS are both provided by the domain controller; in other Implementations of Kerberos, it's possible to have these services be implemented by independent daemons, potentially running on different machines. This is possible because the KDC doesn't need to maintain state across the three subprotocols (that's the client's job by caching tickets).

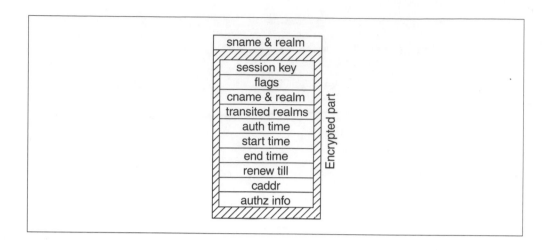

Figure 7.8. Anatomy of a Kerberos ticket

Figure 7.8 shows the basic contents of the ticket data structure. Note that the vast majority of the ticket is encrypted; only the principal to whom the ticket is targeted can actually decrypt the contents,[16] and that principal's name and realm are noted in plaintext at the top of the ticket.

Here's what each field means, briefly:

- **sname & realm** The target principal's name and realm.

- **session key** The all-important session key. Remember that after Alice and Bob authenticate, they each need to end up holding a session key to authenticate the data they send to one another. This is the server's copy of the key. The client receives her copy of the key when she receives the ticket from the KDC.

- **flags** These flags indicate any special circumstances under which the ticket was obtained, as well as any special ways the ticket may be used. I'll talk about a few of these options as I go through the protocol.

---

[16] Of course, because the principal's authority also knows the master key, the authority can also decrypt the ticket. This is important because it's this authority who will actually create the ticket in the first place!

- **cname & realm** The client principal's name and realm, which is used as a double check of the client's identity.

- **transited realms** An ordered list of realms that the client had to visit in order to get this ticket. This will make more sense after the discussion concerning cross-domain authentication and transitive trust relationships in Kerberos.

- **auth time** The time that the client obtained her very first ticket from the KDC (via the Authentication Service). This gives the server confirmation that she proved her identity to her KDC recently.

- **start time (optional)** This optional field is normally omitted (when omitted, the ticket is valid as of the auth time). It is generally only provided when a postdated ticket is used. This allows a client to obtain a ticket for use by a batch process later on after the client has gone home and her normal tickets have expired. A postdated ticket is flagged as such (via the flags field), and is generally also flagged as invalid and must be shipped to the KDC who issued it to be validated before it is used. This (theoretically) allows the KDC to maintain a hotlist of tickets that are known to be stolen.[17]

- **end time** The time after which the ticket becomes invalid and should be rejected by servers. Forcing tickets to expire puts limits on how much time an attacker has to get to a safe location in order to use a stolen ticket.

- **renew till (optional)** Similar to a postdated ticket, a renewable ticket allows a client application to use a ticket for a very long time without requiring the client principal to provide her master key to get a new ticket every eight hours. The ticket is actually renewed each time it's about to expire, which results in a fresh ticket for the client and a fresh session key. As discussed later, this also keeps the authorization attributes stored in the ticket from growing overly stale.

---

[17] I say *theoretically* because Windows 2000 doesn't document whether it maintains such a list or how an administrator would indicate the compromise of a machine and its corresponding tickets to update the list.

- **caddr (optional)** An optional list of client host addresses (for instance, IP addresses on a TCP/IP network) that indicates the machines from which the server should expect requests to originate. Network addresses are relatively easy to spoof, so this is only here to make it a bit more difficult for a bad guy to steal a ticket and a session key and use it from a safe location.

- **authz info (optional)** This field is where any authorization attributes (for Windows, this means group SIDs) are stored.

The KDC confers ownership of a ticket to a legitimate client by discreetly passing a copy of the session key to the client. No server will accept a ticket unless the client can prove that he or she knows the associated session key.

The First Subprotocol: KRB_AS_REQ/REP

When Alice first wants to participate in Kerberos (at the beginning of her workday, for instance), she must prove her identity to one of the KDCs in her realm. The way she does this is somewhat indirect: She requests a ticket by sending the KRB_AS_REQ message (for Authentication Service Request) to the KDC.[18] The KDC sends back a KRB_AS_REP (Authentication Service Reply). Figure 7.9 shows the contents of the request and reply.

The request includes the client's purported principal name and realm as well as the server's name; in this case, this is the client's authority. The request also includes a number of options (the requested start and end times, the requested network addresses from which the ticket may be used, whether the ticket should be renewable, and so on). The key thing to note is that when the KDC receives this request, it doesn't have proof of Alice's identity. As far as the KDC is concerned, it just received a request from a random source that purports to be Alice. And this is all right; read on.

The reply that comes back to Alice contains a ticket targeted at Alice's authority, but remember that a ticket is not enough—the client also needs the corresponding session key associated with the ticket. Thus the KRB_AS_REP message also contains the session key as well as confirmation of the target prin-

---

[18] All communication to the KDC on a TCP/IP network is directed to UDP or TCP port 88.

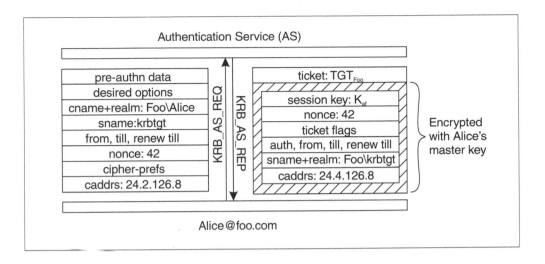

Figure 7.9   The KRB_AS_REQ and KRB_AS_REP messages

cipal and the options that were granted in the ticket. (Recall that Alice cannot see 90 percent of the ticket's contents; it's encrypted so that only the target principal can unlock it.) All this extra information that accompanies the ticket is encrypted with Alice's master key (which the KDC knows, by definition of being Alice's authority). So besides the KDC, only Alice can possibly use the ticket, because only she can decrypt the session key that comes back via the KRB_AS_REP message.

Allowing any random node on the network to send messages to the KDC and receive replies encrypted with a principal's master key opens the system up somewhat to an attacker, because the KDC will always reply with a KRB_AS_REP without knowing whether the requester is a legitimate client. This is the reason for the first optional field, the preauthentication data. The idea is that when Alice wishes to send a KRB_AS_REQ message, she should send some extra information to the KDC to prove her identity so the KDC doesn't just send replies willy-nilly. The most common technique is for Alice to simply encrypt a timestamp with her master key and send the resulting ciphertext as the preauthentication data. Now the attacker can only listen to legitimate requests as opposed to being able to initiate requests at will. So although the KDC doesn't *need* to know the identity of the principal sending the KRB_AS_REQ message, in practice it usually *does* know, and if configured to do so, it will reject any KRB_AS_REQ message without verifiable preauthentication data.[19]

Note the nonce that Alice sends to the KDC (and that the KDC sends back in the encrypted body of the reply). This simple value allows Alice to authenticate the KDC! If the encrypted nonce that Alice receives from the purported KDC decrypts to the value she sent in her request, she can be quite confident that it was the KDC who sent the reply,[20] because besides herself, only the KDC knows her master key. In Kerberos, nobody (not even the authority) escapes without being authenticated.

Alice can now take the ticket and its associated session key and add it to her ticket cache. She can now prove her identity to the KDC at any time (see the next section) and doesn't have to get a new ticket for the KDC until this one expires (typically eight hours later, which for many humans implies the next working day).

Kerberos Authenticators

I keep saying that a ticket isn't any good without an accompanying session key. Let's talk about why this is. What would happen if Alice were to simply send Bob a ticket that she had obtained for him? What exactly does the ticket prove? If Bob can successfully decrypt the ticket, he knows it must have been generated by a KDC from his realm (who else would know how to encrypt something with Bob's master key?) and that it was generated on Alice's behalf (the ticket contains the client's name). But if all Alice sends to Bob is the ticket, how does Bob know that a bad guy didn't record the ticket earlier and is simply replaying it now?

The way to prove that the sender is actually the owner of the ticket is to prove knowledge of the session key buried inside the ticket. If Alice can somehow convince Bob that she knows the session key in that ticket, Bob will be assured of her identity. Who could possibly know the session key? The KDC

---

[19] Windows 2000 allows the administrator to configure, on a per-principal basis, whether or not to require preauthentication in the KRB_AS_REQ message (this is the "Do not require Kerberos preauthentication" checkbox in Active Directory). By default, preauthentication is required.

[20] Replay attacks can be foiled (theoretically) by maintaining a replay cache. It's not documented whether the Windows 2000 implementation does this.

creates and packages the session key inside the ticket, but it's encrypted (along with most of the other information in the ticket) so that only Bob can read it. Recall that the KDC also sends a copy of the session key back to the requester (Alice, in this case) encrypted with the master key of the purported requester. (Look at the KRB_AS_REP message for an example.) Therefore Alice, whose name is listed as the client in the ticket, is the only principal who knows the session key (other than the KDC, who Bob trusts not to impersonate Alice).

NTLM used a challenge/response mechanism to demonstrate knowledge of a key without actually sending the key over the wire. Kerberos takes a different approach and collapses the three-leg handshake into a single leg by using a timestamp. When Alice sends a ticket to the target principal, she proves her knowledge of the session key (and thus her ownership of the ticket) by encrypting a very simple data structure with the session key. This is known as an *authenticator* (see Figure 7.10).

Here's how a server (Bob, say) validates a ticket/authenticator pair from Alice.

1. Bob decrypts the ticket with his master key, thus discovering the buried session key.

2. Bob uses the session key to decrypt the authenticator sent with the ticket.

3. Bob compares the client name in the authenticator with the client name in the ticket, rejecting the request if they don't match.

4. Bob takes the difference between the timestamp in the authenticator and the time on his machine, moving on to step 7 if the difference is within the allowable clock skew (an allowable clock skew of five minutes is typical).

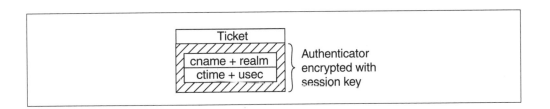

Figure 7.10. The Kerberos authenticator

5. If step 4 failed, Bob sends Alice the current (universal coordinated) time according to Bob's clock. This is simply a less efficient, nonce-based way to prove knowledge of the session key that kicks in if Alice's clock is not well synchronized.

6. Alice sends another authenticator using the corrected time.

7. Bob compares the timestamp in the authenticator with a list of recently received authenticators to verify that this is not a replay (this list is known as the *replay cache*), rejecting the request if a matching timestamp is found.

8. Bob updates his replay cache by adding this new timestamp and deleting any existing timestamps that have grown stale.

Bob has now developed trust in Alice's identity and has discovered a session key that he and Alice can use to authenticate data that they send to one another.

As you can see, machines involved in Kerberos authentication rely on a common time source.[21] Out-of-synch clocks can cause extra round-trips in a Kerberos-based system. It can also paralyze systems that don't implement a fallback nonce-based authentication mechanism as described in steps 5 and 6. I once tried changing a workstation clock on an early beta of Windows 2000 (which didn't implement this) and the system melted down fast.

The Second Subprotocol: KRB_TGS_REQ/REP

When Alice obtained a ticket for her KDC, it was only so that she could later go back to the KDC (proving her identity with her KDC ticket and its associated session key) and obtain tickets for servers on the network that hold secured resources that she needs. Getting to those resources is what Alice really cares about. Fetching that initial ticket was just a required detail that provided Alice entry to the Ticket Granting Service. That initial ticket is thus often referred to as a **ticket-granting ticket**, or **TGT**.

Now that Alice has a TGT, she can send it to the KDC any time she needs to obtain tickets for other principals in the same realm. Let's say that she arrived

---

[21] Windows 2000 uses the Simple Network Time Protocol to keep clocks synchronized automatically.

at work at 9:00 A.M. (and gets her TGT at that point) and then suddenly at 11:30 A.M. a client program she was running decides to make an authenticated COM call to a server running on some other machine on the network (for now, let's assume that the server process is running as a principal named Bob, who is from the same realm as Alice). The Kerberos SSP in the client process sends a request to the KDC on Alice's behalf (one that looks remarkably similar to the one we just saw) requesting a ticket for Bob. This is the Ticket Granting Service (TGS) request and reply, thus the name of the messages (see Figure 7.11).

In this case, the slot for preauthentication data is filled with Alice's TGT/authenticator pair, which proves her identity to the KDC. Alice is requesting a ticket for Bob. Can you see anything else that's different about this pair of messages compared with the KRB_AS_REQ/REP messages?

What you may have noticed is that the reply is *not* encrypted with Alice's master key; rather, it is encrypted with the session key that Alice obtained earlier for use with the KDC. If it were encrypted with Alice's master key, then that key would have to be available to the Kerberos SSP on Alice's machine not only at 9:00 A.M. when she first appeared on the machine and the first subprotocol was executed, but also now at 11:30 A.M. when the ticket request for Bob is satisfied. By encrypting the data with the session key, the system ensures that the only things that AlicesMachine needs to cache on Alice's behalf are her

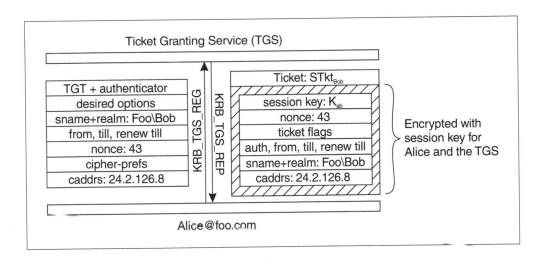

Figure 7.11. The KRB_TGS_REQ and KRB_TGS_REP messages

ticket/session key pairs, *not* her master key. Those session keys are only good for use with their associated tickets, and tickets expire each night when Alice goes home.

It's really quite elegant, unless Alice decides to work a double shift. If she hasn't yet acquired all the tickets she needs for the night, at some point a KRB_TGT_REQ message will fail miserably due to TGT expiration. What should the system do to prevent this?

It turns out that Windows 2000 normally requests a *renewable* TGT that the system can continue to revalidate over and over again (until the *renew-till* time in the ticket). Looking at a network sniff of the unencrypted KRB_AS_REQ from a Windows 2000 Server (build 2195), it's clear that the client does indeed request a renewable TGT (and a look in the ticket cache verifies that the KDC does in fact *issue* one). The Kerberos Policy settings (stored in the directory service and accessible via the Group Policy snap-in) include the following properties:

Maximum lifetime for user ticket = 10 hours

Maximum lifetime for user ticket renewal = 7 days

These numbers were taken from my own installation of Windows 2000 Server (build 2195). The term *user ticket* is an administrator-friendly way of saying TGT. You'll also see the term *service ticket.* This represents any ticket that's not a TGT (the ticket for Bob that Alice just requested is considered a service ticket, for instance).

What happens after the seven-day renewal period expires? One choice would be to prompt the client for her password. Another choice would be to ignore one of the principal tenets of modern Kerberos (that the client's master key shouldn't be cached) and cache it anyway. Microsoft took the latter approach; the master key is cached in the logon session. My only rationalization for this is that a password hash needs to be cached anyway in order to allow the client to perform NTLM authentication with downlevel servers. I must admit that I was disappointed to see this behavior though.[22]

---

[22] Especially since I discovered this immediately after describing how wonderful RFC 1510 was (because it didn't require caching of client passwords) to a group of students at a DevelopMentor Guerrilla event.

The Third Subprotocol: KRB_AP_REQ/REP

The first two subprotocols are really concrete. The client SSP simply forms messages exactly as the Kerberos spec requires, sends them to port 88 of the closest KDC in the client's realm, and gets a reply formatted exactly as specified in RFC 1510. The third subprotocol turns out to be just a small part of a larger conversation that occurs between the client and server when the client wants to establish an authenticated connection with the server. This means that the application (AP) request and reply are piggybacked on top of whatever protocol the client and server happen to be using to get their real work done: raw TCP/UDP, SMB, RPC, or DCOM, for instance. Regardless of the communication protocol, however, the contents of the embedded Kerberos messages are always the same (see Figure 7.12).

Because all the hard work has already been done by the KDC (resulting in a ticket), the application protocol is really quite simple. In fact, the reply is entirely optional and is only used if the client wishes to authenticate the server.

The *options* field in the KRB_AP_REQ message indicates (among other things) whether the client wishes mutual authentication, in which case the server is required to send a KRB_AP_REP message embedded in the reply. The rest of the request message consists of a ticket/authenticator pair that proves the client's identity and gives the server a copy of the session key.

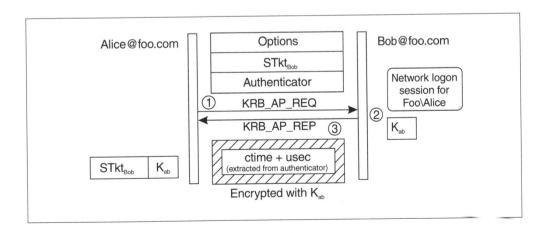

Figure 7.12.   The KRB_AP_REQ and KRB_AP_REP messages

To prove his identity to the client (Alice), the server (Bob) must decrypt the client's authenticator with the session key, extract the timestamp found there, reencrypt it with the session key, and send this back to the client (KRB_AP _REP). If the client requested mutual authentication, she will be expecting to receive the same timestamp she sent in the authenticator; by decrypting the same timestamp from the reply, she concludes that the sender knows the session key (by virtue of being able to decrypt the ticket), and she can feel confident that she now shares a session key with her intended target principal.

Cross-Realm Authentication and the Path of Trust

Kerberos supports cross-realm authentication, as does NTLM; however, the design of Kerberos makes transitive trust relationships between authorities feasible.

Recall what happens when Alice authenticates with another principal (Bob) in her own realm (Foo). Alice performs the first subprotocol with Foo, getting a ticket to Foo's Ticket Granting Service. She then returns this ticket to Foo via the second subprotocol, requesting a ticket for Bob. Foo verifies Alice's identity and issues the ticket, plus a session key for Alice and Bob to use. Alice sends this ticket (plus an authenticator to prove her identity) to Bob. Bob decrypts this ticket with his master key, verifies the authenticator, and believes that Alice is who she says she is, because the ticket says so (the ticket came from Foo, and Bob trusts that Foo verified Alice's identity before issuing the ticket).

What would happen if you replaced Bob in this example with the Ticket Granting Service for another realm (Quux, say)? In other words, if the Ticket Granting Service for realm Quux had an account in realm Foo, Alice would be able to get a ticket for Quux's Ticket Granting Service the same way she got a ticket for Bob. Alice could then prove her identity to Quux's Ticket Granting Service and obtain tickets for principals in Quux's realm. But what does this mean for Quux? The first communication Alice has with Quux is the KRB_TGS_REQ message, in which Alice asks for a ticket for some principal in the Quux realm. Quux can verify that Alice knows the session key inside the TGT (how this works is discussed shortly), but the TGT *wasn't issued by Quux;* it was issued by Foo. Thus Quux must *trust* Foo to have correctly verified Alice's identity. If Foo has been compromised, the request could actually be coming from *anybody* masquerading as Alice. This is the same idea as cross-domain authentication in NTLM: Authority Quux trusts authority Foo to vouch for Foo's principals.

Assuming this trust exists (Quux's administrator trusts Foo's administrator to guard the authentication service for realm Foo), physically what has to happen is that Foo needs to be able to produce a ticket (a TGT) that Quux can consume. Once again, think back to what happens when Alice gets a ticket for Bob: Foo encrypts the innards of Bob's ticket with Bob's master key (which is registered in Foo's security database). So when Alice asks Foo for a ticket to Quux, Foo encrypts this with Quux's master key that is registered in Foo's security database (recall that Quux has registered as a principal in Foo's realm). So when Quux receives Alice's KRB_TGS_REQ message, the ticket is encrypted with the shared key between Foo and Quux, and Quux can decrypt it and verify that Foo has vouched for Alice.

Now consider what happens if Alice is a principal in realm A, and Bob is a principal in realm C. Assume that C trusts B (by registering its Ticket Granting Service as a principal of B's realm), and B trusts A in the same fashion. In order for Alice to authenticate with Bob, she must follow the path of trust: Alice contacts her authority (A), getting a TGT for B. Alice then contacts B, requesting a TGT for C. Alice finally contacts C, requesting a ticket for Bob.

The neat thing about this mechanism is that once Alice is finished with all this work, her ticket cache will contain TGTs for A, B, and C, and she won't have to traverse that particular trust path again until those tickets expire. Because this mechanism is so efficient, it's very natural to implement transitive trust relationships between authorities to simplify administration in a large enterprise. Each domain in a Windows 2000 Active Directory **forest** is linked (directly or indirectly) to all other domains in that forest via bidirectional transitive trust relationships. If an administrator wishes to avoid cross-domain authentication into a particular domain, that domain must be moved into a separate forest.[23]

---

[23] As of this writing, I know of no documented way to disable trust relationships between domains in a forest other than separating the domains into separate forests. This has nothing to do with Kerberos; it's simply Microsoft's way of keeping things simple for administrators. Administrators need to be aware of the implications, however: Each domain in a forest is trusted by all other domains in that forest to correctly authenticate its principals.

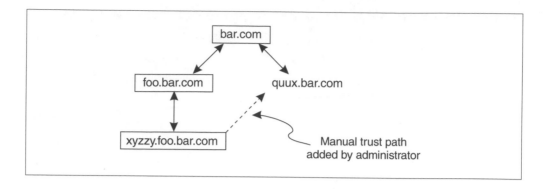

Figure 7.13. A forest of trust

It should now be clear what the *transited realms* field in a ticket represents. When Bob receives the ticket, he'll know (theoretically) every single trust path that was exercised, and if he suspects that realm B (for instance) has been compromised, he can deny Alice's request. The reason I say *theoretically* is that, although this information is present in the ticket, getting at it is not at all straightforward.

One question that hasn't been addressed is this: How does Alice discover the path of trust to get to Bob's realm? How does she know that she needs to go to B in order to get to C? The Kerberos spec doesn't address this in detail, but many implementations simply use the DNS hierarchy (or equivalent) to figure out where to place transitive trusts.[24] Figure 7.13 shows an example of a DNS hierarchy encapsulated in an Active Directory forest. Each node (domain) trusts its parent, and each parent trusts each of its children. Thus the *natural* path of trust from xyzzy.foo.bar.com to quux.bar.com passes through foo.bar.com and bar.com.

Administrators can also add *extra* trust relationships explicitly (perhaps to improve performance or availability) between any two domains that would not

---

[24] As you add new domains to an Active Directory forest, Windows 2000 creates two trust relationships: one from the parent to the child, and one from the child to the parent. So technically, although Windows 2000 uses the DNS hierarchy to figure out where to *establish* trusts initially, at runtime the system discovers the actual trust paths by querying the directory service. This allows the addition of short-circuited trust paths.

normally have a trust (this can be done via the Active Directory Domains and Trusts MMC snap-in). This simply short-circuits the natural trust path, as shown in Figure 7.13.

Figure 7.14 shows an example of cross-realm authentication. Note that once again, there must be a path of trust from the server's authority back to the authority of the client. This is a great rule of thumb for determining whether you might be having authentication problems. Ask yourself the following question: Is there an unbroken path of trust from the target server principal back to the client's authority? Peek in the ticket cache to see how far along the path the client progressed before there was a problem (how to enumerate the ticket cache is discussed later in this chapter).

Delegation of Credentials in Kerberos

Unlike NTLM, in which clients must prove their identities to servers using a master secret (the password hash), Kerberos only requires a client to prove knowledge of a session key, and that session key is associated with a ticket that has built-in limitations on its validity in space and time. Each Kerberos ticket can optionally have network addresses associated with it that limit its validity

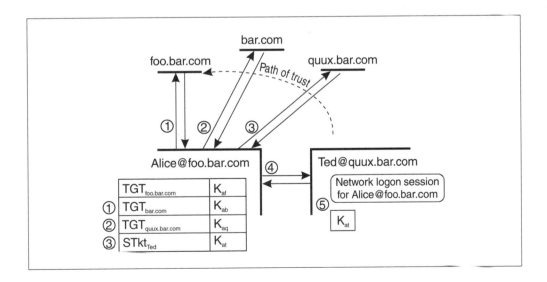

Figure 7.14. Kerberos cross-realm authentication

in space.[25] Each Kerberos ticket is required to have a start and end time that limits its validity in time. Because of these limits, and because the client principal's master key is not needed *at all* to execute the third subprotocol, Kerberos can easily support delegation of credentials. In fact, there are two ways to do this in Kerberos: the fast and loose (but easy) way, and the conservative (but harder) way. I'll discuss both mechanisms and tell you which mechanism Microsoft chose for its implementation.

The Proxy Ticket

Let's say that Alice needs a service from Bob, but in order for Bob to do his work, he'll need to acquire secure network resources on Alice's behalf. (One classic example of this situation is a remote print spooler, which needs to have the client's credentials in order to read the client's file from the file server before printing it.)

As long as Alice knows exactly which principals Bob will need to talk to on her behalf, she can prefetch all the tickets Bob will need ahead of time. To make it concrete, let's say that Bob will need to talk to Ted and Sue, but he'll need to have those conversations while pretending to be Alice. Assuming Alice is comfortable with this, she will talk to her KDC, asking for *proxy* tickets for Ted and Sue. She'll have to specify Bob's network address if she wants to limit the tickets' validity in space, and she'll have to communicate the ticket/session key pairs to Bob discreetly so that he can use them from his machine. This latter problem is easy to solve, because Alice and Bob will first authenticate and exchange their own session key, which can be used to seal their conversation (see Figure 7.15).

The resulting tickets will be marked as proxy tickets, and as such *must* contain special authorization attributes (Kerberos doesn't define what these look like) that put limits on how Alice's credentials can be used (for instance: the holder of this ticket may only print the file named "quux" found on machine "baz" via the share "xyzzy").

---

[25] As mentioned before, network addresses are not intrinsically secure, but marking tickets with an expected source address helps impede the bad guys by forcing them to spoof network addresses if using stolen tickets from "safe" machines.

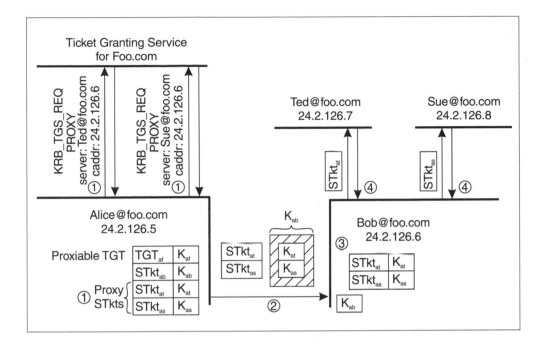

Figure 7.15. Obtaining, communicating, and using proxy tickets

All this configuration (setting specialized authorization attributes, knowing which principals Bob will need to talk to, knowing the network address for Bob, etc.) becomes rather troublesome in an implementation. Imagine the APIs you'd have to call to set something like this up for Alice; it's tough, but then again, delegating a client's credentials shouldn't be taken lightly.

The Forwarded TGT

The fast and loose way for Alice to delegate her credentials is to simply ask the KDC for a *forwarded* TGT that she can give to Bob. She'll hand off this second TGT (she got her first TGT during the initial subprotocol with her KDC) and its associated session key (discreetly) to Bob (see Figure 7.16). Bob can now use this TGT to obtain as many tickets as he likes on Alice's behalf (until the TGT expires).

The difference between the normal TGT that Alice uses and the forwarded TGT that she gives to Bob is twofold: The forwarded TGT has Bob's network

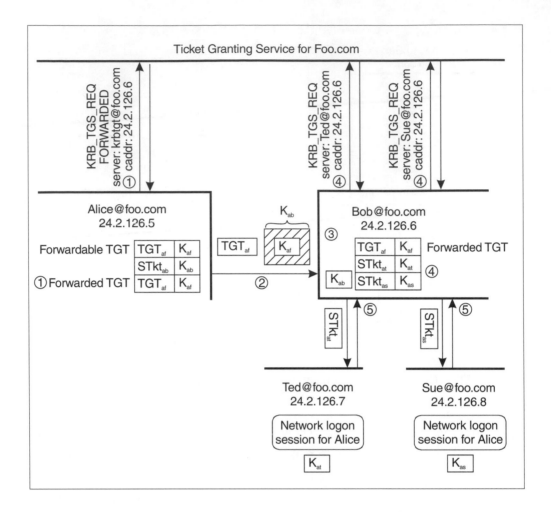

Figure 7.16. Obtaining, communicating, and using a forwarded TGT

address (or *no* network addresses, which means it can be used from *any* machine) and is marked with a flag indicating that it is a forwarded ticket. Unlike proxy tickets, a forwarded TGT does not need to have any special authorization attributes limiting its use. It can be used for *any* purpose.

What has Alice done in this case? She has delegated her identity to Bob for a specific period of time, and has (optionally) specified the network address from which that identity may be used. This is quite easy to implement and is the form of delegation supported by Windows 2000. You should avoid relying on it too much, however, because there's no limit in space as to how far Alice's credentials can be delegated (in other words, Bob can delegate her credentials again to Ted, and Ted to Mary, and so on). In fact, it seems as though the KDC ought to have *some* sort of limits on this potentially dangerous mechanism. It turns out that there are two basic forms of protection provided by the Windows 2000 KDC—read on.

Windows 2000 and Delegation of Credentials

Kerberos includes a special flag that may be set or cleared inside a ticket: OK-AS-DELEGATE.[26] This indicates to the holder of the ticket (Alice) whether the server principal (Bob) is trusted by his KDC to use proxy tickets or forwarded TGTs to delegate client credentials. This is only a hint to a client; the KDC cannot stop the client from ignoring this setting, but the Windows 2000 Kerberos SSP on the client side *does* check this flag, and will refuse to send a forwarded TGT to a server whose ticket doesn't include this flag (even if delegation is requested programmatically via the impersonation level).

In Windows 2000, you can control whether a server's ticket will contain this flag on a per-principal basis. For user accounts, you must check the "Account is trusted for delegation" checkbox, and for computer accounts, you must check the "Trust computer for delegation" checkbox to enable this. By default *no* accounts are trusted for delegation, except for domain controllers; machine accounts for domain controllers are trusted for delegation by default.

In Windows 2000, the first time Alice authenticates with a server whose ticket is marked OK-AS-DELEGATE, the system attempts to obtain a forwarded TGT. This second TGT can then be sent to the server to enable delegation. An administrator can instruct the KDC not to issue a forwardable TGT to a particular client in the first place (thus no forwarded TGTs will be issued to that client, disallowing the client from delegating his or her credentials). The way to do this is to check the "Account is sensitive and may not be delegated" checkbox in the directory service properties for the client's account.

---

[26] Technically, RFC 1510 (issued in 1993) mentions no such flag. This flag is described in the Kerberos revision Internet drafts. (As of this writing, the most recent was filed as draft-ietf-cat-kerberos-revisions-05.txt in March 2000.)

Some Notes on Ticket Expiration

What exactly does an eight-hour ticket lifetime really mean? Does it mean that just before the eighth hour, a TGT can be used to obtain a new ticket that will last another eight hours? The answer is no. Any ticket that the KDC produces is required (by RFC 1510) to limit the end time to that specified in the TGT (there are other limitations as well that can be set via administrative policy). So if Alice's TGT expires at 17:00 and it's now 16:30, any tickets she obtains using that TGT will only be valid until 17:00.

Also remember that during the KRB_AP_REQ/REP handshake, the server obtains the client's global authorization attributes (groups) from the ticket. Thus if the client's ticket is seven hours old, those authorization attributes are also seven hours old. It may be necessary to have the client flush his or her ticket cache and get a new server ticket if these attributes need to be refreshed. It turns out that there is even a documented way of doing this.

Along this line of thought, here's an interesting question. What happens when the administrator of the Foo domain disables Alice's account (by checking the "Account is disabled" box)? If Alice has already obtained a TGT for Foo and a ticket for Bob, she can reauthenticate with Bob as many times as she likes (using the same ticket) until the ticket expires. But what if Alice attempts to acquire a new ticket, perhaps for some other server principal? When Alice contacts the Ticket Granting Service on Foo, presents her TGT, and requests another ticket, the TGS at Foo has full knowledge that Alice's account is disabled, and yet it will continue to issue new tickets to Alice. This troubled me at first,[27] until I postulated what would happen during cross-domain authentication. Assume that Alice had previously obtained a TGT for authority Bar from Foo (this assumes that Bar trusts Foo). Unlike Foo, Bar has no idea that Alice's account is disabled, and will continue to issue new tickets to Alice as long as her TGT is valid. With this in mind, Foo's behavior is reasonable and consistent. All this comes to an end once Alice's original TGT from Foo (specifically, from the Authentication Service at Foo) expires. When the system attempts to automatically renew Alice's TGT, the Authentication Service will reject the request.

---

[27] Mike Woodring at DevelopMentor pointed out this behavior, and it took some thought to rationalize what was going on.

Managing the Kerberos Ticket Cache

Windows 2000 maintains an individual ticket cache for each logon session, and there are a few things you can do programmatically to manipulate the cache for your own logon session (or for someone else's if you are running in the TCB). The function `LsaCallAuthenticationPackage` allows you to make several different types of requests to the Kerberos authentication package, including enumerating the tickets in a ticket cache, requesting new tickets, and purging the cache.

```
NTSTATUS LsaCallAuthenticationPackage(
  HANDLE LsaHandle,                  // in
  ULONG  AuthenticationPackage,  // in
  PVOID  ProtocolSubmitBuffer,   // in
  ULONG  SubmitBufferLength,      // in
  PVOID* ProtocolReturnBuffer,   // out
  PULONG ReturnBufferLength,      // out
  PNTSTATUS ProtocolStatus        // out
);
```

This function is really easy to use; you'll first need to connect to the LSA and look up the Kerberos authentication package index (I'll demonstrate this shortly), but after that, the rest of the parameters to this function represent a way to make any number of requests and get a corresponding reply by filling out a request structure and getting back a response structure. If you successfully contact the target authentication package, the return value from this function will be 0, indicating success, and the *ProtocolStatus* parameter will indicate the actual return value from the authentication package.

Before you can call this function, you'll need to connect to the LSA and obtain an authentication package index:

```
NTSTATUS LsaConnectUntrusted(
  PHANDLE LsaHandle                  // out
);

NTSTATUS LsaLookupAuthenticationPackage(
  HANDLE        LsaHandle,            // in
  PLSA_STRING PackageName,            // in
  PULONG        AuthenticationPackage // out
```

```
);

#define MICROSOFT_KERBEROS_A "Kerberos"
```

The first function is the normal way to connect to the LSA. "Untrusted" simply means that you're not necessarily part of the TCB. You'll still be able to use this handle to manipulate the ticket cache for your own logon session, just not anybody else's.

The second function is simply another hoop that you have to jump through in order to talk to the Kerberos authentication package. The manifest constant you'll need to use to initialize *PackageName* is listed (a helper function for initializing the LSA_STRING data structure is shown in the appendix). After calling this function, you'll have the authentication package index you need to invoke LsaCallAuthenticationPackage.

To enumerate the contents of the ticket cache, you'll use the following two data structures:

```
typedef struct _KERB_QUERY_TKT_CACHE_REQUEST {
  KERB_PROTOCOL_MESSAGE_TYPE MessageType,
  LUID                       LogonId;  // optional
} KERB_QUERY_TKT_CACHE_REQUEST;

typedef struct _KERB_QUERY_TKT_CACHE_RESPONSE {
  KERB_PROTOCOL_MESSAGE_TYPE MessageType;
  ULONG                      CountOfTickets;
  KERB_TICKET_CACHE_INFO     Tickets[ANYSIZE_ARRAY];
} KERB_QUERY_TKT_CACHE_RESPONSE;
```

The *MessageType* of the request should be set to KerbQueryTicket CacheMessage, and the *LogonId* field should be set to 0 to indicate that you'd like to browse the ticket cache associated with your thread's current logon session.

The response is basically a counted array of data structures, each of which tells you a little bit about the ticket being enumerated:

```
typedef struct _KERB_TICKET_CACHE_INFO {
  UNICODE_STRING ServerName;
  UNICODE_STRING RealmName;
  LARGE_INTEGER  StartTime;
```

```
    LARGE_INTEGER   EndTime;
    LARGE_INTEGER   RenewTime;
    LONG            EncryptionType;
    ULONG           TicketFlags;    // from RFC 1510
} KERB_TICKET_CACHE_INFO;
```

Visit my Web site for a sample program (`tktview.exe`) that enumerates and prints information about all the tickets in your ticket cache using these functions.

Purging your ticket cache is also quite straightforward, and is simple enough to be shown here as an example. You'll still use the same functions as before to make the call, but you'll specify a different message structure:

```
typedef struct _KERB_PURGE_TKT_CACHE_REQUEST {
  KERB_PROTOCOL_MESSAGE_TYPE MessageType;
  LUID                       LogonId; // optional
  UNICODE_STRING             ServerName;
  UNICODE_STRING             RealmName;
} KERB_PURGE_TKT_CACHE_REQUEST;
```

Once again, if you're running in the TCB, you can purge the ticket cache for *any* logon session. If you're not, you must set the *LogonId* field to 0 to indicate that you'd like to purge the ticket cache for the logon session of the calling thread. (The following example relies on a couple of helper functions that are provided at my web site.)

```
void _purgeTicketCache() {
  // connect to the LSA (doesn't require TCB)
  HANDLE hLSA;
  NTSTATUS s = LsaConnectUntrusted(&hLSA);
  if (s)
    _lsaErr(L"LsaConnectUntrusted", s);

  // look up the index for the Kerb authentication pkg
  LSA_STRING sPackage;
  _initString(sPackage, MICROSOFT_KERBEROS_NAME_A);
  ULONG nAuthnPkg;
  s = LsaLookupAuthenticationPackage(hLSA, &sPackage,
                                     &nAuthnPkg);
```

```
if (s)
  _lsaErr(L"LsaLookupAuthenticationPackage", s);

// set up the request message
KERB_PURGE_TKT_CACHE_REQUEST request;
ZeroMemory(&request, sizeof request);
request.MessageType = KerbPurgeTicketCacheMessage;

// make the call
NTSTATUS sPkg;
s = LsaCallAuthenticationPackage(hLSA, nAuthnPkg,
                         &request, sizeof request,
                         0, 0, &sPkg);
if (s)
  _lsaErr(L"LsaCallAuthenticationPackage", s);

// figure out what actually happened
switch (sPkg) {
case 0:
  wprintf(L"Successfully purged ticket cache.\n");
  break;
case SEC_E_NO_CREDENTIALS:
  wprintf(L"Ticket cache was already empty.\n");
  break;
default:
  _lsaErr(L"KerbPurgeTicketCacheMessage", sPkg);
  break;
  }
}
```

Why might you want to purge your ticket cache? Well, although a ticket cache is great from the perspective of making authentication efficient, it also can lead to stale security contexts. When Alice sends her ticket to Bob, that ticket contains Alice's authorization attributes (group SIDs) *at the time she obtained the ticket* (which means this information could be several hours old). Alice can easily fix this by purging her ticket cache, which will force her SSP to obtain fresh tickets on her behalf the next time she authenticates with Bob. Fortunately, authorization attributes don't change that often, but if you run into a situation in which you've been recently added to a group and yet you are not being granted the access you now deserve to a remote resource, remember this tip.

Benefits and Drawbacks of Kerberos

The benefits of Kerberos are as follows:

- It is fully documented (RFC 1510).

- It is built in to Windows 2000.

- Authentication results in the exchange of a session key.

- Kerberos supports the use of centralized authorities.

- It supports cross-domain authentication.

- It supports mutual authentication.

- It supports delegation of credentials.

- Ticket caching reduces round-trips, making the protocol less expensive and less sensitive to network outages.

- Ticket validity is limited in space and time.

- Because clients cache state (via tickets), the KDC can remain stateless across the three subprotocols (think load balancing and redundancy).

- According to RFC 1510, the client's master key may be forgotten after the first subprotocol ends, but Windows 2000 doesn't follow this particular suggestion in order to give the user a more satisfying experience (that is, until her master key is stolen).

Kerberos has the following drawbacks:

- Clocks must be synchronized (although the added support for slightly out-of-skew clocks in Windows 2000 really means that clocks *should* be closely synchronized for optimal performance).

- The client and server must be connected to each other (the protocol does not support disconnected operation such as authentication of MSMQ messages).

- Kerberos requires the use of a centralized authority. (If you use local accounts, even Windows 2000 falls back to using NTLM.)

- Kerberos v5 uses ASN.1 DER encoding, which is pretty obscure (part of the legacy of OSI); be happy you get to use Microsoft's implementation on Windows 2000 and you don't have to write your own.

- Authorization attributes in tickets may become stale and need refreshing.

SSPI

Consider for a moment the vast differences between the NTLM and Kerberos authentication protocols (see Figure 7.17). In NTLM, there is communication between client and server, followed by communication between the server machine and its authority. In Kerberos, on the other hand, there is communication between the client and his or her authority, followed by communication between client and server. In NTLM, there is no intrinsic client-side or server-side caching, so each client authentication request causes the server to communicate with its authority. In Kerberos, if a valid ticket exists in the cache, the client may not even need to talk to his or her authority at all.

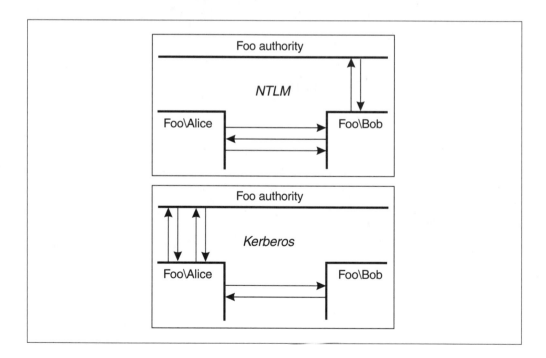

Figure 7.17. Comparing NTLM and Kerberos from a 10,000-foot vantage point

DISTRIBUTION

With all these differences, what do these protocols have in common? They ultimately result in a logon session for the client on the server machine. Both the client and server always discover a session key, and this key can be used to sign or seal messages passed between them. RFCs 1508 and 1509 describe an interface called the Generic Security Service API (GSSAPI) that abstracts the commonalities between most authentication protocols and hides the implementation details. Microsoft's version of this interface is known as the Security Service Provider Interface (SSPI). This is the abstract interface to all those SSPs that I've been alluding to throughout the chapter.

The idea behind GSSAPI and SSPI is that clients and servers want to have secure conversations over lots of different communication protocols: raw sockets, RPC, Java RMI, DCOM, CORBA, and so on. Rather than having each individual communication protocol tie itself closely to one particular network authentication protocol, it becomes easier to mix and match communication and authentication protocols by simply leaving space in the network packets to hold an opaque token generated by a security service provider. GSSAPI and SSPI thus define several functions that a communication subsystem should call to allow the selected SSP (NTLM or Kerberos, for instance) to do its work. Because the communication subsystem is only worried about enabling a network conversation between client and server (and knows nothing of authorities), it can easily transport opaque tokens back and forth between the client-side SSP and the server-side SSP, but any communication to a client or server's authority is the SSP's business.

Let's make this concrete by describing the fundamental methods exposed by SSPI. This first set of functions is used to establish authentication and exchange a session key:

- **QuerySecurityPackageInfo** Allows the communication subsystem to ask the SSP to describe itself; this includes capabilities such as sealing and signing, as well as the size of the token that the SSP will require the communication subsystem to transport between the client and server versions of the SSP.

- **AcquireCredentialsHandle** Called on both client and server SSPs before any authentication takes place, this function allows the

SSP to attach to a set of existing network credentials (this may involve making network round-trips to an authority, but that's the SSP's business; the caller doesn't care about this detail). This function also allows the caller to provide an alternate set of credentials (typically an authority/principal/password tuple).

- **InitializeSecurityContext** Called on the client side to give the SSP a chance to prepare an outgoing token[28] (and perhaps process an incoming token from the server-side SSP). The NTLM SSP, for instance, will prepare a Negotiate message the first time the client-side communication subsystem calls this function. The Kerberos SSP, on the other hand, will look up a ticket for the target server principal and prepare a KRB_AP_REQ message. (If no ticket exists, the Kerberos SSP will first synchronously send a KRB_TGS_REQ message to the client's KDC and wait for the response in order to *get* that ticket.)

  Often this function will be called more than once. Because NTLM requires a three-way handshake, this function will be called to generate the Negotiate token. After the communication subsystem sends this token and receives a Challenge token, it will call this function a second time, giving the client-side SSP a chance to process the Challenge token and produce an Authenticate token to send back to the server-side SSP. The return value from this function indicates to the caller whether the SSP expects another round of token exchanges or whether authentication is complete (or whether it failed, of course). For the Kerberos SSP, if mutual authentication is being used, this function will need to be called a second time to process the incoming KRB_AP_REP message that authenticates the server to the client.

- **AcceptSecurityContext** Called on the server side to give the SSP a chance to process the incoming token from the client-side SSP (and perhaps produce an outgoing token to send back to the client). For

---

[28] Please note that the tokens referred to here are simply opaque byte arrays that are exchanged between client and server (for instance, the Authenticate, Challenge, and Response messages, and the KRB_AP_REQ and KRB_AP_REP messages). These are *not* the access tokens (kernel objects) that were discussed in depth in Chapter 4.

NTLM, this allows the SSP to process the Negotiate token and produce the Challenge token. On the second pass, the Response token is accepted (and perhaps passed through to the server machine's authority). For Kerberos, this allows the SSP to process the KRB_AP_REQ token and produce (if required) a KRB_AP_REP token. As with its client-side sibling, the return value of this function tells the server-side communication subsystem whether another token needs to be exchanged with the client or not (and whether or not authentication succeeded). Upon a successful final pass, this function causes the system to generate a new network logon session for the client.

- **ImpersonateSecurityContext** Called on the server side after authentication is complete to ask the SSP to place a token for the client's logon session on the caller's thread.

- **RevertSecurityContext** Called on the server side to undo the effect of a call to ImpersonateSecurityContext.

- **QuerySecurityContextToken** (Windows 2000 only) Called on the server side after authentication is complete to directly retrieve a handle to the client's token. On older platforms the only way to get access to the token is to call ImpersonateSecurityContext and OpenThreadToken, followed by RevertSecurityContext, which feels a lot like eating a cheeseburger with your arm wrapped around the back of your head.

Once authentication is complete, regardless of whether NTLM or Kerberos (and generally any other supported protocol) was used, a session key has been exchanged and the client and server can use this session key to sign and seal messages. The following set of functions are used for this purpose.

- **MakeSignature** The communication subsystem (on either the client or server side) calls this function to ask the SSP to sign a message with the session key. The caller needs to provide room in the message for the resulting MAC. (The space required can be determined by calling QueryContextAttributes.)

- **VerifySignature** The communication subsystem calls this function to verify the MAC for an incoming message using the session key.

- **EncryptMessage** The communication subsystem (on either the client or server side) calls this function to ask the SSP to encrypt a message with the session key. For legal purposes, this function is only supported on Windows 2000 and later service packs of Windows NT.[29]

- **DecryptMessage** The communication subsystem calls this function to decrypt incoming messages using the session key. The same legal stipulation applies here as well.

Figure 7.18 shows that InitializeSecurityContext and AcceptSecurityContext are the key hooks used by SSPI to ride on top of many different network communication mechanisms. Note how the last call to AcceptSecurityContext in the case of NTLM causes the server-side SSP to perform synchronous pass-through authentication. Also note how in the case of Kerberos, the first call to InitializeSecurityContext causes the client-side SSP to look for appropriate tickets in the ticket cache; if they cannot be found (or if they've expired), the SSP goes and gets the tickets it needs from the KDC. The communication subsystem is completely unaware of this; it just keeps calling these functions and passing tokens to its peer until the SSP says it's done authenticating.

The main reason I'm bothering to drill down to the level of SSPI is to give you a more intuitive feel for what authentication protocols do, and how various communication subsystems integrate with a variety of authentication pro-

---

[29] These functions are actually implemented by the NTLM SSP on all versions of Windows NT 4; the legal issue (as I understand it—I'm a programmer, not a lawyer) has to do with keeping random folks from developing SSPs with strong encryption algorithms that the U.S. military cannot easily break, and exporting them to countries of which the U.S. government does not approve. There are two versions of Microsoft's SSPs: a North American version (that uses reasonably strong encryption) and an "exportable" version (that uses weak encryption that can easily be broken by the U.S. government). In fact, this is the primary difference between the North American and Exportable versions of Windows. So why were these functions later documented and supported? Microsoft now has a program for signing SSPs in the same way that CryptoAPI CSPs (Cryptographic Service Providers) are signed. An independent software vendor can present a CSP/SSP to Microsoft for signing, but it's the vendor's responsibility to satisfy U.S. government export regulations.

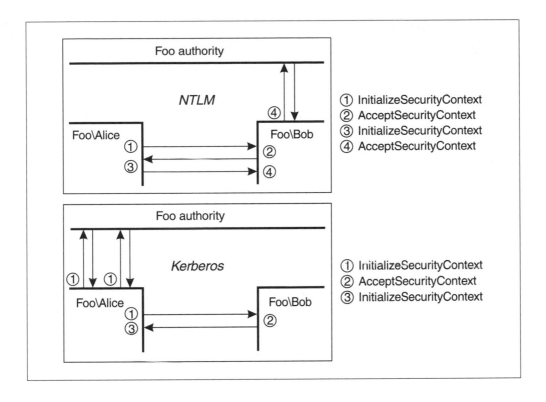

Figure 7.18. SSPI abstracts the differences between authentication protocols

tocols. When you call functions such as `ImpersonateNamedPipeClient`, `RpcImpersonateClient`, and `CoImpersonateClient`, you'll know that deep down, these are simply mapped to a call into the appropriate SSP, asking it to place the token (which was already discovered via an earlier authentication handshake) on your thread. Most people won't program to SSPI directly.

Another reason for mentioning SSPI is this: If you have your own custom authentication protocol, don't attempt to implement it *on top of* existing communication protocols such as RPC and COM; rather, implement an SSP that slips under the covers and allows you to collaborate directly with the guts of the communication subsystem. For instance, by implementing an SSP, when RPC asks you to sign an outgoing packet, you won't just be signing the payload, you'll be signing the RPC headers as well.

SPNEGO: Simple and Protected Negotiation

Windows 2000 supports several different authentication protocols, including (among others) Kerberos and NTLM. The former is preferred to the latter, but NTLM must still be implemented in order to support older versions of Windows. Here's an example of a classic problem with a multiprotocol-capable communication subsystem: Imagine a Windows 2000–based client that needs to talk to servers running on Windows 2000 and Windows NT 4. What should it do? Always use the lowest-common denominator, NTLM?

The answer is that it should negotiate the most secure protocol that the client and server both support. Imagine a naïve approach to solving this problem: The client simply sends a list of supported protocols in order of preference, and the server responds by selecting one (or rejecting all of them). First of all, this adds an extra round-trip, and second, it's possible for a bad guy who has compromised a router between the client and server to change the server's response to a less secure protocol that is easier to attack (thus performing what is known as a **downgrade attack**).

The first problem is easy to solve: simply piggyback the first token from the client's preferred authentication protocol into the negotiation token. This way, if the server also supports the client's favorite protocol, the preferred authentication exchange is already underway (thus eliminating the extra round-trip). If the server *doesn't* support the first protocol in the list, it'll cost an extra round-trip to tell the client which protocol the server *does* support. This is a reasonable trade-off for a significant gain in interoperability.

The second problem is more difficult, but one reasonable approach is as follows: After negotiation and authentication are complete, the server echoes back to the client the original list of protocols that was presented to the server in the first negotiation token, signing this packet with the session key exchanged during authentication. This allows the client to verify that the server did indeed receive the full, unadulterated list of protocols, as opposed to a watered-down version substituted by a bad guy. (Of course, if a bad guy in the middle can instantly break the client's weakest authentication protocol during the authentication exchange, he or she would discover the session key and could alter the server's echoed list at will and recalculate its MAC, thus faking the client into believing that the negotiation was protected when it was in fact downgraded. I said the method was *reasonable,* not *perfect*.) Naturally, the negotiation can only be protected if the authentication protocol ultimately settled on supports signing messages (both NTLM and Kerberos support this).

What I've just described is known as **SPNEGO,** which stands for Secure and Protected Negotiation, and there is an SPNEGO SSP that does just this on Windows 2000. The SPNEGO SSP is used as the default provider in many communication subsystems (including COM) to promote maximum interoperability. As with Kerberos, SPNEGO is an open standard; it is documented in RFC 2478.

Summary

- The NTLM protocol is built into most versions of Windows. It is a simple protocol, but has lots of limitations.

- Kerberos is a robust protocol that was developed under heavy public scrutiny and is documented in RFC 1510.

- Most authentication protocols can be abstracted away from the communication subsystems that use them; GSSAPI and SSPI are examples of interfaces that allow such loose coupling.

- GSSAPI (RFCs 1508 and 1509) and SSPI expose functions that allow a communication subsystem to collaborate with a security service provider (SSP). The SSP creates and processes what look like opaque tokens to the communication subsystem, which carries them to the SSP on the other side of the wire. The two SSPs (client-side and server-side) can therefore help to piggyback an authentication protocol that authenticates the client (and often the server) and allows them to both discover a session key. Afterward, this session key can be used to sign or seal messages sent by the communication subsystem.

- SPNEGO (RFC 2478) allows GSSAPI/SSPI-based communication subsystems to negotiate the best security service provider, and makes downgrade attacks difficult for the bad guys.

Chapter 8

The File Server

What's a chapter like this doing in a book on security for programmers? Well, very often the file server is used as an important component in a distributed system. Often, it's taken for granted as well—until the problems start to rear their ugly heads . . .

> Access is denied.
>
> Logon failure: bad user name or password.
>
> The credentials supplied conflict with an existing set of credentials.

One reason these problems often seem so mysterious is that the documentation doesn't lay out a conceptual model of how security in the file server really works. The goal of this chapter is to remedy that. Having a solid conceptual model will not only make you more comfortable developing distributed systems using the file server, but will also help you on a day-to-day basis as you're using Windows to get work done.

LAN Manager

The Windows file server is built on top of a Microsoft proprietary wire protocol known as Server Message Block (SMB). In December 1997, Microsoft published an Internet draft proposal with the Internet Engineering Task Force (IETF) for a protocol named CIFS (Common Internet File System) that was basically a subset of SMB that was Internet friendly,[1] so you'll often hear the SMB protocol referred to as CIFS. This text will stick with the term SMB.

The SMB protocol has a server-side component that listens for incoming requests (this is packaged in the Server service), and a client-side component that issues those requests (this is packaged in the Workstation service).

To avoid confusion and too much tongue tangling, I'm going to define some terms to be used in this chapter:

- **lmserver** The file server that listens for SMB requests
- **lmclient** The client-side daemon that sends SMB messages to the server on the client's behalf
- **lmsession** An SMB session, as opposed to any other type of sessions that I'll talk about (such as a logon session)

The "lm" prefix stands for **LAN Manager,** the root technology that resulted in the SMB protocol that is used in Windows for Workgroups, Windows NT, and Windows 2000. When you program against these components, you include a header file called `lm.h`, so the prefix seemed pretty natural here.

LAN Manager Sessions

The first thing you need to know about the file server is that it is session oriented. A client that wishes to read or write a file must first establish a session with the file server. The system sets up implicit sessions on your behalf so often that you may not even be aware that they are there. This is desirable for an end user, but as a distributed systems programmer you should be keenly aware of how sessions affect your designs.

On each machine running the Server service, lmserver maintains a list of open SMB sessions. On each client running the Workstation service, lmclient also maintains a list of open SMB sessions (see Figure 8.1). An authentication

---

[1] This draft expired six months later, and as of this writing, no further progress in IETF has been made (and no plans have been announced). Regardless, if you want to get information about SMB in MSDN, you should search for CIFS. If you really want to know how SMB works, spend some time at http://www.samba.org, where a group of very smart programmers have basically reverse-engineered much of LAN Manager into an open-source product that runs on UNIX.

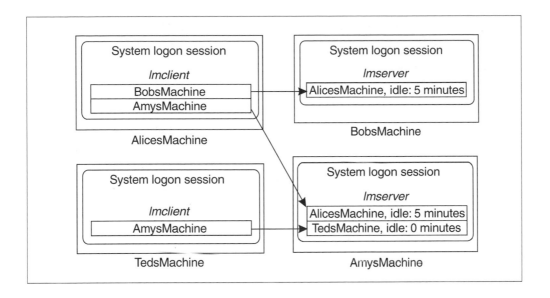

Figure 8.1. **LAN Manager sessions**

handshake is required to open a session. While a session is open, however, no further authentication is performed, unless SMB signing is negotiated (this is covered later).

Think about what sessions meant before Windows 2000, when the de facto authentication protocol was NTLM. If the file server were not session oriented, each time Alice (on AlicesMachine) opened a file on BobsMachine the system would have to perform an authentication handshake. This isn't terribly expensive if you only consider the extra network authentication tokens passed between Alice and BobsMachine, but if Alice is using a centralized authority the overhead gets tremendously high: Alice's authority must be contacted to participate in NTLM pass-through authentication for each request. And if Alice and BobsMachine aren't in the same domain, it's even worse (see Chapter 7 for the details). Thus, authenticating once and maintaining an open session makes the system seem more responsive to Alice, and it also helps eliminate lots of network requests for domain controllers. (The comparison with Kerberos, which relies on *client*-side caching of tickets, is interesting because Kerberos reduces the need for server-side sessions somewhat, although some sort of session would still be necessary if only to allow files to remain open between requests.)

Remember what happens at the end of a client/server authentication handshake in Windows. The server-side SSP talks to the Local Security Authority and establishes a network logon session and a token for the client. The server can then ask the SSP for the client's token in order to peruse the client's identity and authorization attributes. In the case of lmserver, *the thread handling the request will always impersonate the client while carrying out the request;* this is the canonical example of the "pass the buck" access control strategy described in Chapter 3, and it works well in this case because lmserver provides (among other things) a network front end to an already secure file system.[2]

Because lmserver needs to be able to impersonate the client at each request, but the authentication handshake only occurs when the lmsession is first established, clearly the lmsession must hold a reference to the client's network logon session (in SSPI terminology, you'd say that the lmsession holds a security context handle). This way, the lmserver thread only has to call `ImpersonateSecurityContext` whenever it needs to execute a new request from the client.

So how long does each lmsession remain open? This isn't clearly documented, but there are a number of observations that I've made while studying both Windows 2000 and Windows NT 4. It appears as though lmserver occasionally makes a sweep of open sessions and closes those sessions that have no files (or other devices) open and that have been idle for a certain amount of time.[3]

One reason it's important to close these sessions occasionally is to allow a refresh of the client's security context. As long as an lmsession is open, lmserver receives no new information about the client's current authorization attributes.

---

[2] Of course, I'm assuming you're *not* using a FAT file system, which is possible but not very interesting for this discussion.

[3] Knowledge Base article Q138365 describes a previously undocumented registry parameter named `AutoDisconnect` as controlling the number of minutes an lmsession must be idle before it is closed. This appears to apply to lmsessions' setup in the presence of an explicit client-side *use record* (use records are discussed shortly). This does not appear to control implicit lmsessions constructed without a use record. My own personal experiments on Windows 2000 indicate that implicit lmsessions are often terminated after as little as ten seconds of idle time.

The network logon session being held open by the lmsession becomes stale in this case. This can become a problem if a particular lmsession is rarely idle, because the lmserver won't be able to automatically time out that session. What does all this mean? It means that if you are added or removed from a group this change won't have any effect on an open lmsession.

If this ever becomes a problem, one workaround is to force the session to close by calling `NetSessionDel`:

```
NET_API_STATUS NetSessionDel(
  LPWSTR servername,        // in, optional
  LPWSTR UncClientName,     // in, optional
  LPWSTR username           // in, optional
);
```

servername is the Universal Naming Convention (UNC) name[4] of the machine whose lmserver you want to contact. You can choose up to two criteria for which sessions should be closed: You can filter based on the client host address (*UncClientName*) or based on the client principal (*username*). An undocumented feature (bug?) in this function prevents you from calling it without specifying at least one of these filters (the function returns ERROR_INVALID _PARAMETER in this case).

The danger in calling the `NetSessionDel` function is that any open files (or other resources such as named pipes) will be forced closed and data may be lost; to be safe, therefore, only do this when you know your sessions are idle. Because of this danger, the caller must be a member of the Administrators or Account Operators alias on the server machine, or the call will fail. Interestingly enough, because the LAN Manager API is implemented using RPC over SMB (named pipes), when you make the call to `NetSessionDel` you are actually using an lmsession to make the RPC call, and if you've indicated that you want to close your own session, you'll close the session you're using to make the `NetSessionDel` call in the first place! The function will indeed operate as documented, but you'll get an RPC error when the function returns, which shouldn't surprise you.

---

[4] A UNC machine name is always prepended with two backslashes (for example, \\BobsMachine). Most of the LAN Manager APIs require this type of machine name.

One safe thing you can do with sessions is enumerate them:

```
NET_API_STATUS NetSessionEnum(
  LPWSTR   servername,       // in, optional
  LPWSTR   UncClientName,    // in, optional
  LPWSTR   username,         // in, optional
  DWORD    level,            // in
  LPBYTE*  bufptr,           // out
  DWORD    prefmaxlen,       // in
  LPDWORD  entriesread,      // out
  LPDWORD  totalentries,     // out
  LPDWORD  resume_handle     // out, optional
);
```

The first three parameters are the same as those to `NetSessionDel`, except that you can pass NULL for all of them and this function actually works as advertised. Depending on the level of information you request, you don't necessarily need any particular authorization attributes at all. Here's an example that enumerates all lmsessions on a specified server machine (this example doesn't require any particular authorization attributes):

```
void _enumAllSessions(wchar_t* pszServer) {
  SESSION_INFO_10* prgInfo;
  DWORD cRead, cTotal;
  NET_API_STATUS s = NetSessionEnum(pszServer, 0, 0,
                           10, (BYTE**)&prgInfo,
                           MAX_PREFERRED_LENGTH,
                           &cRead, &cTotal, 0);
  if (s)
    _err(L"NetSessionEnum", s);

  for (DWORD i = 0; i < cRead; ++i) {
    SESSION_INFO_10& info = prgInfo[i];
    wprintf(L"Client Host:      %s\n",
            info.sesi10_cname);
    wprintf(L"Client Principal: %s\n",
            info.sesi10_username);
    wprintf(L"Session started %d sec ago\n",
            info.sesi10_time);
    wprintf(L"Session has been idle for %d sec\n\n",
```

```
      info.sesi10_idle_time);
   }
   // standard cleanup for LAN Manager APIs
   NetApiBufferFree(prgInfo);
}
```

Windows 2000 and Windows NT both provide user interfaces by which you can view (and manually close) individual sessions. In Windows 2000, go to the Computer Management snap-in[5] and drill down as follows: System Tools, Shared Folders, Sessions. This shows the lmsessions that the local computer is serving up. To get the same view on a remote computer, run MMC directly (from the Start menu, run `mmc.exe` and add the Computer Management snap-in, at which point the system will allow you to choose which computer you'd like to manage). In Windows NT, you can get virtually the same view by going to the Control Panel applet named Server and pressing the button labeled Users; by using the Server Manager tool, you can connect to remote machines as well. Note that whenever you are looking at a remote machine's lmsessions, you'll always see the one that the system used to make the `NetSessionEnum` call in the first place.[6]

Clients and Sessions

While writing this chapter, I came across some documentation in the recently released Windows 2000 platform SDK that really pointed to the need for this chapter:

> A *session* is a link between a workstation and a server. A session is established the first time a workstation makes a connection to a shared resource on the server. Until the session ends, all further connections between the workstation and the server are part of the same session.

This does a pretty good job of describing how lmsessions work, but it does the reader a terrible disservice by making it sound as though multiple

---

[5] One easy way to launch this snap-in is to right-click My Computer and choose Manage.

[6] If you're feeling brave (and you're an administrator on the remote machine), close that connection and you'll get the RPC error described earlier.

simultaneous Imsessions cannot exist between a given client machine and a given server machine. This is in fact not the case at all, and we'd suffer horribly if it were.

Imagine that a service on AlicesMachine is designated to run as some daemon principal—let's call it Quux. If code running inside this service were to call `CreateFile` to access a file on BobsMachine, the Imclient on AlicesMachine would silently open an authenticated Imsession for Quux with BobsMachine. Now, just to make sure that this Imsession stays open, let's say that Quux holds this remote file open all day long. What happens when Alice logs in to AlicesMachine and executes the following from a command prompt?

```
copy \\BobsMachine\SomeShare\AlicesFile.txt
```

If the previously quoted description were true, the Imserver on BobsMachine would use Quux's security context to open `AlicesFile.txt`. This is clearly wrong; the system should have authenticated Alice and should be using Alice's security context to access the file.

Here's a more accurate description:

> An Imsession is a link between a client's logon session and a server. An Imsession is established the first time code running in a client's logon session makes a connection to a shared resource on the server. Until the Imsession ends, all further connections between the client's logon session and the server are part of the same Imsession.

Because Quux is running in a private daemon logon session, it'll have its own private Imsession to BobsMachine. Alice will also have her own private Imsession to BobsMachine. These are completely independent and coexist peacefully. Even if a service was running as Alice (unlikely, but it drives the point home), and Alice was simultaneously logged on as an interactive user, the service has its own private logon session and thus will have its own Imsession to BobsMachine, independent of what Alice is doing in her interactive logon session. Any code running in Alice's logon session that contacts the Imserver on BobsMachine will use Alice's Imsession. Any code running in the service's logon session that does the same will use the service's private Imsession.

Client		Server	
host_addr	port	host_addr	port

Figure 8.2. TCP/IP associations

Client		Server
host_addr	logon luid	host_name

Figure 8.3. LAN Manager associations

I remember once seeing a particularly effective diagram of how a TCP/IP association works.[7] Each TCP association is a four-tuple (see Figure 8.2). The server listens on a particular host address and port, and many clients can connect from various host addresses simultaneously. In fact, a single server listening on a single port to a single client host can experience multiple simultaneous connections to that client host, because each connection can come from a different port on the client.

You can think of lmsessions in a similar way. The association on the client side consists of the client's host address coupled with the client's logon session LUID (think of this as the port). The server side consists of just the server's address because there is only a single lmserver that does all the listening (as opposed to raw TCP, where many servers might be listening on different ports). Figure 8.3 shows this relationship.

Now that it's been established that each logon session on a client machine can have its own private lmsession on a given server, here's where things start to get interesting. When an lmsession is established between a logon session

---

[7] I'm not sure if Tim Ewald came up with this originally or not, but it sure was a great diagram, Tim.

for Alice and a machine called BobsMachine, whose credentials do you think are used to authenticate that session? In other words, when an lmserver thread on BobsMachine impersonates the security context associated with this lmsession, whose identity does it take on? The obvious answer is that it takes on Alice's identity. But it turns out that this is just the *default* behavior. Alice can explicitly control the credentials she uses if she desires. This can be quite powerful, as you'll see.

Use Records

If Alice wants more control over her session with BobsMachine, she can establish an explicit **use record**[8] with her lmclient. If you've ever mapped a drive letter, you've established a use record as a byproduct of having redirected a local device.[9] A use record consists of a remote resource and (optionally) a set of credentials.

You can add a use record interactively from the command line:[10]

```
net use \\BobsMachine /u:user@domain.com *
Type the password for \\BobsMachine:
```

This example specifically provides an alternate set of credentials to make things interesting. The asterisk at the end of the command isn't a typo; this is how you indicate to the NET.EXE utility that you'd like it to prompt you for a password. Although technically you can establish several use records to BobsMachine, each indicating a different share, pipe, or printer, remember that only one lmsession can ever be established between your logon session and that remote

---

[8] Note that this is my own terminology. The MSDN documentation refers to this as a *connection*, which is sort of misleading; a use record can exist without any SMB connection active at all. Please bear with me, and once you understand the basic model of how LAN Manager works, you can call these things whatever you want.

[9] I'm only using this as an example that most people can relate to; generally, you'll want to avoid mapping drive letters programmatically from your software products. Drive letter mappings should normally be managed by the administrator of a machine, where they are generally either used as a convenience for interactive use or as a crutch for legacy software that doesn't know about UNC paths.

[10] The format of the user name in the following commands follows the Windows 2000 convention known as UPN (User Principal Name). For earlier versions of Windows NT, use the older Authority\Principal naming convention.

machine at a given moment in time.[11] Thus, unless you're mapping drive letters it's pretty pointless to do the following:

```
net use \\BobsMachine\ShareOne /u:user@domain.com *
net use \\BobsMachine\ShareTwo /u:user@domain.com *
net use \\BobsMachine\ShareThree /u:user@domain.com *
```

This is redundant. In fact, if you were to try to do this instead:

```
net use \\BobsMachine\ShareOne /u:jose@domain.com *
net use \\BobsMachine\ShareTwo /u:ranjiv@domain.com *
net use \\BobsMachine\ShareThree /u:sally@domain.com *
```

you'd find that the second and third lines would fail mysteriously with the error "The credentials supplied conflict with an existing set of credentials." The lmclient component is trying to tell you that you'll only ever be able to establish a single lmsession from your current logon session to BobsMachine, and thus you must pick a single set of credentials and stick with them.

So assuming you avoid the redundancy and type

```
net use \\BobsMachine /u:user@domain.com *
```

(followed by the password when prompted), you've actually done two things. First and foremost, you've established a use record with your local lmclient daemon, which will remember the record for the duration of your logon session. (When I say it *remembers,* I mean it remembers that you want all SMB traffic originating from your logon session and directed at BobsMachine to use the credentials you've specified.) Second, you've primed the connection by actually establishing a live lmsession (and authenticating; so if you accidentally typed the wrong password, you'll find out right away).

If you were to now type

```
net use
```

you'd see output that looks something like this:

---

[11] Thanks to Mike Nelson for pointing out a twisted way to get more than one connection between a client logon session and a server machine: Use a different host name string for the server (e.g., use the dotted-decimal IP address for the first, and the DNS name for the second). This doesn't scale very well, but it certainly was clever!

```
Status    Local    Remote              Network
------------------------------------------------------
OK                 \\BobsMachine\IPC$  Microsoft...
```

Note that NET.EXE takes \\BobsMachine as shorthand for the interprocess communication (IPC) pipe that SMB uses as a bootstrap. This is just a detail. The important thing to understand is that all SMB traffic to a given server from a given client-side logon session will use the *same* lmsession.

The Status field (OK) currently indicates that as far as the lmclient daemon knows, there is in fact a live lmsession established between your logon session and BobsMachine. If you were to leave the lmsession idle for 20 minutes or so and run net use again, you'd see this indicator change to Disconnected, which indicates that the lmsession has timed out and closed. No problem, though: If you try to talk to BobsMachine over SMB again (from the same logon session), the lmclient daemon will use the credentials you specified earlier to establish another authenticated lmsession. Another invocation of net use will show OK, because you once again have a live session. I'm trying to make it painfully obvious that the lmsession can come and go independently of the client-side use record, which always sticks around (at least until the client terminates his or her logon session or removes the use record explicitly).

Here's another way of adding a use record:

```
net use \\BobsMachine
```

This establishes a use record to BobsMachine using a default set of credentials (this will be taken from my logon session unless I've already established one or more use records with BobsMachine; in the latter case, lmclient will use whatever credentials were specified in the earlier use records).

Let's start fresh once again. Say Alice establishes her first use record to BobsMachine:

```
net use \\BobsMachine
```

Imagine that later in the day (from her same logon session) she wants to use an alternate set of credentials to talk to BobsMachine. She must first delete any existing use records to BobsMachine before adding a new one using different credentials (this avoids the "conflicting credentials" error that can be so painful):

```
net use \\BobsMachine /d
net use \\BobsMachine /u:user@domain.com *
```

How Can I Do This Programmatically?

If you are wondering why I'm showing you how to use NET.EXE, a LAN Manager utility, it's because it's the easiest way for me to explain how lmsessions and use records work, and you can interactively follow along on your own machine.[12] (Surprisingly enough, you don't even need a network: You can use lmclient and lmserver on the same machine in the various ways I've been describing.) Once you understand how the net use command works, you'll find that the programmatic API is similar:

```
#include <lm.h>
#pragma comment(lib, "netapi32.lib")
NET_API_STATUS NetUseAdd(
    LPWSTR   UncServerName,  // reserved, must be 0
    DWORD    level,          // in
    LPBYTE   buf,            // in
    LPDWORD  ParmError       // out
);

typedef struct _USE_INFO_2 {
    LPWSTR   ui2_local;      // optional
    LPWSTR   ui2_remote;
    LPWSTR   ui2_password;   // optional
    DWORD    ui2_status;     // unused for NetUseAdd
    DWORD    ui2_asg_type;
    DWORD    ui2_refcount;   // unused for NetUseAdd
    DWORD    ui2_usecount;   // unused for NetUseAdd
    LPWSTR   ui2_username;   // optional
    LPWSTR   ui2_domainname; // optional
} USE_INFO_2;
```

---

[12] Also, NET.EXE is incredibly useful. I *never* use the network neighborhood browser; it's just too darn slow. With NET.EXE, I can immediately connect with the server of my choice. As a hardcore Windows user, you should spend some time getting familiar with this tool, especially if you eschew the GUI tools and crave a command-line interface.

Remember that a use record is established between a client-side logon session and a server machine. The logon session is discovered implicitly; it's the logon session of the thread that calls NetUseAdd. If you'd like to specify alternate credentials (which is the primary reason you'd call this function in the first place), you'd specify info level 2 and fill out a corresponding USE_INFO_2 structure. In this structure, you'd need to set *ui2_remote* to a UNC path to the target resource; *ui2_domainname*, *ui2_username*, and *ui2_password* to the alternate credentials you'd like to use; and *ui2_asg_type* to USE_WILDCARD (you don't need to indicate the type of resource when calling NetUseAdd):

```
void _establishUseRecord( wchar_t* pszResource,
                          wchar_t* pszAuthority,
                          wchar_t* pszPrincipal,
                          wchar_t* pszPassword) {
    USE_INFO_2 ui2;
    ZeroMemory(&ui2, sizeof ui2);

    // NetUseAdd obfuscates and then rehydrates the
    // data that ui2_password points to for some reason,
    // so be sure to pass a writable pointer!
    wchar_t szPassword[256];
    lstrcpy(szPassword, pszPassword);

    ui2.ui2_remote     = pszResource;
    ui2.ui2_domainname = pszAuthority;
    ui2.ui2_username   = pszPrincipal;
    ui2.ui2_password   = szPassword;
    ui2.ui2_asg_type   = USE_WILDCARD;

    DWORD nParmErr;
    NET_API_STATUS s = NetUseAdd(0, 2,
                    (BYTE*)&ui2, &nParmErr);
    if (s)
      _err(L"NetUseAdd", s);
}
```

Here's a usage example:

```
_establishUseRecord(L"\\\\BobsMachine\\IPC$",
                L"Foo", L"Alice", L"heffalump");
```

Note that *pszResource* must indicate an SMB resource, not just a machine name. NET.EXE conveniently appends \IPC$ if you just provide a machine name; this is what I do by convention as well in my own programs. Remember, you'll only have a single lmsession from your logon session to the target machine no matter which resource (file share, printer, or pipe) you choose.[13]

Pay attention to the comment in the previous code above: For some reason, NetUseAdd will temporarily obfuscate the password *in place,* so if you pass a pointer to a hardcoded password string, you'll get an access violation (if you're lucky, it might even happen before you ship your product). The previous code provides a workaround (when experimenting with security, I'll often hardcode passwords), but you could almost look at this as an undocumented *feature.* If you're hardcoding cleartext passwords into production software, this access violation isn't the worst of your problems! Generally you'll get credentials from humans (interactively) or from a password stash (the Windows password stash is discussed in the appendix).

You can programmatically enumerate all the use records for a logon session by calling NetUseEnum (the logon session is naturally determined by the security context of the thread that makes the call):

```
#include <lm.h>
#pragma comment(lib, "netapi32.lib")
NET_API_STATUS NetUseEnum (
  LPWSTR   UncServerName,        // reserved, must be 0
  DWORD    Level,                // in
  LPBYTE   BufPtr,               // out
  DWORD    PreferedMaximumSize,  // in
  LPDWORD  EntriesRead,          // out
  LPDWORD  TotalEntries,         // out
  LPDWORD  ResumeHandle          // out, optional
);
```

---

[13] Technically, the reason that I use IPC$ is because with any other resource name lmserver performs an access check against the DACL on the chosen resource. Thus it's possible for NetUseAdd to return ERROR_ACCESS_DENIED in this case. Since I'm just setting up a logical connection to a particular machine, I prefer to set up the use record in peace (sans any access checks on a particular resource), and then allow each piece of code that accesses individual resources to handle this on a case-by-case basis.

Here's an example that prints a bit more information than NET.EXE does; this code displays the client credentials stored in the record (sans the password; NetUseEnum doesn't give you that).

```
void _enumUseRecords() {
  USE_INFO_2* prgui;
  DWORD cRead, cTotal;
  NET_API_STATUS s = NetUseEnum(0, 2, (BYTE**)&prgui,
                                MAX_PREFERRED_LENGTH,
                                &cRead, &cTotal, 0);
  if (s)
    _err(L"NetUseEnum", s);
  for (DWORD i = 0; i < cRead; ++i) {
    USE_INFO_2& ui = prgui[i];
    wprintf(L"Resource:      %s\n", ui.ui2_remote);
    wprintf(L"Local Mapping: %s\n", ui.ui2_local);
    wprintf(L"Status:        %d\n", ui.ui2_status);
    wprintf(L"Type:          %d\n", ui.ui2_asg_type);
    wprintf(L"Ref Count:     %d\n", ui.ui2_usecount);
    wprintf(L"Authority:     %s\n", ui.ui2_domainname);
    wprintf(L"Principal:     %s\n", ui.ui2_username);
    wprintf(L"\n");
  }
  NetApiBufferFree(prgui);
}
```

Note that each use record has a reference count (*ui2_usecount*). This means that if you call NetUseAdd three times for the same resource, you have to call NetUseDel three times. To avoid this, there is a special flag you can pass to NetUseDel called USE_FORCE that will force the reference count to zero and remove the use record.

```
#include <lm.h>
#pragma comment(lib, "netapi32.lib")
NET_API_STATUS NetUseDel(
    LPWSTR UncServerName, // reserved, must be 0
    LPWSTR UseName,       // in
    DWORD  ForceCond      // in
);
```

```
#define USE_NOFORCE              0
#define USE_FORCE                1
#define USE_LOTS_OF_FORCE        2
```

Whoever came up with these constants had a sense of humor. USE_NOFORCE decrements the reference count and only removes the record if the reference count drops to zero.[14] USE_FORCE says to decrement the reference count all the way to zero and remove the use record.

Note that when you remove a use record manually via NetUseDel, if it was the last use record for the target machine and an lmsession is currently active, the system will consider terminating the lmsession. The first two force flags will only terminate the lmsession if there are no resources currently open. The third flag, USE_LOTS_OF_FORCE, does what you think it does: It terminates the lmsession with extreme prejudice, regardless of whether any files, printers, or pipes are open.

Here's the natural way to remove a use record:

```
void _removeUseRecord(wchar_t* pszResource) {
  NET_API_STATUS s = NetUseDel(0, pszResource,
                               USE_FORCE);
  if (s)
    _err(L"NetUseDel", s);
}
```

NULL Sessions

NULL sessions were defined in Chapter 7, and now I'd like to show you a case where they can be useful. If you have a system where authentication is not needed or desired (perhaps you don't have a centralized authority and you don' t want to bother keeping a bunch of local accounts synchronized), you can use NULL sessions to turn off authentication in all SMB traffic. The way to do this is simple: Just establish a use record that specifies empty credentials. In fact, you can even do this via NET.EXE:

---

[14] The reference count is mainly an annoyance in my opinion; presumably, in early versions of LAN Manager it was useful.

```
net use \\BobsMachine /u: *
Type the password for \\BobsMachine:
```

Note that I used the /u switch to indicate a user name, but I left the user name blank. (Once again, the asterisk tells NET.EXE to ask me for a password; if you forget this, it'll try to use the password material cached in your logon session, which isn't what you want.) When NET.EXE prompts you for a password, just hit Enter to provide a blank password. If you go look at the list of lmsessions on BobsMachine, you'll see an entry with a blank user name. This is a NULL session.

From now on, any SMB traffic from your logon session to BobsMachine will use this NULL session. Given this, consider that each lmserver resource (file share, printer, pipe) has a DACL on it that indicates who should be allowed to use the resource via an lmsession. As long as that DACL grants access to one of the SIDs in the NULL session (Everyone is the classic example), it would seem as though you'd be granted access to that resource. However, *very* early in the history of Windows NT, administrators were being surprised by this behavior (no big shock there) and weren't aware that at least as far as LAN Manager was concerned, "Everyone" also included anonymous users connecting via NULL sessions. So in version 3.5 of Windows NT, some registry settings were added to the configuration for lmserver that provided additional protection from NULL sessions. The most important of these settings was RestrictNullSessionAccess. If you look under the following registry key

```
HKLM\SYSTEM\CurrentControlSet\
Services\LanmanServer\Parameters
```

you'll likely not see this registry entry at all (it's not there by default). If it's absent, the default setting is TRUE, which indicates that NULL sessions are to be denied access to all LAN Manager resources (IPC$ appears to be an exception). You can add this value and set it to FALSE if you want to turn this feature off.[15] Alternatively, you can leave this setting on, and open holes for NULL

---

[15] More fine-grained ways of granting and denying access to NULL sessions are discussed in Chapter 7, using the Authenticated Users SID introduced in Windows NT 4 Service Pack 3.

sessions at individual share points or pipes by adjusting the following MULTI_SZ registry values: NullSessionPipes and NullSessionShares. These are simply lists of resource names that NULL sessions may access (the DACL on the resource still needs to grant access to the NULL session; this is commonly done via the Everyone SID).

Programmatically establishing a use record that uses a NULL session is quite easy:

```
_establishUseRecord(L"\\\\BobsMachine\\IPC$",
                    L"", L"", L"");
```

Dealing with Conflict

What if you try to establish a use record with a certain set of credentials (a NULL session is just one example) but there's a conflicting use record already established? You have two choices: the brute-force method, and a somewhat twisted but elegant method. Brute force is simply deleting the existing use record, potentially creating horrible race conditions with other processes, or, even worse, orphaning open file handles by specifying USE_LOTS_OF_FORCE.

The second option is to give yourself a new sandbox to play in. As a TCP/IP programmer, when you want a private client connection to a server, you use a new, dynamically assigned client-side port. With SMB, the equivalent of a client-side port is a logon session, so if you can create a new logon session (directly or indirectly), you have your own private world where you can create lmsessions to your heart's content, satisfied that you won't conflict with any-body else.

Imagine, for instance, creating a dummy local account and calling LogonUser to establish a logon session for that account just to get yourself a new SMB "port." After impersonating this logon session, your thread now has a new "port" and can call NetUseAdd to specify the *real* credentials that you want to use across the wire (it could even be a NULL session). What's neat about this approach is that you won't kick anybody else in the head on the local machine by stomping on their lmsessions and use records. Hey, I warned you up front that it was somewhat twisted!

Drive Letter Mappings

If you understood the description of lmsessions and use records, then this chapter has done its job. However much I hate to even *think* about drive mappings (except in the past tense), enough software in the world still relies on this DOS legacy that I'd be remiss not to mention the issue.

Many of the observations made so far in this chapter come from little hints in the documentation and tons of experimentation. From what I can tell with the experimentation I've done with drive mappings, when you establish a drive mapping you are doing two orthogonal things simultaneously (which often confuses people). First, you are establishing a use record, with all the semantics that this entails. Drive mappings are nothing special in this regard; each use record still is confined to its creator's logon session, and only a single set of credentials may be used for each association between a client logon session and a server host. Second, you are establishing a *machine-wide alias*[16] for the corresponding UNC path. All logon sessions on the machine see the same set of drive mapping aliases, but each logon session has its own set of lmsessions.

Let's look at an example. Say that a daemon, Quux, is logged on as a service on AlicesMachine. Quux establishes a drive mapping, redirecting the X drive to point to \\BobsMachine\ShareForQuux. Quux will have its own private lmsession to this resource, and when it uses the X drive mapping, lmserver on BobsMachine will see Quux making those requests. No problem.

Now let's say that Alice logs on interactively (think new logon session) and decides to use drive X (she won't be able to see it via the `net use` command, but the drive mapping alias is available nonetheless). Alice's logon session does not yet have an lmsession to BobsMachine because she just logged on (assume there are no persistent connections; I'll cover those shortly). When Alice uses drive X, because she has no use record for BobsMachine, the system will simply map X to the UNC path \\BobsMachine\ShareForQuux, set up an implicit lmsession to BobsMachine authenticated using Alice's credentials, and attempt to access the resource on her behalf. If ShareForQuux doesn't grant access to Alice, she'll be denied.

---

[16] For terminal services, this would be a terminal services session-wide alias, naturally.

When using drive letter mappings from an interactive logon session where the interactive user's profile is available, these mappings can be made *persistent,* which simply means that they will be automatically reestablished the next time the user logs in interactively:

```
net use x: \\BobsMachine\c$ /p:yes /u:user@foo.com *
```

The /p:yes switch indicates to NET.EXE that this is a persistent connection.[17] Besides all the other stuff that normally goes on as a result of mapping a drive letter, this also causes a new key to be created in the user's profile (HKEY_CURRENT_USER\Network\x in this case) named after the device name, which contains the target UNC path and the authority and principal names (but not the password) of the client-side credentials to be used to set up the use record. The next time the user logs in, Winlogon runs a program called USERINIT.EXE, which puts up that (somewhat annoying) little dialog that tells you that it's trying to reestablish your persistent network connections. All this program is doing is walking through the registry setting up use records and drive letter aliases. If you've specified alternate credentials, you'll have to wait while the system attempts to authenticate using the alternate authority/principal pair but with your current password (which usually won't work) before you are prompted for a correct password for the principal.

I can't imagine a modern distributed application needing to use drive letter mappings in the first place, let alone setting up persistent connections programmatically (this is something the end user should manage). But if you're writing a utility that does this sort of thing, you'll want to check out the WNetAddConnection2 function. This function basically does the work of NetUseAdd and optionally adds the persistent connection registry key mentioned earlier.

Named Pipes

Named pipes (and mailslots, which are similar, security-wise) are all about hooking into the SMB infrastructure in Windows and using it to perform inter-

---

[17] This is the default setting whenever you map a drive letter via NET.EXE, so technically, I didn't even need to say /p:yes. The /p:no switch causes the drive mapping not to be persistent (and thus it doesn't write any information to the user profile).

process communication, which may or may not include network communication. If you're using this technology in your distributed system, clearly you should have a very good grasp of all the concepts introduced in this chapter—lmsessions, use records, and so forth—because they all apply to you. As a named pipe server, your service is seen by the world as if you were simply a file; all your communications are funneled through lmclient and lmserver, using (typically authenticated) lmsessions.[18]

When a client sets up a use record with a set of explicit credentials (or even if he or she uses the default credentials), those credentials will be used to set up the lmsession between the client's logon session and a server, and all files, printers, and pipes on that server will be accessed using those same credentials. Use records can quickly become tricky to manage because they are global resources in the client's logon session; if you're not careful, processes can start to fight over them. RPC and COM benefit from divorcing themselves from SMB (although it is possible to use RPC over SMB; this is the way many of the administrative tools in Windows work[19]). In RPC and COM, the authentication settings are much more fine grained, as discussed in Chapter 9.

A named pipe server calls `CreateNamedPipe` to expose a named pipe, and although most of the arguments to this function have nothing to do with security, the last argument certainly does:

```
HANDLE CreateNamedPipe(
    LPCTSTR lpName,          // in
    DWORD   dwOpenMode,      // in
    DWORD   dwPipeMode,      // in
    DWORD   nMaxInstances,   // in
```

---

[18] Note that connecting to a named pipe via a machine name of "." (for instance, "\\.\pipe\mypipe") appears to cause the system to use a different transport (specifically, the local interprocess communication transport), which doesn't use SMB. This is purely based on experimentation and hints left in MSDN here and there.

[19] This is a trick I've used quite often when administering domains in Windows NT 4. If I happen to be working at a machine that's connected to the network but is not a member of the domain I'd like to muck with (and thus I cannot log into the machine using my domain credentials), I simply set up a use record with the remote domain controller using my domain credentials so that whenever I run any of the administrative tools, such as User Manager, Server Manager, or the Registry Editor (connecting to a remote registry), these tools will use the credentials I specified in my use record. (I always am careful to delete the use record before I leave the workstation.) NET.EXE is your friend in more ways than one.

```
  DWORD    nOutBufferSize,    // in
  DWORD    nInBufferSize,     // in
  DWORD    nDefaultTimeOut,   // in
  LPSECURITY_ATTRIBUTES lpSecurityAttributes // in, optional
);
```

The security descriptor specified via *lpSecurityAttributes* is important: It determines who is allowed to access the pipe. The lmserver component will perform automatic access checks on your behalf based on the DACL you've specified here. If you don't specify a DACL, you'll get the default DACL in your token, which, unless you've changed it, will only allow you and the System logon session to access the pipe, which is probably not what you want. Check out Chapter 6 for details on setting up a security descriptor.

Once the named pipe is created, a client can connect to it by calling `CreateFile`:

```
HANDLE CreateFile(
  LPCTSTR lpFileName,               // in
  DWORD   dwDesiredAccess,          // in
  DWORD   dwShareMode,              // in
  LPSECURITY_ATTRIBUTES lpSecurityAttributes, // in, optional
  DWORD   dwCreationDisposition,    // in
  DWORD   dwFlagsAndAttributes,     // in
  HANDLE  hTemplateFile             // in, optional
);
```

Most developers are intimately familiar with this function, but when used with a named pipe, there are some security-related flags that are worth mentioning. These flags are specified via the *dwFlagsAndAttributes* parameter, and are known as the security quality-of-service options:

SECURITY_ANONYMOUS

SECURITY_IDENTIFICATION

SECURITY_IMPERSONATION

SECURITY_DELEGATION

SECURITY_CONTEXT_TRACKING

SECURITY_EFFECTIVE_ONLY

If you read Chapter 4, the first four flags should ring a bell; this is the level of trust the client (who is opening a named pipe) places in the server he or she is authenticating with. The server (as we'll see) will be able to impersonate the client; by controlling this level of trust, the client controls the strength of security context available to the server.[20]

The next flag, SECURITY_CONTEXT_TRACKING, is a rather odd beast, and I really had to dig to find any documentation on it. It turns out that it only works with the local interprocess communication transport. (If the client specifies a machine name other than ".", this flag is ignored.) When this flag is set, each outgoing call from the client is sensitive to the current security context of the client. That is, when the server impersonates the client, the server will always see the client's current security context. If the client opens a pipe and sends a message while impersonating Alice, the server sees Alice. If the client starts impersonating Aaron and sends another message through the same pipe handle, the server now sees Aaron. This is very similar to the way dynamic cloaking works in COM, as is shown in Chapter 9. This is clearly incompatible with the way lmsessions work (one set of credentials is used to authenticate the connection, period), which is the reason for the restriction that the flag only works with the IPC transport (which short-circuits the normal lmsession mechanism).

As with the previous flag, SECURITY_EFFECTIVE_ONLY is only implemented by the local interprocess communication transport. This flag allows the client to restrict the server's use of his or her privileges quite severely. The only privileges that will appear in the token that the server obtains after authenticating the client will be those privileges that were actually enabled in the client's token at authentication time.

One final note: If you decide to specify any of these flags, you must indicate that you are specifying security information via yet another flag—SECURITY_SQOS_PRESENT.

---

[20] On Windows 2000, I've successfully gotten the first three impersonation levels to work across the wire, but CreateFile failed mysteriously each time I tried to use delegation-level impersonation.

SMB Signing

Recall that after an authentication handshake, the client and server discover a shared session key that can be used for sealing or signing messages that they send to one another. SMB supports this feature,[21] and you can control whether SMB traffic is signed or not via the security policy editor in Windows 2000. Unfortunately, there is a single setting for the entire machine, so a single application cannot adjust this setting without affecting other applications.

There are basically two settings on both the client and the server side, resulting in four possible permutations per entity (one of which is meaningless). For instance, the settings on the client side are as follows:

Digitally sign client communication (when possible)

Digitally sign client communication (always)

If the first setting is enabled, SMB signing is *enabled;* the client prefers to sign SMB traffic as long as the server supports it. Enabling the second setting only makes sense if the first setting is also enabled, and this goes one step further: It *requires* the server to support SMB signing; otherwise, the SMB negotiation will fail. This results in the client having three effective states for SMB signing: required, enabled, or disabled.

On the server side, a similar pair of settings is available:

Digitally sign server communication (when possible)

Digitally sign server communication (always)

This results in the server also having three effective states for SMB signing: required, enabled, or disabled.

Table 8.1 shows what happens in each of the possible combination of cases. The OK column specifies whether the SMB connection will be established, and the Signed column indicates whether the resulting SMB traffic will be signed.

The Windows 2000 policy editor really just adjusts a couple of registry settings (documented in Knowledge Base article Q161372). You can adjust these registry settings directly if you're running an earlier version of Windows.

---

[21] As of Windows NT 4 Service Pack 3.

Table 8.1. SMB Signing

Client	Server	OK?	Signed?
Disabled	Disabled	Yes	No
Enabled	Disabled	Yes	No
Required	Disabled	No	—
Disabled	Enabled	Yes	No
Enabled	Enabled	Yes	Yes
Required	Enabled	Yes	Yes
Disabled	Required	No	—
Enabled	Required	Yes	Yes
Required	Required	Yes	Yes

Summary

- Spending some time to understand the file server can help you build more robust distributed systems, and it can also help you understand how to use Windows more effectively from day to day.

- The file server is session oriented.

- At most one Lan Manager session may exist between a client logon session and a server machine. However, because multiple client-side logon sessions may exist simultaneously, multiple lmsessions may therefore exist between a client machine and a server machine.

- Each lmsession can use an alternate set of credentials to communicate with the file server.

- Client-side "use records" allow you to set up alternate credentials or drive mappings.

- One interesting application of a use record is to set up a NULL session with a server.

- `NET.EXE` is your friend.

- Drive mappings are nothing more than a client-side use record plus a machine-wide alias from a drive letter to a UNC path.

- SMB signing allows a client machine and server machine to negotiate use of a session key for signing SMB traffic.

Chapter 9

COM(+)

I often joke with students who sit through my security course at DevelopMentor that one of the objectives of the course is to produce 24 new developers who have some inkling of what COM security is all about. That generally gets a good laugh out of the crowd. Why is it that COM security seems so unapproachable to most developers? I'm convinced that the reason lies in all the chapters prior to this one. There's just an incredible amount of infrastructure underneath, and if one isn't familiar with the basic mechanisms that make up the Windows security model (such as logon sessions, window stations, network authentication, etc.), it's a pretty tough journey. But once you have a basic understanding of these mechanisms, COM security adds just a few more concepts and some extra details.

This chapter progresses from RPC to COM security, and then shows how COM+ configured components factor into the picture. It starts from the ground up because each layer builds on the previous layer, and understanding the historical progression of the technology is helpful in understanding why security in COM+ works the way it does. COM+ as implemented in Windows 2000 is simply an evolution of MTS, so most of the things I'll say about COM+ also apply to MTS. Rather than cluttering the text with "COM+/MTS," I'll simply use the term *COM+* to refer to both systems, unless I'm specifically pointing out where they differ. Also, please note that this chapter covers COM+ as it was shipped with the operating system in February 2000.

The MSRPC Security Model

Understanding the concepts and model of RPC security is fundamental to understanding how COM security works. I originally planned to have a separate chapter on RPC security (because I felt that it would be useful on its own for any RPC programmers left out there), but I realized that most COM programmers would skip that chapter. So instead, I've incorporated the discussion of RPC security fundamentals into this chapter, and if you are here to understand COM security, I strongly recommend you don't skip this section.

MSRPC has an extremely simple security model that builds on the basic concepts of Windows security that were outlined in earlier chapters. MSRPC is designed to be network protocol agnostic; the client and server simply need to agree on a particular protocol, and MSRPC will load client- and server-side DLLs that know how to send RPC packets over TCP, UDP, IPX, SPX, SMB, AppleTalk, or whatever. That's quite a feat. MSRPC is also designed to be authentication protocol agnostic. The client and server simply need to agree on a particular protocol, and MSRPC will load client- and server-side DLLs that know how to complete an authentication handshake using NTLM, Kerberos, SSL, SPNEGO, or whatever (see Figure 9.1). Chapter 7 discussed SSPI, which is what MSRPC uses to abstract itself from the differences among various authentication protocols.

In MSRPC, it's possible for a server (Bob) to listen on multiple network protocols simultaneously. Bob typically indicates these protocols by making a call to `RpcServerUseProtseq` once for each protocol that he wants to support. When a client (Alice) wants to talk to the server, she must pick a single protocol and construct a binding handle that is annotated with that protocol's identifier. Any calls Alice makes to Bob using this binding handle will be made using

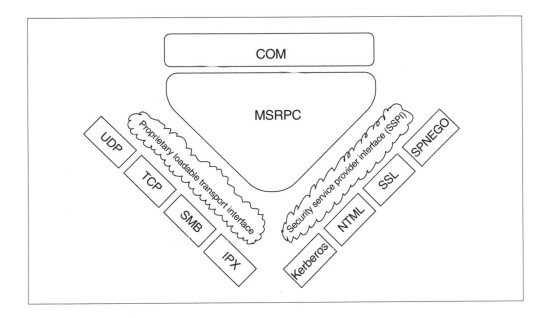

Figure 9.1 MSRPC's agnosticism

the protocol she's specified (and as long as it's one of the protocols that Bob is listening on, things are good).

Similarly, it's possible for Bob to engage in authentication via a number of different authentication protocols. Bob indicates this list of protocols by making one or more calls to RpcServerRegisterAuthInfo. When Alice wants to contact Bob using a particular SSP, she must annotate her binding handle with this information before making any calls. As long as Alice chooses an SSP that Bob has registered, the SSPs will work together to authenticate Alice.

The Client Selects

Alice obtains a binding handle directed at a particular server by calling RpcBindingFromStringBinding, but before she can make any authenticated calls with that handle, she needs to annotate the handle with the authentication settings (including an SSP) that she wants to use. The function Alice calls to choose these settings is RpcBindingSetAuthInfoEx. This function is really important to understand, so each argument will be discussed (COM developers, pay attention here—you'll need this background later).

```
RPC_STATUS RpcBindingSetAuthInfoEx(
  RPC_BINDING_HANDLE Binding,                // in
  unsigned char PAPI *ServerPrincName,       // in, optional
  unsigned long AuthnLevel,                  // in
  unsigned long AuthnSvc,                    // in
  RPC_AUTH_IDENTITY_HANDLE AuthIdentity,     // in, optional
  unsigned long AuthzSvc,                    // in
  RPC_SECURITY_QOS *SecurityQOS              // in
);
```

Binding specifies an RPC binding handle to the server. This function is all about setting some state in the binding so that when Alice makes remote procedure calls to Bob using its handle, the MSRPC runtime will know how to represent Alice when it comes to authentication.

Recall from Chapter 7 that in Kerberos, the client needs to know the principal name of the server in order to obtain a ticket to send to that server. This is what the *ServerPrincName* parameter to RpcBindingSetAuthInfoEx is used for. Under Kerberos, authentication will fail unless the client specifies this principal name (in other words, Alice cannot pass NULL for *ServerPrincName*). If Alice doesn't know ahead of time what the server's identity is (and she doesn't care, she just wants to be able to get a ticket for the server), she can call RpcMgmtInqServerPrincName to obtain the principal name that the server has advertised (the server specifies this in his call to RpcServerRegisterAuthInfo).

The *AuthnSvc* parameter allows Alice to choose which SSP she wants to use. Any outgoing RPCs will use the protocol that the client chooses (if the server doesn't support that protocol, the RPC will fail). Here are the manifest constants that represent the mainstream SSPs:

```
#define RPC_C_AUTHN_GSS_NEGOTIATE   9
#define RPC_C_AUTHN_WINNT           10
#define RPC_C_AUTHN_GSS_SCHANNEL    14
#define RPC_C_AUTHN_GSS_KERBEROS    16
```

In this list, GSS_NEGOTIATE represents SPNEGO, and WINNT represents NTLM (the latter is the only one with built-in support on Windows NT 4; the others were introduced in Windows 2000).

AuthzSvc is a manifest constant that allows Alice to choose an *authorization* service. This is an artifact of MSRPC's DCE heritage, and unless you are using a third-party DCE security provider, you should specify RPC_C _AUTHZ_NONE for this parameter.

If Alice chooses the GSS_NEGOTIATE authentication service, she can indicate an ordered list of authentication services that she prefers by passing a pointer to a SEC_WINNT_AUTH_IDENTITY_EX structure via the *AuthIdentity* parameter:

```
#define SECURITY_WIN32
#include <security.h>
typedef struct _SEC_WINNT_AUTH_IDENTITY_EX {
    unsigned long  Version;
    unsigned long  Length;
    LPTSTR         User;
    unsigned long  UserLength;
    LPTSTR         Domain;
    unsigned long  DomainLength;
    LPTSTR         Password;
    unsigned long  PasswordLength;
    unsigned long  Flags;
    LPTSTR         PackageList;
    unsigned long  PackageListLength;
} SEC_WINNT_AUTH_IDENTITY_EX;
```

The list of authentication services is a single string with the comma-delimited names Kerberos, NTLM, and/or SCHANNEL.[1] If all Alice wants to do is choose the packages used for negotiation, she should pass NULL for the *User*, *Domain*, and *Password* fields, and the SSP will obtain her network credentials automatically by looking at the security context of her thread (more on this later).

Whereas security package negotiation was introduced in Windows 2000, another feature that *AuthIdentity* can be used to enable is choosing an alter-

---

[1] As of this writing, although the SCHANNEL SSP integration for RPC and COM is enabled in Windows 2000, it's not yet fully documented (or fully debugged), which is why I'm not spending any time discussing it in this chapter.

Table 9.1 Values for choosing credentials

User	Domain	Password	Result
0	0	0	Uses the default credentials for the thread
"amy@foo.com"	" "	"password"	Uses amy@foo.com
"amy"	"foo.com"	"password"	Uses amy@foo.com
" "	" "	" "	Uses NULL session (NTLM only)

nate set of credentials, which is supported on older platforms as well.[2] Table 9.1 provides a few examples of values that Alice could specify for the *User*, *Domain*, and *Password* fields to dictate the client-side credentials to be used with the binding handle.

Here are the other details you should know if you plan on using this structure. The *Version* field should be set to SEC_WINNT_AUTH_IDENTITY_ VERSION, and the *Length* field should be set to the size of the structure. Because you can pass either Unicode or multibyte strings, the *Flags* field must indicate your choice via one of the following flags:

```
#define SEC_WINNT_AUTH_IDENTITY_ANSI        0x1
#define SEC_WINNT_AUTH_IDENTITY_UNICODE     0x2
```

A couple of other flags are listed in MSDN without adequate documentation:

```
#define SEC_WINNT_AUTH_IDENTITY_MARSHALLED  0x4
#define SEC_WINNT_AUTH_IDENTITY_ONLY        0x8
```

The first flag is used internally and (at least as of this writing) Microsoft doesn't provide documentation of the format for the expected "marshalled" structure (thus I mention this flag only for completeness). The second flag appears to be for use with non-Windows implementations of Kerberos, because it allows you to obtain a ticket without any authorization attributes, the structure of which is

---

[2] Use the SEC_WINNT_AUTH_IDENTITY structure on older platforms.

not defined by Kerberos. Just for kicks I tried using this flag and was treated to a NULL session on the server, which doesn't seem terribly useful.

Note that this data structure is *not* sent across the wire; rather, it is passed discreetly to the client-side SSP, who uses it to determine how to authenticate outgoing requests (for example, which tickets to obtain and which password to use to answer an NTLM challenge).

Security Quality of Service

The information passed via `SecurityQOS` should be familiar if you happened to read Chapter 8. These are the security quality-of-service flags that provide extra information about the client's wishes:

```
typedef struct _RPC_SECURITY_QOS
{
  unsigned long Version;
  unsigned long Capabilities;
  unsigned long IdentityTracking;
  unsigned long ImpersonationType;
} RPC_SECURITY_QOS;
```

If you want proof of the server's identity, set the RPC_C_QOS_ CAPABILITIES_MUTUAL_AUTH flag in the `Capabilities` field of this structure. This causes the RPC runtime to request mutual authentication; in the case of Kerberos, this means that the KRB_AP_REQ message will contain an option indicating that the server should prove knowledge of the session key in the ticket (as discussed in Chapter 7) and reply with a KRB_AP_REP message. The end result is that if Alice requests mutual authentication and her first call to the server succeeds, she's assured that the server is indeed running under the credentials she specified via `ServerPrincName`. If the server is running as some other principal, Alice's calls to the server will fail. (In my experience, the error code has always been RPC_S_SEC_PKG_ERROR: "A security package specific error occurred.")

Interestingly enough, if you're using SPNEGO and you pass NULL for `ServerPrincName`, MSRPC will choose NTLM over Kerberos.[3] What it boils

---

[3] I didn't find this behavior documented in MSDN; this is based on my own experience with Windows 2000 build 2195.

down to is this: As a client, if you know the server principal name (or think you know), you should always specify it explicitly if you want to have any chance of using Kerberos.

The *IdentityTracking* field determines when (chronologically) the MSRPC runtime should select the client's default credentials (in other words, the credentials to be used when the client passes NULL for *AuthIdentity*). The two possible settings for this field are as follows:

```
RPC_C_QOS_IDENTITY_STATIC

RPC_C_QOS_IDENTITY_DYNAMIC
```

The first option (the default) says that the MSRPC runtime will only select client-side credentials when the client calls `RpcBindingSetAuthInfo(Ex)`, and will continue to use those same credentials for that binding handle until another call to `RpcBindingSetAuthInfo(Ex)` causes a different set of credentials to be cached.

Here's an example to illustrate:

1. A thread in a process hosted in Alice's logon session calls `RpcBindingSetAuthInfoEx (RpcBSAIEx)`.

2. All RPCs using this binding handle now use Alice's credentials.

3. The thread now begins impersonating Mary and makes an RPC using this binding handle; the outgoing call *still* uses Alice's credentials.

4. While still impersonating Mary, the thread calls `RpcBSAIEx` again on the same binding handle. Now outgoing calls through this binding handle use Mary's credentials.

5. The thread stops impersonating Mary.

6. All RPCs using the binding handle *still* use Mary's credentials.

7. The thread (no longer impersonating) calls `RpcBSAIEx` one more time. All new RPCs using this binding handle use Alice's credentials once more.

As you can see by this example, the binding handle holds a "sticky" reference to the client's network credentials (if you recall from the discussion of SSPI in

Chapter 7, this is physically a client-side SSPI credential handle obtained by calling `AcquireCredentialsHandle`). Since static (sticky) tracking is used by default, you should be very aware of your thread's security context when you call `RpcBindingSetAuthInfo(Ex)`, unless you are passing explicit credentials via *pAuthIdentity*.

The second tracking option (DYNAMIC) says that MSRPC should gather the client's credentials at each outgoing call. Unlike the file server (where dynamic tracking only works locally), MSRPC happily implements dynamic tracking over the wire and thus reauthenticates at the next RPC if your thread's security context has changed since your last RPC.

All this talk about identity tracking is only interesting if the thread making outgoing RPCs happens to also use impersonation occasionally. The DYNAMIC tracking option makes MSRPC work very much like the operating system works locally, and is considerably more intuitive to most people than static tracking.

ImpersonationType indicates the amount of trust the client places in the server via the same four impersonation levels that were discussed in Chapter 4; the manifest constants are different, but the concept remains the same. If Bob impersonates Alice, the token he gets will have the impersonation level that Alice specifies, so this limits what Bob can do with Alice's credentials:

```
#define RPC_C_IMP_LEVEL_ANONYMOUS      1
#define RPC_C_IMP_LEVEL_IDENTIFY       2
#define RPC_C_IMP_LEVEL_IMPERSONATE    3
#define RPC_C_IMP_LEVEL_DELEGATE       4
```

MSRPC supports the ANONYMOUS level over the local interprocess communication transport (ncalrpc) only. For other transports, it silently promotes this level to IDENTIFY.

One final setting that's not shown here is the rather esoteric "effective-only" flag that may be specified in the binding string itself. This is equivalent to the SECURITY_EFFECTIVE_ONLY flag discussed in Chapter 8, and again, it only has an effect if the client and server are on the same machine and are using the local interprocess communication transport. For instance, the binding string

```
"ncalrpc[Security=identification static true]"
```

indicates not only that the impersonation level is identification and the identity-tracking setting is STATIC, but also that only the enabled privileges in the client's token should be present in the token seen by the server. Don't be surprised if you see this behavior for local COM servers as well, because effective-only is the default setting and COM provides no facility for changing this. Because this feature only works locally, you won't see this behavior across the wire, which is a good thing because privileges are granted on a per-machine basis and thus the privileges that happen to be present in Alice's token on AlicesMachine may be completely different from the privileges that reside in Alice's token on BobsMachine.

Authentication Levels

The only parameter to RpcBindingSetAuthInfoEx that has not yet been covered is *AuthnLevel*. This parameter allows Alice to choose exactly how much protection she desires from her SSP. Recall from Chapter 7 that during an authentication exchange, Alice and Bob each discover a session key that they can use to sign or seal packets that they send to one another. *AuthnLevel* allows Alice to control exactly how this session key should be used:

```
#define RPC_C_AUTHN_LEVEL_NONE           1
#define RPC_C_AUTHN_LEVEL_CONNECT        2
#define RPC_C_AUTHN_LEVEL_CALL           3
#define RPC_C_AUTHN_LEVEL_PKT            4
#define RPC_C_AUTHN_LEVEL_PKT_INTEGRITY  5
#define RPC_C_AUTHN_LEVEL_PKT_PRIVACY    6
```

These constants are purposely arranged in order of increasing security.

If Alice cranks this level all the way up to PKT_PRIVACY, the entire message (headers and payload) will be signed and the payload will be sealed with the session key. Because *AuthnLevel* provides equal protection for the request and response packets, both [in] and [out] parameters are protected. What does Bob know when he receives a call at this authentication level? He knows that the parameters were hidden from eavesdroppers, and because the packet is signed with the session key, he knows that it came from Alice and that it hasn't been tampered with. (If tampering is detected, the MSRPC runtime fails the call at the door and Bob's procedure isn't invoked at all.)

If Alice doesn't require confidentiality, she might instead choose PKT_INTEGRITY to save some CPU cycles. Here, the SSP signs the entire packet contents with the session key (forming a **MAC**), but the payload is not encrypted. Thus MSRPC can still detect any tampering with the payload or headers and can guarantee to Bob that every last fragment of the RPC request was actually sent by Alice (because she is the only other party who knows the session key). If MSRPC cannot verify the MAC, the call will be rejected immediately with an error.

To avoid signing the entire payload, the authentication level PKT indicates that only the headers should be signed. This saves even more CPU cycles, at the risk of allowing tampering with the payload to go unnoticed.

To avoid signing each fragment of a large RPC request or response, the authentication level CALL indicates that only the headers of the first fragment should be signed. This is a rather obscure setting, and is in fact not implemented by any of the mainstream SSPs. If Alice chooses this level, it'll be silently promoted to PKT.

To avoid signing or sealing anything at all, Alice can choose authentication level CONNECT. This indicates that at connection time (in other words, at TCP connection establishment, SMB session establishment, etc.), the normal authentication handshake should take place, resulting in the exchange of a session key, as usual. However, the session key is not to be used *at all* for the remainder of the connection. This saves even more CPU cycles, but it also leaves Alice hoping that a determined attacker isn't smart enough to realize that he or she can simply hijack Alice's connection and start sending packets to Bob (or intercepting Alice's packets, changing them, and *then* sending them to Bob). Bob won't know that these packets are coming from a bad guy. He won't really know the true origin of *any* packets arriving via this connection, nor will Alice know the true origin of the response. Clearly this level only will work if Alice chooses to make RPC calls over a connection-oriented transport such as TCP or SMB. If Alice chooses a datagram transport (for instance, UDP[4]), CONNECT is silently promoted to PKT.

---

[4] In COM, RPC over UDP is used by default between two Windows NT 4 machines. Both Windows 9x and Windows 2000 use RPC over TCP.

The last level is NONE, which indicates that no authentication handshake should occur at all. If the client chooses this level, none of the other parameters to RpcBindingSetAuthInfoEx have any meaning, and so they will be ignored (note that if you choose this authentication level you must also set the authentication service to RPC_C_AUTHN_NONE). This is the default setting in RPC; if Alice forgets to call RpcBindingSetAuthInfoEx on her binding handle, no authentication handshake will be performed at all, and thus no network logon session (not even a NULL session) will be established on Bob's machine as a result of RPCs coming from Alice; thus, Bob won't be able to get a token to discover who the client is.

As you can see, RpcBindingSetAuthInfoEx allows Alice to specify boatloads of configuration information so that her SSP knows how to represent her on the wire. In summary, Alice can choose which authentication protocol to use (*AuthnSvc*), how much protection she wants (*AuthnLevel*), a name to use in order to verify the server's identity (*ServerPrincName*), whether she wants to use an alternate set of credentials (*AuthIdentity*), and how much she trusts the server to impersonate her (*SecurityQOS.ImpersonationType*). All these settings are chosen at Alice's discretion.

Solving Race Conditions

As a client, you can call RpcBindingSetAuthInfoEx any time you want to change the security settings on a binding handle. MSRPC will simply reauthenticate the next time you make a method call using that binding handle. This means, for example, that you can dynamically switch between PKT_PRIVACY and PKT_INTEGRITY so that you only pay the price for encryption on the RPCs that send or receive truly sensitive data. In fact, sometimes it's convenient to have two separate binding handles that point to the same server endpoint but differ in security settings. When you make calls using the first handle, they will go out at PKT_INTEGRITY; when you make calls using the second handle, they will go out at PKT_PRIVACY.

This technique is traditionally used to solve race conditions in which multiple threads are competing for a single binding handle. By giving each thread its own binding handle, that thread has autonomy to adjust the authentication settings at any time without introducing race conditions. MSRPC provides a couple of functions to make this easy:

```
RPC_STATUS RPC_ENTRY RpcBindingCopy(
  RPC_BINDING_HANDLE   SourceBinding,
  RPC_BINDING_HANDLE*  DestinationBinding
);

RPC_STATUS RPC_ENTRY RpcBindingInqAuthInfoEx(
  RPC_BINDING_HANDLE   Binding,
  RPC_CHAR PAPI*       ServerPrincName,
  unsigned long PAPI*  AuthnLevel,
  unsigned long PAPI*  AuthnSvc,
  RPC_AUTH_IDENTITY_HANDLE PAPI* AuthIdentity,
  unsigned long PAPI*  AuthzSvc,
  unsigned long        RpcQosVersion,
  RPC_SECURITY_QOS*    SecurityQos
);
```

By making a copy of an existing binding handle via RpcBindingCopy, and then asking for the current authentication settings via RpcBindingInqAuth InfoEx, the thread can then adjust only the settings it wants to tweak (most often this is used to change the authentication level, as suggested earlier).

What If Authentication Fails?

Imagine what would happen if Alice chooses an authentication level of PKT_ PRIVACY and makes an RPC to Bob, requesting sensitive medical records. First of all, if she's using Kerberos, her SSP will verify Bob's identity assuming she's requested mutual authentication. Second, she is going to expect that those medical records will be encrypted so nobody can discover their contents as they travel across the wire; that's confidential information for Alice.

What are some reasons why the authentication handshake Alice requested might fail? In practice, the most common reason is that there is no path of trust from Bob's authority to Alice's authority, which means that there is no way to allow Alice and Bob to securely exchange a session key. Without a session key, Bob cannot prove (via Kerberos, at least) his identity to Alice. Without a session key, Bob also cannot encrypt those medical records to send back to Alice. None of Alice's requirements can be met if authentication fails. So the question is, what should MSRPC do in this case? Allow the call to succeed? Or fail the call immediately?

The answer is that the call fails (as you probably expected it would). Note that the reason it failed is because Alice and Bob's SSPs could not make *Alice* happy; it has nothing to do with what Bob wants. If Alice requests authentication, and authentication fails, the call will *always* fail. The error code you might expect in this case would be something like "Gee, sorry Alice, Bob's happy to accept anonymous callers, but since you requested authentication protection and Bob can't make it happen, we had to fail the call (if you want, you may try again without authentication and the call will likely succeed)." However, to avoid giving attackers *any* information about a failure that would help them adjust their penetration strategy, the call simply fails with ERROR_ACCESS_ DENIED.

This is a fantastic example of why it can be difficult to debug security-related errors: The system is designed to make this hard for an outsider. But if you've been paying attention, you probably already know exactly how to figure out what went wrong in this case. As a good guy, you (or an administrator that you can contact) will have access to the server and can enable auditing of logon and logoff events (I can't recommend this enough). By looking in the audit log, you'll see the reason the SSP gave for failing Alice's authentication request (probably "bad user name or password," but it could also be something as silly as "password needs to be changed at first logon"). You can also use Alice's Kerberos ticket cache (discussed in Chapter 7) to find more clues. The more you know about how authentication works, the more quickly you'll be able to diagnose problems in the field.

The Server Detects

Yes, there's a little rhyme that weaves its way through this chapter: The client selects, and the server detects. Remember this rhyme and you'll be well on your way to understanding RPC and COM security.

Alice can select any authentication protocol and any authentication level she likes (even *NONE*) and make calls to Bob. In MSRPC, Bob receives all incoming authenticated calls (assuming Alice's requests can be satisfied by the

SSPs). What might surprise you at first is that in MSRPC, Bob receives all incoming anonymous calls as well (where the caller chose not to use authentication at all). It's up to Bob to detect the settings chosen by the client and act accordingly (a highly secure server would likely reject all anonymous calls, for instance).[5]

When one of Bob's procedures is invoked by the MSRPC runtime on Alice's behalf, Bob takes his server-side binding handle and passes it to *RpcBindingInqAuthClient*. (Technically, `ClientBinding` is an optional parameter; if you pass NULL, the MSRPC runtime assumes you want information about the current caller for the thread.)

```
RPC_STATUS RpcBindingInqAuthClient(
    RPC_BINDING_HANDLE  ClientBinding,    // in, optional
    RPC_AUTHZ_HANDLE*   Privs,            // out, optional
    unsigned char**     ServerPrincName,  // out, optional
    unsigned long*      AuthnLevel,       // out, optional
    unsigned long*      AuthnSvc,         // out, optional
    unsigned long*      AuthzSvc          // out, optional
);
```

First note that this function will fail[6] if the client chose not to authenticate at all (either by specifying an authentication level of NONE or by not calling `RpcBindingSetAuthInfoEx`). Bob should always be careful to check for this condition, because it indicates an anonymous caller.

Bob can pass NULL for any of the [out] parameters that he's not interested in. (For instance, *AuthzSvc* isn't interesting to people not using DCE security, and *AuthnSvc* and *ServerPrincipalName* aren't going to be surprising because they will come from the set Bob registered earlier via `RpcServerRegisterAuthInfo`.)

---

[5] The function `RpcServerRegisterIfEx` provides a bit of help to those writing secure RPC servers; after calling this function, RPC will automatically reject any unauthenticated calls (calls that arrive at an authentication level of NONE) as long as you provide a security callback function. RPC will call this function once for each new client that makes a call to the interface, and you can make access control decisions at that time.

[6] The error code in this case is RPC_S_BINDING_HAS_NO_AUTH (the S means "status code," not "success" as it does in a COM HRESULT).

AuthnLevel indicates the level of protection selected by the client (and thus the level being used for the duration of this remote procedure call). This is one of the first things Bob is going to care about. Is the client-selected level satisfactory to him? (Bob cannot change the level at this point, but he can choose to return an error code and ignore the client's request if he's not satisfied with the client's choice.) Bob might even look at the [in] parameters Alice passed in her request and determine that because she's asking for really sensitive information, he'll fail the call unless she chose PKT_PRIVACY; for less sensitive requests, Bob may be satisfied with PKT_INTEGRITY. The choice is left entirely up to Bob; MSRPC makes no judgments here.

This explanation should make it clear why MSRPC allows anonymous callers through by default: It assumes that the server is smart enough to reject anonymous calls to sensitive procedures.

Privs is an interesting parameter that might convince Bob to pay attention to the *AuthnSvc* parameter as well, since *Privs* basically allows him to get a pointer to some SSP-specific data structure designed to be used for making authorization decisions (hence the name). For the NTLM and Kerberos SSPs, this pointer will refer to the client principal name in Authority\Principal format. If all you need is the client's name, this is the cheapest way to get it, because this information is always sent across the wire in an NTLM or Kerberos exchange and is sitting there in the server-side SSP's security context, waiting for you to ask for it.[7]

If Bob needs more information than is provided by RpcBindingInqAuth Client, he can impersonate Alice and open her token (via OpenThread Token, as discussed in Chapter 4).

```
RPC_STATUS RpcImpersonateClient (
    RPC_BINDING_HANDLE BindingHandle  // in, optional
);

RPC_STATUS RpcRevertToSelf();
```

This of course assumes that Alice hasn't chosen an impersonation level of RPC_C_IMP_LEVEL_ANONYMOUS (if she has, OpenThreadToken will fail).

---

[7] You must not free this string; you're just getting a peek into the SSP's internal data structures.

RPC Security Wrapup

That's all there is to it. RPC security is fundamentally a very simple model, exposed via a very small set of functions. The client *selects* an SSP and a group of authentication settings, and MSRPC uses those settings to authenticate (or not) with the server. As long as the client has chosen an SSP that the server is happy with (or has made an anonymous, unauthenticated call), authentication will proceed according to the client's wishes. If authentication fails, the call fails. If authentication succeeds (or if it's an anonymous call), the server *detects* the client's chosen settings and reacts appropriately. MSRPC doesn't attempt to provide a default access control policy; the server receives all anonymous and successfully authenticated calls and makes its own choices.

As a result of this simplicity, RPC security is quite straightforward to use and debug in the field. To wrap up this section, I've provided an example of an RPC client and server using the functions described previously. Here's the client code:

```
long sum = _addViaRPC(2, 2,
                    L"ncacn_ip_tcp:BobsMachine",
                    L"bob@foo.com");

long _addViaRPC(long a, long b,
                wchar_t* pszBindingString,
                wchar_t* pszExpectedServerPrincipal) {
  // get a binding handle to the server
  RPC_BINDING_HANDLE h;
  RPC_STATUS s = RpcBindingFromStringBinding(
                    pszBindingString, &h);
  if (s)
    _err(L"RpcBindingFromStringBinding", s);

  // select authn settings on the binding handle
  RPC_SECURITY_QOS sqos = {
    RPC_C_SECURITY_QOS_VERSION,
    RPC_C_QOS_CAPABILITIES_MUTUAL_AUTH,
    RPC_C_QOS_IDENTITY_STATIC,
    RPC_C_IMP_LEVEL_IDENTIFY
  };
```

```
s = RpcBindingSetAuthInfoEx(h,
            pszExpectedServerPrincipal,
            RPC_C_AUTHN_LEVEL_PKT_INTEGRITY,
            RPC_C_AUTHN_GSS_KERBEROS,
            0,
            RPC_C_AUTHZ_NONE,
            &sqos);
if (s)
  _err(L"RpcBindingSetAuthInfoEx", s);

long sum = 0;
__try {
  sum = Add(h, a, b); // here's the actual RPC
}
__except(EXCEPTION_EXECUTE_HANDLER) {
  _err(L"RPC", GetExceptionCode());
}
RpcBindingFree(&h);
return sum;
}
```

Here's the implementation of Add in the server. Note that the server verifies the client's authentication level (only after carefully checking the error code returned from RpcBindingInqAuthClient):

```
long Add(RPC_BINDING_HANDLE h, long a, long b) {

  // server detects the client's authn settings
  RPC_AUTHZ_HANDLE hPrivs;
  DWORD nAuthnLevel;
  RPC_STATUS s = RpcBindingInqAuthClient(h,
              &hPrivs, 0, &nAuthnLevel, 0, 0);

  // don't allow anonymous callers to slip through
  if (s)
    RpcRaiseException(ERROR_ACCESS_DENIED);

  // make sure we're happy with the caller's authn level
  if (nAuthnLevel < RPC_C_AUTHN_LEVEL_PKT_INTEGRITY)
    RpcRaiseException(ERROR_ACCESS_DENIED);
```

```
    // here's a really low-tech auditing mechanism ;-)
    wprintf(L"Add invoked by %s\n", (wchar_t*)hPrivs);

    return a + b;
}
```

Here's the code that the server calls from main to service RPC requests. Most of it is just boilerplate RPC, but notice the first two API calls: The first selects a network transport; the second selects a network authentication protocol (Kerberos).

```
void _listenForRPCRequests() {
  // choose a network transport: TCP
  RpcServerUseProtseq(L"ncacn_ip_tcp",
      RPC_C_PROTSEQ_MAX_REQS_DEFAULT, 0);

  // choose a network authentication protocol: Kerberos
  RpcServerRegisterAuthInfo(L"bob@foo.com",
                            RPC_C_AUTHN_GSS_KERBEROS,
                            0, 0);

  // see which TCP port we were allocated
  RPC_BINDING_VECTOR* pbv;
  RpcServerInqBindings(&pbv);

  // register protseq/port/uuid with the endpoint mapper
  RpcEpRegister(RpcCalc_v1_0_s_ifspec, pbv, 0, 0);

  // register our RpcCalc interface with the RPC runtime
  RpcServerRegisterIf(RpcCalc_v1_0_s_ifspec, 0, 0);

  // turn on the fire hose!
  RpcServerListen(0, RPC_C_LISTEN_MAX_CALLS_DEFAULT,
                  FALSE);
}
```

The COM Security Model

With a basic understanding of how RPC security works, you'll be surprised how easy COM security can be. The first thing you must understand is how a COM proxy is built (see Figure 9.2). Note that each interface proxy holds a pointer to

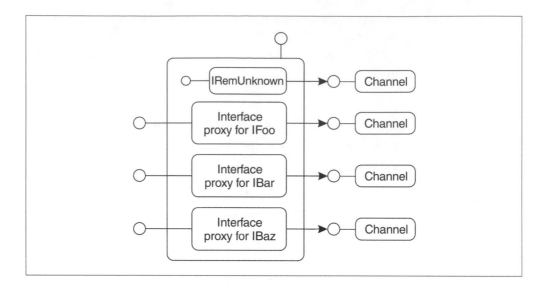

Figure 9.2   Anatomy of a COM proxy

a channel object. Each interface proxy is responsible for marshaling stack frames to and from transmission buffers provided by the channel; the interface proxy itself could care less about security or even where the call will be dispatched. The channel ultimately wraps the services provided by MSRPC, and you can probably guess what each of those channel objects really holds under the sheets: an RPC binding handle.

The Client Selects

Remember the RPC security rhyme? It's the same rhyme in COM, except that the binding handles you're configuring are buried down in the channel objects shown in Figure 9.2. The COM interface you use to configure these binding handles is known as `IClientSecurity`, and it should look remarkably familiar considering what you've seen so far.

```
[local, ...]
interface IClientSecurity : IUnknown {
    HRESULT QueryBlanket(
            [in]  IUnknown*      pProxy,
            [out] DWORD*         pAuthnSvc,
```

```
              [out]  DWORD*        pAuthzSvc,
              [out]  OLECHAR**     pServerPrincName,
              [out]  DWORD*        pAuthnLevel,
              [out]  DWORD*        pImpLevel,
              [out]  void**        pAuthInfo,
              [out]  DWORD*        pCapabilites
              );
         HRESULT SetBlanket(
         [in]  IUnknown*      pProxy,
         [in]  DWORD          dwAuthnSvc,
         [in]  DWORD          dwAuthzSvc,
         [in]  OLECHAR*       pServerPrincName,
         [in]  DWORD          dwAuthnLevel,
         [in]  DWORD          dwImpLevel,
         [in]  void*          pAuthInfo,
         [in]  DWORD          dwCapabilities
         );
         HRESULT CopyProxy(
         [in]   IUnknown*     pProxy,
         [out]  IUnknown**    ppCopy
    );
}
```

First of all, notice that this interface is marked [local]. This means it's never remoted: This interface is implemented by the proxy manager directly (see Figure 9.3) and is simply used to adjust the settings on the binding handles that COM has squirreled away down in the channel. Apparently somebody on the COM team had a sense of humor; instead of configuring *authentication settings* as we do in RPC, we configure a *security blanket*[8] in COM to do the same thing.

Take a look at the three methods of IClientSecurity, and notice the striking resemblance to three MSRPC APIs I've already described:

---

[8] In case this cultural reference doesn't ring a bell, a security blanket is the blanket that a young person typically gets attached to around the age of 2. This naming convention was introduced *after* the COM specification was released; the COM specification (Chapter 8, Security) still refers to a function known as CoSetProxyAuthenticationInfo (which doesn't exist). "Blanket" is easier to pronounce than "AuthenticationInfo," so I guess we should be grateful.

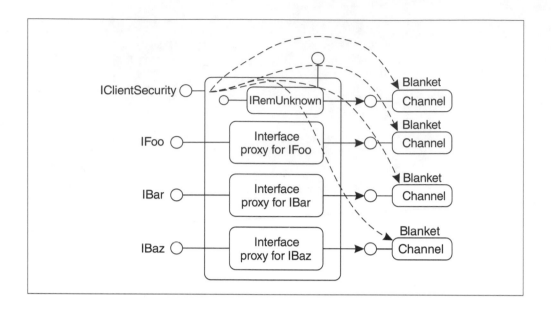

Figure 9.3 Security blankets in a proxy

COM	RPC
ICS::SetBlanket	RpcBindingSetAuthInfoEx
ICS::CopyProxy	RpcBindingCopy
ICS::QueryBlanket	RpcBindingInqAuthInfoEx

Whereas the RPC APIs expect to operate on binding handles, IClient Security expects to operate on interface pointers to proxies. At the end of the day, however, it's really just the same old RPC security model.

Here's an example:

```
void _sendASecretToBob(ISecret* pSecret) {
  IClientSecurity* pcs;
  pSecret->QueryInterface(IID_IClientSecurity,
                          (void**)&pcs);
  pcs->SetBlanket(pSecret,
                  RPC_C_AUTHN_GSS_KERBEROS,
                  RPC_C_AUTHZ_NONE,
```

```
                    L"bob@foo.com",
                    RPC_C_AUTHN_LEVEL_PKT_PRIVACY,
                    RPC_C_IMP_LEVEL_IDENTIFY,
                    0, 0);
    // assuming we can authenticate with Bob, the call
    // will be encrypted using a Kerberos session key
    pSecret->HeresASecret(L"The answer to life, "
                          L"the universe, "
                          L"and everything is 42.");
    pcs->Release();
}
```

This code tells the proxy manager that we want to tweak the authentication settings of the binding handle associated with *pSecret* to use Kerberos authentication with encryption and so forth. Just as with RPC, if the system can't make the client happy (for instance, if authentication fails), the call will fail with E_ACCESSDENIED. This happens *regardless* of what the server wants, because we always have to satisfy the client's request for authentication before we worry about making the server happy. If you want to control the settings used in the proxy manager's internal calls to IRemUnknown, you must pass the non-delegating unknown as the first parameter.[9]

There are three shortcuts that make SetBlanket and friends a bit easier to call (each shortcut API takes the same parameters as its respective cousin in IClientSecurity):

---

[9] What's IRemUnknown anyway? For those of you not familiar with the DCOM wire protocol (Kindel 1998), be aware that calls to QueryInterface, AddRef, and Release on a standard proxy (via any of the interfaces exposed by the proxy) are not directly remoted (IUnknown is actually declared [local] in IDL). Instead, when AddRef is called, it's implemented locally in the proxy manager (PM) by bumping up the proxy's local reference count. Similarly, Release simply decrements this count, and when the count transitions to zero, a single call to IRemUnknown::Release notifies the target stub manager in a single round-trip. The PM implements QueryInterface locally by handing out an interface proxy that's already been aggregated, except when you ask for an interface that you've never asked the PM for before. In this case, the PM uses IRemUnknown::RemQueryInterface to do the deed, aggregating an interface proxy upon success so that later calls to QueryInterface for that interface can be satisfied locally.

If you want to control the authentication settings for any calls that the PM issues through IRemUnknown, you must explicitly obtain the nondelegating unknown (known in some circles as the *thumb,* or *vertical lollipop*) of the PM by calling QueryInterface for IID_IUnknown and using the resulting pointer as the target of your adjustments.

```
HRESULT CoSetProxyBlanket   (/* same as SetBlanket */);
HRESULT CoQueryProxyBlanket(/* same as QueryBlanket */);
HRESULT CoCopyProxy        (/* same as CopyProxy */);
```

This saves you from having to call `QueryInterface` for `IClientSecurity`, in case you felt that was too much of a hassle. Here's an example using the shortcut:

```
void _sendASecretToBob2(ISecret* pSecret) {
  CoSetProxyBlanket(pSecret,
                    RPC_C_AUTHN_GSS_KERBEROS,
                    RPC_C_AUTHZ_NONE,
                    L"bob@foo.com",
                    RPC_C_AUTHN_LEVEL_PKT_PRIVACY,
                    RPC_C_IMP_LEVEL_IDENTIFY,
                    0, 0);
  // assuming we can authenticate with Bob, the call
  // will be encrypted using a Kerberos session key
  pSecret->HeresASecret(L"But what is the question?");
}
```

Besides using interface pointers instead of binding handles in `IClient Security`, note that the `RPC_SECURITY_QOS` data structure has been unfolded into two top-level parameters: *dwImpLevel* and *dwCapabilities*. The impersonation level constants are the same ones used in RPC. Here are the flags that you can pass via *dwCapabilities*:[10]

```
// simplified excerpt from objidl.idl
EOAC_MUTUAL_AUTH     = 0x0001
EOAC_STATIC_CLOAKING  = 0x0020
EOAC_DYNAMIC_CLOAKING = 0x0040
EOAC_DEFAULT         = 0x0800
```

The first flag should look familiar: It's a request for mutual authentication, but COM ignores this flag and always requests mutual authentication on your behalf if the SSP in use supports it.

---

[10] All these flags were introduced in Windows 2000; you must pass 0 for dwCapabilities in earlier versions of Windows.

I'll talk about EOAC_DEFAULT a bit later. For now, let's talk about a Windows 2000 feature called cloaking.

Cloaking

Cloaking is just a fancy-schmancy new term for something we've had all along in named pipes and RPC: control over identity tracking.[11] In Windows NT 4, the one and only identity-tracking mode was that of the default in RPC: static, or sticky, tracking. Whenever you'd call SetBlanket, the blanket would cache the current identity of the calling thread. (If Bob's thread was impersonating Alice when he called SetBlanket, the blanket took on Alice's identity until he called SetBlanket again.)[12]

Windows 2000 exposes the dynamic identity-tracking model as well (it's not clear why this wasn't an option in Windows NT 4, since MSRPC has supported this model for years). What's interesting is that Windows 2000 added a *third* option that RPC doesn't intrinsically support, and made it the default. I'll call this the "ignore the thread token" tracking option, because it does just that: COM completely ignores thread tokens when determining the credentials to use for the outgoing call; it always uses the *process* token to pick up credentials for the outgoing call. Figure 9.4 shows the differences among the three models.

Here's how the cloaking constants map onto the behaviors I've described above:

EOAC_STATIC_CLOAKING	static (sticky) identity tracking
EOAC_DYNAMIC_CLOAKING	Dynamic identity tracking
0x0000	"Ignore the thread token" identity tracking

---

[11] Cloaking sounds so much more *impressive* than identity tracking, don't you think? Kind of like COM+ sounded cooler than ActiveX, which sounded cooler than OLE. Sheesh.

[12] This feature (in COM) was not documented for a *long* time (apparently it was just assumed that people were familiar with how the default static identity tracking worked in RPC and wouldn't be surprised); it wasn't until the MSDN drop that shipped with Visual C++ 6.0 that this behavior was explicitly documented.

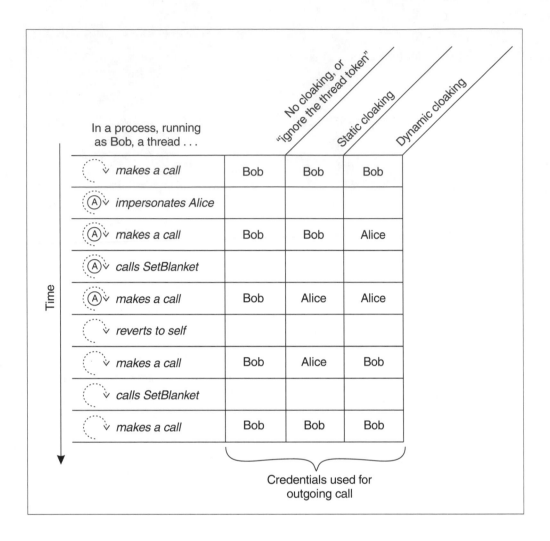

In a process, running as Bob, a thread ...	No cloaking, or "ignore the thread token"	Static cloaking	Dynamic cloaking
makes a call	Bob	Bob	Bob
impersonates Alice			
makes a call	Bob	Bob	Alice
calls SetBlanket			
makes a call	Bob	Alice	Alice
reverts to self			
makes a call	Bob	Alice	Bob
calls SetBlanket			
makes a call	Bob	Bob	Bob

Credentials used for outgoing call

Figure 9.4   Cloaking in action

CopyProxy (Considered Useless)

Remember `RpcBindingCopy`? That function was traditionally used to solve race conditions between threads that were sharing binding handles. If one thread wanted to temporarily elevate the authentication level on a handle, it could make a clone of the handle and make the change on the clone to avoid interfering with any other threads using the original handle. There is a similar function for COM clients called `CopyProxy` that results in the same behavior.

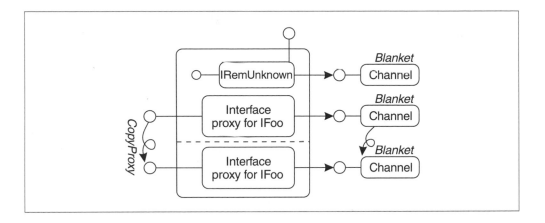

Figure 9.5 The effect of `CopyProxy`

The resulting proxy looks rather strange (see Figure 9.5) because the result is a second interface pointer (attached to the same proxy manager) that implements the same interface as the first. But deep down in the guts of the channel, it has its own private binding handle, and so any blanket settings you apply to it won't have any affect on the original interface pointer.

In COM, you shouldn't ever need to worry about calling `CopyProxy` to avoid race conditions between threads, because if you're a savvy COM(+) developer, you'll realize that you should never share interface pointers directly between threads unless they point directly to objects that you *know* are context neutral (such as the `IStream` pointer returned from `CoMarshalInterThread InterfaceInStream`).[13] Proxies are not considered context neutral by any stretch of the imagination; the interceptors set up between the proxy and stub are based on the differences between the client and object's contexts, and using one proxy from another context results in (at best) an error or (at worst) completely undefined behavior.

---

[13] Technically, if you *know* that your threads are both in the same context (which is possible in the multithreaded apartment, especially in base COM clients), you don't have to do this, but this is a really dangerous path to go down.

If you are already being careful to marshal interface pointers between threads, you'll never have the race conditions that RPC programmers suffer, because each thread (technically, each *context*) will have its own proxy and thus its own set of binding handles.

Another reason RPC programmers used to call `RpcBindingCopy` was to have two different handles that only differed by authentication level, because each time you change the authentication level on a binding handle you'll be reauthenticated at the next call in order to synchronize the client- and server-side SSPs. I have some good news for you: Based on network traces I've performed, it appears as though each channel has the capacity to have multiple binding handles *without any assistance from you;* if the authentication level on a particular interface pointer starts out at `PKT_INTEGRITY`, say, and then you adjust it to `PKT_PRIVACY` by calling `SetBlanket`, MSRPC will simply reauthenticate you in order to synchronize the client- and server-side SSPs. However, since the channel has cached the original (`PKT_INTEGRITY`) binding handle, when you readjust the blanket back to `PKT_INTEGRITY`, the system simply starts using the old binding handle again (you can switch back and forth between these two levels all you want at this point without any further network overhead). This means that you don't need to use `CopyProxy` to optimize overlapped calls at different authentication levels—just adjust the authentication level whenever you feel like it, and COM will do all the binding handle caching behind the scenes to make sure things are as efficient as possible. (This optimization is not documented, so caveat emptor.)

I can't think of any really compelling reason to call `CopyProxy`, but if you find it absolutely necessary, one thing to watch out for is that the cloned interface pointers it creates are not visible via `QueryInterface`. So if you write a helper component in C++ that adjusts the blanket settings for a VB or scripting programmer (`IClientSecurity` isn't very friendly to either of those environments), you should not call `CopyProxy`, then configure the copy and hand *the copy* back to the caller. Virtually all these higher-level environments will automatically perform a `QueryInterface` on any interface pointer they obtain, which means the original caller will never see the fine work that you've done because they'll end up using the original pointer they gave you in the first place.

NTLM and Proxies to Local Objects

For local cross-process calls, COM uses the local interprocess communication transport (always), coupled with the NTLM protocol, which in this particular case doesn't bother to perform an SSPI authentication handshake at all, the premise being that once Alice has a logon session on AlicesMachine, she should be able to use that same logon session to talk to *any* resources on that machine, including COM servers (recall that an SSPI handshake results in a new network logon session for the client). Instead of establishing a new logon session for Alice, the NTLM SSP simply duplicates Alice's token (using the impersonation level specified in the blanket) and gives it to the server-side SSP, where it is picked up by the channel and used in access checks (and potentially impersonation if the server chooses to impersonate).

This affects your life in a very profound way. For one thing, SetBlanket is not nearly as useful for proxies to local (as opposed to remote) objects, because it's designed to specify settings for an SSP to use in an authentication handshake (alternate credentials, authentication levels, and so on). COM is not going to perform an authentication handshake in this case, so most of the parameters to SetBlanket are simply ignored (leading to much confusion and gnashing of teeth by developers who aren't aware of this special case).

Because COM uses the local interprocess communication transport in this example, the payload is never visible to network adapters or to any bad guys on the network. Thus while encryption is not used for confidentiality, the authentication level will still be fixed at RPC_C_AUTHN_LEVEL_PKT_PRIVACY, which will make any local server happy.

The two settings that Alice *can* control here are the impersonation level and the identity-tracking policy (cloaking), which allows Alice to choose which token gets duplicated: her process token or potentially a thread token if she happens to be impersonating.

Alice should choose the impersonation level she uses in calls to local servers with caution. If Alice makes a call to a local server (Bob), Bob can impersonate her, and his thread will now be running in her logon session. If Alice's logon session has network credentials (which is natural for most logon sessions, except potentially a network logon session), Bob will be able to use those credentials if Alice has specified an impersonation level of `RPC_C_IMP_LEVEL_IMPERSONATE` or higher. (If this surprises you, see the section in Chapter 4 entitled Trust.) The `SecurityImpersonation` authentication level (as of this writing) does *not* prevent a local server from accessing the client's network credentials as one might conclude based on its documentation. To protect against this, Alice can use `RPC_C_IMP_LEVEL_IDENTIFY`; however, be aware that this will prevent Bob from obtaining even *local* resources on Alice's behalf.

One final note regarding local COM communications: One option that is enabled by default on every RPC binding handle that uses the local interprocess communication transport is the "effective-only" mode discussed earlier, which means the only privileges that will be present in the token obtained by the server will be those that were enabled at the time the client made a call. This surprises almost everyone who impersonates a local client and tries to enable privileges. If Alice wants Bob (a local COM server) to be able to use one of her privileges while he's impersonating her, she'll have to enable that privilege in her token before making the call into Bob.

I thought that I could be clever and get around these ugly limitations by forcing my client to use Kerberos for local calls. However, for some reason, as of this writing MSRPC doesn't allow Kerberos to run over the local interprocess communication transport (which COM always uses for local out-of-process communication), and thus if you try to force Kerberos via `SetBlanket`, you'll get an error code of `RPC_S_UNKNOWN_AUTHN_SERVICE`. So it goes.[14]

The Server Detects

When an incoming call arrives, the server can discover information about the caller's authentication settings, just as with RPC:

```
[local, ...]
interface IServerSecurity : IUnknown {
    HRESULT QueryBlanket(
        [out] DWORD*    pAuthnSvc,
```

---

[14] Apologies to Kurt Vonnegut.

```
        [out] DWORD*      pAuthzSvc,
        [out] OLECHAR**  pServerPrincName,
        [out] DWORD*      pAuthnLevel,
        [out] DWORD*      pImpLevel,    // reserved, mbz
        [out] void**      pPrivs,
        [in,out] DWORD* pCapabilities
    );
    HRESULT ImpersonateClient();
    HRESULT RevertToSelf();
    BOOL IsImpersonating();
}
HRESULT CoGetCallContext(REFIID riid,
                         void **ppInterface);
HRESULT CoQueryClientBlanket(/* same as above */);
HRESULT CoImpersonateClient();
HRESULT CoRevertToSelf();
```

To get a pointer to `IServerSecurity`, the object must (during a method call) reach up and ask COM for this information by calling `CoGetCallContext` (calling this function outside the scope of a method call is meaningless and results in an error). Once again, there are shortcuts provided that save you a call to `CoGetCallContext`.

Notice the similarities to RPC security:

COM	RPC
ISS::QueryClientBlanket	RpcBindingInqAuthClient
ISS::ImpersonateClient	RpcImpersonateClient
ISS::RevertToSelf	RpcRevertToSelf

There's really nothing different here. The explanations provided in the section on RPC security hold here equally well; the only difference is that you are using a COM interface to get this information as opposed to making an RPC API call.

What I've not yet addressed is how a server selects the SSPs it wants to use. Instead of making several calls to `RpcServerRegisterAuthInfo`, once per SSP, COM provides a single API that takes a counted array of data structures that describe the requested SSP and its parameters (the two relevant parameters are highlighted below):

```
typedef struct tagSOLE_AUTHENTICATION_SERVICE {
    DWORD     dwAuthnSvc;
    DWORD     dwAuthzSvc;
    OLECHAR*  pPrincipalName; // advertised name
    HRESULT   hr;
} SOLE_AUTHENTICATION_SERVICE;

WINOLEAPI CoInitializeSecurity(
    PSECURITY_DESCRIPTOR          pSecDesc,
    LONG                          cAuthSvc,
    SOLE_AUTHENTICATION_SERVICE  *asAuthSvc,
    void                         *pReserved1,
    DWORD                         dwAuthnLevel,
    DWORD                         dwImpLevel,
    void                         *pAuthList,
    DWORD                         dwCapabilities,
    void                         *pReserved3
);
```

While the details of the other arguments to `CoInitializeSecurity` will be covered shortly, for now, here's a direct translation of the earlier RPC example in COM. The programming model here is the same: The client *selects* authentication settings, and the server *detects* them. Here's the client code (note that I used the shortcut `CoSetProxyBlanket` to save some typing):

```
long sum = _addViaCOM(2, 2, pCalc, L"bob@foo.com");
long _addViaCOM(long a, long b,
                ICalc* pCalc,
                wchar_t* pszExpectedServerPrincipal) {
  // set security on the binding handle behind pCalc
  CoSetProxyBlanket(pCalc,
                RPC_C_AUTHN_GSS_KERBEROS,
                RPC_C_AUTHZ_NONE,
                pszExpectedServerPrincipal,
                RPC_C_AUTHN_LEVEL_PKT_INTEGRITY,
                RPC_C_IMP_LEVEL_IDENTIFY, 0, 0);
  // now make the call using those settings
```

```
  long sum;
  HRESULT hr = pCalc->Add(a, b, &sum);
  if (FAILED(hr))
    _err(L"Add", hr);

  return sum;
}
```

Here's the server code that calls CoInitializeSecurity to choose Kerberos as the only supported SSP:

```
void _listenForCOMRequests() {
  CoInitializeEx(0, COINIT_MULTITHREADED);
  SOLE_AUTHENTICATION_SERVICE as = {
    RPC_C_AUTHN_GSS_KERBEROS,
    RPC_C_AUTHZ_NONE,
    L"bob@foo.com", 0
  };
  CoInitializeSecurity(0,
                       1, &as,
                       0,
                       RPC_C_AUTHN_LEVEL_NONE,
                       RPC_C_IMP_LEVEL_IDENTIFY,
                       0, 0, 0);
  // class object registration omitted for brevity
  Sleep(INFINITE); // this server never stops ;-)
}
```

Finally, here's the implementation of Add:

```
struct Calc : ICalc {
  // IUnknown implementation omitted...
  STDMETHODIMP Add(long a, long b, long* pSum) {
    DWORD nAuthnLevel;
    RPC_AUTHZ_HANDLE hPrivs;
    HRESULT hr = CoQueryClientBlanket(0, 0, 0,
                                      &nAuthnLevel,
                                      0, &hPrivs, 0);
    // don't allow anonymous callers to slip through
    if (FAILED(hr))
```

```
        return E_ACCESSDENIED;

    // make sure we're happy with the caller's authn level
    if (nAuthnLevel < RPC_C_AUTHN_LEVEL_PKT_INTEGRITY)
        return E_ACCESSDENIED;

    // yet another low-tech auditing mechanism...
    wprintf(L"Add invoked by %s\n", (wchar_t*)hPrivs);

    *pSum = a + b;
    return S_OK;
    }
};
```

Note the similarity to the RPC implementation: This code is careful to check the result of `CoQueryClientBlanket`, which will fail if the client has chosen to make a call at authentication level NONE. It then verifies that the caller is using an authentication level that's reasonable, audits the request to standard output, and finally does the work of adding two numbers.

COM Interception

So far, I've shown you the most basic features of COM security that enable you to use it deliberately, very carefully writing your client and server code to use authentication in exactly the way you choose. Once you understand this basic model, you can now start to fathom the subtle features that COM adds to the RPC security model to make your life easier (and your applications more secure) via interception.

First, notice that RPC servers (and COM servers that use this model) must verify at each and every entry point whether their caller is even authenticated, let alone whether the caller is allowed to do what he or she is trying to do. What if you were to forget to check the return value from `CoQueryClientBlanket`? An anonymous caller could slip through. One answer is to wrap all that code up in a subroutine, but then you have to remember to actually *call* that subroutine. A better option is to let the server-side COM channel intercept the call and perform the authentication check on your behalf before the call even reaches your server's code. If you could set a process-wide low-water mark, saying "No callers may enter my code unless they have been authenticated at least to the level of PKT_INTEGRITY" (for instance), you could eliminate a tremendous amount of risk.

This is exactly what the *dwAuthnLevel* parameter to CoInitialize Security is all about: setting an automatic process-wide low-water mark. Note that the previous code sets this value to NONE in order to accept the entire gamut of possible calls, from unauthenticated calls all the way up to encrypted calls. This follows the MSRPC model of security. If you want to allow COM's interception layer to automatically block underauthenticated callers, you can raise this level to something higher than NONE. Now the implementation of Add becomes considerably simpler (I've removed the log of the caller's identity to show that I don't even have to bother calling CoQueryClientBlanket at all if I don't want to):

```
// only calls that have satisfied the process-wide
// low-water mark will get through the channel and
// actually execute code in this server
STDMETHODIMP Add(long a, long b, long* pSum) {
  *pSum = a + b;
  return S_OK;
}
```

Another thing you can do to make life easier is rely on COM to choose an appropriate set of SSPs for you at runtime, depending on the version of the operating system. By passing (−1, 0) for the counted array of authentication service structures, you turn over control to COM.[15]

```
CoInitializeSecurity(0,
    -1, 0,  // let COM choose the SSPs
    0,                                  // Choose a
    RPC_C_AUTHN_LEVEL_PKT_INTEGRITY, // low-water mark
    RPC_C_IMP_LEVEL_IDENTIFY,
    0, 0, 0);
```

---

[15] On Windows 2000, the default providers include Kerberos, NTLM, and SPNEGO (among others).

Now that the server has set a low-water mark, Alice (a client) will not be able to make calls into the server process[16] unless she chooses at least `PKT_INTEGRITY` (which means that she must be able to be authenticated, which means there must be a trust path from the server machine back to her authority, naturally). If Alice attempts to make a call using an authentication level lower than `PKT_INTEGRITY`, the COM channel will answer her request on the server's behalf by returning `E_ACCESSDENIED`, which is exactly what the server code used to do manually. There's nothing but goodness here for servers.

The Low-Water Mark and Anonymous Callers

Be aware that the low-water mark isn't enough to keep out determined bad guys who know how COM works. Once you specify a low-water mark higher than NONE, COM requires that each caller successfully establish a logon session on the server box. There are a couple of logon sessions that the client can establish without truly proving his or her identity: a NULL session and a Guest logon. Although the details have changed across various service packs,[17] what I can tell you is that you should simply assume that no matter what you set your low-water mark to (from NONE to `PKT_PRIVACY`), anonymous callers using NULL sessions or the Guest logon will be able to slip past this check. The answer to controlling these types of logons lies in access control. If you want to block access to anonymous callers, grant access to Authenticated Users as opposed to Everyone (see Chapter 7 for more details). Basic access control in COM is discussed a bit later in this chapter.

Simplifying the Client's Life

What if a client chooses an authentication level that does not satisfy the server's low-water mark? If the server's low-water mark is `PKT_INTEGRITY`, and the client calls `SetBlanket` with CONNECT level authentication, the server-side channel will block all the client's calls. This isn't a good way to make friends and influence people. So COM provides a hint during a process known as *OXID*

---

[16] Technically, on Windows 2000 the server can open discreet "notches" in this low-water mark using COM+ library applications, as I'll describe a bit later in the chapter.

[17] See Brown (1999c).

resolution that occurs (under the hood) every time the client unmarshals an interface pointer.[18] This hint tells the client-side COM infrastructure exactly what the server's low-water mark is, and thus allows the channel to automatically configure the binding handle with an authentication level *at least as high as the server's*. Another thing that the client-side COM infrastructure discovers during OXID resolution is the server's advertised principal name.[19] This will be the default server principal name specified on the client's binding handle (more on this later).

How does this change the model? The answer is not by much. The client is *still* in charge of selecting the authentication settings, and the server can still detect those settings. The only difference is that with COM, the server gets a chance to *recommend* a default authentication setting to the client.

COM's client-side channel infrastructure can retrieve these settings from the local OXID resolver's cache at any time, and thus the blanket settings for each remotable interface pointer exposed via the standard proxy start life with settings that will at least satisfy the server.

This is all well and good for the server, but what about the client? If it were possible for the client to contribute to these default settings on a process-wide basis, the client might not have to call `SetBlanket` at all. There are in fact a group of client-side default settings, which base COM clients can control by calling `CoInitializeSecurity`.

```
WINOLEAPI CoInitializeSecurity(
    PSECURITY_DESCRIPTOR            pSecDesc,
    LONG                           cAuthSvc,
    SOLE_AUTHENTICATION_SERVICE    *asAuthSvc,
    void                           *pReserved1,
    DWORD                          dwAuthnLevel,
    DWORD                          dwImpLevel,
    void                           *pAuthList,
```

---

[18] A caching mechanism in the OXID resolver makes this pretty efficient. See Kindel (1998) for the details on OXID resolution.

[19] If the server explicitly passed an array of SOLE_AUTHENTICATION_SERVICE structures in his call to CoInitializeSecurity, the "advertised" server principal name is whatever was specified in the *pPrincipalName* field of that structure. If the server instead passed (–1, 0) to get the default SSPs, COM looks at the server's security context to determine these settings.

```
DWORD                               dwCapabilities,
void                                *pReserved3
);
```

The four settings that are meaningful for clients are highlighted. *dwImpLevel* is the default impersonation level. *pAuthList* provides a counted array of alternate credentials;[20] it's possible for a single client process to use different authentication protocols to contact different servers, so each entry in this array corresponds to the default credentials to use for a particular authentication service. *dwCapabilities* allows you to specify the default cloaking behavior for your application (the identity-tracking mode, that is). The cloaking constants and what they mean were discussed earlier, but suffice it to say that usually you'll choose EOAC_DYNAMIC_CLOAKING or no cloaking at all.

Putting the client- and server-side defaults together, Table 9.2 shows how COM arrives at the default blanket settings for each interface pointer on a standard proxy; this is what you get as a client if you don't call SetBlanket at all. Once again, these are just the defaults; the client can always call SetBlanket to make surgical adjustments or to completely reset the authentication settings.

For each parameter to SetBlanket, there is a corresponding constant that you can use to indicate to COM that you'd like to revert to the default value as shown in Table 9.2. (This feature was added in Windows 2000.)[21] These constants are as follows:

```
RPC_C_AUTHN_DEFAULT            0xFFFFFFFF
RPC_C_AUTHZ_DEFAULT            0xFFFFFFFF
COLE_DEFAULT_PRINCIPAL         (OLECHAR*)  0xFFFFFFFF
RPC_C_AUTHN_LEVEL_DEFAULT      0
RPC_C_IMP_LEVEL_DEFAULT        0
COLE_DEFAULT_AUTHINFO          (void*)  0xFFFFFFFF
EOAC_DEFAULT                   0x0800
```

---

[20] This feature (process-wide defaults for alternate credentials) was added in Windows 2000.
[21] On Windows NT 4, there was no way to specifically revert to the default negotiated blanket settings unless you had previously called QueryBlanket and remembered what those settings were yourself (which was common practice).

Table 9.2 Default blanket settings in COM

Blanket Setting	Suggested by	How COM Arrives at a Default
Authentication service	Server	COM does its best to use the strongest authentication service supported by both the server and client.
Server principal name	Server	COM uses the name advertised by the server during OXID resolution. The name advertised by a server can be controlled programmatically via the `asAuthSvc` parameter to the server's `CoInitializeSecurity` call.
Authentication level	Client *and* server	COM uses the highest (most secure) of the two suggestions.
Impersonation level	Client	COM uses the impersonation level specified via the *dwImpLevel* parameter in the client's `CoInitializeSecurity` call.*
Cloaking flags	Client	COM uses the identity-tracking (cloaking) mode specified by the client via the *dwCapabilities* parameter in the client's `CoInitializeSecurity` call.
Alternate credentials	Client	COM uses whatever alternate credentials (if any) the client provides via the *pAuthList* parameter in the client's `CoInitializeSecurity` call.

* Recall that RPC bumps ANONYMOUS-level calls up to IDENTIFY if they go across the wire; this happens with COM as well. However, it is possible to use the ANONYMOUS impersonation level in local COM calls. This is generally a bad idea, however, because if the server-side COM channel attempts to perform access control (which it will do unless access control in the server is completely turned off), it'll fail to open the client's token (ANONYMOUS tokens cannot be opened). Generally the safest bet is to stick with IDENTIFY unless you have a good reason not to.

The following sample code creates a new COM object and adjusts the impersonation level on the resulting interface pointer while leaving all the other blanket settings at their default values:

```
MULTI_QI mqi = {&IID_ICalc};
COSERVERINFO csi = {0, L"BobsMachine"};
CoCreateInstanceEx(CLSID_Calc, 0, CLSCTX_ALL, &csi,
                   1, &mqi);
```

```
// at this point, pCalc has a default blanket
ICalc* pCalc = (ICalc*)mqi.pItf;

CoSetProxyBlanket(pCalc,
  RPC_C_AUTHN_DEFAULT,
  RPC_C_AUTHZ_DEFAULT,
  COLE_DEFAULT_PRINCIPAL,
  RPC_C_AUTHN_LEVEL_DEFAULT,
  RPC_C_IMP_LEVEL_IMPERSONATE,  // here's the change
  COLE_DEFAULT_AUTHINFO,
  EOAC_DEFAULT);

// pCalc now has an impersonation level of IMPERSONATE
```

dwAuthnLevel: One Setting with Two Meanings

As a server, the *dwAuthnLevel* parameter to CoInitializeSecurity specifies your low-water mark. The COM channel will reject any calls that come in at a lower authentication level, and your server's code won't be invoked at all. This low-water mark will be advertised to all your clients during OXID resolution so that their proxies will start life with an authentication level at least as high as the one you desire.

As a client, the authentication level means something different entirely. It's no longer about a low-water mark. It's about negotiating what authentication level you want to use by default for outgoing calls. By bumping up your authentication level, you can elevate the default authentication level on all your proxies. For instance, if a server has a low-water mark of NONE and your authentication level is PKT_INTEGRITY, the proxy you get from that server will start life at PKT_INTEGRITY, the higher of the two settings (see Figure 9.6).

A client can always adjust (via SetBlanket) the authentication level of any proxy before making an outgoing call. The client can make these adjustments using the full range of authentication settings (of course, if the client dips below the low-water mark of the server, the client's call will be rejected by the server-side channel). This is convenient in the case where a client needs to make calls to secure as well as nonsecure servers.

A server can't adjust the low-water mark once it's been set. All clients that make calls into the server must come in at least as high as this process-wide

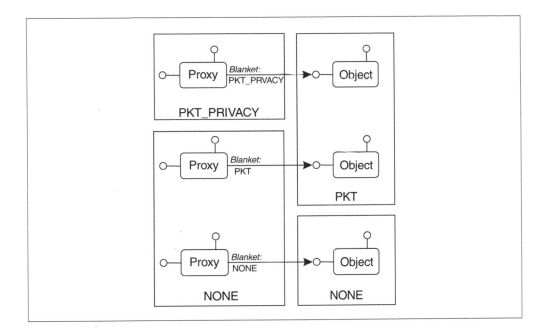

Figure 9.6 Negotiating a default authentication level

setting. A server that wants to receive calls from secure *and* nonsecure clients (clients who cannot be authenticated) has traditionally been a tremendously difficult problem to solve without dropping the server's process-wide low-water mark to NONE, which isn't usually a desirable option. COM+ library applications provide an interesting workaround that I'll discuss later in this chapter.

What if your COM client also acts as a server (perhaps because it receives callbacks)? You have a single setting that controls two very different mechanisms. Carefully consider the authentication setting for your applications with this in mind.

Activation Requests

MSRPC doesn't support any sort of activation mechanism; it's assumed that by the time the client begins issuing calls to the server, the server is already running and listening for incoming calls. COM makes no such assumption, and provides several functions (`CoCreateInstanceEx` being the most popular) that will lazily start a server process if there isn't already one laying around. This is a very simple one-off solution that works by having a daemon on the server machine that *always* listens for activation requests. This daemon is known as the COM Service Control Manager (SCM), and it runs in the RPC subsystem in the System logon session on *every* machine running Windows 2000 or earlier versions of Windows NT.[22] When Alice calls `CoCreateInstanceEx`, the COM library passes this request to her local SCM, which uses an RPC interface known as `IRemoteActivation` to contact the remote SCM.[23]

The whole idea of an activation request (`CoCreateInstanceEx` and friends) is to bootstrap the client (Alice) by giving her an interface pointer to a server (often launching the server at the same time). At the time Alice issues the activation request, she has no interface pointer to the server; thus, she has no binding handle to the server. There are no advertised default settings from the server. So the obvious question is, What sort of authentication settings does COM use for activation requests? There are two answers to this question.

First of all, Alice can control these settings explicitly by specifying a `COAUTHINFO` data structure:

```
typedef struct _COAUTHINFO {
    DWORD   dwAuthnSvc;
    DWORD   dwAuthzSvc;
    LPWSTR  pwszServerPrincName;  // use SPN for Kerb24
    DWORD   dwAuthnLevel;
    DWORD   dwImpersonationLevel; // at least IMPERSONATE
    COAUTHIDENTITY __RPC_FAR *pAuthIdentityData;
    DWORD   dwCapabilities;
} COAUTHINFO;
```

These settings should look awfully familiar: They are the same parameters Alice would normally pass when calling `SetBlanket`. After she fills out this

---

[22] …at least back through Windows NT 3.51.

[23] Technically, in Windows 2000, an undocumented interface known as `IRemote SCMActivator` (000001A0-0000-0000-C000-000000000046) is preferred. For this text, I'll refer to the interface documented in Kindel (1998), `IRemoteActivation`. For our purposes, the differences between the two are unimportant.

[24] If you're using Kerberos, be sure to use the SPN form of the server machine's name here (for example, "HOST/bobsmachine.foo.com"). If you're using NTLM, set this value to NULL.

structure, she passes it to `CoCreateInstanceEx` by attaching it to a `COSERVERINFO` structure:

```
typedef struct   _COSERVERINFO {
    DWORD        dwReserved1;
    LPWSTR       pwszName;
    COAUTHINFO*  pAuthInfo;  // hang it here!
    DWORD        dwReserved2;
}   COSERVERINFO;
```

It's important to note that *pAuthInfo* is only used to indicate to the SCM the authentication settings it should use for this particular call to `IRemote Activation`. The pointer Alice receives from `CoCreateInstanceEx` will be set up using the defaults shown in Table 9.2 (`COAUTHINFO` generally doesn't affect these defaults). The only exception to this rule is the authentication service negotiation. Here's an example:

```
ICalc* _createCalculator() {
  COAUTHINFO cai = {
    RPC_C_AUTHN_GSS_KERBEROS,
    RPC_C_AUTHZ_NONE,
    L"HOST/bobsmachine.foo.com",
    RPC_C_AUTHN_LEVEL_PKT_INTEGRITY,
    RPC_C_IMP_LEVEL_IMPERSONATE,
  };
  COSERVERINFO csi = {0, l"bobsmachine.foo.com", &cai};
  MULTI_QI mqi = {&IID_ICalc};
  HRESULT hr = CoCreateInstanceEx(CLSID_Calc, 0,
              CLSCTX_REMOTE_SERVER, &csi, 1, &mqi);
  if (FAILED(hr))
    _err(L"CoCreateInstanceEx(CLSID_Calc)", hr);
  return (ICalc*)mqi.pItf;
}
```

This code explicitly requests that Kerberos be used for the activation request. The resulting interface pointer will use Kerberos by default as well. Note also that the code uses an impersonation level of `IMPERSONATE`. It's critical that Alice give the local SCM a strong enough token (in other words, a strong enough impersonation level) to allow access to her network credentials.[25] If Alice had instead specified IDENTIFY-level impersonation, the activation request would have failed.

Now what if Alice had instead passed NULL for *pAuthInfo* (like most folks do)? The answer is that Alice's SCM will do its very best to establish an authenticated connection to the remote SCM, but if all tries at authentication fail (over all possible network protocols supported by COM on Alice's machine), it will back off and try again without authentication. Is this good? Well, it works quite well assuming that authentication succeeds. But (to take an example) if the client and server are in different domains, and there isn't a trust path from the server's authority to the client's authority, you have two choices: Either wait five minutes or so for CoCreateInstance(Ex) to succeed (only after failing authentication will it retry again without authentication), or be explicit and pass a COAUTHINFO structure saying that you don't want authentication at all (you specify this by setting the authentication service and level to NONE):

```
HRESULT _activateUnauthenticated(REFCLSID  clsid,
                                 wchar_t*  pszHost,
                                 CLSCTX    clsctx,
                                 DWORD     cmqi,
                                 MULTI_QI* rgmqi) {
    COAUTHINFO cai = {
      RPC_C_AUTHN_NONE,
      RPC_C_AUTHZ_NONE,
      0,
      RPC_C_AUTHN_LEVEL_NONE,
      RPC_C_IMP_LEVEL_IMPERSONATE   // meaningless now
    };
    COSERVERINFO csi = {0, pszHost, &cai};
    return CoCreateInstanceEx(clsid, 0, clsctx,
                              &csi, cmqi, rgmqi);
}
```

[s25] Recall that OLE32.DLL implements CoCreateInstance(Ex) by making an interprocess request to the local SCM. As I discussed on page 365, for local interprocess communication, IMPERSONATE gives local servers access to the client's network credentials.

This handy helper function can be used in systems where authentication is not desired. (Hey, some folks just want to turn *off* security, and to do this, you have to turn off *authentication*.)

FAQ: Can I Use Kerberos without Calling SetBlanket?

Think about this problem for a moment. Both RPC and COM guarantee mutual authentication when using the built-in Kerberos SSP. To guarantee mutual authentication, the client's SSP must verify (via Kerberos) the server's identity. This means obtaining a ticket for that server principal (Bob, say), handing it to him, and asking him to prove that he knows the session key buried inside the ticket. Because the ticket is encrypted with a key that only Bob should know, this shouldn't be a problem if Bob really is the principal that the client (Alice) thinks he is.

Here's the problem. How does Alice figure out the server principal in the first place? If Alice simply relies on the default negotiation algorithm and doesn't call SetBlanket to specify a server principal name, what will the server be proving? He'll be proving that he is who he *advertised* he was during OXID resolution. This isn't terribly interesting and doesn't help Alice much, unless she's content to make a call to the server, verify that Kerberos was used, and then read the server principal name by calling CoQueryProxyBlanket. What would a program do with this information? How could it validate it?

This is a really difficult problem to fix. The directory service in Windows 2000 provides some infrastructure for automating the *authenticated* discovery of principal names for services,[26] but unfortunately, as of this writing COM doesn't participate in this scheme. In talking with a buddy of mine on the COM team at Microsoft, I found out that COM still *does* make an attempt to select Kerberos by default. The way it works is this: During an activation call (CoCreateInstanceEx and friends), the client's SCM sets up an authenticated connection with the server's SCM using SPNEGO (assuming the caller didn't use an explicit COAUTHINFO structure specifying otherwise). If Kerberos is negotiated during that activation request, then the client now at least knows that the server does in fact support Kerberos. Because the SCM runs in the

---

[26] See the documentation for Service Connection Points in MSDN for details.

System logon session, it runs with the machine's credentials; thus, COM can make an educated guess at the server principal name by looking at the host name used by the client in the activation request. Assuming the machine name was specified as bobsmachine.foo.com, COM uses "RPCSS/bobsmachine.foo.com" as the server principal name, which Kerberos translates to "HOST/bobsmachine.foo.com", which should work assuming that this name is registered for the server in the directory service (which will normally be the case for any machine that is a member of a Windows 2000 Kerberos domain; see the MSDN documentation for `DsWriteAccountSpn` for more details). Because COM caches SCM-to-SCM connections on a per-client logon session basis, your application may not be the one that ends up making this negotiation happen; the negotiation may have already occurred using a non-Kerberos friendly host name. If the activation request successfully authenticates using Kerberos as the negotiated protocol, COM remembers this, and the resulting proxy will also use Kerberos by default.

The moral of the story is this: Unless you're careful, you won't end up using Kerberos by default for DCOM authentication (you'll often end up negotiating down to NTLM). Want a solution? During activation requests, use a `COAUTHINFO` that demands Kerberos. If you get an interface pointer via some other mechanism, demand Kerberos by calling `SetBlanket`. In both these cases, you'll need to specify a valid principal name for the target. Of course this won't work if the server doesn't actually *support* Kerberos, but generally speaking, you'll know this (perhaps via configuration information) ahead of time. One hopes that in the future COM will integrate with the directory service a bit better in order to mitigate this headache.[27]

If you are using Kerberos in an attempt to delegate the client's credentials, be aware that in order to send the server a forwarded TGT, the server principal

---

[27] If you choose to call `SetBlanket` as suggested here, don't forget to call it for `IUnknown` as well; otherwise, calls to `Release` (which eventually translate on the wire to `IRemUnknown::RemRelease`) will silently fail with `E_ACCESSDENIED`. You can see this happening if you are using Visual C++ and you open the output window; you'll see a first chance exception (which is trapped and silently discarded by the proxy) that maps to `E_ACCESSDENIED`. You must explicitly `QueryInterface` for `IID_IUnknown` and call `SetBlanket` on *that* interface pointer in order to annotate the binding handle used for `IRemUnknown` calls. The Universal Delegator (Brown 1999b) is an example of a tool that can help you automate this.

(or the server's machine account if the server runs in the System logon session) must be marked "Trusted for delegation" in the directory. Also, the client's account must *not* be marked "Account is sensitive and may not be delegated." If this is true, and the client specifies an impersonation level of RPC_C_IMP _LEVEL_DELEGATE, the client-side SSP will send a forwarded TGT to the server, thus delegating the client's network credentials (see Chapter 7 for more details on Kerberos and delegation of credentials).

More COM Interception: Access Control

If a server (Bob) sets his low-water mark to something other than NONE, he is stating that every single external client that makes calls into him is *required* to establish a logon session of one form or another on his machine so that he has the chance to get a token and examine the client's security attributes. Although Bob can do this manually in each of his method implementations, the COM channel is perfectly happy to perform an automatic process-wide access check on Bob's behalf. This is what the first parameter to CoInitializeSecurity (*pSecDesc*) is all about.

COM caches this security descriptor, and the channel calls AccessCheck at each incoming client request, using the client's token, the cached security descriptor, and an access mask of COM_RIGHTS_EXECUTE (defined in OBJBASE.H):

```
#define COM_RIGHTS_EXECUTE 1
```

If access is granted, the call will be dispatched to the object. If not, the call will *not* be dispatched, and the client will receive the error code E_ACCESS DENIED. The generic mapping used for the call to AccessCheck is empty (whoops), so be absolutely sure to grant or deny the specific right COM_RIGHTS_EXECUTE and avoid using generic permissions in the DACL. If you want to turn off this access check completely, pass NULL for *pSecDesc* in your call to CoInitialize Security.

Because COM uses the security descriptor exactly as you provide it, you must provide a fully formed descriptor (this is annoying, but true). This means you must populate the descriptor with an owner and group SID; otherwise, an internal test run of `AccessCheck` will fail miserably and `CoInitialize Security` will complain.[28] You could go ahead and call `CreatePrivate ObjectSecurity` yourself to populate these settings automatically from the defaults in your token, but another bizarre requirement of `CoInitialize Security` is that the descriptor must be in absolute form (`CreatePrivate ObjectSecurity` returns a self-relative security descriptor). This is also annoying, but once you understand the fragilities of `CoInitializeSecurity`, it's quite easy to work around them and amaze your friends.

One thing you should watch out for is to *always grant access permissions to the System logon session*. If you forget to do this, bad things will happen when a client attempts to activate your server. During OXID resolution your local OXID resolver (OR) will attempt to reach into your COM server to ask it to load an RPC transport and start listening. Because the OR runs in the System logon session, it will be denied if you've forgotten this magical step, and the poor devil who's activating your server will get an error code that ranges from `E_OUT OFMEMORY` to `E_ACCESSDENIED`, depending on the weather.

You can pass two other forms of information via *pSecDesc* (besides a security descriptor) that indicate a COM server's access control policy. The first option is to pass an AppID, which is the mechanism typically used by surrogate processes (as is discussed shortly). The second form that you can pass is an implementation of `IAccessControl`, a COM interface that represents a discretionary access control policy that can be used on platforms where the security descriptor APIs are not present (Windows 9x, UNIX, etc.). The data structures used by this interface are deprecated. (They enjoyed brief popularity during the early betas for Windows NT 5, but the functions that used them were obsolete by the time Windows 2000 beta 2 shipped.) In short, avoid this interface unless you're forced to use it because your COM server runs on Windows 9x or UNIX (in which case you probably have bigger problems anyway). If you

---

[28] It's hard to believe that whoever implemented this function went to all the trouble of verifying that the caller passed a fully formed security descriptor, instead of just calling `CreatePrivate ObjectSecurity` like the rest of us to get the owner and group from the caller's token automatically. But that would have made `CoInitializeSecurity` too consistent with the rest of the Windows API and would have seriously jeopardized the job security of COM developers worldwide.

pass an `IAccessControl` pointer, be sure to indicate this by passing `EOAC_ACCESS_CONTROL` via the *dwCapabilities* parameter.

Plugging Obscure Security Holes

`CoInitializeSecurity` allows you to pass a set of capability flags. How the cloaking flags work has already been described, along with the fact that COM ignores the mutual authentication flag. What this chapter has not yet talked about is two of the more esoteric flags, `EOAC_DISABLE_AAA` and `EOAC_SECURE_REFS`.

The first of these flags (introduced in Windows 2000) plugs a minor security hole during activation. Because the client (Alice) is required to use an impersonation level of at least `IMPERSONATE` during an activation request, if the target COM server is designated to run As Activator (in `DCOMCNFG.EXE`, this is the "Launching user" option), it will run in the network logon session established by the SCM when authenticating Alice. Anything that server does (at least locally) will be done on Alice's behalf, and if it does evil things, Alice probably won't be happy.

Prior to Windows 2000, there wasn't any way for Alice to protect herself from As Activator servers other than not to make COM calls to them at all. But because Alice can't necessarily tell how a remote COM server is configured at any given time, this meant she couldn't safely make *any* COM activation requests to servers whose configuration she doesn't control. By specifying `EOAC_DISABLE_AAA` via `CoInitializeSecurity` in Windows 2000, however, Alice can tell her local SCM to communicate to the target SCM that she isn't willing to allow any COM servers to run in her logon session.[29]

Another really twisted attack can be executed by anyone who is knowledgeable about how `IRemUnknown` works. If Alice makes a COM call to Fred (a bad guy), and she gives Fred a copy of an interface pointer that she holds, Fred can marshal that interface pointer to get its context-neutral representation, tweak the count of public references in that representation, and then call `CoReleaseMarshalData`, forcing a call to `IRemUnknown::Release` that

---

[29] As of this writing, this feature doesn't appear to work at all (Windows 2000 build 2195), so this is all theory at this point; I hope that this will be fixed in a service pack.

can release *all* public references to the remote stub. This causes the stub to shut down, and leaves Alice holding a dangling reference (her next call through the proxy will fail).

The obvious solution to this problem is for Alice not to give away her pointer in the first place. (There's a growing camp of COM developers who believe that clients should *never* share their references with other clients.)[30] If Alice doesn't buy into this first solution but wants to be protected from this attack, she should specify `EOAC_SECURE_REFS` in her call to `CoInitializeSecurity`. This causes an extra round-trip to the server each time she unmarshals an interface pointer; the extra round-trip is a call to `IRemUnknown::RemAddRef` requesting a private reference specifically for Alice. The stub manager will keep track of this reference separately, so that if Alice gives her pointer to Fred, and Fred drops the stub's public reference count to zero, the stub will stick around because it still has an outstanding *private* reference for Alice (which cannot be released by Fred, only by Alice). If Alice doesn't like this extra round-trip, maybe she should reconsider sharing pointers with Fred.

Security in In-Process Servers?

One of the limitations of `CoInitializeSecurity` is that it can only be called once per process. This is a reasonable limitation given the race conditions that would arise if it could be called multiple times, but what the heck do you do if you're writing a DLL?

By the time a DLL is loaded, the process-wide security settings have already been configured, either because the client called `CoInitializeSecurity` explicitly or because COM went ahead and made best guesses on the client's behalf. That's right—if you forget to call `CoInitializeSecurity`, COM will configure your settings automatically (I'll talk more about this later).

From a security standpoint, DLLs are just guests in the host process. This means that they run in the same logon session as the client (the DLL has the same security context as its host process). So there's not much to say here, other than you can't really control the security environment of an in-process server independently from that of its host.

---

[30] See Ewald (2000).

Surrogates and Declarative Security

As of Windows NT 4 Service Pack 2, a feature known as DLL surrogates was introduced, which allows arbitrary COM servers packaged in DLLs to be hosted out-of-process (to allow them to be sandboxed, remoted, etc.).

The way this works is a thing of beauty. The developer simply creates a unique GUID that represents a logical application, and registers this under HKEY_CLASSES_ROOT\AppID in the registry of the machine where the DLL will be hosted. She then adds a named value DllSurrogate under this key (containing an empty string by default, or the name of a custom surrogate EXE):

```
HKCR\AppID\{DEADBEEF-0000-0000-0000-ABBADABBADOO}
    DllSurrogate=""
```

Now the developer chooses COM classes from any DLL installed on the machine, and directs them to run in her logical application by adding a named value AppID linking the class back to the application:

```
HKCR\CLSID\{12341234-1234-1234-1234-123412341234}
    AppID="{DEADBEEF-0000-0000-0000-ABBADABBADOO}"
```

She can do this for as many classes in as many different DLLs as she likes (see Figure 9.7). The result is that COM will treat each logical application as a separate out-of-process server, and the natural allocation of processes will be one process per application. This is simply a declarative way to paste together a process (Figure 9.7 also shows the results). The default surrogate process is known as DLLHOST.EXE.

Each of these processes will probably want to configure security, but because a DLL cannot call CoInitializeSecurity for the reasons outlined earlier, these settings must be configured declaratively, and it makes complete sense to place these declarations in the registry as part of the definition of the logical application (the AppID).

Besides DllSurrogate, there are a number of other named values you can specify under your AppID key in order to configure the process-wide security settings for the application:

- **AuthenticationLevel** This maps directly to the dwAuthnLevel parameter in *CoInitializeSecurity*, and sets the process-wide

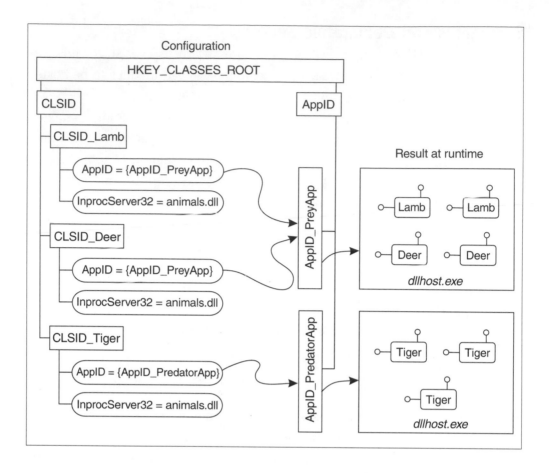

Figure 9.7 Configuring base COM surrogates via AppIDs

default authentication level.[31] Remember that this is the low-water mark when the application acts as a server; when the application acts as a client, it contributes (along with the server's advertised authentication level) to negotiating the default authentication level for proxies.

- **AccessPermission** Controls who is allowed to make calls into the process (this maps directly to the *pSecDesc* parameter in

---

[31] This per-application authentication level was introduced in Windows NT 4 SP4. Prior versions of Windows only supported the machine-wide setting that I'll discuss shortly.

`CoInitializeSecurity`). The format is that of a serialized (self-relative) security descriptor.

- **LaunchPermission** Controls who is allowed to launch processes via activation requests. The format is that of a serialized (self-relative) security descriptor. More on this later.

- **RunAs** Selects a logon session for the application to run in. More on this later.

The surrogate process (`DLLHOST.EXE` or your own custom surrogate) will call `CoInitializeSecurity` in a special way in order to pick up the first two settings (`LaunchPermission` and `RunAs` are only used by the SCM at activation time). Instead of passing a security descriptor via the first parameter (*pSecDesc*), the surrogate will pass a pointer to a GUID. This GUID is none other than the AppID, the identifier for the logical application that the process is hosting. To instruct `CoInitializeSecurity` to interpret the first parameter as a GUID rather than a security descriptor, the surrogate passes the special flag `EOAC_APPID` via *dwCapabilities*. This tells COM to *ignore all the rest of the parameters* to `CoInitializeSecurity` and pick up the process-wide security settings by looking in the registry under the specified AppID, where these settings can be configured declaratively.

At this point I should note that there is also a set of machine-wide security settings that will be used if the respective setting under the AppID key cannot be found. These settings are configured via named values that fall under the `HKLM\Software\Microsoft\OLE` key:

- **EnableDCOM** Set this to 'Y' to enable the local SCM to accept incoming activation requests via `IRemoteActivation`. Otherwise, all incoming remote activation requests and outgoing remote method calls will fail.[32]

- *LegacyAuthenticationLevel* This is the machine-wide default authentication level. It's interesting to note that this setting defaults to

---

[32] On a Windows 2000 client with this setting disabled, I found that I could successfully make outgoing activation calls, but each method call I made through the resulting interface pointer failed with an HRESULT of `RPC_E_REMOTE_DISABLED`.

RPC_C_AUTHN_LEVEL_CONNECT. Authentication is required in COM by default, as opposed to its close cousin RPC, where the client must explicitly request authentication. In fact, if you delete this named value from the registry completely, *CONNECT* will be the implied setting.

- **LegacyImpersonationLevel** This is the machine-wide default impersonation level. This setting defaults to *RPC_C_IMP_LEVEL _IDENTIFY*. Note that this setting cannot be set on a per-AppID basis; this seems to me to be an oversight.

- **LegacyMutualAuthentication** Maps to *EOAC_MUTUAL_AUTH*, which is ignored anyway.

- **LegacySecureReferences** Maps to the *EOAC_SECURE_REFS* capability. Note that this cannot be set on a per-AppID basis.

- **DefaultAccessPermission** This is the machine-wide default access permission. The format is that of a serialized (self-relative) security descriptor.

- **DefaultLaunchPermission** This is the machine-wide default launch permission. The format is that of a serialized (self-relative) security descriptor.

Note that there are no registry settings for choosing a default authentication service; the only way to configure this is to explicitly call `CoInitialize Security` (without using `EOAC_APPID`) and specify all the arguments manually.

The horribly bug-ridden but ever-so-lovable tool used by developers to configure AppIDs is `DCOMCNFG.EXE` (Figure 9.8). The figure maps the GUI controls to the corresponding registry settings listed here.

COM Servers Packaged as Services

It's possible to indicate to the COM SCM that you'd like it to call `Start Service` as opposed to `CreateProcess` when a COM activation request requires a COM server to be launched. To do this, you of course need to write a service, install it via `CreateService`, and link all your classes to an AppID

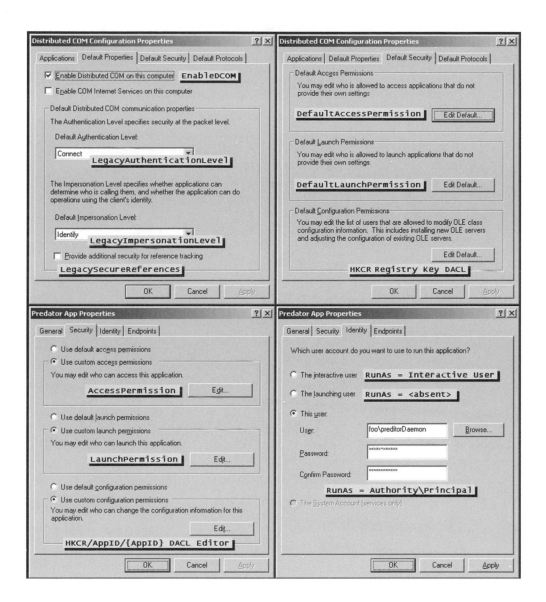

Figure 9.8 DCOMCNFG decoder ring

(in the same fashion described earlier for surrogates, although in this case because you're providing the host process, it's *your* responsibility to expose all the class objects from your service via `CoRegisterClassObject`).

You indicate the name of your service to the COM SCM via the `Local Service` named value under the AppID. If you want a specific set of parameters passed to your service when it's started via the COM SCM, you can specify these via the `ServiceParameters` named value.

Why write a COM server as a service? That's a really good question, since the COM SCM already provides a facility for starting servers on an as-needed basis (services are great for hosting RPC servers that have no such activation service). There are two good reasons for writing a COM server as a service: First, writing a service is the natural way to run in the System logon session (which is part of the TCB and has godlike authority over the local machine). Second, if you want your COM server to start at boot time, before anyone gets a chance to activate it via a normal COM activation request, the System SCM would be happy to bootstrap you as the system loads.

If you're writing five servers that need to be started at boot time (or need to run in the TCB, heaven forbid), do you really need to write five services? I hope Chapter 4 has helped you realize that you only need at most one service to bootstrap the others. Don't just write your COM server as a service because that radio button in the ATL wizard looks cool. Writing a COM server as a service just means that you have twice as much configuration to get right.

Be sure to call `CoInitializeSecurity`, either specifying your settings directly or by using the `EOAC_APPID` trick to cause COM to look up your settings in the registry. As you'll see in the next section, forgetting to call this function often leads to unpredictable behavior.

Legacy Out-of-Process Servers

When a process that uses COM hasn't bothered to call `CoInitialize Security` explicitly, COM will set up the default process-wide security settings automatically using the various registry settings described earlier. If COM can find an AppID for your server, then at least you can control this application's settings individually. Otherwise, COM will pick up the machine-wide settings, which most legacy COM applications share. If you have an existing out-of-process server for which you need to control security settings, yet you aren't allowed (for whatever reason) to change the source code to call `CoInitialize Security`, you're not entirely out of luck, although the feature I'm about to describe may not give you much hope.

You can create an AppID for your server after the fact, but because you cannot call `CoInitializeSecurity` to indicate which AppID is yours, you must instead create a subkey under `HKCR\AppID` and name it after your EXE's filename. (Hey, I'm just the messenger here, so don't throw tomatoes at me.) This key should have a single named value under it that links your EXE to its AppID:

```
HKCR\AppID\legacy.exe
  AppID="{DEADBEEF-0000-0000-0000-ABBADABBADOO}"
```

The problems with this approach are numerous. The obvious problem is uniqueness, and using a long filename to ensure that your name is unique will likely just complicate things.[33] Relying on this mechanism is also troublesome because as soon as somebody renames the EXE, the mapping is lost and suddenly all the security settings you've been relying on are no longer in effect. I call this the *Fragile EXE-to-AppID Mapping Problem,* it's so darn prevalent. The ATL wizard (at least as of this writing) doesn't generate a call to `CoInitializeSecurity`; rather, it writes registry scripts that give you an EXE-to-AppID mapping. This mapping falls down quite badly for people who have two different names for their EXEs, one for debug and one for release builds.

I'll stop ranting now. In summary, don't rely on this mapping, period. Call `CoInitializeSecurity`, specifying your settings directly or simply telling COM where to find an AppID that holds your declarative settings. Or, don't write an EXE at all—just write a DLL and use a surrogate process (configured components fall under this latter umbrella, as you'll see a bit later).

---

[33] The classic example of this problem can be found in the ATL wizard in Visual C++ 6.0. Being the good folks that they were, the ATL team designed the registrar to expand `%MODULE%` in your registry script to the *short filename* of your server to compensate for a silly bug in the Windows NT 4 version of `CreateProcess`. This means that at runtime, COM will see an EXE named `ReallyLongFileName.EXE` as `REALLY~1.EXE`. This won't match the AppID name, because the ATL wizard sets that key to the long filename. Whoops.

Launching Servers via the COM SCM

When the COM SCM goes to launch a server in response to an activation request, it asks itself two questions:

1. Is the caller allowed to launch this COM server?
2. Which logon session should I run this COM server in?

To answer these questions, the COM SCM cannot rely on the server process calling `CoInitializeSecurity` (or any other function) because, well, the server isn't even running yet. So the COM SCM looks for a security descriptor and a `RunAs` setting in either the COM+ catalog (for configured components) or in the registry.

In the case of a base COM component, the SCM looks up the CLSID being activated under `HKCR\CLSID`, and discovers the `AppID` named value. Then it traverses over to `HKCR\AppID` and looks up the `LaunchPermission` named value. If this information cannot be found (either because there is no CLSID-to-AppID mapping, or because there is no `LaunchPermission` named value), the SCM looks at the machine-wide `DefaultLaunchPermission` setting to get this information. If this key is not found, all launch requests will be denied.

Once this security descriptor is found, the SCM performs an access check using this security descriptor, the token from the client's logon session (established during the `IRemoteActivation` request), and an access mask of (once again) `COM_RIGHTS_EXECUTE`.[34] If access is denied, the activation request fails and the activator receives the failure code `E_ACCESSDENIED`.

If the client's activation request reached the server at an authentication level of `NONE`, there will be no client logon session from which to get a token in order to call `AccessCheck`. In this special case, the SCM grants the request based on whether the Everyone SID has been granted `COM_RIGHTS_EXECUTE` permissions. The moral of the story here is that if you want unauthenticated users to be able to launch your COM server, you must grant `LaunchPermission` to the Everyone SID.

---

[34] As with access permissions, this check also uses an empty generic mapping, so avoid using generic permissions in this security descriptor as well.

Assuming the activation request gets past the launch permission access check, the SCM must now determine the security context in which to host the server process. (All processes must run inside a logon session; the question is, which one?) If you choose to host COM objects in a service, it's not the COM SCM that needs to worry about this; rather, it's the System SCM, so you can configure this when you call `CreateService` (see Chapter 4). Otherwise, the COM SCM will need to pick an appropriate logon session, and to do this, it will follow the CLSID-to-AppID mapping and look under the AppID for the value named `RunAs`. There are three possibilities:

- **RunAs=<absent>** **(As Activator activation)** Run As Activator occurs when there is no `RunAs` named value at all (thus this is the default setting for base COM servers). The COM server will always run in the logon session of the activator, established during the call to `IRemoteActivation`. This means that there *must be* a logon session for the client; thus, activation will fail if the client request comes in at an authentication level of NONE. This also means that each client principal will get his or her own personal copy of the server process.[35]

- **RunAs="Interactive User"** In this case, the SCM will look for the existence of an interactive user (specifically, someone who logged on via Winlogon). If there is one, the COM SCM will discover the interactive user's token using an undocumented mechanism[36] and start the server process running with a copy of that token, at the same time directing the server onto the interactive window station. If no interactive user is present, all activation requests will fail. If an interactive user happens to be present and your server starts in her logon session and then she logs off, your server gets toasted along with the other processes running in her logon session.

---

[35] This is regardless of whether the server specified REGCLS_MULTIPLEUSE in its call to CoRegisterClassObject. Security takes precedence over application semantics—sorry.

[36] On Windows NT 4, the mechanism is pretty simple: The SCM just looks for the shell process and makes a copy of its token for the new server process. On Windows 2000, the mechanism is more sophisticated because Terminal Services sessions are in the picture, but the end result is the same.

- **RunAs="Authority\Principal"** In this case, the SCM attempts to establish a batch-style logon session using the authority and principal specified here, and the password stored in the password stash at index `SCM:APPID`, where `APPID` is the stringized GUID for the application. The SCM then launches the server in this logon session.

Figure 9.9 shows how these settings affect the logon session (and window station) in which the application will be hosted. Internalizing this picture will help you develop a more intuitive feel for how COM servers work.

With these facts out on the table, here are some interesting corollaries. First of all, the default setting of Run As Activator makes lots of sense for the thousands of applications that use COM for binding user interfaces together using OLE. These applications weren't designed to be activated by remote users, and thus would be prime candidates for exploitation by a bad guy. Because the default is Run As Activator, if some bad guy (Fred, say) *does* attempt to launch Microsoft Word on AlicesMachine via DCOM, it won't work unless the system can establish a logon session for the bad guy on AlicesMachine. Even if Fred is clever and figures out how to get COM to use a NULL session or a Guest logon, it's unlikely that these security contexts will make it past the DACL in `DefaultAccessPermission` for the machine. Even if Fred makes it past all of these hurdles, the server application will run in a logon session that was established with his authorization attributes, which will severely limit what he can do. (Look, if the bad guy is the domain administrator, you have worse problems than COM security to worry about.) Also, because this is a daemon logon session, the application will run in a noninteractive window station and won't be able to do nasty things like put up dialog boxes requesting passwords, or send keystrokes to the shell to do evil deeds.

All this being said, Run As Activator is truly miserable if you have designed your server specifically to service remote activation requests from multiple client principals. Unless you enjoy having multiple copies of your server being launched (one per client principal, which can get *really* expensive and kills any chance of pooling database connections), don't leave the `RunAs` setting absent for a base COM server of this type.

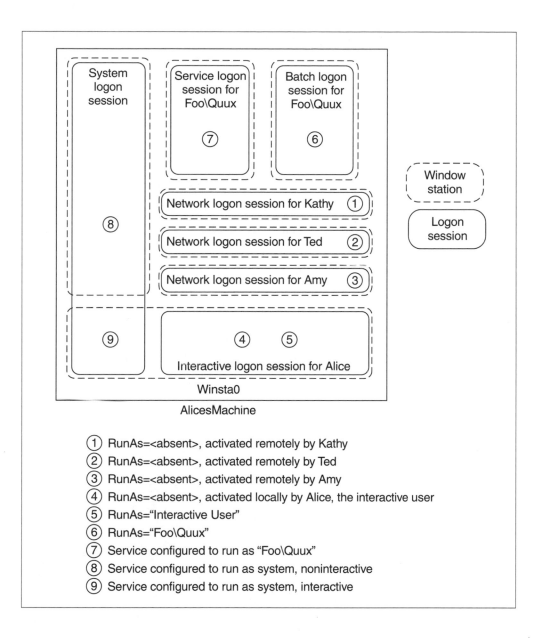

Figure 9.9 **RunAs** decoder ring

Run As Interactive User is great for debugging in the lab, because it forces your server application into the interactive window station. (Of course, this only works if somebody is logged on interactively, so make sure you have someone log in to the server box interactively before configuring your server to run in this mode.) If your server puts up a dialog box (even accidentally, for instance because of an ASSERT firing), you'll be able to see it.

The other benefit to this setting is that you'll always be able to start the server process in a debugger. Regardless of whether you are writing a classic EXE server or a DLL that will be hosted in a base COM or COM+ surrogate process, *somebody* needs to call CoRegisterClassObject(CLSCTX_LOCAL _MACHINE) to expose your class objects to the world. When class objects are registered in this scope, COM follows the CLSID-to-AppID mapping to find a RunAs setting, and if found, it will compare this setting with that of the caller's security context. If it doesn't match, the COM SCM will assume you're a bad guy trying to spoof the legitimate server and will reject the call with CO_E _WRONG_SERVER_IDENTITY.[37] For services, COM ignores the RunAs setting and instead looks at the service configuration to make this determination. All this being said, however . . .

Never, never, never *ship* code that configures itself to run as the interactive user unless you are absolutely sure that it is safe. No, I take that qualification back. Don't ever do it, period. If your code has any weakness that an attacker can exploit (or if it can be used to do obviously dangerous things like deleting files), and an administrator happens to be logged on interactively to a machine where your program is configured to run as the interactive user, an attacker can exploit that bug in the security context of the administrator. (The administrator's interactive logon session will have network credentials; imagine what damage could be done with a domain administrator's credentials!) This is really bad news. It also brings up all kinds of ethical issues: By activating a COM server in this way, it's as if you've silently reached out and hypnotized the user into

---

[37] When debugging a COM+ server application, the symptoms will be quite subtle: You'll start the debugger, and the surrogate process will start and exit almost immediately without giving you a clue as to what went wrong (in my own testing, I didn't even find any breadcrumbs left behind in the event log, which surprised me). If you experience this behavior, after verifying that you have the correct debugging command line, dllhost.exe /ProcessID:{*your-appid-goes-here*}, immediately go and check the server's identity setting.

launching your application by double-clicking it; even worse, you've told him that he won't remember having done this when he wakes up. No user deserves to be subjected to this.

Run As Distinguished Principal is great for distributed COM servers that are being installed in a production system. This type of server runs in a daemon logon session and thus has no dependencies on the presence of an interactive user. Because the server always runs in the same security context, it will have a more stable environment. The server principal *must* be granted the right to a batch logon (naturally), so your installation program should set this up. (Typically you'll add the server's account at installation time as well; see the appendix for tips on how to set this up.)

DCOMCNFG.EXE is a really great tool for switching base COM servers back and forth between Run As Interactive User and Run As Distinguished Principal in the lab.[38]

A Note on Choosing a Server Identity

When running a COM(+) server as a distinguished principal, you should think carefully before choosing a server identity. If your server will not be running on a domain controller, I strongly recommend that you consider using a local account (your setup application can install this automatically; see the appendix for details). By using a local account, you reduce the damage that can be done by an attacker who compromises the server machine and learns the password by looking at the password stash. Local accounts are absolutely the way to go if your server doesn't require access to secure network resources.

However, if your server needs to be authenticated on the network, the decision becomes a bit harder. You can either create a matching user name and password on the target machine(s) where your server needs to be authenticated, or break down and use a domain account that is limited as much as possible (you can restrict the privileges and types of logons it can have throughout the domain using Group Policy, for instance). If you choose to use the matching user name and password kludge, you should consider writing a program to automatically synchronize passwords (the appendix will help with this).

---

[38] For configured components, as you'll see, you can simply use the Component Services snap-in.

Access Checks in the Middle Tier

In Chapter 3, I promised to provide further explanation for why the imperson-ation model doesn't work well in a three-tier system. Having the middle tier sim-ply impersonate the remote client and use her credentials to call into the back tier (typically a database) opens a whole host of problems. First of all, as men-tioned in Chapter 3, in order for this to work, the client must delegate her cre-dentials to the server. This in itself is reason for concern. Besides the fact that it won't work at all on Windows NT 4 (which uses NTLM), requiring clients to expose their credentials to delegation simply broadens the surface area open to an attacker (by compromising a server machine, the bad guy can now obtain network credentials for clients that delegate them). Limiting the use of delega-tion is like vaccinating your kids. It tends to limit the spread of sickness through-out a system.

Another major problem is that impersonation in the middle tier completely annihilates any chance of pooling connections to the database. Because each database connection represents an authenticated session (similar to the way LAN Manager sessions work, as described in Chapter 8), these are principal-sensitive resources. If the middle tier wishes to delegate the client's credentials to the database it must open a database connection for each client principal.

Three-tier systems are often built as such not just to separate business logic from database schemas (usually the customer really doesn't give a darn how object oriented your internal implementation is), but rather to offload as many machine instructions as possible from the database and transfer them to a middle-tier server farm where hardware is cheap and can be replicated as needed. By performing access checks in the middle tier and pooling database connections, the middle tier communicates with the database using a single set of credentials that the database can quickly authenticate (at database connec-tion time via a handshake, and thereafter using a session key). The database trusts the middle tier to perform access checks and can therefore focus on doing what it does best: executing SQL queries and stored procedures as blazingly fast as it possibly can.[39] Figure 9.10 shows the two diametrically opposed strategies.

---

[39] See Ewald (2000) for more information on building scalable three-tier systems.

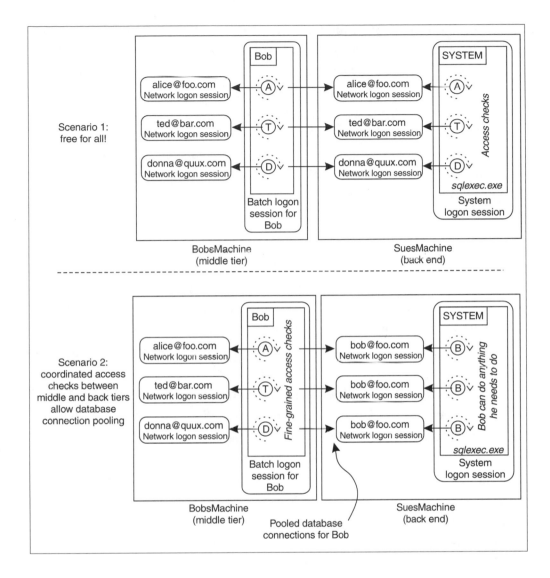

Figure 9.10 Two strategies for access control

Now that I've explained the need for access checks in the middle tier, let's look at how COM+ helps to automate this.

The COM+ Security Model: Configured Components

As I was writing this chapter, I noticed an interesting pattern. I started the chapter talking about RPC security and then migrated into base COM security, and now I'm going to start exploring the added security features that COM+ configured components offer. I noticed that there is an awful lot of *code* at the start of the chapter, but as I move toward this section, I see less and less code and more and more explanations of automated mechanisms and declarative settings. This pattern follows the evolution of middleware on the Windows platform from RPC to COM to MTS and COM+. More and more of the boilerplate code common to middle-tier COM servers is being pushed down into the runtime where its behavior can be controlled via declarative attributes.

Surrogates are a fantastic example of this: Just configure a logical application via an AppID, set up some declarative security settings, attach some CLSIDs to it (declaratively), and you're off and running—you have a secure distributed COM server and all you did was write some DLLs that don't concern themselves with authentication or access checks. By declaring a RunAs setting, the COM SCM will set up an environment that's right for you (logon session, window station, etc.). By declaring a set of access permissions, the COM channel will intercept all incoming calls and perform an access check on your behalf.

COM+ (and its baby brother, MTS) takes the idea of surrogates and interception to new heights. The problem with base COM was that it could only do so much, because it was relatively nonintrusive.[40] If you wanted finer-grained access control, you had to provide it yourself, because base COM had no idea how your program was structured. In COM+, the logical application introduced with base COM surrogates is now a first-class citizen. COM+ applications still have a GUID that identifies them, but you won't see any AppID in the registry, because there are loads of new settings and this information is tucked away in the COM+ catalog.[41] The COM+ catalog has knowledge of the structure of the configured components and the applications that house them, and can be used to configure fine-grained security settings.

What you'll find with most of the security settings in COM+ is that generally the COM+ catalog is just another way of declaratively specifying many of

---

[40] Although many would argue that this was a feature.

[41] Because MTS was hacked on top of COM in Windows NT 4, it stores some of its settings in the catalog and other settings under the AppID in the registry, in order to play ball with base COM. The COM+ team had no such limitations, because they were changing the guts of COM itself.

the settings that have already been covered. It's mostly a matter of figuring out which setting does what (and getting your head around the role-based security infrastructure).

Another thing that you'll find is that COM+ performs access checks at *application* boundaries as well as *process* boundaries, which means that library applications often have a bit more autonomy when it comes to security. This is different from Windows NT 4, where security checks for configured (and nonconfigured) components were only performed when a call entered the process (see Figure 9.11). Note that once the boundary has been crossed, no further access checks are performed (this is indicated via dashed lines between components).

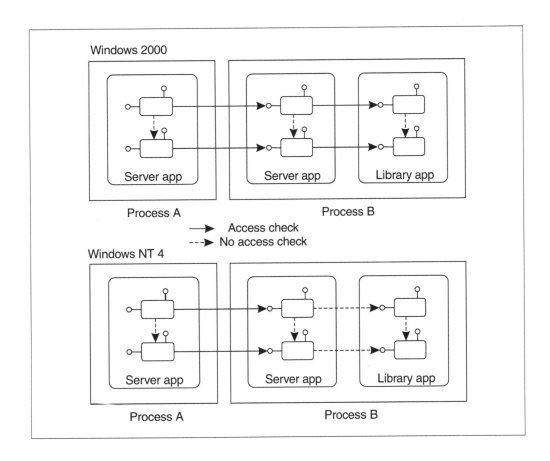

Figure 9.11   Security boundaries

Catalog Settings

The quickest way to get the lowdown on the security-related settings that can be configured in COM+ is to enumerate the properties in the catalog. The first object we'll look at is the `LocalComputer` object. This object exists mainly as an abstraction over existing machine-wide registry settings; for instance, many of the security settings described earlier as falling under `HKLM\Software\Microsoft\OLE` can be edited via this catalog object (this directly accesses the registry settings without you having to write registry code).[42]

- **DCOMEnabled** Maps to the machine-wide registry setting `EnableDCOM`
- **DefaultAuthenticationLevel** Maps to the machine-wide registry setting `LegacyAuthenticationLevel`
- **DefaultImpersonationLevel** Maps to the machine-wide registry setting `LegacyImpersonationLevel`
- **SecureReferencesEnabled** Maps to the machine-wide registry setting `LegacySecureReferences`
- **SecurityTrackingEnabled** While this property is mentioned in the documentation, I've not been able to find anyone at Microsoft who will own up to what it means or where it is used. The concensus appears to be that it's completely unused, so you should ignore it.

Here's an example script that displays the default authentication level for the local computer:[43]

```
set cat = createObject("comAdmin.comAdminCatalog")
set cc = cat.getCollection("LocalComputer")
cc.populate
set c = cc.item(0)
msgbox c.value("DefaultAuthenticationLevel")
```

---

[42] Although this is academically interesting and is included here for completeness, you should clearly use caution when modifying any machine-wide settings. If your application doesn't own the machine, you have no place altering any of these settings because you could very easily break other applications.

[43] This and the following scripts are designed to work with COM+; there is a separate, but similar, scripting model for MTS.

Now let's look at the security-related properties on each `Application` object:

- **Activation** Indicates whether the application is a server or library application. The former activates out-of-process, and the latter activates in-process. Many security settings only make sense for server applications; I'll call these out as I come to them.

- **Identity** May be either `Interactive User` or the name of a distinguished principal.[44] (Note that Run As Activator is not supported for configured components, and as of this writing, there is no support for running configured components in the System logon session.)[45] If you want to set this value programmatically, make sure you also set the password before committing your changes. This property is only valid for server applications. Because each library application is hosted in the client's process, a library application cannot control its security identity.

- **Password** The password associated with the identity (unused for `Interactive User`). This property is write-only.

- **Authentication** For a server application, this is the process-wide authentication level and can take on any of the normal authentication levels discussed earlier. This is set to the equivalent of `RPC_C _AUTHN_LEVEL_PKT` by default. For a library application, this setting may either be `DEFAULT` or `NONE`. The former says that the channel will use the process-wide authentication level, whereas the latter says that objects in the library application may be called using any authentication level, including `NONE`. I'll talk more about the design implications of this feature later.

- **AuthenticationCapability** A bitfield that allows you to control identity tracking (cloaking) as well as `EOAC_SECURE_REFS`. As of this

---

[44] According to my experiments on Windows 2000 build 2195, this name must be of the form Authority\Principal as opposed to the UPN form, more modern principal@authority.

[45] Encouraging developers to keep their application code out of the System logon session is a really good thing in my opinion.

writing, this property isn't visible via the Component Services snap-in, but can be controlled programmatically via the catalog interface. The default setting is dynamic identity tracking (EOAC_DYNAMIC _CLOAKING). This is a process-wide setting, and although it's also present in library applications, it is ignored in that context as of this writing. The reason dynamic identity tracking was chosen as the default is that threads in IIS Web applications (which are essentially COM+ applications) are always impersonating, and it's architecturally critical to be able to delegate the thread's security context to other COM objects that the Web application creates. More on this in Chapter 10.

- **ImpersonationLevel** The process-wide default impersonation level for the application. The default setting is the equivalent of RPC_C_IMP _LEVEL_IMPERSONATION, which is somewhat surprising considering base COM's usual conservative approach to security.

- **ApplicationAccessChecksEnabled** Determines whether the interception layer should automatically perform access checks. By setting this value to False, any caller who satisfies the authentication low-water mark will be able to make calls into the application without the COM channel performing any access checks at all. This is great for temporarily turning off access checks in the lab when debugging, because it affects the entire application. Access checking is turned off by default, apparently with the assumption that you'll set up role-based security and then enable access checks once you've made these decisions.

- **AccessChecksLevel** Determines the extent of the access checks that should be performed, as well as the level of security context bookkeeping that should be maintained by the channel. This is a very important (server app only) setting that will be discussed in conjunction with COM+ roles. This setting is not present in MTS.

Here's a script that enumerates all the COM+ server applications installed on the local machine, displaying the identity setting for each via a message box:

```
function getApplicationCollection
  set cat = createObject("comAdmin.comAdminCatalog")
  set ac = cat.getCollection("Applications")
  ac.populate
  set getApplicationCollection = ac
end function

set ac = getApplicationCollection()
for each a in ac
  if 1 = a.value("Activation") then
    s = s & a.name & ": " & a.value("Identity") & chr(13)
  end if
next
msgbox s
```

Besides the COM+ roles that I discuss in detail later, there is one remaining security-related attribute in the catalog, specified on a per-class basis:

- **ComponentAccessChecksEnabled** Determines whether component-level access checks should be performed for calls originating from outside the application targeting this component. This setting is enabled by default. This and the other access check settings are summarized in the section Making Sense of COM+ Access Checks.

Applications and Role-Based Security

Preparation

Unless you explicitly turn on access checks for an application, the only protection you'll have is the authentication low-water mark for your application. All calls that satisfy this authentication requirement will be allowed through. To ask the channel to perform access checks on your behalf, you must turn on the application-level property called ApplicationAccessChecksEnabled. This setting (as well as virtually all the others I'll discuss) can be configured either via script, or interactively via the Component Services snap-in. The benefit of using a script during development is that it ensures a repeatable configuration (misconfiguration bugs are common in COM+ development), and the script can be checked into source control, where changes can be carefully tracked.

The following script enables access checks for an application named `Pet Store App`:

```
function findObject(coll, name)
  for each obj in coll
    if name = obj.name then
      set findObject = obj
      exit function
    end if
  next
end function

set ac = getApplicationCollection()
set a = findObject(ac, "Pet Store App")
a.value("ApplicationAccessChecksEnabled") = true
ac.saveChanges
```

If you're planning on using COM+ role-based security in your application, you'll want to instruct the channel to perform these checks based on fine-grained catalog settings. Each application has a property that controls the granularity of access checks: `AccessChecksLevel`. This (COM+-only) setting can have the following values:

- **COMAdminAccessChecksApplicationComponentLevel** Indicates that the role-based access checks on each class, interface, and method should be enforced. This is the default level, and is almost always what you want. As you'll see later, this setting also turns on some extra bookkeeping in the channel.

- **COMAdminAccessChecksApplicationLevel** Indicates that the role assignments to each class, interface, and method should be completely ignored. As long as the caller is in at least one of these roles, he or she may call any method on any interface on any class in the application. This level basically renders roles meaningless and throws you back to the days of base COM, where there was a single DACL that controlled access to all objects in the process.

Here's a script that forces component-level access checks. Note that I've used the WSF (Windows Script File) format so that I can include the type library for the COM+ catalog (I found this GUID by peeking in the `COMADMIN.DLL` component with `OLEVIEW.EXE`). This allows me to use the enumerations in the type library as opposed to hardcoding constants.

```
<?xml version="1.0" ?>
<job>
<reference
   guid="{F618C513-DFB8-11D1-A2CF-00805FC79235}" />
<script language="VBScript"> <![CDATA[

set ac = getApplicationCollection()
set a = findObject(ac, "Pet Store App")
a.value("AccessChecksLevel") = _
   COMAdminAccessChecksApplicationComponentLevel
ac.saveChanges

]]></script>
</job>
```

So at this point, I've shown you how to turn on access checks for the application and set the access checking level to enable meaningful role-based checks, but there's one more setting that needs to be configured before you can be sure that your class will be protected via role-based security. Each class has a property called `ComponentAccessChecksEnabled` that must be set in order to enable role-based access checks:

```
set ac = getApplicationCollection()
set a = findObject(ac, "Pet Store App")
set cc = ac.getCollection("Components", a.key)
cc.populate
set c = findObject(cc, "PetStores.PetStore.1")
c.value("ComponentAccessChecksEnabled") = true
cc.saveChanges
```

After turning on these checks, if you were to try to use any of the components in the application, you'd find yourself completely locked out (E_ACCESS DENIED). The application wouldn't even launch. Role-based security is additive (each caller is implicitly denied unless a role specifically grants him or her access), and currently the pet store application has no roles defined at all (the next section discusses how to approach this task).

Designing with Roles

When designing a COM+ application, the designer discovers the various categories of users that need to be distinguished with respect to security. During implementation, these categories are made concrete by adding roles to the application. Chapter 3 introduced the notion of logical roles. (You might want to revisit Figure 3.1, which pretty much sums it up.)

The following script adds three roles to a pet store application (the results are shown in Figure 9.12):

```
set ac = getApplicationCollection()
set a = findObject(ac, "Pet Store App")
set rc = ac.getcollection("Roles", a.key)
rc.add.value("Name") = "Customers"
rc.add.value("Name") = "Workers"
rc.add.value("Name") = "Supervisors"
rc.saveChanges
```

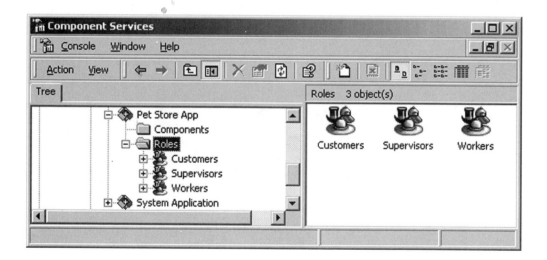

Figure 9.12   Defining roles

DISTRIBUTION

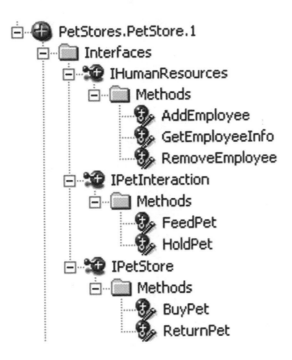

Figure 9.13 Sample pet store application

After discovering the roles in an application, the designer needs to determine which methods clients in each role should be allowed to invoke. During implementation, these decisions are made concrete by assigning roles to methods (COM+ only), interfaces, and classes. Roles can be assigned either via script or via the Component Services snap-in (you'll find a Security tab on the property sheet for each class, interface, and method).[46] Figure 9.13 shows a sample pet store application with its expanded set of interfaces and methods (there's only one class to keep things simple).

The only interfaces you'll see in the catalog for a configured class are those that are listed in the coclass statement in the type library; it's completely possible that an object might actually implement several other interfaces as well that aren't advertised via the coclass statement. This doesn't mean that these

---

[46] The MTS user interface is considerably more cumbersome, but it gets the job done.

interfaces escape role-based access checks; what it does mean is that you'll have less granularity of control.

Here are the rules:

- A role assigned to a class grants callers in that role access to *all methods of all interfaces* implemented on any instances of the class. This also includes interfaces that are not advertised via the coclass statement. This is the most coarse-grained role assignment.

- A role assigned to an interface of a particular class grants callers in that role access to all methods of that interface for any instances of the class. This is only possible for interfaces that are advertised via the coclass statement.

- A role assigned to a method of an interface of a particular class grants callers in that role access to that method of that interface for any instances of the class. Once again, this level of granularity is only possible for interfaces exposed via the coclass statement. This is the most fine-grained role assignment (and is not supported by MTS).

Note that if two configured classes implement the same interface, each of those classes has a separate role-assignment space for its interfaces; for example, the role assignments for interface quux on class foo are completely orthogonal to the role assignments for interface quux on class bar.

Dealing with Dispatch Interfaces

Dispatch interfaces can be tricky, depending on how much of a COM purist you are. If you agree with the general consensus in the COM community that dual interfaces are a thing of the devil,[47] then you'll need to do some fancy footwork to get your dispatch interface recognized by COM+. The approach I normally use for supporting scripting clients *and* vtable-friendly clients is as follows. I provide a hidden interface (one that I don't expose via `QueryInterface`) that represents the union of all the methods on my normal custom interfaces that I want scripting clients to be able to see. I then implement `IDispatch` by dele-

---

[47] Search the DCOM listserver archives for "Why do we still need duals?" and follow the thread that Chris Sells started back in 1997 that rocked the COM community on its heels.

gating to the `ITypeInfo` implementation of this interface that I slurp out of my type library.[48] In any case, because this is a hidden interface, the catalog doesn't see it and has no idea what the `DISPID`s are in order to allow you to configure roles for each `DISPID`. (The COM+ interceptor is happy to perform role-based access checks on `IDispatch::Invoke` as long as you configure each `DISPID` with the roles that can access it.) My solution to this conundrum is to cruft up a classic dispinterface declaration in my type library block that maps one-to-one to my hidden union interface:

```
// interface IFoo, IBar, IQuux, and IBaz
// omitted for brevity
[uuid(4056311C-E848-473B-B43C-CB4B29D2864B)]
library Foo
{
  [
    object,
    uuid(A51F6D55-AD0E-4EE3-A284-A0805B996BAF),
    pointer_default(unique)
  ]
  interface IHiddenUnion : IUnknown
  {
    [id(1)] HRESULT Foo();
    [id(2)] HRESULT Bar();
    [id(3)] HRESULT Quux();
    [id(4)] HRESULT Baz();
  }
  [
    uuid(A5148D55-AD0E-4EE3-A284-A0805B996BAF)
  ]
  dispinterface UseThisToConfigureMethodsForScripts {
  properties:
  methods:
    [id(1)] void Foo();
    [id(2)] void Bar();
```

---

[48] For a nice description of how to map multiple COM interfaces onto a dispatch interface, surf to http://www.sellsbrothers.com/tools/multidisp. Chris Sells also has a great tool called Simple Object II that automates this style of programming; you can download it from http://www.sellsbrothers.com/tools.

```
      [id(3)] void Quux();
      [id(4)] void Baz();
    }
    [
      uuid(0863E813-6C99-4296-983F-7A5C06588E4B),
    ]
    coclass MyConfiguredClass
    {
      interface IFoo;
      interface IBar;
      interface IQuux;
      interface IBaz;
      dispinterface UseThisToConfigureMethodsForScripts;
    };
  }
```

Note that I was careful to explicitly define DISPIDs for my hidden union interface and that I matched these DISPIDs in the dispinterface, method for method. Also note that I exposed this single dispinterface from my coclass statement, which causes the COM+ catalog to provide slots for configuring role-based security on each method (each method is identified by its DISPID in a dispinterface).

The following script assigns the Supervisors role to the PetStore class (thus granting access to all methods of all interfaces of the class). Next it assigns Workers to the IPetInteraction interface so that they can hold and feed the pets. Finally, it assigns Customers to the HoldPet method and the IPetStore interface (so they can hold, buy, and return pets, but not feed them).

```
sub addRoleToClass(cc, className, roleName)
  set c = findObject(cc, className)
  set rc = cc.getCollection("RolesForComponent", c.key)
  rc.add.value("Name") = roleName
  rc.saveChanges
end sub

sub addRoleToInterface(cc, className, itfName, roleName)
```

```
      set c = findObject(cc, className)
      set ic = cc.getCollection("InterfacesForComponent", _
                                 c.key)
    ic.populate
    set i = findObject(ic, itfName)
    set rc = ic.getCollection("RolesForInterface", i.key)
    rc.add.value("Name") = roleName
    rc.saveChanges
  end sub

  sub addRoleToMethod(cc, className,  itfName, _
                         methName, roleName)
    set c = findObject(cc, className)
    set ic = cc.getCollection("InterfacesForComponent", _
                               c.key)
    ic.populate
    set i = findObject(ic, itfName)
    set mc = ic.getCollection("MethodsForInterface", i.key)
    mc.populate
    set m = findObject(mc, methName)
    set rc = mc.getCollection("RolesForMethod", m.key)
    rc.add.value("Name") = roleName
    rc.saveChanges
  end sub

  set ac = getApplicationCollection()
  set a = findObject(ac, "Pet Store App")
  set cc = ac.getCollection("Components", a.key)
  cc.populate
  className = "PetStores.PetStore.1"
  addRoleToClass       cc, className, "Supervisors"
  addRoleToInterface cc, className, "IPetStore", "Customers"
  addRoleToMethod     cc, className, "IPetInteraction", _
                                     "HoldPet", "Customers"
```

The pet store application is now complete (at least security-wise) as far as the designer is concerned, and he or she can ship it by exporting the application. However, until an administrator installs the application and assigns concrete SIDs to the roles, everyone will be denied access.

Deploying with Roles

Defining roles and assigning them to classes, interfaces, and methods is the job of the application designer, who knows the semantics of the application. At deployment time, the administrator installing the application can assign users and groups to these roles via the Component Services snap-in. Once the administrator has made these concrete assignments, if he needs to replicate the application on several machines in a server farm, he can export the application *again,* this time specifying the option to "Export user identities with roles." Note that this won't work very well if he's assigned aliases (local groups) to any roles (other than those that are part of the BUILTIN domain, including Administrators, Guests, etc.), because the SIDs for custom aliases only make sense on the local machine. This also applies to local user accounts.

If the administrator wants to copy *all* the COM+ applications on a server to another server in the farm, he can use the utility COMREPL.EXE (located in the %SYSTEMROOT%\Com directory). This tool exports all applications from a source machine and imports them on the destination machine, effectively copying not only the catalog information but also the components themselves.

Making Sense of COM+ Access Checks

If you look in the Component Services snap-in and consider the various checkboxes and radio buttons that control access checks, and then also consider that the process hosting a server application might host a number of library applications as well, it can be very confusing to figure out exactly how a particular configuration will affect any given call.

I find that the easiest way to understand these settings is to think of several *ordered hurdles* that you must cross before you can successfully make a call into a configured component. Remember, the target component lives in a single COM+ application (which could be a server *or* a library application), and the application lives in a single process. Each COM+ server process will host exactly one server application (which controls many process-wide settings, such as the security identity and default impersonation level) and zero or more library applications (a library application has much less control over its security environment than a server application, naturally). Figure 9.14 shows an example.

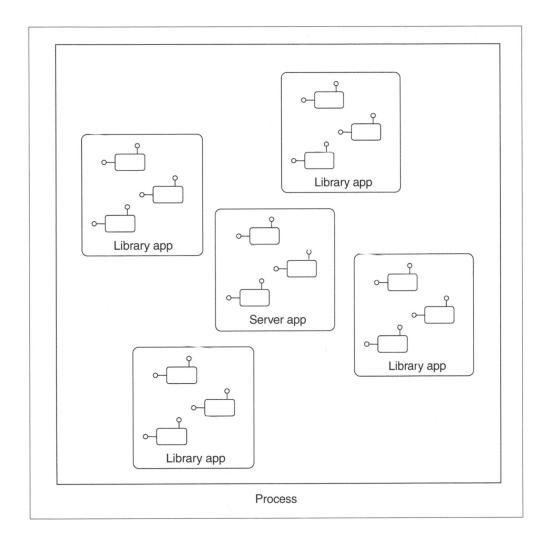

Figure 9.14 A typical COM+ process

Three access control hurdles stand in the way of making a successful call. If you don't get past one of them, you're immediately denied access and cannot move on to the others. These hurdles occur in the following order and at the following points (see Figure 9.15, where it is assumed that causality A caused the process to launch, after which casuality B and C entered the already running process):

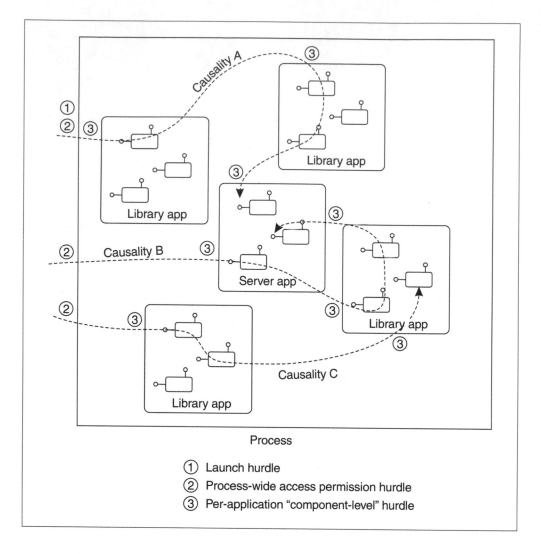

Figure 9.15 The three hurdles

1. As an activation request causes the COM SCM to consider launching a server process

2. As a call enters a process[49]

3. As a call enters an application[50]

---

[49] This includes activation requests, IRemUnknown calls, and normal method calls.

[50] This does not include activation requests or IRemUnknown calls.

The first hurdle is special because it's evaluated by the COM SCM only when a server process needs to be launched in response to an activation request. If the process is already running, this hurdle is essentially removed from the picture (similar to the LaunchPermission setting for base COM servers). If a caller is denied access by the first hurdle, the server process won't be launched at all.[51]

The first two hurdles are controlled entirely by the configuration of the single *server* application in the process. The caller satisfies both of these hurdles as long as he or she is a member of at least one of the roles *defined* for the application (note that the role doesn't even have to be assigned to any components). The ApplicationAccessChecksEnabled property on the single server application in the process directly enables or disables both these hurdles (see Figure 9.16).[52] Note that if the server application hands out pointers to objects hosted in a library application in the same process, those objects are also subject to the second hurdle; a library application that grants everyone all access to its components will still be subject to the process-wide hurdles imposed by the server application in the process.[53]

The third hurdle indicates whether or not the call will be able to enter the application. This setting is configured on both server *and* library applications individually. Note that the COM+ documentation refers to this as a *component-level* access check, which almost universally gives the (incorrect) impression that COM+ performs intrinsic access checks for calls between components in the same application. The key thing to keep in mind is that COM only performs this check when a call crosses into the application. Once inside the application, the COM+ channel performs no further access checks.

The reason for the "component-level" label is that the application-entry access check that the channel performs is sensitive to the component targeted by the call (technically, it's sensitive to the targeted *method* on that

---

[51] Note that this differs from MTS, which granted Everyone launch permission. This is clearly a tremendous improvement in the model.

[52] Turning off ApplicationAccessChecksEnabled does truly remove the first barrier (launch permissions) completely; unauthenticated activation requests will now cause the server to launch.

[53] However, by turning off both authentication and access checks for a library application, you open the somewhat esoteric "notch" that I'll describe later in the chapter, which *does* allow calls to slip past the second hurdle.

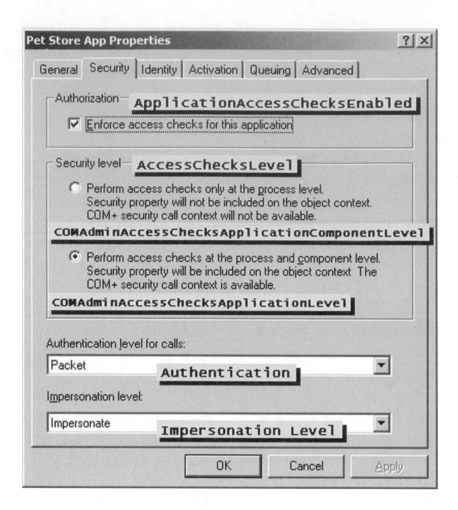

Figure 9.16 COM+ catalog security properties

component). As long as the caller is a member of at least one role assigned to the target method (or its host interface or class), he or she will satisfy this final hurdle.

Three settings need to be aligned in order for this third hurdle to be erected in front of a particular call. The first and second settings must be configured on the application that hosts the component targeted by the call. The second setting is necessary in order to install interceptors into the channel that perform the fine-grained bookkeeping necessary to implement this level of access con-

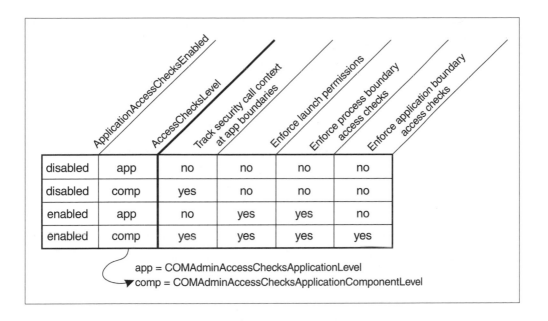

ApplicationAccessChecksEnabled	AccessChecksLevel	Track security call context at app boundaries	Enforce launch permissions	Enforce process boundary access checks	Enforce application boundary access checks
disabled	app	no	no	no	no
disabled	comp	yes	no	no	no
enabled	app	no	yes	yes	no
enabled	comp	yes	yes	yes	yes

app = COMAdminAccessChecksApplicationLevel
comp = COMAdminAccessChecksApplicationComponentLevel

Figure 9.17   Access control decoder ring

trol (I'll talk more about this setting a bit later). The third setting must be enabled on the component targeted by the call:

1. `ApplicationAccessChecksEnabled = True`

2. `AccessChecksLevel = COMAdminAccessChecksApplicationComponentLevel`[54]

3. `ComponentAccessChecksEnabled = True`

Figure 9.17 provides a summary of the various options for enabling or disabling these hurdles.

---

[54] Although MTS applications don't have an `AccessChecksLevel` setting, this behavior most closely resembles the way MTS works. As long as you've turned on MTS access checks at both the application and component level, fine-grained role-based checks will always be in force; there's no setting equivalent to `COMAdminAccessChecksApplicationLevel` that turns off fine-grained component-level role checks and leaves process-wide checks intact. Using the hurdle analogy, in MTS, hurdles 2 and 3 are tied together, whereas in COM+ it's possible to enable hurdle 2 while hurdle 3 is disabled.

As mentioned in footnotes 49 and 50 regarding the second and third hurdles, COM+ deals with `CoCreateInstance` and `QueryInterface` in a unique way. You are allowed to create instances of *any class exposed by the server process* as long as you can get past the first two (process-wide) hurdles, even if you're not granted access (via role assignments) to any methods on that class. Also, in order to allow optimizations in the COM remoting architecture, you'll be able to call `QueryInterface` for *any interface* regardless of its role assignments. The access checks for the third hurdle don't kick in until you begin making non-`IUnknown` method calls. (I mention these special cases only so that you won't be surprised by this behavior.)

As a final note, the System logon session is not subject to any of these hurdles in COM+ applications, thus eliminating the silly problem in base COM that I described earlier which occurs when you forget to grant access to SYSTEM.

Which Components Need Role Assignments?

Most of the COM+ services provided via interception are predicated on the notion that as a client of a configured component you will not share any references to that object with anyone else. Let's say that there exist two configured components, A and B. If a client creates component A, and A creates B, A should generally avoid returning a reference to B back to the client. Ewald (2000) discusses the problems this can lead to if A and B share a synchronization or transaction domain, but sharing object references can make your life more difficult from a security perspective as well.

Designating a small set of classes as the entry point into an application tremendously simplifies the security model. It is these "gateway" classes that need to be assigned roles; the other internal helper classes should have role-based checks enabled (via the `ComponentAccessChecksEnabled` property), but should have *no roles assigned to them whatsoever*. This guarantees that external clients will not be able to make method calls directly to these objects, and reduces the surface area that you expose to external clients (which means less potential security holes to plug). As for library applications, in general, I prefer to simply be honest and open them wide by setting `ApplicationAccess ChecksEnabled` to `False`. Figure 9.18 shows the basic strategy.

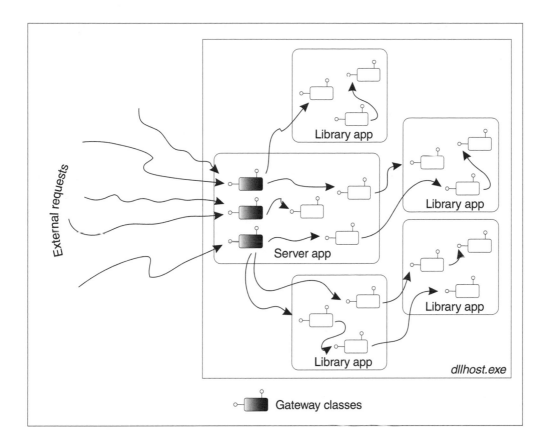

Figure 9.18   Gateway into a COM+ application

Security in COM+ Library Applications

COM+ library applications (unlike MTS library packages) have some distinct security settings. One can define roles in a library application and assign them to classes, interfaces, and methods, just as with a server application. Although academically interesting, the security of this mechanism is questionable at best, because any in-process component is subject to the whims of its client, who (if clever) can simply reach past the interceptor and call directly into the object.[55]

---

[55] Perhaps we'll see a day when processes are subdivided into separate security domains, but Windows 2000 certainly does not provide this feature.

One might rationalize the need for role-based access checks in library components by suggesting that they could be employed in a reusable fashion by other server applications and handed directly back to the client, who would then be subject to the common access checks defined by the library application. However, this argument doesn't hold water because the library application will still be subject to the process-wide access control settings on the single server application in the process, which often eliminates this benefit. Besides, as mentioned previously, sharing object references (especially transactional components) is looked on with disdain by the COM+ plumbing.

With all that said, there is an interesting use of library application role-based access checks related to a particular type of Web application architecture; Chapter 10 explores this use.

The one feature of library application security that is really unique and worth talking about in this chapter is the authentication level. Although a library application cannot fully control its authentication level, it can provide a "notch" in the low-water mark of its host. Suppose the host application's low-water mark was PKT_INTEGRITY, but the application desperately needed to receive a callback from another server that could not be authenticated. In base COM, there was no way for a process to change its low-water mark to allow unauthenticated callbacks (all COM channels in a process respected the single process-wide authentication level). In COM+, however, each library application has the choice of retaining the authentication level set by the server application in the process, or choosing the equivalent of RPC_C_AUTHN_LEVEL_NONE, thus creating the notch mentioned earlier. By giving out a reference to a component in a library application configured in this fashion, it's now possible to receive unauthenticated callbacks to that object, despite the process-wide low-water mark. (Yes, this is sharing an object reference, but in this case, you'll likely only be using this object to tunnel into the application via an unauthenticated call; the object will almost invariably be nontransactional.)

Although most security experts will probably shun this feature, I've talked to many developers whose projects have ground to a halt because they couldn't get a callback to work because of lack of bidirectional trust relationships. Many of these folks cried out (via the listserver at discuss.microsoft.com) for per-apartment authentication-level control. This feature addresses this need (albeit in a different way).

Note that if you choose to use this feature, the default authentication level for the proxy will still be negotiated based on the low-water mark of the process hosting the library package (which will usually not be (RPC_C_AUTHN_LEVEL _NONE), so whoever tries to make an unauthenticated call back into the notch will need to call SetBlanket explicitly in order to drop the authentication level to NONE; otherwise, COM will attempt to authenticate the request.

Here's a script that opens this notch by creating a library application aptly named Notch Library (note that you must also turn off ApplicationAccess ChecksEnabled in order for this trick to work):

```
<?xml version="1.0" ?>
<job>
<reference
  guid="{F618C513-DFB8-11D1-A2CF-00805FC79235}" />
<script language="VBScript"><![CDATA[

set ac = getApplicationCollection()
set a = ac.add
a.value("Name") = "Notch Library"
a.value("Activation") = COMAdminActivationInproc
a.value("Authentication") = COMAdminAuthenticationNone
a.value("ApplicationAccessChecksEnabled") = false
ac.saveChanges

]]></script>
</job>
```

After running this script, you'd add your callback component into the Notch Library application, and at runtime, you'd create an instance of this component to hand off to anyone who needed to send you unauthenticated messages. If you care a whit about security, you'll want to use this feature like wasabi: A little bit goes a long way.[56]

---

[56] In case you don't share my enthusiasm for good sushi, wasabi is the green mustard traditionally served with such a dish.

Fine-Grained Access Control: IsCallerInRole

COM+ poses the following questions to determine whether to grant or deny access:

1. Who is the caller?
2. What class of object is the caller accessing?
3. What are the caller's intentions?

The first question is answered by authentication, and the third question is answered based on the method that the caller is invoking. The second question is just a more coarse-grained form of "What object is the caller accessing?" which comes close to the ultra-fine-grained object-centric model of access control discussed in Chapters 3 and 6.

If you look at the traditional usage of COM+ in **OLTP** applications, configured components rarely represent entities (individual objects), but rather are more suited to representing sessions (operations performed on groups of objects).[57] Because each instance of a configured class is often treated as equivalent (a session), it doesn't make sense to bother putting a DACL on each instance of an object. However, what *does* make sense is to allow the session object to perform logical access checks based on specific patterns of input. For instance, one classic example is when a withdrawal request above a certain amount will only be accepted if a supervisor (as opposed to a teller) submits it.

COM+ provides an extensibility point via a method known as `IsCaller InRole` on the security call context.[58] A very simple function, it allows you to extend the logic of the intrinsic role-based access control infastructure in COM+ to include your own rules. Note that because this is simply an extension of the implicit role-based security provided by COM+, this application logic is also turned on and off via the same catalog-based settings described earlier: `ApplicationAccessChecksEnabled` and `ComponentAccessChecks Enabled`. If either of these settings is `False`, `IsCallerInRole` will always

---

[57] See Ewald (2000).

[58] The security call context object was introduced in COM+; in MTS, `IsCallerInRole` is available via `IObjectContext`.

return `True`, which is quite nice because it allows you to temporarily strip out all access checks from an application during development without having to modify your code. If this worries you because (for example) you're using role-based access checks to keep people from physical harm, you can check to see if access checks have been turned off by calling `IsSecurityEnabled`.[59] These APIs are very straightforward to use.[60]

```
[dual, ...]
interface ISecurityCallContext : IDispatch {
HRESULT get_Count(
              [out, retval] long* plCount);
HRESULT get_Item(          [in] BSTR name,
              [out, retval] VARIANT* pItem);
HRESULT get__NewEnum(
              [out, retval] IUnknown** ppEnum);
HRESULT IsCallerInRole(  [in] BSTR bstrRole,
              [out, retval] VARIANT_BOOL* pfInRole);
HRESULT IsSecurityEnabled(
              [out, retval] VARIANT_BOOL* pfIsEnabled);
HRESULT IsUserInRole(    [in] VARIANT* pUser,
                         [in] BSTR bstrRole,
              [out, retval] VARIANT_BOOL* pfInRole);
}
HRESULT CoGetCallContext(REFIID iid, void** ppv);
```

It's important to note that unless your application is configured for component-level access checks (via the `AccessChecksLevel` property in the catalog), this interface will not be available via `CoGetCallContext` (you'll get `E_NO INTERFACE` if you ask for it).

You may have noticed that I didn't recommend use of the `IsUserInRole` method. This method was specifically provided for supporting Queued Components (QC), where because of the disconnected nature of the system, neither

---

[59] Note that while this can help guard against *accidental* misconfiguration, it clearly adds no real security; the same administrator who disabled access checks could also remap roles.

[60] Aside from the complete lack of a localization strategy for strings used as role names (granted, localization is a little more important for shrink-wrapped software than for the problems COM+ was designed to solve).

NTLM nor Kerberos can be used to establish a server-side logon session for the caller. Instead, QC uses a certificate to verify the signature of each incoming authenticated message, including the caller's SID, which may then be passed to `IsUserInRole` to dynamically determine whether the SID maps to a particular role. The drawback of this mechanism is performance: Because the system hasn't established a logon session, `IsUserInRole` must make network round-trips to the client and server's authority in order to download the authorization attributes (group SIDs) to compare against the role membership table in the application. In short, avoid this function if at all possible.

Call Context Tracking

As each COM causality[61] meanders through a set of configured components, the COM channel performs bookkeeping at each application boundary crossing. This may be as simple as remembering the SID of the caller who rode the causality into the very first configured component in the object graph, and it may be as detailed as maintaining snapshots of all the blanket settings for any call that crossed an application boundary. Setting a server application's `AccessChecksLevel` property to `COMAdminAccessChecksApplication ComponentLevel` causes the channel to perform this more detailed tracking throughout the server process.

Look back at the definition of `ISecurityCallContext`. Note that besides `IsCallerInRole` and friends, it acts as a collection of other named pieces of information. Here are those names and what they mean:

- **NumCallers** The count of items in the `Callers` stack.

- **Callers** A stack of objects representing security information for calls that have been made in the current causality; each call that crosses an application boundary is pushed onto the stack associated with the causality. Each object in the stack records the caller's SID and name, the authentication service and level of protection, and the imperson-ation level in use.

---

[61] A causality in COM is a network-wide logical thread of execution. See Ewald (2001) for more details.

- **MinAuthenticationLevel** A quick way to determine the weakest link in the call chain; this is the lowest authentication level found in the `Callers` stack.

- **DirectCaller** The first element in the `Callers` stack (this represents the most recent call that crossed an application boundary). This information is available via the `ISecurityProperty` interface as well, which is also supported by MTS.

- **OriginalCaller** The last element in the `Callers` stack (this represents the very first call in the current causality that crossed an application boundary). This information is available via the `ISecurity Property` interface as well, which is also supported by MTS.

Although I don't expect that many will iterate through the `Callers` collection at runtime and try to make any sense of it, it's certainly useful for debugging. `OriginalCaller` is great for auditing who started the causality (this will generally be the original client in the chain), and it eliminates the need for impersonation in the middle tier simply for the sake of auditing. Each of the objects in the `Callers` collection implements the `ISecurityIdentity Coll` interface, which is just a classic automation collection without any additional unique methods. Here are the various properties you can access via the collection:

- **SID** An array of bytes representing the SID of the caller

- **AccountName** The caller's authority and principal names as a string

- **AuthenticationService** One of the RPC_C_AUTHN_*XXX* constants indicating the authentication service used by the caller

- **AuthenticationLevel** One of the RPC_C_AUTHN_LEVEL_*XXX* constants indicating the level of protection used by the caller

- **ImpersonationLevel** One of the RPC_C_IMP_LEVEL_*XXX* constants indicating the level of impersonation selected by the caller

Tips for Debugging COM Security Problems

COM security pulls together virtually all the concepts discussed in Parts I and II of this book, and is therefore one of the most complex beasts to troubleshoot unless you've begun to internalized the way Windows security works. Here are some tips.

- Don't rush.

- Approach troubleshooting systematically. Avoid the temptation to randomly turn knobs hoping to get things working.

- As soon as you discover a problem, record the exact function call that is returning an error, and exactly which error code it is. Document the server's security settings. If the problem occurs when the client makes a COM method call to the server, consider modifying the client code (in a nonobtrusive way) to call `CoQueryProxyBlanket` and record the exact settings on the proxy blanket before the call was made.

- Start from a known configuration. If need be, run a script to configure your client and server so that you don't end up chasing ghosts. Keep a written log of each change you make. Pay close attention to the identity setting of the server.

- Draw a diagram showing the logon sessions that the client and server are running in, and whether or not they will have network credentials.

- Turn on auditing of logon and logoff events and pay attention to the security event logs. This will tell you two things: whether the SCM was able to create the *server's* batch (or service) logon session in order to host the server process at launch time, and whether the client could be authenticated (assuming the client is remote).

- Shut down the server process each time you reconfigure it. Most COM security settings are cached for the lifetime of the process.

- When running debug builds of your COM servers, seriously consider Run As Interactive User. Of course, you'll need to have someone interactively log in to the server machine to make this work; consider logging in using the daemon account you'd normally run your server under to get as close to a production scenario as possible.

- For nonconfigured components, make absolutely sure that you grant access to the System logon session. If you want unauthenticated activation requests to launch your server, be sure to grant launch permissions to the Everyone SID.

- In the process of debugging, don't bother trying to use `DebugBreak` (or `_asm int 3`) inside implementations of COM method calls in your servers. Your stub will just catch this exception and return an error code to the client. Instead, start the server in a debugger, or attach a debugger at runtime.

- Make sure your server's DLL or EXE file and any proxy-stub DLLs don't have any weird DACLs on them that might cause problems.[62]

- Do *not* convince yourself that callbacks are in any way special. Each COM call has a client and a server, and in the case of a "callback" the roles are reversed, but all the same mechanisms are in place: The client (formerly the server) must be able to be authenticated by the server (formerly the client) unless the authentication setting in the blanket is `RPC_C_AUTHN_LEVEL_NONE`.

- If the client is impersonating before making the call, be conscious of the security context tracking mode (cloaking settings) configured in the proxy blanket.

- Always keep in mind the order of the security-related hurdles that you have to cross in order to make a successful COM call. This is key to isolating the problem.

  1. You have to satisfy the client's request for authentication. If the default negotiated blanket (or the result of the client calling `Set Blanket`) is something other than `RPC_C_AUTHN_LEVEL_NONE`, then authentication must succeed or the call will fail *regardless of the server's low-water mark*. This is one reason that I advocated recording the actual settings on the proxy by calling `CoQuery`

---

[62] I once lazily dropped a proxy-stub DLL onto my desktop and registered it there, then later had to debug an error (`E_ACCESSDENIED`) that I was getting when calling `QueryInterface` through a proxy. The server was running under a daemon account and couldn't load the proxy-stub DLL; the problem was that my desktop (protected by a pretty tight DACL) conferred a similar DACL (via inheritance) to the DLL when it was placed there. I nearly died laughing once I figured out what I had done, but it was pretty painful to debug at the time.

`ProxyBlanket`. If the client requested authentication, verify that it succeeded by checking the server's audit log.

2. You have to satisfy the server's authentication low-water mark.

3. You have to get past launch permissions (only if the server isn't running when you make your activation request). If the server process launches in response to your activation request, that's your indication that you made it past this step.

4. You have to get past the process-wide access permission DACL. Legacy COM components relying on an EXE-to-AppID mapping should make absolutely sure this isn't broken at this point.

5. Finally (for configured components only), you have to get past any role-based access checks that have been enabled.

Summary

- COM security starts with the basic model of RPC security and adds value through defaulting mechanisms and automated access control schemes such as role-based security.

- In RPC and COM security, the client selects the authentication settings and the server detects them.

- The authentication level controls how much the session key (established during authentication) will be used.

- The server-side channel uses the process-wide authentication level as a low-water mark, but a COM+ library application can override this by opening up a hole that allows unauthenticated calls through.

- Local COM calls behave radically differently with regard to security (and blanket configuration) than those calls going across the wire.

- Try to stick with an impersonation level of `RPC_C_IMP_LEVEL _IDENTIFY` if at all possible. This provides protection for the client, while giving the server a token strong enough to perform access checks against.

- COM+ roles help decouple design-time and implementation-time decisions from deployment-time decisions.

- Remember the fundamentals when it comes to debugging COM security.

Chapter 10

IIS

As you well know, not everyone on the Internet runs Windows. There are many other platforms that can be reached across the Internet that have absolutely no idea how to send or receive DCOM packets. Because of the vast commercial enterprises farming the Internet using HTTP, and the vast numbers of consumers who want to jump on the fabled information superhighway, an incredible amount of research, development, and most importantly, standardization has gone into hardware and software for making HTTP sing on just about any platform you can imagine. Most pagers these days can access the Web. There are refrigerators in the works that will automatically order groceries over the Internet when your supplies are running low. If you want to tap this well, you have to buy into HTTP and Web server technology, and if you want to secure your transactions, you have to learn ways of authenticating in the face of firewalls and an incredible variety of client platforms.

This chapter is all about putting a Web front end on your COM+ distributed application. You'll find that there is virtually no code in this chapter, because the job is mainly an administrative task (I assume you already know how to program ISAPI, ASP, or CGI apps). If this chapter does its job, by the time you're done reading it you'll feel more comfortable working with Internet Information Server (IIS) because you'll have a more clear understanding of the security context that your application will be running in given any particular configuration. (There are so many different configuration options that it's easy to become confused, and this often leads to a general sense of unease.) The chapter begins by explaining how authentication works on the Web using public key cryptography and certificates, then works through the various client authentication options, and ends by providing some tips to help you use IIS as a gateway into a COM+ application.

Authentication on the Web

When you go online and plan a trip, you typically send sensitive information across the wire, such as information about where you're going to be and special needs that you might have; often you'll even send your credit card number across the wire to purchase tickets or reserve a room or a rental car. It's amazing to me that so many people are willing to do this without understanding how their conversations are secured. Most consumers who care about security look for the little key in Netscape's Communicator or the little padlock in Microsoft's Internet Explorer (IE) and feel comfortable that these conversations are being encrypted so that a bad guy cannot see this sensitive information. But what's the point of encrypting a message if you don't know who you're sending the message to? How do you know that it's really Amazon.com on the other end of the wire and not a bad guy? I'm pretty confident that Jeff Bezos doesn't have lunch with each and every Amazon customer and exchange a secret passphrase that can later be used to generate session keys. What we need is some form of authentication that scales to the global Internet.

Chapter 7 described in reasonable detail a couple of authentication protocols that can be used to prove the identity of one principal to another electronically: NTLM and Kerberos. Can we apply either of these technologies to this particular problem?

Consider NTLM. NTLM is all about proving the identity of the client to the server, which is usually satisfactory in a controlled environment such as a single business. The client is never cryptographically assured of the server's identity, but it's also much harder for internal servers to be spoofed than it is on the Internet at large. On the Web, where compromise of a router is a much more likely scenario, the focus reverses and protecting the consumer from spoofed servers is of critical importance. E-commerce sites typically still need to have some form of client authentication, but often this is as simple as correlating a credit card number with a billing address. Client authentication is pushed off to the credit card authority. Even if we were to reverse NTLM so that the client challenges the server, this requires the server to have a shared secret with each client (or that client's authority), which is pretty much equivalent to having the CEO of Amazon.com whisper a shared passphrase in your ear at lunch.

What about Kerberos? Kerberos has specific provisions for mutual authentication. The client can in fact verify the identity of the server during the authentication handshake, and any information that the client encrypts with the resulting session key and sends to the server is only useful to the one true server with which the client originally authenticated, because that server also knows the session key and can decrypt the incoming message.

When it comes to scalability, Kerberos is certainly a move in the right direction; by issuing tickets that have an expiration time on the order of ten hours, we reduce the load on the authority significantly, as opposed to a protocol such as NTLM, where the authority must be contacted for each authentication request.

So why doesn't Amazon.com use Kerberos to prove its identity to its clients? Well, when used in the conventional way, Kerberos requires the client to prove his or her identity to the server. Having the server prove its identity to the client is a nifty optional feature of Kerberos, but this doesn't help Amazon.com, who would now be forced to cryptographically authenticate each and every client, which once again puts Amazon.com in the business of whispering secrets to clients on lunch breaks.

However, what if we were to use Kerberos in reverse? Perhaps the server could present a ticket to the client to prove the server's identity, as opposed to the other way around. Figure 10.1 shows how this might work. The client makes a request to the server, and the server sends a ticket plus an authenticator to the client to verify its identity. The ticket contains the server's name, an expiration date, and a key that the client and server can use to secure their conversations. This information was encrypted by the authority (not the server), so as long as the client trusts that authority, she'll trust that the ticket was not forged. If the client can decrypt this information (checking the authenticator to make sure the server really sent this message and that it wasn't stolen or replayed), she can happily use the key in the ticket to send confidential messages to the server.

Look at all the good ideas we've been able to leverage from Kerberos: Kerberos tickets *do* contain a key that can be used to establish an encrypted session, and they *do* contain an expiration date that helps make the authentication protocol scale better than something like NTLM, and they *do* have the notion of ownership (the server's name is in the ticket and anyone who purports to be the server must prove knowledge of the secret key associated with the ticket). The glaring problem is that the ticket also has a *fixed target* (in our case, the target is the client). If Amazon.com wants to prove its identity to Alice, it must obtain a ticket targeted at Alice. If Amazon.com wants to prove its identity to Mary, it must obtain a ticket targeted at Mary. This means that *everyone*

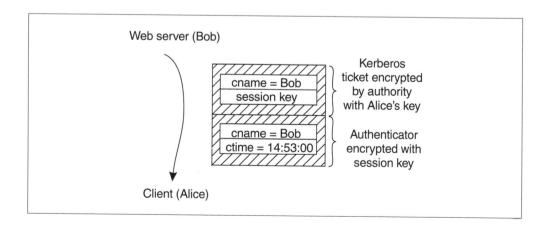

Figure 10.1 Kerberos in reverse?

must register with a Kerberos authority, even clients. A client cannot simply be an anonymous Internet user and have any chance of verifying a server's identity using this scheme.

Why does this limitation exist? Because the Kerberos KDC relies entirely on conventional cryptography to prove the origin of its tickets. Using the reverse-Kerberos scheme that I've concocted, when Alice receives a ticket from Amazon.com, that ticket is encrypted with a secret key shared by Alice and the authority. The only reason Alice trusts the contents of the ticket is that she can decrypt it successfully, and thus she knows it came from her authority. It's not feasible at all to have Amazon.com (or its Kerberos authority) register as a principal with every client's authority on the Internet in order to weave a chain of secret keys across the Web. It just won't scale (once again, we've resorted to whispering secrets).

If, on the other hand, there were some way for an authority to encrypt a ticket with a special private key in such a way that *anyone* could decrypt it using a *different* key that was not a secret (but instead was a well-known value), we'd be just about half-way to a solution. When Alice receives this ticket from Amazon.com, if she can decrypt it with the well-known key for the authority, she will trust that the contents were really produced by that authority.

This doesn't completely solve the problem, though. If anyone in the world can decrypt the ticket with the authority's well-known key, this also means that anyone can see the secret key inside that Alice will use to encrypt data that she sends to Amazon.com. These sorts of tickets *cannot hold secrets*. So instead of a secret, the authority can put a well-known key for Amazon.com in the ticket. Similar to the key the authority used to encrypt the ticket, anyone can use this well-known key to encrypt a message, but only Amazon.com knows the corresponding private key to decrypt that message. In this scenario, the ticket doesn't need to be encrypted at all because it holds no secrets. Instead, the authority could simply *sign* the ticket using the special private key I mentioned earlier. Anyone in the world who trusts that authority could then verify this signature using the authority's well-known key.

This seemingly bizarre idea for a cryptosystem in which two paired keys are used (one public and one private) was invented in the mid-1970s by Whitfield

Diffie,[1] and it's known as **public key cryptography.** The tickets we're talking about now are no longer Kerberos tickets, but rather **digital certificates.**

Public Key Cryptography

Without going into the mathematics involved in making it work,[2] the idea behind public key cryptography is quite simple. Instead of having a single secret key that can be used for encryption and decryption, the key is split into two parts: a **public key** and a **private key.** Only a single entity knows the private key, but the public key is just that—public. Most public key cryptosystems work in the following way: If you encrypt some **plaintext** with key A, you can only decrypt the resulting **ciphertext** with key B (see Figure 10.2). Because two different keys must be used for encryption and decryption, public key algorithms are also known as **asymmetric algorithms,** whereas conventional cryptosystems that use a single key are known as **symmetric algorithms.**

Here's an example of a public key algorithm. In DSA (the Digital Signature Algorithm[3]), key A is a private key and key B is the corresponding public key. This means that only one person can encrypt the plaintext into ciphertext,

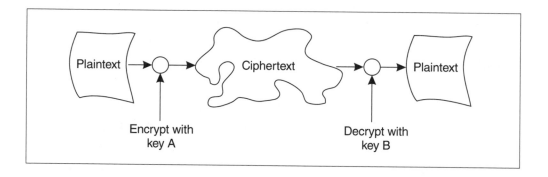

Figure 10.2 Public key cryptography

---

[1] As far as us civilians know, at least. It's entirely possible that this technology had been discovered years before by a major government; this is one sort of discovery that a government would want to keep to itself.

[2] See Schneier (1996) for an approachable introduction to the math.

[3] Part of the DSS (Digital Signature Standard) specification.

but many people can decrypt it. Clearly this method cannot be used to send secrets, because anyone with the public key can decrypt the ciphertext, but this sort of mechanism is exactly what is required for signatures. By calculating a one-way hash of some plaintext and encrypting that hash with a private key, anyone who knows the corresponding public key can verify the signature. After verifying a digital signature of this type, you know that the plaintext wasn't tampered with since it was originally signed, and you know that the only entity that could have created the signature was the one who knows the associated private key.

By far the most well-known digital signature algorithm is RSA, named after its inventors, Rivest, Shamir, and Adleman. This algorithm can be used to create digital signatures as with DSA, but it can also be used to send secrets. In this mode, we reverse the way the keys are used so that anyone who knows the public key can encrypt a block of plaintext, but only the holder of the private key can decrypt the resulting ciphertext. What's convenient about RSA is that it works both ways: The same algorithm can be used to encrypt secrets as well as create signatures by reversing the way the keys are used (see Figure 10.3).[4]

One thing that stands out about asymmetric algorithms is that although they are great for producing and verifying signatures for which only a hash value needs to be encrypted or decrypted (a hash value is typically between 128 and 256 bits of data), they are really poor performers for encrypting bulk data. Symmetric algorithms are hundreds of times faster at bulk encryption. In practice, if Alice wants to send an encrypted message to Bob leveraging his public key, she can do something as simple as generating a random *conventional* key and sending it to Bob encrypted with his public key. She can then send Bob as much data as she likes, and encrypt it using a symmetric algorithm. Thus in practice, public keys are used for two different purposes: generating digital signatures and exchanging symmetric keys (also known as session keys).

---

[4] Although it's a bad idea to use the same key pair to do both; usually one key pair is used for signatures and another is used for encryption (Schneier 1996).

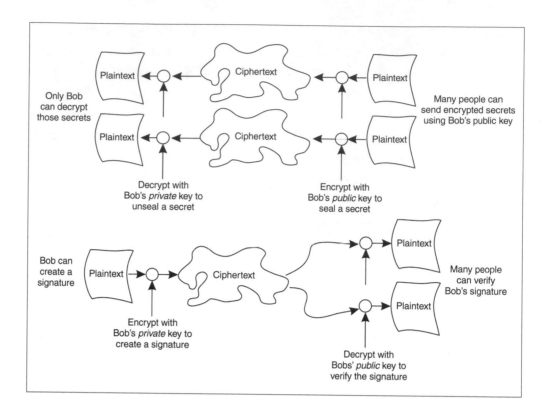

Figure 10.3　RSA encryption and signature generation

Certificates

I remember that when I first learned about public key cryptography, I initially thought it was the silver bullet that would solve all key exchange problems. What I quickly realized, however, was that when used properly it can lead to a more scalable cryptosystem, but that key exchange is still hard.

With a conventional cryptosystem, all keys are secret keys. When the KDC constructs a Kerberos ticket and embeds a session key inside, the contents of that ticket must be carefully encrypted so that a bad guy cannot discover the embedded session key. This also means that if a bad guy were to tamper with the ticket, in an attempt to change the session key to a value he or she knows, the server receiving the ticket would detect this because the ticket would not decrypt properly. (The results would be a garbled mess, and Kerberos implementations watch for this sort of funny business.)

However, when you send your *public* key across the wire, it's tempting to think that it doesn't need any protection. Granted, it's not a secret, so you don't need to hide it as Kerberos hides its session keys inside tickets, but imagine what would happen if a bad guy were to tamper with the key in transit. If Bob sent his public key to Alice, and Fred intercepted that message and replaced Bob's public key with his own before sending the message on to Alice, any secrets that Alice subsequently sent to Bob using the compromised key would be readable by Fred. Granted, if Bob receives any of these messages *directly*, if he's paying any attention at all he'll see that they decrypt to complete gibberish (only Fred can successfully decrypt messages encrypted with his own public key), but if Fred has hijacked a router between Alice and Bob, it's all over. Fred can simply intercept each of Alice's encrypted messages, decrypt them, read them, modify them to his liking, and then encrypt them using Bob's real public key. Neither Alice nor Bob will have a clue that Fred is in the middle. If Bob also asks Alice for her public signature key, Fred can substitute his own key; now Fred will be able to sign messages to Bob, and Bob will be tricked into thinking that Alice was the signer (Figure 10.4 shows the scam). The crux of the problem is that in order for Alice or Bob to be able to safely use public keys

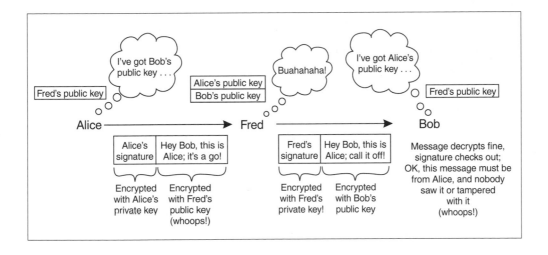

Figure 10.4 The "Fred in the middle" attack

that they receive electronically, they must have some way to verify the identity of the person who owns the corresponding private key.

Can't Bob just sign the key he sends to Alice, so that Alice can verify that it really came from Bob? This is like asking which came first, the chicken or the egg. Alice can't verify any of Bob's signatures until she obtains his public signature key, and how will she ever verify *that* key? The point that I'm trying to drive home here is that secure key exchange is just plain hard, even with public keys (which are not secrets). Two popular solutions to the problem are as follows:

1. Exchange initial public keys with your friends (even face to face if necessary) so that Fred *can't* get in the middle. Then treat those friends as trusted authorities. This is the model used by PGP (Pretty Good Privacy).

2. Use a hierarchy of trusted authorities. This is the model used by X.509.

PGP and Cumulative Trust

Here's the idea behind PGP in a nutshell: Alice and Bob are friends, so they exchange public keys simply by sending them via email, but then they meet at lunch (or call each other on the phone) and authenticate those keys. The way this is done is quite simple. For instance, for Alice to verify Bob's public key, she calculates a hash of the key she received in the mail, and Bob takes a hash of the key he sent. Alice then reads the hash value aloud (either over the phone or over a ham sandwich). Now that they trust the validity of each other's keys, in the future, Alice and Bob can sign or seal packets that they send to one another. If Bob wants to introduce Alice to Mary, he can send Alice a signed message containing Mary's public key, and Alice, because she trusts Bob, adds this key to her "keyring" (presumably Bob met Mary face to face or obtained her key electronically from someone he trusts and with whom he had previously exchanged keys). This "web of trust" expands into a community of users who trust one another's public keys.[5]

---

[5] This is tremendously simplified, of course. See Zimmerman (1995) for more detail.

Each public key that Alice receives electronically from Bob comes wrapped in a tight little package called a *certificate*. The certificate contains a public key along with (typically) an email address identifying the owner of that public key, plus an expiration date; the contents are signed with Bob's private key. Bob in this case is the certifying authority. Because Alice trusts Bob, when she validates his signature she develops trust in Mary's public key.

X.509 and Hierarchical Trust

The X.509 model of trust asserts that there is a rigid hierarchy of authorities (your buddy can't simply act as an authority). In the degenerate case there is just one authority whose public key is well known. If Alice needs to obtain Bob's public key, she simply asks him for it electronically, and Bob sends Alice a certificate (see Figure 10.5) that contains a public key and an X.509 distinguished name, along with (among other things) an expiration date and the name of the authority that issued the certificate. The contents of the certificate are signed with the private key of the issuing authority, and since this authority is well known, Alice can verify Bob's certificate by simply using the well-known public key of the authority.

In the real world, there are several authorities whose public keys (contained in self-signed certificates) actually ship with Web browsers such as Communicator and IE. Many individual companies also maintain their own

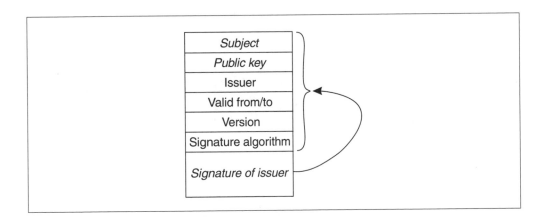

Figure 10.5   An X.509 certificate

certificate authorities (CAs) so that they can issue certificates internally; this works well as long as the certificates are only used within that particular company. In order to broaden the scope of trust for these internal certificates, it's possible for the company's certificate authority to be validated by one of the well-known authorities, forming a tree of trust (see Figure 10.6).

In Figure 10.6, the company Foo may choose to accept Bob's certificate that was issued by Bar, because Bar has been certified by an authority that Foo trusts. This manifests itself by a chain of certificates, starting with Bob's certificate, which is signed by Bar, and Bar's certificate, which is signed by Quux. Quux is a root authority and thus signs its own certificate; this is the sort of well-known certificate that gets distributed with software such as a Web browser. As long as Foo trusts one of the certificates in the chain (in this case, Quux), Foo develops trust in Bob's certificate. This is a simplified explanation; for more information on developing a **public key infrastructure** (**PKI**) such as this, see Adams (1999), Feghhi (1999), and Ford (1997).

Web servers use X.509 certificates to prove their authenticity to clients. Each client can obtain the Web server's certificate, ask it for proof of its identity, and traverse up the hierarchy of trust until a trusted certifying authority is found.

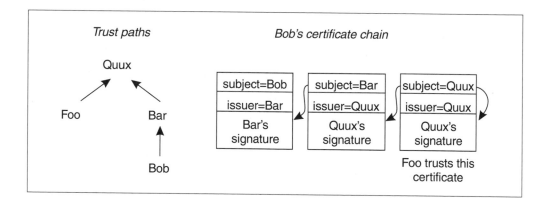

Figure 10.6 A hierarchy of trust and a resulting certificate chain

Interlude: Some Acronyms and Terms

This section contains a rather terse description of some of the acronyms and terms that you'll commonly hear on the Web security playground. I wanted to provide this to give you some idea of the history of authentication on the Web; by putting these acronyms into context, I can focus on the dominant protocol.

SSL, PCT, and TLS, Oh My!

In 1994, Netscape Communications developed and popularized a network authentication protocol known as the Secure Sockets Layer (SSL 2.0). In 1995, Microsoft countered with a protocol known as Private Communication Technology (PCT 1.0), which was an improvement on SSL 2.0. Around the same time Netscape released an independent suite of improvements via the SSL 3.0 protocol, which dominates the Web as of this writing. SSL 3.0 was submitted to the IETF as an Internet draft ("Secure Sockets Layer 3.0 Specification") in 1996, and an IETF working group was formed to come up with a recommendation. In January 1999, RFC 2246 was issued by the IETF, documenting the result of this group's efforts: the Transport Layer Security protocol (TLS 1.0), which is virtually indistinguishable from SSL 3.0.[6]

After the world embraced SSL 3.0 and TLS, Microsoft gave up on PCT with a sigh (the following quote was taken from the November 1999 MSDN build):

> Developers are not encouraged to use PCT because it is Microsoft proprietary and has been completely superseded by SSL 3.0 and TLS.

No matter how much I'd like to use the term *TLS* throughout the rest of this chapter (because it's been standardized), the world still refers to the protocol as SSL; thus, because there is so little difference between TLS and SSL, I'll

---

[6] I searched long and hard to find the differences between SSL and TLS and finally came up with an Internet draft that specified the proposed modifications to SSL made by the authors of the TLS RFC. This draft has expired, of course, but in case you're interested, you can search the Web for draft-ietf-tls-ssl-mods-00.txt. The most important change mentioned in this document that made it into TLS is a revision to the MAC calculation algorithm, but other minor changes were also proposed, such as the addition of more detailed error codes and a change in the way clients who have no certificates respond to a server's request for a client certificate.

cave in and refer to the protocol as *SSL* as well. The name change just confuses people.

SCHANNEL

You may have heard the term SCHANNEL (which stands for "secure channel"); this is the name of the SSP in Windows that implements all four of the authentication protocols discussed earlier: SSL 2.0, PCT 1.0, SSL 3.0, and TLS 1.0. SCHANNEL is a Windows-specific term that is often bandied about in MSDN documentation as an umbrella term for all these authentication protocols.

HTTPS

The Internet Assigned Numbers Authority (IANA) reserved port 443 for HTTP over SSL (although all the different flavors of SSL, including PCT and TLS, also use this port); HTTPS is the name of the URL scheme used with this port. Thus, http://www.develop.com implies the use of vanilla HTTP to port 80, and https://www.develop.com implies the use of HTTP over SSL to port 443.

Secure Sockets Layer

At the heart of SSL (a.k.a. TLS) is the *record protocol* that provides message framing, typing, and fragmentation, as well as compression, encryption, and MAC generation and verification.[7] SSL assumes that a connection-oriented transport is in use (TCP being the canonical example), and unless the message fragments are received in the correct order from the underlying communication protocol, the receiver won't be able to decrypt the stream (each fragment isn't guaranteed to be independently decryptable).

To encrypt or generate/verify MACs, obviously both endpoints need to share a secret key, otherwise known as a session key. SSL uses a higher-level protocol known as the *handshake protocol* on top of the record protocol to exchange this key and authenticate the client and server to one another. Authentication is technically optional, and there are three modes in which SSL can be used:[8]

---

[7] The concept of a MAC (message authentication code) was discussed in Chapter 7.

[8] Note that it's possible to negotiate a cipher suite with a NULL bulk data encryption algorithm, which allows authentication without encryption. Although Web browsers don't use this option, it's interesting to consider for other, more intelligent user agents.

1. Mutual authentication
2. Server-only authentication (the client knows who the server is)
3. No authentication (deprecated)

The third option is silly if you think about it. Exchanging sensitive data over an encrypted but unauthenticated link is like two spies sitting alone in a dark corner of an obscure restaurant, whispering secrets to one another without either of them having a clue who the other one is. The vast majority of commercial HTTPS traffic over the Web today uses option 2, wherein the client is anonymous (as far as SSL is concerned), but the server is authenticated.

SSL uses a four-way handshake in all three cases (see Figure 10.7); this discussion will focus on the elements of this handshake necessary for authen-

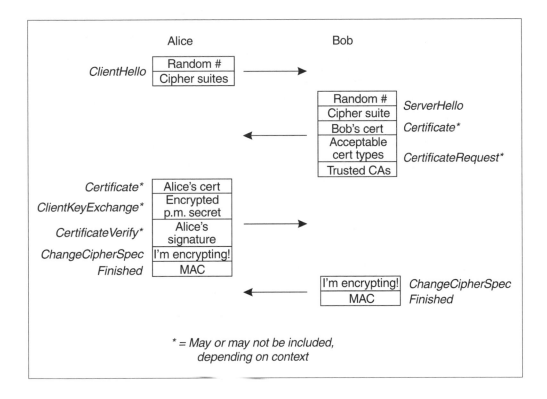

Figure 10.7   Establishing a new SSL session

tication and key exchange.[9] The client (Alice) first sends a Client Hello message to the server (Bob) to indicate that she wants to establish a new SSL session. This message contains a random number generated by Alice, as well as an ordered set of preferred cipher suites (each cipher suite indicates a key exchange algorithm, a bulk encryption algorithm, and a MAC algorithm).

Bob looks at the incoming request, selects a cipher suite from Alice's proposed list (assuming one is acceptable), and sends a Server Hello message back to Alice. This message includes a random number generated independently by Bob, along with the cipher suite that Bob chose from Alice's list. If Bob chose a cipher suite whose key exchange algorithm requires him to prove his identity (only the deprecated option 3 does not), he'll send his X.509 certificate as well.[10] Depending on the key exchange algorithm, Bob might also need to include extra information to allow key exchange or satisfy U.S. export restrictions,[11] but to keep things simple, let's assume that the certificate Bob sends to Alice can also be used directly for key exchange. Finally, as long as Bob has provided his certificate, he is allowed to include a request for Alice's certificate, which forces Alice to prove her identity.

When Alice receives this information from Bob, she can verify Bob's certificate. This includes checking the signature of the root authority with her copy of the authority's well-known public key (certificate verification is revisited in the upcoming section Certificate Revocation). At this point, Alice knows that she has a public key for Bob, but she really doesn't have any proof that it's actually

---

[9] See RFC 2246 if you want more detail.

[10] Technically, this can be a list of certificates if Bob's certificate wasn't signed by an authority that Alice trusts. In practice, this means that Bob sends back a chain of certificates up to but not necessarily including the self-signed certificate for a well-known root authority such as VeriSign or Thawte, with which all Web browsers are already equipped. As of this writing, most of the Web sites we know and love (www.amazon.com, for example) have certificates that are signed directly by a well-known root authority such as VeriSign. This is actually one of the minor differences between SSL and TLS; in SSL, the server was always required to send the entire certificate chain, including the self-signed certificate for the root authority.

[11] This might include parameters for the Diffie-Hellman key exchange algorithm or an independent RSA public key no longer than 512 bits to satisfy U.S. export restrictions for key exchange. This allows strong authentication with weak encryption; the U.S. military is happy to allow Alice to know the name of the tall, dark, and foreign person she's having cybersex with, as long as they get to watch!

Bob on the other end of the wire. No session key has been exchanged, but Alice is now going to remedy that.

Alice sends the following information to Bob: her certificate (if it was requested),[12] and another random number (known as the premaster secret) that has been encrypted with Bob's public key.[13] If Bob requested a certificate from Alice, she will also include her signature on all the data she's sent to or received from the record layer so far during the handshake.

Up until now, the SSL record layer has been streaming data using the NULL bulk data encryption algorithm; nothing has been encrypted. Alice now streams out a Change Cipher Spec message, which basically says, "Until I say otherwise, I'm going to instruct my record layer to use the cipher suite we just negotiated." This means that Alice needs to calculate keys for bulk data encryption and MAC generation/verification, both of which are ultimately just functions of the premaster secret and the two random numbers generated independently by the client and server during the first two messages. Finally, Alice streams out a Finished message, which is encrypted by the record layer. This message includes a MAC of all the data she's sent to or received from the record layer so far during the handshake.

When Bob receives Alice's transmission, he verifies her certificate (assuming that he asked her for one), obtains the premaster secret by decrypting it using his private key, and (once again, assuming he requested her certificate) verifies Alice's signature on the handshake messages he's seen so far using the certificate she sent. (He's now developed trust that it really is Alice on the other end of the wire.)

Bob now receives Alice's Change Cipher Spec message, calculates the keys for bulk data encryption and MAC generation/verification, and instructs his record layer to start using the new cipher suite to decrypt the incoming transmission. This allows Bob to read the Finished message, which is at the tail of

---

[12] When Alice sends her certificate to Bob, she also may send a chain of certificates, although in this case SSL provides a way for Bob to indicate to Alice the root certificate authorities that he trusts so that she doesn't have to guess.

[13] If Diffie-Hellman key exchange was negotiated, this information will instead be parameters for a Diffie-Hellman key exchange (assuming those parameters weren't already specified in the server's certificate).

Alice's transmission. After verifying the MAC in the Finished message, Bob develops trust that the entire handshake and cipher suite negotiation wasn't tampered with, because this MAC protects the entire set of handshake messages exchanged so far.

Finally, Bob sends a Change Cipher Spec message back to Alice (instructing his record layer to use the new cipher suite to encrypt outgoing messages), followed by a Finished message (which once again includes a MAC of all messages exchanged so far).

Alice receives the Change Cipher Spec message, instructs her record layer to decrypt incoming messages using the negotiated cipher suite, and reads the Finished message from Bob. If the message decrypts successfully and she can verify the MAC Bob sends to her, she develops trust in Bob's identity (only Bob could have decrypted the premaster secret she sent, which was required for him to be able to generate the MAC).

At this point, Alice and Bob have negotiated a cipher suite, exchanged shared keys for bulk data encryption and message authentication, and Alice knows that she's talking to Bob. Bob may also (if he asked for a client certificate) know Alice's identity.

Certificate Revocation

One of the biggest potential traps of using certificates is the tendency for people to assume that a certificate is valid simply because its signature can be verified and it's not yet expired. In a password-based authentication system, if Bob's password is compromised, he can simply change his password. In NTLM the authority immediately enforces this change for all new authentication requests[14] because the authority is involved in every single network authentication exchange. In Kerberos, this change is usually enforced in something less than ten hours (after Bob's outstanding TGTs expire). So what happens in a certificate-based system if Bob's *private key* is compromised? Well, Bob notifies his authority and obtains a new certificate, and the authority "revokes" the old certificate.

---

[14] Barring replication latency between domain controllers.

But what does this mean for Alice, who contacts a server that she presumes is run by Bob but really has been hijacked by Fred (who has an illegitimate copy of Bob's old private key)? Fred can simply send Bob's old certificate (which won't expire for a year or so) back to Alice and can prove ownership of the certificate because he now holds the associated private key. Unless Alice specifically checks for *revocation,* she'll never know that she's really talking to Fred. Once again, public key cryptography is not a silver bullet. Alice still needs to contact an authority to verify that Bob's certificate hasn't been revoked.

Bob's authority publishes a **certificate revocation list (CRL)** that Alice can obtain occasionally, perhaps once a day or once a week; she can use her current copy of the list to validate Bob's certificate. As an example, IE 5 has a security option entitled "Check for server certificate revocation" that forces the browser to download a CRL (or retrieve a freshly cached one) and verify that each server-side certificate hasn't been revoked. If you think about it, one reason that certificates have expiration dates is to keep CRLs from growing infinitely long.

From Theory to Practice: Obtaining and Installing a Web Server Certificate

Now that I've described how SSL authentication works, you'll find that it's mainly an administrative task to enable it in IIS. Recall that for SSL to be effective, the server must have a certificate so that at least one of the parties can be authenticated. If you look at the properties for a Web site in IIS, you'll notice on the Web Site tab that the entry for SSL Port is disabled by default. IIS will not support SSL without a server-side certificate.

Obtaining and installing a Web server certificate for an established company is very straightforward.[15] IIS provides a wizard that makes it easy. IIS allows you to have multiple Web sites exposed from a single machine, and each of these Web sites can have a certificate (or not); the point here is that you must set them up independently. Choose the Web site for which you want to obtain

---

[15] The following description assumes IIS 5.0; IIS 4.0 had a tool called Key Manager that was used to manage the acquisition and installation of server-side certificates. The procedure is very similar in any case.

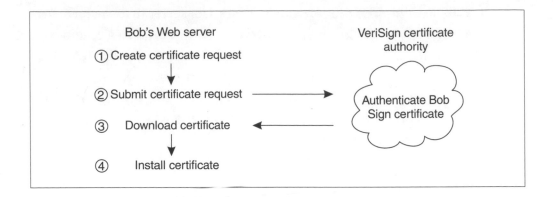

Figure 10.8   **Requesting and installing a certificate**

a certificate, bring up its property sheet, and choose the Directory Security tab. Press the Server Certificate button to invoke the wizard.

The wizard allows you to create certificate requests, install new certificates, remove an existing certificate, and so forth. Each of these activities requires answering a few straightforward questions. Unless you're planning on using your own enterprise certificate authority[16] to issue a certificate directly, obtaining and installing a certificate will be a four-step process (see Figure 10.8). The first step is to create the request. To do this, you need to choose the strength for the key in the certificate (you should use 1024 bits or greater), along with some strings that will end up in the certificate exactly as you type them in the wizard:

- **Name** Some friendly name that you can use to distinguish this certificate from any others you might obtain.[17]

- **Organization Name** The name of your company.

- **Organizational Unit** Typically the name of your department.

- **Common Name** This is the name that will be used to authenticate the URL being used to access the Web server, so it should match the

---

[16] When installing Certificate Services on a Windows 2000 domain controller, you can choose to have it integrate with Active Directory, becoming an "enterprise" certificate authority.

[17] This isn't important for authentication, but will be included as an extra property in the certificate.

DNS name that you expect clients to use (for instance, the common name for DevelopMentor's Web site is "www.develop.com").

- **Country/Region** Self-explanatory.
- **State/Province** You cannot use an abbreviation here (specify "Texas" instead of "TX").
- **City/Locality** No surprises here.

After this, the wizard asks you to choose the name of a text file where it will dump the request. By the time this file is created, the wizard will have made calls into the CryptoAPI to generate a public/private key pair for the certificate, storing the private key on the local machine. This public key will be included along with the other information you've entered in the text request file, which you can send to your certificate authority (for instance, VeriSign or Thawte[18]). The resulting file contains a base-64 ASCII rendering of all the information in the request:

```
-----BEGIN NEW CERTIFICATE REQUEST-----
```
```
MIIDBjCCAm8CAQAwcTERMA8GA1UEAxMIcXV1eC5jb20xDzANBgNVBAsTBkJyYWlu
czEWMBQGA1UEChMNRGV2ZWxvcE11bnRvcjERMA8GA1UEBxMIVG9ycmFuY2UxEzAR
BgNVBAgTCkNhbGlmb3JuaWExCzAJBgNVBAYTAlVTMIGfMA0GCSqGSIb3DQEBAQUA
A4GNADCBiQKBgQDFUxFtzr170yxptKuGI1590Sta5z2dVE1LfjAn+q4T1uZE3DiH
HXNRHW1eS9W2aeMZhRnYRi5U8eOdG3RUO4YXy4B1sqfy5I0qjjySA89ghVd/6JcA
K1nhGJL9FPJ6XKVUNLez7NpSCFlYs5foyTqyxDkHzTnQwRwkkwQ9dlbnfwIDAQAB
oIIBUzAaBgorBgEEAYI3DQIDMQwWCjUuMC4yMTk1LjIwNQYKKwYBBAGCNwIBDjEn
MCUwDgYDVR0PAQH/BAQDAgTwMBMGA1UdJQQMMAoGCCsGAQUFBwMBMIH9BgorBgEE
AYI3DQICMYHuMIHrAgEBHloATQBpAGMAcgBvAHMAbwBmAHQAIABSAFMAQQAgAFMA
QwBoAGEAbgBuAGUAbAAgAEMAcgB5AHAAdABvAGcAcgBhAHAAaABpAGMAIABQAHIA
bwB2AGkAZABlAHIDgYkAXxNuAz6gcBaZUdef8WQ2PAroKMW8sprcKv7QD2encz6/
Wct9DZ5CkGynLGy0f+Lff7ViSDJqxYWaJ68ddqgXyAqIilF63kivPTiC6yxLaNX6
5v3cnKFx4UrUrGXZtub7M7/NuxSipOW0Vv7yCHganypxDyRzp6IhulEnL4APEH4A
AAAAAAAADANBgkqhkiG9w0BAQUFAAOBgQBljJb1ZhWOwOLfzfHbC3yxGkXDy9w3
NA7uhQOvgntnqmSmdHP9nsM3DnxwaHb3EVxMKbAuLsSRDAE1KGqeamvQ3uFjuuL0
5q4nKhX25LyGFDSc6h1OHcv+0ugZ/9klsiViSeEGpMwllUf057o7q1Vls4HN22vM
wkcejcttDjo3Kw==
```
```
-----END NEW CERTIFICATE REQUEST-----
```

---

[18] Thawte was actually acquired by VeriSign in December 1999.

The second step is to send the request to the authority. You'll typically paste this into the authority's Web-based certificate application form, along with contact information, proof of domain ownership, and proof of your right to do business under the specified organization name. Third-party certificate authorities will charge you a fee for this service. (Fees vary depending on the level of service and security; as of this writing you can expect to pay approximately $100 to $1000 for a certificate that expires in a year.)

The third step is when the authority issues (or denies) your request. Assuming the authority can determine that you are who you say you are (by checking addresses, making phone calls, etc.), you'll receive email (typically within a few business days) indicating that your certificate request has been granted and that you can download your certificate, which will again take the form of a file (the contents will look very similar to the certificate request).

The fourth and final step is to install the downloaded certificate. If you now revisit the certificate wizard, it'll allow you to process the response; just give it the path to the file you downloaded from the authority and you should be off and running.

Note that during this request/response phase, the private key remains on the computer where you generated the request. Be aware that if you delete the "pending" request using the wizard (before you install the certificate), the private key will be erased and you'll have to start all over again. If you've already paid money to a third-party authority to sign your public key, this can be painful, so watch out.

Once you've installed the certificate, you can export the certificate *along with its corresponding private key* to a file that you can drop on a floppy and put in an offline vault in case the Web server crashes and the private key becomes unrecoverable. To do this, bring up the property page for the Web site, go to the Directory Security tab, and press the View Certificate button. Go to the Details tab on the resulting dialog, and choose Copy to File. If you choose to export the private key, you'll be asked for a password that will be used to encrypt the file. If you were really concerned about security, you could store the password in a *separate* vault, but to be honest, you should be more worried about someone simply compromising the Web server and stealing the private key from there. (Unfortunately, for a Web server, there's not much sense in keeping the private key offline, because it is needed to establish each new HTTPS session.)

After installing a certificate, you'll notice that the SSL Port field on the Web Site tab of the Web site's property sheet is now enabled, and defaults to the standard port number for HTTPS, 443. You should now be able to access your Web site from a browser using the https: scheme.

What Is Server Gated Cryptography?

You may be wondering what the Server Gated Cryptography checkbox in the IIS cerificate wizard is all about. Prior to January 2000, United States export laws strictly prohibited the export of software that used strong encryption (128-bit SSL bulk data encryption keys fall under this category). Browsers built by Microsoft and Netscape were therefore subject to these laws and normally do not use 128-bit encryption unless the client specifically downloads an upgrade. Microsoft therefore proposed an extension to SSL called **Server Gated Cryptography (SGC)**. SGC allows a server certificate to include a special annotation that indicates that the server has been approved to use strong encryption (certain types of businesses including banks and online merchants were excluded from the older export laws). If a browser that supports SGC detects this, it will negotiate the use of strong (128-bit) bulk data encryption with that server. As of this writing, VeriSign issues SGC certificates (this is part of their Global Site Services program), but they are considerably more expensive than a normal certificate.

However, now that U.S. export laws have been relaxed, SGC is not nearly as critical to global trade over the Internet. Clients can now download strong encryption packs for their browsers that work with or without SGC support on the server side. There are still some limitations, but they generally only apply to embargoed countries (see http://www.microsoft.com/exporting for more details).

Requiring HTTPS via the IIS Metabase

In IIS, once you've installed a server certificate, any virtual directory may be accessed via HTTP or HTTPS. If you want to *require* HTTPS for a particular resource, you can use the metabase to do so. If you're not already familiar with the metabase, it's simply a hierarchical data structure that mimics the layout of your Web site. The metabase tree is what you're looking at when you manage the Web site using the IIS MMC snap-in. The metabase uses an attribute inheritance scheme somewhat similar to the DACL inheritance scheme used in Windows 2000: When you change an attribute on a node, it propagates to all children of that node, except for those children that have provided their own definition of the attribute.

The attribute that controls whether HTTPS is required is *AccessSSL*. Here's a script that turns on this attribute for a virtual directory known as "Secure" on the default Web site:[19]

```
set vd = getObject("IIS://localhost/W3SVC/1/Root/secure")
vd.accessSSL = true
vd.setInfo
```

In the metabase, once a child node has defined an attribute, the flow of inheritance is interrupted at that node (exactly the same way SE_DACL _PROTECTED works in a security descriptor, as described in Chapter 6). If you want to remove the attribute from an object and unblock the flow of inheritance for that attribute, you must use the PutEx method:

```
set vd = getObject("IIS://localhost/W3SVC/1/Root/secure")
vd.putEx 1, "AccessSSL", ""
vd.setInfo
```

If you enable AccessSSL on a virtual directory, as long as no children provide their own definitions, they will automatically inherit the new setting, and all the resources subordinate to that directory will require the client to use HTTPS. (If the client attempts to access any of these resources via vanilla HTTP, she'll get an error instructing her to switch to HTTPS.) As with most metabase settings, you can control this setting on a per-file basis if you need that level of granularity. To access this property via the user interface, bring up the property sheet for the resource in question and choose Directory Security for a Web site or virtual directory object, or File Security for an individual file, and then press

---

[19] If you're not familiar with administering IIS programmatically, take a look at the IIS reference (just surf to http://localhost/iishelp on your Web server to get the help index). Also check out the Inetpub\AdminScripts directory for some example scripts.

the Edit button in the section labeled Secure Communications. Most of the metabase keys this chapter describes have pretty obvious user interface representations, but some aren't accessible via the user interface at all (I'll point these out as I get to them).

The following list provides some related settings that might interest you, along with notes as to how they affect the behavior of IIS.

- **AccessSSL**   This attribute was discussed previously; it requires use of HTTPS to access the resource.

- **AccessSSL128**   This setting only makes sense if you've also turned on AccessSSL; it further limits cipher-suite negotiation to 128-bit or better bulk encryption keys. Most user agent software produced in the United States uses a relatively weak key by default to satisfy older U.S. export laws, so if you plan on using this feature, make sure all your clients are using software that can negotiate 128-bit encryption keys.

- **AccessSSLNegotiateCert**   Causes the server to request a client certificate during SSL negotiation. If the client doesn't present a certificate (which is legal according to SSL), IIS will not fail the connection request. Thus some clients will present certificates, whereas others will not. This assumes that the AccessSSLRequireCert attribute is set to False.

- **AccessSSLRequireCert**   This option only makes sense if you've also turned on AccessSSLNegotiateCert; this indicates that clients must provide a certificate in order to access the resource.

- **AccessSSLMapCert**   Enables automatic mapping of client certificates to Windows security accounts. This is discussed in more detail in the section entitled Client Authentication.

- **AccessSSLFlags**   Technically, all the previous options are stored in this one single attribute; the individual attributes simply provide an easier way to set these bits. The main reason I'm mentioning this is because all these settings are inherited as a unit. See the IIS documentation if you want the precise bit mappings.

Managing Web Applications

Back in the old days with IIS 3.0, the Web server simply ran in a single process known as `INETINFO.EXE`, which lurked in the System logon session. All server-side Web applications therefore ran in the System logon session, which is really dangerous. Let me give an example why.

Interlude: The Buffer Overflow Attack

Consider the following C++ code:

```
void foo() {
  char buf[256];
  GetStringFromTextBox(buf);
}
```

This ultra-simplified code reads a string from a text box on a user-submitted form. Imagine that this code were housed in an Internet Server API (ISAPI) DLL running inside `INETINFO.EXE`, and that the user actually typed 300 characters into the text box. Because `GetStringFromTextBox` doesn't pay any attention to how much memory `buf` points to, it will happily overflow the buffer. Is this bad? It's incredibly bad. Because `buf` is on the stack, any overflow will quickly overwrite the return address on the stack, and when `foo` returns, it won't return to the caller, it'll return to whatever address was overwritten on the stack.

Crackers find great fun in sending unexpectedly long strings to applications as input and just waiting for one of them to explode. Once they discover a bug like this, it's just a matter of shortening the string until the program doesn't crash anymore. Now they know the exact length of the buffer and have a darn good idea where to write their own return address onto the victim's stack. By crafting an input string that contains binary executable machine instructions, all the cracker has to do is figure out the address of the buffer on the stack[20] and point the return address into the buffer. The most elegant attack I've seen

---

[20] This becomes quite easy if she can get a Dr. Watson crash report (in other words, if she can reproduce the bug on her own machine).

460   DISTRIBUTION

documented[21] is one in which the cracker sends a small program as input that loads WININET.DLL and calls a few functions that download an executable program of the attacker's choosing onto the victim's hard drive. The program then launches the downloaded executable and quietly shuts down the victimized process in an attempt to hide the fact that something is horribly awry. (Note that simply using a safer language than C or C++ can help alleviate this problem.)

Imagine if this attack were carried out on an ISAPI application running in the System logon session. The attacker has now compromised the TCB of the machine and it's game over. It's funny, I remember when people were worried about ISAPI DLLs *crashing* the Web server; now that you've seen that a buggy ISAPI DLL can allow an attacker to *hijack* the Web server's process, I hope that the imperative for moving this code out of the System logon session is clear.

Introducing the Web Application Manager

IIS 4.0 addressed this problem in an elegant way. By separating the core Web server functionality present in INETINFO.EXE from the code needed to invoke ISAPI applications, it is possible to run ISAPI applications in separate processes, sandboxing them in lesser-privileged logon sessions. This separation was implemented by having the core Web server talk to the ISAPI environment via an (undocumented) COM interface. IIS 4.0 offered two choices for each Web "application" (each virtual directory is considered a separate application): The application could run in-process inside INETINFO.EXE, or it could run in its own separate process. In either case, a logical COM object representing the environment for each application was registered and added to the MTS catalog as a configured component. This component was named the **Web Application Manager** (or **WAM** for short). This is one case where COM's claim of "local-remote transparency" does in fact ring true; using a COM interface allows the Web server to interact with in-process as well as out-of-process WAMs polymorphically.

---

[21] It's hard to say if this essay will still be on the Web by the time you are reading this book, but if it is, it's great reading: http://www.cultdeadcow.com/cDc_files/cDc-351. Don't visit this site if you're easily offended by street talk. If you find that this site is unavailable, visit my Web site and I'll mirror it there.

Unfortunately, IIS 4.0 didn't go quite far enough, and since each "isolated" Web application chews up another process, the default setting for each new Web application was to run in-process. IIS 5.0 makes out-of-process Web applications more attractive by providing *three* options for isolation:

1. Low (IIS Process)
2. Medium (Pooled)
3. High (Isolated)

Options 1 and 3 are exactly the same as what IIS 4.0 provided; in the first case, the application code runs in INETINFO.EXE, and in the last case, the application code runs in its own dedicated process. What's interesting is the new option 2, which places all pooled applications into a *single* process that runs outside INETINFO.EXE (and in a separate logon session, as you'd expect). This new option is the default in IIS 5.0, and is a great way to mitigate threats like the buffer overflow attack. (Don't get me wrong—the attack is still possible, but hijacking a process in the TCB is *very* different from hijacking one outside the TCB, assuming that the administrator has erected effective perimeter defenses around the TCB.)[22]

The process isolation level is represented by a metabase attribute named AppIsolated, an inheritable attribute that can be set on a per-application basis (the current IIS 5 docs indicate that this value can be set on subdirectories inside an application, but this has no effect). This attribute can have one of three values:

0: Low (IIS Process)

1: High (Isolated)

2: Medium (Pooled)

Because each WAM runs in the context of a configured COM+ application, you can actually use the Component Services snap-in to look at the two WAM-

---

[22] For an extreme example of carelessness, if everyone is granted all access to critical registry keys and system files, then the TCB can be compromised by simply replacing components of the operating system itself. Sandboxing a server in a lesser-privileged logon session won't help unless the administrator secures the perimeter of the TCB.

hosting applications that IIS creates by default when it is installed with the operating system:

IIS In-Process Applications

IIS Out-Of-Process Pooled Applications

The first application is designated as a library application, so that when INETINFO.EXE creates an instance of the WAM for an in-process application, the WAM will load into that same process. The second application is designated as a server application, so that when INETINFO.EXE creates an instance of the WAM for a pooled application, that object will be served up from a single COM+ surrogate process.

If you look at the properties for the second application listed earlier, you'll notice that it is designated to run as a distinguished principal: IWAM_*MACHINE*, where *MACHINE* is the NetBIOS name of the machine at the time IIS was installed. This is a local account that is created by the system at IIS install time. Every Web application that you designate to run at the third level of isolation (Isolated) causes IIS to create another distinct COM+ application configured in a similar way.

To demonstrate the differences between these levels of process isolation, imagine creating six virtual directories, App1 through App6, and configuring them as follows:

App1: Low (IIS Process)

App2: Low (IIS Process)

App3: Medium (Pooled)

App4: Medium (Pooled)

App5: High (Isolated)

App6: High (Isolated)

Figure 10.9 shows the results if all these applications are in use simultaneously. Traversing over to the Component Services snap-in, here is the complete list of COM+ applications that are now hosting WAMs:

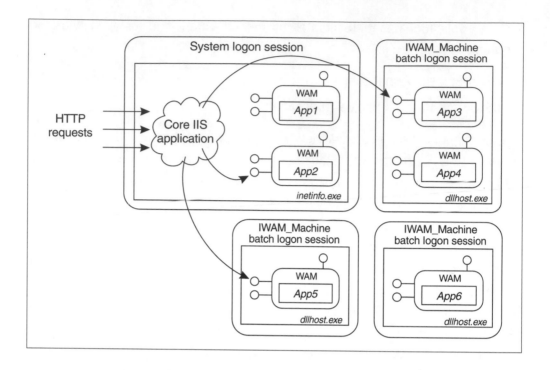

Figure 10.9   Runtime profile of Web applications

IIS In-Process Applications

IIS Out-Of-Process Pooled Applications

IIS-{Default Web Site//Root/App5}

IIS-{Default Web Site//Root/App6}

As Figure 10.9 makes clear, App5 and App6 are configured to run in separate server applications, also under the auspices of IWAM_MACHINE.

IIS actually doesn't hardcode the account name and password for IWAM_ MACHINE; you can get and set these values via the metabase. If you change these values, IIS will use the new values from then on for the identity of all new COM+ applications it creates. Here's some code that displays the user name and password for the IWAM_MACHINE account (you must do this programmatically; these attributes aren't exposed via the IIS snap-in):

```
set w = getObject("IIS://localhost/W3SVC")
msgBox w.wamUserName & chr(13) & w.wamUserPass
```

If you make changes, be aware that IIS doesn't attempt to synchronize your changes with the security database (you can, of course, do this programmatically; see the appendix). If you change this to a user name of "Foo\Bob" with a password of "shazam," you'd better make sure that the Foo domain does in fact have an account called Bob, and that its password is indeed "shazam." Also note that I used the older-style authority\principal form for the name, because COM+ currently chokes on server identities in UPN form (bob@foo.com), as mentioned in Chapter 9.

Before you make a change like this, recall from Chapter 9 that it's usually safest to use a local account for a server's identity unless you absolutely need something different. Anyone with administrative access to the metabase can read this user name and password, so leaving this as a local account severely restricts the damage that can be done if the machine is compromised and the password disclosed.

Client Authentication

Although Figure 10.9 is interesting, it doesn't provide the full picture. Every WAM thread that performs work in response to an HTTP request from a client does so while impersonating. Which account that thread actually impersonates depends on a number of factors, but it's critical to remember that each WAM thread that makes calls to the file system, an ISAPI application, or an Active Server Pages (ASP) application (which is really just a stylized form of ISAPI) does so while impersonating *somebody*.

The various ways that IIS can determine the identity of the client, and thus obtain a logon session for the WAM thread to impersonate, are listed here in order of preference:

1. Anonymous (no authentication)

2. Certificate-Based Authentication

3. Integrated Windows Authentication

4. Digest Authentication

5. Basic Authentication

Each resource can have its own configuration for authentication, and you can select one or more of these options via the metabase. The metabase attributes for enabling or requiring client certificates were discussed previously. As for the other options, the `AuthFlags` attribute (a bitfield) controls which authentication options are allowed.[23] Here are the bit values you can use with this attribute:

0x00000001: Anonymous

0x00000002: Basic

0x00000004: Integrated Windows Authentication (SPNEGO)

0x00000010: Digest

Anonymous (No Client Authentication)

You may have noticed from the previous list that IIS prefers not to authenticate its clients. Authenticating each client consumes CPU resources and increases network traffic. Many large commercial Web sites typically don't rely on the operating system to perform authentication; rather, authentication is done at the application level (perhaps by asking for a credit card number and verifying the billing address, or even by asking for an application-defined password).

IIS has the notion of an "anonymous Internet user" account, which defaults to IUSR_MACHINE, another local account (similar to IWAM_MACHINE) that's created when IIS is installed. For a given resource, if the Anonymous option is enabled, IIS will check to see if the requested resource (HTML file, ASP script, GIF file, etc.) can be successfully accessed by this account. If the DACL on the file grants access to the anonymous Internet user account, IIS will execute the client's request under the auspices of that account, as opposed to trying any of

---

[23] There are also three subflags (`AuthAnonymous`, `AuthNTLM`, and `AuthBasic`), but they are rather out of date. There is no corresponding `AuthDigest` setting, and `AuthNTLM` should really be renamed `AuthNegotiate` because it now means SPNEGO.

the more expensive authentication options.[24] This means that IIS will impersonate the anonymous Internet user account and open the file while impersonating. If instead the DACL denies access to the anonymous Internet user, IIS will move on to the next authentication option in the list (access will be denied if no other option is enabled for this resource).

Note that I've been careful to label this account in abstract terms; this is because it doesn't always have to be IUSR_MACHINE. Rather, each individual Web resource (Web site, virtual directory, file system directory, file) in the IIS metabase has the following (inheritable) attributes:

- **AnonymousUserName** The name of a valid user account that IIS will use to establish a logon session for anonymous Internet users when they request this particular resource
- **AnonymousUserPass** The password for the account just described
- **AnonymousPasswordSync** A boolean attribute with magical properties that I'll describe shortly

By default, the `w3svc` node in the metabase (the root of all Web nodes) sets `AnonymousUserName` to `IUSR_MACHINE`, and `AnonymousPasswordSync` to `True`. This latter property is quite magical; when set, it causes `INETINFO.EXE` to obtain a logon session without providing a password by invoking a special subauthentication DLL in the LSA that basically says "Sure, I'll give you a logon" without checking the password at all. This is a nifty feature, but be aware that it's only supported for local accounts.[25] If this feature alarms you, remember that `INETINFO.EXE` runs in the System logon session and is therefore part of the TCB. This is just an example of a member of the TCB doing whatever it pleases on the local machine.

Based on my own experimentation with IIS 5.0, if you use the password synchronization option, the resulting logon session for the anonymous user will be a network logon session with no network credentials, which makes sense

---

[24] One exception to this rule is as follows: If the server requests a certificate and the client presents one, and if a mapping to a Windows user account can be found (I'll cover this shortly), IIS will use the mapped account as opposed to simply accessing the resource as the anonymous Internet user.

[25] Although with experimentation, I was able to get it to work with domain accounts as well. If you try to configure a domain account with this magic setting via the Internet Services snap-in, you'll get a rather rude message that says "This isn't supported; are you sure?" Caveat emptor.

because IIS obtained the logon session without providing a password. On the other hand, if you don't use this feature and you specify a password explicitly, the logon session will be an interactive logon session with network credentials. (Of course, if you're using a local account, these network credentials won't buy you much unless you've created a matching user name and password on some other machine.)

Another thing to be aware of is that when two or more resources share the same anonymous account settings (which is typically the case), IIS does its best to cache a single logon session and impersonate that one logon session for all those resources, even across isolated application boundaries (Figure 10.10 shows an example). If you've read Chapter 8, this should make you think, "I'm probably sharing a logical LAN Manager client port with other Web applica-

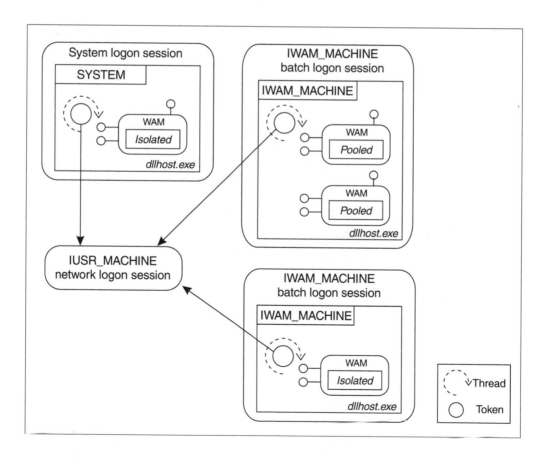

Figure 10.10   **A typical set of logon sessions for anonymous Internet users**

DISTRIBUTION

tions." If you try to use alternate credentials to access a remote file server by calling `NetUseAdd`, you might succeed, but you'll be changing the credentials used for that server for *all other Web applications* that are also using the anonymous logon. It's also possible that someone has already beat you to the punch, in which case you'll run into the dreaded conflict of credentials that was discussed in Chapter 8. Watch your step here. This is one case in which having your application set to an isolation level of High can be a good thing because you can always call `RevertToSelf` to get to your own application's private batch logon session (for IWAM_MACHINE), at which point you can call `NetUseAdd` without tromping on any other applications.

Certificate-Based Client Authentication

Earlier in the chapter I described the SSL protocol and explained that as long as the server has a certificate, the server is allowed to request a certificate from the client. I also described the metabase attributes that allow you to control whether IIS should request or even *require* a client certificate.

Before IIS will accept a client certificate, it must verify that that certificate is valid. This involves comparing the current date with the valid from/to dates in the certificate, followed by verifying the signatures in the certificate chain. Finally, IIS must determine whether any of the certificates in the chain are trusted. By default, each Web site trusts all certificates that haven't expired, so it's a good idea to create a certificate trust list (CTL) for your Web site that limits this trust to certificates for a selected set of trusted authorities. To do this, bring up the property sheet for the Web site, choose the Directory Security tab, and then press the Edit button that takes you to the certificate-related settings. Check the box that says "Enable certificate trust list." This tells IIS not to trust any authorities except the ones that you put in the CTL. Press New to invoke a wizard that will help you build the CTL; it's pretty straightforward once you've figured out which certificate authorities you need to trust.

As IIS validates certificates, it needs to check for revocation, which can be time-consuming. By default IIS skips this step, but you can control this via the `CertCheckMode` metabase attribute on each Web site (this is not available via the IIS snap-in; it must be set programmatically). Setting this value to a number greater than 0 forces IIS to check for revocation (which may involve downloading a CRL from a certificate authority, or simply looking in a cached CRL). If you are serious about client authentication, you should enable this check.

At this point, another metabase attribute becomes useful: `AccessSSL MapCert`, which is really just another bit that can be set or cleared in the `AccessSSLFlags` attribute that was mentioned early in the chapter. If this attribute is set to `True`, IIS will attempt to map the client's certificate onto a Windows user account via one of two mechanisms: Either IIS will use its own internal table of mappings from certificates to user accounts/passwords, or it will ask its domain controller to perform the mapping based on settings in the directory service. You can control which method is used via the metabase attribute `SSLUseDSMapper`. (This is a global setting on the `W3SVC` node in the metabase, accessible via the Web Service Master Properties in the user interface; as of this writing, you cannot control this on a per–Web site basis.) By default `SSLUseDSMapper` is set to `False`, which indicates that IIS should perform its own internal mapping.

An administrator can configure the internal IIS certificate-to-account mapping via the IIS snap-in. Each Web site has its own set of account mappings, which can be edited by going to the property sheet for the Web site, choosing the Directory Security tab, and pressing the Edit button that takes you to the certificate-related settings. After checking "Enable client certificate mapping," which is just the `AccessSSLMapCert` metabase setting, press Edit to configure the certificate-to-user-account mappings.

There are two ways to map certificates to user accounts in IIS: one certificate to one account, or many certificates to one account. The first method requires you to obtain a certificate from the user (typically packaged in a base-64-encoded ASCII file), whereas the second method allows you to simply specify a set of criteria for the various components of the distinguished name for the subject and issuer in the certificate (for instance, you can detect certificates issued by VeriSign in which the subject's organization is ACME Corporation and map these certificates onto a particular user account). With the many-to-one option, you can either grant *or deny* access to a matched certificate. Denying access is easy—you just need to indicate that this is your intention via a radio button.

If you want to grant access (using the one-to-one or many-to-one option), you'll need to provide a user account and password, which IIS will tuck away in the metabase. If you want to configure this mapping programmatically via script, you'll want to check out the `IIsCertMapper` interface; this interface currently allows you to set up one-to-one mappings, but does not provide for many-to-one mappings, which must be set up via the IIS snap-in.

If IIS authenticates a client via one of these internal certificate mappings, the result will be an interactive logon session with the network credentials of the account (which makes sense, because the logon session was created locally with a password). If, instead, IIS delegates authentication to the directory service, it will establish a network logon session that will (naturally) not have network credentials. If a match cannot be found, or if the client did not submit a certificate,[26] IIS will move on to the next authentication option in the list, or will deny access if no further options are available.

If Alice was issued a certificate from an enterprise security authority in her domain (one that's integrated with the directory service), her certificate will have enough information in it for the directory service to determine which account is Alice's. For other clients, it's possible to set up certificate mappings manually in the directory service: Bring up the Active Directory Users and Computers snap-in, turn on the Advanced Features option via the MMC View menu, then right-click on any user account and choose Name Mappings to do this.

Certificates are the most natural and, when used properly, can be the most secure way to authenticate clients over the Internet, but there are also other options available if issuing client certificates doesn't make sense for your application.

Basic Authentication

Basic Authentication is the native authentication mechanism that is built into HTTP. The client sends an HTTP request to the server, and the server sends back a failure, demanding that the client prove his or her identity by sending a

---

[26] This of course assumes that you haven't turned on the `AccessSSLRequireCert` attribute, which causes IIS to immediately fail the connection during the SSL handshake if the client doesn't provide the requested certificate.

user name plus a base-64-encoded ASCII password. Base 64 is not an encryption algorithm; rather, it's an expansion algorithm that allows Internet-unfriendly characters to be represented by friendly ones, and is therefore completely reversible without a key. Thus Basic Authentication only makes sense over an SSL encrypted link with strong server-side authentication. As long as you know who you're sending the password to, and as long as you are assured that nobody but that server will see the password, Basic Authentication works just fine, assuming you trust the server with your cleartext password.

If you attempt to turn this authentication mechanism on via the IIS snap-in, you'll get a very nasty warning that says, "Don't do this unless you plan on using SSL to secure the connection." This is great advice; you should *require* SSL for any resources where you plan to allow Basic Authentication. If you can't afford a public key infrastructure, this combination will serve you well.

When IIS receives the client's user name and password, it will check the `LogonMethod` attribute in the metabase to determine which type of logon session to establish. There are three options:

0: Interactive logon (the default)

1: Batch logon

2: Network logon

The first two result in a logon session with network credentials; the network logon naturally does not have network credentials. Which one should you choose? Well, a batch-style logon will be pretty tough for most clients to establish, because no principals are granted this logon right by default. An interactive logon is more wide open in this respect, depending on the type of machine your server runs on (domain controllers severely limit the right to an interactive logon). However, establishing an interactive logon can be considerably more expensive than establishing a batch or network logon (as I discussed in Chapter 4). Generally, everyone is granted a network logon on any machine, including domain controllers. (Whether it's good security practice to run a public Web server on a domain controller is another question entirely; you should avoid doing this in my opinion, as I'll discuss shortly.)

One thing you should be aware of when using Basic Authentication is that Web applications (CGI, ISAPI, ASP) will have access to the client's cleartext password via a server variable named AUTH_PASSWORD. I know of no way of disabling this, which is too bad, considering IIS has already used the password to authenticate the client; letting this information leak through to scripts is dangerous. (Just because you trust the TCB of a server with your password doesn't mean you want to trust all its scripts with your password as well.) However, even if this little flaw didn't exist, trusting the TCB of the Web server with your credentials may be more than a security-conscious client is willing to do. In that case, consider using a client-side certificate, which is ultimately a client's safest bet.

Digest Authentication

Digest Authentication is a relative newcomer (it was introduced with HTTP 1.1 and was first implemented by Microsoft in IIS 5 and IE 5), but it will likely have limited use as certificate-based authentication becomes more and more popular. Digest Authentication is somewhat similar to NTLM: It's a simple challenge/response protocol that allows a client to prove knowledge of a password without transmitting the password across the wire. It does not provide mutual authentication, and it does not provide a way to exchange a session key for data encryption or MAC generation. It also requires password storage for users to be weakened significantly. (The passwords must be stored in such a way that the domain controller can decrypt them to obtain a plaintext password; this is known as using *reversible encryption*.)

Probably the most dangerous thing of all is that the only way this mechanism can be used is if the Web server resides on the same machine as the domain controller (to have access to those cleartext passwords). Exposing a public Web server from a domain controller opens some serious security risks; you'd better make absolutely sure that all the applications on your server are sandboxed or bug-free, because a compromise of the TCB of a domain controller is a compromise of the domain itself.

I mention this protocol only for completeness. If you care about securing the transactions on your Web server, you'll get a server certificate and use SSL to encrypt the session. The authors of the spec (RFC 2069) state their position as follows:

Digest Authentication does not provide a strong authentication mechanism. That is not its intent. It is intended solely to replace a much weaker and even more dangerous authentication mechanism: Basic Authentication. An important design constraint is that the new authentication scheme be free of patent and export restrictions.

Most needs for secure HTTP transactions cannot be met by Digest Authentication. For those needs SSL or SHTTP are more appropriate protocols. In particular, Digest Authentication cannot be used for any transaction requiring encrypted content. Nevertheless, many functions remain for which Digest Authentication is both useful and appropriate.

Integrated Windows Authentication

The Integrated Windows Authentication option tells IIS to engage the user agent in a native Kerberos or NTLM handshake piggybacked on HTTP. These extensions are not supported by non-Microsoft browsers, which significantly limits the option's appeal for use with clients on the Internet at large. Another problem with using Kerberos or NTLM is that neither protocol gets along very well with firewalls. For instance, the Kerberos KDC listens on port 88 for TCP or UDP requests; can you imagine any administrator in his or her right mind opening this port to allow random crackers on the Internet to have direct conversations with the most trusted entity in the domain? I think not. Microsoft and Cisco have proposed extensions to Kerberos to work around this problem (see the Internet draft "Initial Authentication and Pass Through Authentication Using Kerberos V5 and the GSS-API"), but this still won't solve the browser problem; most browsers expect to use certificates to authenticate their clients.

Within the perimeter of the firewall in the confines of a Windows-only enterprise, however, this is a very convenient option. Alice doesn't need to be issued a certificate to participate. She just has to agree to use Internet Explorer, and the system will use the network credentials that were established when she logged in via Winlogon to authenticate her to IIS servers on the company intranet.

The result of this form of authentication is (naturally) a network logon session on the server. (This assumes the client is not running her browser on the same machine as the Web server; in that case often the client's local interactive logon session will be used directly.)

If authentication fails using the client's default credentials (either because of problems with authentication or because the client has not been granted access to the resource), Internet Explorer will pop up a dialog asking for alternate credentials, allowing the client to retry.

Server Applications

Three classes of server applications are in common use with IIS today: raw ISAPI applications, ASP script-based applications, and Common Gateway Interface (CGI) applications. All these applications are ultimately derived from the basic CGI model that provides a set of variables describing the client and server environment as well as the request, along with input and output streams for reading and writing the request and response bodies. The interface that exposes these variables and streams to the application differs significantly among the three types of applications, but the basic information provided is similar. Table 10.1 lists some interesting variables that are security related.

Table 10.1   Security variables for server applications

Variable	Definition
AUTH_TYPE	Indicates the authentication mechanism that IIS used to obtain the logon session for the client.
REMOTE_USER, AUTH_USER, LOGON_USER	Although the IIS documentation discusses each of these separately, giving them slightly different semantics, in practice they're generally the same, and refer to the client principal that was authenticated in authority\ principal form.
AUTH_PASSWORD	For Basic authentication, this is the cleartext password that the client specified (better trust those ASP scripts!). For Digest Authentication, this is the set of values computed by the digest (see RFC 2069 for details). For all others, this is blank.
SERVER_PORT_SECURE	0 indicates HTTPS is not in use; 1 indicates HTTPS is in use.
HTTPS	"off" indicates HTTPS is not in use; "on" indicates HTTPS is in use.

Table 10.1   Security variables for server applications (continued)

Variable	Definition
CERT_FLAGS	This is a bitfield with the following masks: 0x0001: A client certificate was received. 0x0002: The issuer is not a trusted authority.
CERT_SUBJECT	The common name of the subject listed in the client certificate.
CERT_ISSUER	The distinguished name of the issuer listed in the client certificate.
CERT_SERIALNUMBER	The client certificate serial number.
CERT_COOKIE	The hash value of the client certificate.
CERT_SERVER_ISSUER, HTTPS_SERVER_ISSUER	The distinguished name of the issuer listed in the server certificate.
CERT_SERVER_SUBJECT, HTTPS_SERVER_SUBJECT	The distinguished name of the subject listed in the server certificate.
CERT_KEYSIZE, HTTPS_KEYSIZE	The strength, in bits, of the negotiated bulk encryption key.
CERT_SECRETKEYSIZE, HTTPS_SECRETKEYSIZE	The strength, in bits, of the server's private key exchange key.

I wrote a simple script that echoes back these security-related variables, and ran it several times while changing the authentication options on the server. Table 10.2 shows my results when running over HTTP (note that I've omitted all the certificate-related fields because naturally they were all empty). Here are the values that I didn't have room for in the table:

```
<dpw1>
    username="quux\alice", realm="preston", qop="auth",
    algorithm="MD5", uri="/b/x.asp",
    nonce="2150219db2046391643468100000031fabb800044f103d689
    0a9e076c63f6", nc=00000001,
    cnonce="d2694a8e9e65dd4607378e132f284eb4",
    response="e03cce66fa29f14dccd16bb8835c924e"
```

Table 10.2 Resulting variables over HTTP

Variable	Anonymous	Basic	Digest	Integrated
AUTH_TYPE		Basic	Digest	Negotiate
REMOTE_USER		quux\alice	quux\alice	QUUX\alice
LOGON_USER		quux\alice	quux\alice	QUUX\alice
AUTH_USER		quux\alice	quux\alice	QUUX\alice
AUTH_PASSWORD		woosel	<dpw1>	
SERVER_PORT_SECURE	0	0	0	0
HTTPS	off	off	off	off

Table 10.3 Results of using variables over HTTPS

Variable	Anonymous	Basic	Digest	Integrated	Client Certificates
AUTH_TYPE		Basic	Digest	Negotiate	SSL/PCT
REMOTE_USER		quux\alice	quux\alice	QUUX\alice	QUUX\alice
LOGON_USER		quux\alice	quux\alice	QUUX\alice	QUUX\alice
AUTH_USER		quux\alice	quux\alice	QUUX\alice	QUUX\alice
AUTH_PASSWORD		woosel	<dpw2>		
SERVER_PORT_SECURE	1	1	1	1	1
HTTPS	on	on	on	on	on
CERT_FLAGS					1
CERT_SUBJECT					<subject>
CERT_ISSUER					<issuer>
CERT_SERIALNUMBER					<serial>

Variable	Anonymous	Basic	Digest	Integrated	Client Certificates
CERT_COOKIE					<cookie>
CERT_SERVER_ISSUER	<sissuer>	<sissuer>	<sissuer>	<sissuer>	<sissuer>
HTTPS_SERVER_ISSUER	<sissuer>	<sissuer>	<sissuer>	<sissuer>	<sissuer>
CERT_SERVER_SUBJECT	<ssubject>	<ssubject>	<ssubject>	<ssubject>	<ssubject>
HTTPS_SERVER_SUBJECT	<ssubject>	<ssubject>	<ssubject>	<ssubject>	<ssubject>
CERT_KEYSIZE	56	56	56	56	56
HTTPS_KEYSIZE	56	56	56	56	56
CERT_SECRETKEYSIZE	512	512	512	512	512
HTTPS_SECRETKEYSIZE	512	512	512	512	512

The results of the same script invoked via HTTPS are shown in Table 10.3. This table makes it very clear which elements relate to the server-side certificate as opposed to the client-side certificate. (Both client and server certificates in this case were generated by quux.com, the enterprise certificate authority in my test system.) Here are the values that I didn't have room for in the table:

```
<dpw2>
    username="quux\alice", realm="preston", qop="auth",
    algorithm="MD5", uri="/b/x.asp",
    nonce="fb210da32ca30592643468100000cc6d97809692660cb7d6
    b596f5e731c1", nc=00000001,
    cnonce="8e7206169ad8e237f3fb08d525cc2378",
    response="f5faa59c9eeeb7ded74ea8ade38b77cf"
<serial>
    29-92-0f-64-00-00-00-00-00-0b
<cookie>
    6f245f3a7b3e0d19c84e03786bbf6e41
<subject>
    CN=alice
<issuer>
    E=no@mail.com, C=US, S=CA, L=Torrance, O=quux.com,
    OU=lab, CN=Quux Authority
<ssubject>
    C=US, S=CA, L=Torrance, O=quux.com, OU=lab,
    CN=wendoline
<sissuer>
    E=no@mail.com, C=US, S=CA, L=Torrance, O=quux.com,
    OU=lab, CN=Quux Authority
```

Notes on ISAPI Applications

ISAPI applications are hosted by the appropriate WAM depending on how the Web application is configured in the metabase with respect to process isolation. Each thread that enters the ISAPI DLL will be impersonating; the particular account being impersonated will depend on the mechanisms described earlier. One interesting difference between IIS 4 and IIS 5 is that on the earlier platform, calls to GetObjectContext failed with CONTEXT_E_NOCONTEXT. This made it impossible for the ISAPI DLL to call IObjectContext::Create Instance, which was required in Windows NT 4 to flow the impersonation token to the configured component being created (in order to perform role-based access checks based on the *client* as opposed to IWAM_MACHINE or SYSTEM). This requirement was removed in IIS 5 (Brown 1999d), and the client's security context appears to flow correctly, at least according to my own experiments.

Notes on ASP Applications

Although ASP is implemented as an ISAPI DLL, it provides its own thread pool and transfers incoming requests from the WAM thread onto its own thread before making calls into your scripts. Never fear, ASP also transfers the token on the WAM thread to its own thread before making the call, so threads entering ASP scripts will *always* be impersonating, using the mechanisms described earlier.

As mentioned previously for ISAPI applications, in IIS 4 it's critical that you call `IObjectContext::CreateInstance` when creating configured components; otherwise, the thread's security context will not be propagated to the new object. This can either cause all calls to be denied (typical if your WAM is running under IWAM_MACHINE) or cause all calls to be allowed, because SYSTEM is not subject to role-based access checks (this happens if your WAM is running in-process in `INETINFO.EXE`). This is not a problem at all in IIS 5.

So for IIS 4, it's critical that scripts use `Server.CreateObject` to instantiate objects (using <object> tags is also safe). Forgetting to do this can lead to unpredictable and unsafe behavior.

Another interesting security-related tidbit is that if a client submits a certificate, you can access all the various information in that certificate from ASP by using the `Request` object's `ClientCertificate` method. Here's a simple ASP script that echoes back all the attributes in the client's certificate in a table:

```
<table border=1 cellpadding=3>
<thead><td>Key</td><td>Value</td></thead>
<% for each key in Request.ClientCertificate %>
<tr><td><%= key %></td>
<td><%= Request.ClientCertificate(key) %></td></tr>
<% next %>
</table>
```

Notes on CGI Applications

Just as ISAPI and ASP applications run in the logon session of the client (or the anonymous Internet user)—or at least their threads run in that logon session via impersonation—so too do CGI applications, except that the entire process is directed into the client's logon session, as opposed to just a thread in that process. This is a great sandboxing measure for CGI applications, but there is a metabase attribute that can be used to force a particular CGI application (or a whole host of them; this attribute is inheritable, as are most metabase attributes) into the System logon session. This attribute is known as `Create ProcessAsUser`, and it's set to `True` by default, which is where you should leave it unless you really know what you're doing.

Setting this attribute to `False` causes CGI applications to run in the System logon session, in the noninteractive window station. (Not that the latter is in any way a sandbox; when running as `SYSTEM` you can pretty much move to any window station you desire.)

IIS as a Gateway into COM+

The primary reason for incorporating a Web server in a distributed three-tier application is to broaden the reach of the application to a multitude of platforms. (Imagine trying to use DCOM to reach clients on all the various flavors of UNIX, or on a handheld like the Palm OS or a simple appliance like a pager.) A Web-based front end is the de facto architecture for reaching across the Internet at large.

However, the natural architecture for a classic three-tier Windows-based distributed application is to use a Web server simply as a gateway into a more structured environment built with COM+ components. From a security standpoint, this type of architecture makes a lot of sense and can help you avoid an overabundance of application-level security checks. Once again, the less security-related code in your application, the better off you'll be.

Because IIS provides a plethora of authentication services that you can choose declaratively, all you have to do is figure out a way to smoothly move the client's security context from the WAM into your COM+ components and let COM+ role-based access checks do the heavy lifting. ASP goes to great pains

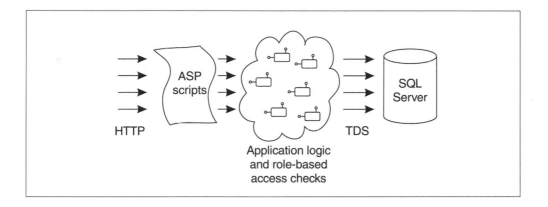

Figure 10.11   Natural three-tier architecture with a Web front end

to do its part, by transferring the client's token from the WAM thread to the ASP thread. COM+ also gives you a boost by using dynamic cloaking in all COM+ applications by default. Because the WAM is a configured component, it runs in a process where dynamic cloaking is enabled, and thus each outgoing COM call you make from an ISAPI application or ASP script will go out using the client's security context. (Recall that dynamic cloaking implies that outgoing COM calls are sensitive to the current thread token; without cloaking turned on, COM ignores the thread token for outgoing calls.) Things didn't work nearly as smoothly in Windows NT 4, as detailed in Brown (1999d).[27] Figure 10.11 shows natural three-tier architecture in which IIS acts as the gateway into a collection of COM+ components in the middle tier.

If you plan on collocating the Web server and your COM+ applications on the same machine (as in Figure 10.12), the security architecture will be very natural and obvious. (There might even be a farm of these machines, each with a Web server and a set of equivalent COM+ applications, but that's not a problem.) The key is having the Web application and the components it uses located on the same machine. Because dynamic cloaking is turned on in the WAM by default, when you make calls from your scripts into your local COM+

---

[27] If you've ever wondered what the MTS Trusted Impersonators group in Windows NT 4 was for, you'll enjoy reading this article.

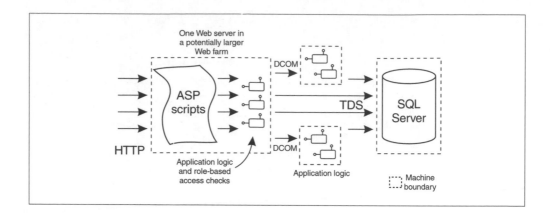

Figure 10.12   Collocating role-based access checks on the Web server

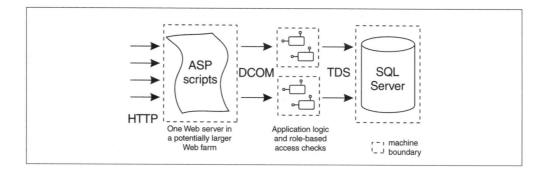

Figure 10.13   Separating role-based access checks from the Web server

components, role-based access checks will occur naturally against the client's security context.

On the other hand, if you plan on putting the Web server on one machine and your COM+ components on a separate machine (see Figure 10.13), you have to make sure that the client's logon session on the Web server will have network credentials in order to survive the hop from the Web server machine to the other machine where the role-based access checks will occur. If the client's logon session doesn't have network credentials, you'll end up making the call using a NULL session; if your client was in fact authenticated, you've basically just dropped that information on the floor.

Table 10.4 shows when the logon session for the client will have network credentials and when it won't, depending on the type of authentication in use (this table assumes the client is on a different machine than the Web server). As you can see, the options are not very pretty. Practically speaking, if the client is authenticated (and therefore not using the anonymous Internet user account), unless you're using Basic Authentication you likely won't have network creden-

Table 10.4 Authentication and network credentials

Scenario	Network Credentials?	Which Credentials?
Anonymous; password sync on	No	
Anonymous; password sync off	Yes	Anonymous Internet user account in effect at that node in the meta-base, typically IUSR_MACHINE
Certificate based; directory service mapping on	No	
Certificate based; directory service mapping off	Yes	User account specified in IIS internal mapping
Basic Authentication; interactive logon method	Yes	Client-specified user name and password
Basic Authentication; batch logon method	Yes	Client-specified user name and password
Basic Authentication; network logon method	No	
Digest Authentication	No	
Integrated Windows Authentication	No	

tials, and you won't be able to pass the access control responsibilities on to COM+ components on a different machine in the middle tier.

If you're adamant about using this multihop architecture, you might consider using a COM+ library package, configured with role-based security, as a layer between you and the remote objects that your script would normally talk to directly. These library components can mimic the remote object's interfaces (in fact, this code can be generated automatically based on a type library if you're smart about it), and can simply delegate calls to the remote object.

The beauty of this model is twofold. First, you don't want to be making calls from ASP scripts directly to remote objects, because most scripting languages double the number of round-trips required to make each method call (think `IDispatch::GetIDsOfNames` followed by `IDispatch::Invoke`). If you generate the code for the library component layer in a vtable-friendly language such as Visual Basic, Java, or C++, the `IDispatch` round-trips will be negligible because they'll happen locally between your script and the library components. When the library components actually make calls across the wire they can use vtable interfaces and execute the call in a single round-trip.

Second (back to security), your role-based checks will now work as desired because the COM+ interceptors in the library application will see the client's security context. Note that this trick requires Windows 2000, because MTS library packages have no notion of role-based security.

Miscellaneous Topics

This section contains some miscellaneous tips and traps to watch out for.

Using Client IP Addresses to Control Access

Because HTTP is designed to run over TCP/IP, and TCP/IP headers include the source IP address and port, it's possible to grant or deny access purely on the basis of the client's host address. Although this is an interesting feature that is commonly used to block unsophisticated pranksters from accessing Web resources on a server, unless this policy is backed up with IPSec (which authenticates host addresses cryptographically using Kerberos), simply relying on a client's advertised host address to determine access restrictions is very insecure. Spoofing a network address in a TCP request is relatively easy in the big scheme of things. If you decide to use this feature and want to set this up via a script, you'll use the methods defined under the `IIsIPSecurity` interface.

Mapping Virtual Directories to UNC Paths

Mapping virtual directories to UNC paths is an interesting feature that IIS supports. Instead of having a virtual directory map to a file system on a local device, you can direct it to a remote host by specifying a UNC path (\\machine\share). Remember, though, IIS is *always impersonating* when it accesses files for a client, and depending on the authentication mechanism you've chosen, the logon session being impersonated will likely not have network credentials. Thus, there are three metabase attributes for every virtual directory that come into play when a UNC path is in use:

- **UNCUserName** The user name that should be used in lieu of the actual client's identity to access the resource. According to my own experiments, this must be in authority\principal form, rather than UPN (principal@authority) form.

- **UNCPassword** The corresponding password for the account.

- **UNCAuthenticationPassthrough** Instead of setting a user name and password, you can set this attribute to True (the default setting is False) to indicate that you want to attempt to delegate the client's credentials if possible to make the additional network hop to the remote file system.

  If all parties involved support Kerberos, and the computer that hosts the Web server has been designated "trusted for delegation," then if the client's account has not been marked "sensitive and cannot be delegated" the Lan Manager client will ask for a forwarded TGT for the Web server to use to delegate the client's credentials and make the call. This of course assumes that you've enabled Kerberos authentication for the virtual directory (by selecting Integrated Windows Authentication). There are so many constellations that must align correctly for this to work that it's questionable whether it's worth it to even enable this option, but as you'll see, it's probably no worse than using a hardcoded user account.

When you hardcode a user account and password, IIS simply verifies that the client can be authenticated (period) according to the `AuthFlags` attribute for the target resource. Thus, if you have allowed anonymous access, everyone gets past this hurdle. Once the authentication requirement is satisfied, IIS now ignores the real client's identity and instead establishes an interactive logon session for the user specified via `UNCUserName`. (This will of course fail if the specified user has not been granted the interactive logon right on the machine hosting the Web server.) IIS impersonates this logon session (as it would normally impersonate the client's logon session, or IUSR_MACHINE) and executes the request. This means that if you are targeting an ASP script via UNC redirection, that ASP script will never see the actual client authenticated by IIS; rather, it will see the user principal specified via `UNCUserName`. This can lead to security holes unless you're paying attention, so watch your back.

Using RevertToSelf to Reenter the TCB

Imagine that you had a Web application that ran at a process isolation level of Low (in other words, inside `INETINFO.EXE`). Although this can be dangerous, it can also allow you to do very powerful things. However, because all threads that call into your application from the WAM will be impersonating *someone,* you need to rejoin the TCB temporarily if you need to execute privileged code (for instance, if you want to call `LogonUser`).

The following piece of code shows how this can be done (I've packaged this in a nonconfigured, in-process COM component so that you can call it directly from an ASP script):

```
HRESULT Foo::DoSomethingPowerful() {
  HANDLE htok;
  OpenThreadToken(GetCurrentThread(),
                  TOKEN_IMPERSONATE,
                  TRUE, &htok);
  RevertToSelf();
  // we're now executing in the TCB!
  SetThreadToken(0, htok);
  CloseHandle(htok);
  return S_OK;
}
```

This code temporarily removes the thread token, causing the WAM thread to execute in the security context of the process, in this case INETINFO.EXE, and the System logon session. Note that the code carefully places the token back on the thread before returning to the WAM; restoring the environment this way protects the application from any assumptions that ASP or the WAM might make, and is purely a precautionary measure.

Calling this code from a Web application configured at Medium or High isolation also allows you to run in the security context of the host process, but in this case it won't be the System logon session; rather, it'll be (typically) IWAM_MACHINE, which is not very privileged at all, at least by default, and thus is much less interesting.

Debugging Authentication Settings

If at any time you want to find out what security context your ASP script is running in, you can download a little component that I built called the token dumper (from http://www.develop.com/books/pws). This COM component exposes a single method that scripts can invoke:

```
HRESULT TokenDump([in]             long  grfOptions,
                  [out, retval] BSTR* pbstrResult);
```

The options allow you to limit the output in some ways (see the documentation that comes with the tool for details); just pass -1 if you want to get *all* the output. This function will dump the token contents into a pretty-printed HTML stream, including the details of the thread *and* process tokens. I've found this tool invaluable in debugging secure Web applications. Here's how to use it in an ASP script:

```
<%= createObject("tokdumpsrv.tokdump").tokenDump(-1) %>
```

Where to Get More Information

IIS documentation ships with the product itself; just go to a machine that has IIS installed and surf to http://localhost/iishelp. As of this writing, the IIS 5 documentation is somewhat out of date, but one hopes that the next service pack will fix this. The Platform SDK also includes this documentation as well; I'd expect this to be updated sooner than the IIS product documentation, but only time will tell.

Summary

- Public key cryptography reduces the need for shared secrets.
- Public key cryptography does *not* reduce the need for trust.
- Signatures created with a private key can be verified by anyone, because the public key is not a secret.
- Certificates provide a way of authenticating a public key.
- At its essence, a certificate is a name and a public key bound together by the signature of a trusted third party.
- A certificate revocation list (CRL) is a published list of certificates that have been revoked for one reason or another; when authenticating, it's important to check the certificate against a current CRL before assuming it's valid. Both IE and IIS provide this option.
- Often a hierarchy of trust will be necessary for two parties in different organizations to develop trust in each other's certificates, which results in a chain of certificates, each signed by a more widely trusted authority.
- An administrator can install a certificate trust list (CTL) for each Web site to indicate the certificates (typically for root authorities) that he or she is willing to trust in a client certificate chain.
- SSL 3.0 is the de facto authentication protocol used with HTTP. TLS 1.0 is essentially just SSL 3.1 with the IETF's stamp of approval, and PCT is a dead technology.
- SCHANNEL is the name of the security service provider that implements the aforementioned authentication protocols.
- SSL runs in three modes: mutual authentication, server-only authentication, and no authentication (which is deprecated).
- HTTPS is simply HTTP over SSL on a designated default port (443). All communication over HTTPS is encrypted using a conventional session key exchanged during SSL authentication.

- The IIS metabase is a hierarchical store of attributes that parallels the structure of the Web sites for a particular machine. Attributes in the metabase are normally inheritable to make administration easier.
- The Web Application Manager (WAM) was introduced to move Web applications into safer environments than the System logon session. These sandboxes not only protect the Web server from crashing but also significantly reduce the threat imposed by buggy Web applications and the crackers who exploit them.
- IIS provides a plethora of client-side authentication options, each of which has pluses and minuses depending on the environment in which it is used.
- IIS is often used as an HTTP gateway into a world of COM+ components. It's designed to make it easy to pass through the client's identity so that COM+ interceptors can provide role-based security checks.
- Whenever you place a network hop between the Web server and the COM+ components that perform role-based access checks, life becomes much less automatic, and you need to start thinking about how to get network credentials for that hop or how to move those access checks into the Web server process itself.

Appendix

Some Parting Words

One thing I often rant about is the necessity of an intelligent setup program for a distributed application. After you've installed your application's files and registered your COM servers, you're not near being done. Simply throwing up a readme file in the administrator's face telling him the accounts he needs to add, the privileges he needs to grant, and the other random things he needs to do in order for your application to function is a recipe for disaster (although it'll keep lots of technical support staff employed at your company).

I personally like the idea of a smart setup program that gives the administrator a customized interview about how he plans to deploy your application. You are an expert in your problem domain; you know your application's needs and how it was designed to be used. Pay some big bucks to a user interface wizard and have her design a friendly interview that gathers all the information you need, and once you've performed the interview, tell the administrator exactly what you plan to do and why you plan on doing it (perhaps via a summary, akin to the way many Visual C++ wizards summarize the code they will generate when you press the Finish button). When the administrator confirms that this is acceptable, go make those changes yourself. Add the accounts you need to run your COM servers. Add the groups and aliases that make sense for

your application. Add the SID-to-role mappings to your COM+ applications.
Here are some tips for making this work.

Well-Known SIDs

Never hardcode the names of well-known SIDs (Everyone, Administrators, etc.)
into any application (including your setup application); you'll have a heck of a
time localizing it for other languages. Instead, construct them programmatically.
Here's a C++ class that I've found useful in this regard:

```
struct WellKnownSid : SID {
  void _init(BYTE iaFragment,
             BYTE subAuthCount,
             DWORD firstSubAuth) {
    ZeroMemory(IdentifierAuthority.Value,
               sizeof IdentifierAuthority.Value);
    Revision                    = SID_REVISION;
    SubAuthorityCount           = subAuthCount;
    IdentifierAuthority.Value[5] = iaFragment;
    SubAuthority[0]             = firstSubAuth;
  }
  WellKnownSid(BYTE iaFragment,
               DWORD firstSubAuth)
               : secondSubAuth(0) {
    _init(iaFragment, 1, firstSubAuth);
  }
  WellKnownSid(BYTE iaFragment,
               DWORD firstSubAuth,
               DWORD _secondSubAuth)
               : secondSubAuth(_secondSubAuth) {
    _init(iaFragment, 2, firstSubAuth);
  }
  DWORD secondSubAuth;
};
```

There are two constructors for creating well-known SIDs with this class: The
first takes a single subauthority, and the second takes two subauthorities. This
is all you need to build all the well-known SIDs. For instance, to construct the
well-known SID for Everyone, use the first constructor:

```
WellKnownSid everyone(1, SECURITY_WORLD_RID);
```

To construct the well-known SID for the Administrators alias, use the following:

```
WellKnownSid admins(5, SECURITY_BUILTIN_DOMAIN_RID,
                        DOMAIN_ALIAS_RID_ADMINS);
```

Notice that the first code snippet passed 1 for the *iaFragment* parameter, and the second passed 5. This is because although there are six well-known 48-bit identifier authorities, only the last byte varies from 0:

```
// excerpt from winnt.h
#define SECURITY_NULL_SID_AUTHORITY        {0,0,0,0,0,0}
#define SECURITY_WORLD_SID_AUTHORITY       {0,0,0,0,0,1}
#define SECURITY_LOCAL_SID_AUTHORITY       {0,0,0,0,0,2}
#define SECURITY_CREATOR_SID_AUTHORITY     {0,0,0,0,0,3}
#define SECURITY_NON_UNIQUE_AUTHORITY      {0,0,0,0,0,4}
#define SECURITY_NT_AUTHORITY              {0,0,0,0,0,5}
```

Thus the first SID constructed in the previous code is S-1-1-0 (the identifier authority is 1, and the single subauthority is 0). The second SID is S-1-5-32-544 (the identifier authority is 5, and the two subauthorities are 32 and 544).

Tables A.1 and A.2 show how to build all the well-known SIDs with the manifest constants found in `winnt.h`. The SIDs in Table A.2 represent well-known aliases in the BUILTIN domain, so the first subauthority will always be `SECURITY_BUILTIN_DOMAIN_RID`, which I've omitted for brevity.

If you download the code fragments for this book from http://www. develop.com/books/pws, you'll find constants for each of these well-known SIDs that you can cut and paste into your own header file.[1]

Printing SIDs in Human Readable Form

Sometimes it's convenient to print SIDs from DACLs or tokens (my token dump component is an example of the latter). Windows 2000 introduced a couple of functions to make it easy to convert back and forth between a binary and a string representation of a SID (similar to what we've had for years with GUIDs

---

[1] You may eventually see this code (or something very similar) released with Visual C++ in the future. This is one of the suggestions I've made to the folks working on the ATL/MFC frameworks.

in COM). The next page includes a helper function that uses one of these conversion functions to print a SID on Windows 2000, and also provides a formatting routine for earlier versions of Windows (this function is referenced in earlier chapters of the book).

Table A.1. Well-known SIDs

Well-Known SID	IA	First Subauthority
Everyone	1	SECURITY_WORLD_RID
Local	2	SECURITY_LOCAL_RID
Creator Owner	3	SECURITY_CREATOR_OWNER_RID
Creator Group	3	SECURITY_CREATOR_GROUP_RID
Dialup	5	SECURITY_DIALUP_RID
Network	5	SECURITY_NETWORK_RID
Batch	5	SECURITY_BATCH_RID
Interactive	5	SECURITY_INTERACTIVE_RID
Service	5	SECURITY_SERVICE_RID
Proxy	5	SECURITY_PROXY_RID
Enterprise Controllers	5	SECURITY_ENTERPRISE_CONTROLLERS_RID
Anonymous Logon	5	SECURITY_ANONYMOUS_LOGON_RID
Self	5	SECURITY_PRINCIPAL_SELF_RID
Authenticated Users	5	SECURITY_AUTHENTICATED_USER_RID
Restricted	5	SECURITY_RESTRICTED_CODE_RID
Terminal Server	5	SECURITY_TERMINAL_SERVER_RID
System	5	SECURITY_LOCAL_SYSTEM_RID

IA = Identifier authority.

Table A.2. Well-known SIDs in the BUILTIN domain

Well-known SID	IA	Second Subauthority
Administrators	5	DOMAIN_ALIAS_RID_ADMINS
Users	5	DOMAIN_ALIAS_RID_USERS
Guests	5	DOMAIN_ALIAS_RID_GUESTS
Power Users	5	DOMAIN_ALIAS_RID_POWER_USERS
Account Operators	5	DOMAIN_ALIAS_RID_ACCOUNT_OPS
System Operators	5	DOMAIN_ALIAS_RID_SYSTEM_OPS
Print Operators	5	DOMAIN_ALIAS_RID_PRINT_OPS
Backup Operators	5	DOMAIN_ALIAS_RID_BACKUP_OPS
Replicator	5	DOMAIN_ALIAS_RID_REPLICATOR
RAS Servers	5	DOMAIN_ALIAS_RID_RAS_SERVERS
Pre-Windows 2000 Access	5	DOMAIN_ALIAS_RID_PREW2KCOMPACCESS

IA = Identifier authority.

```
#if _WIN32_WINNT >= 0x500
void _printSid(void* psid) {
  wchar_t* psz;
  if (!ConvertSidToStringSid(psid, &psz))
    _err(L"ConvertSidToStringSid");
  wprintf(psz);
  LocalFree(psz);
}
#else
void _printSid(void* psid) {
  // formatting algorithm borrowed from mssdk
  // sample "textsid", by Scott Field
  const SID_IDENTIFIER_AUTHORITY& ia =
    *GetSidIdentifierAuthority( psid );
  wchar_t szIdentifierAuthority[20];

  if (!ia.Value[0] && !ia.Value[1]) {
```

```
      // decimal form
      wsprintf(szIdentifierAuthority, L"%u",
              (ULONG)(ia.Value[5]        ) +
              (ULONG)(ia.Value[4] <<  8) +
              (ULONG)(ia.Value[3] << 16) +
              (ULONG)(ia.Value[2] << 24));
    }
    else {
      // hex form
      wsprintf(szIdentifierAuthority,
              L"0x%02hx%02hx%02hx%02hx%02hx%02hx",
              (USHORT)(ia.Value[0]),
              (USHORT)(ia.Value[1]),
              (USHORT)(ia.Value[2]),
              (USHORT)(ia.Value[3]),
              (USHORT)(ia.Value[4]),
              (USHORT)(ia.Value[5]));
    }

    // S-R-IA
    wprintf(L"S-%d-%s", int(((SID*)psid)->Revision),
                        szIdentifierAuthority);

    //        -SA-SA-SA-SA
    const int nSubAuthorities = *GetSidSubAuthorityCount(psid);
    for (int i = 0; i < nSubAuthorities; ++i)
      wprintf(L"-%d", int(*GetSidSubAuthority(psid, i)));
  }
#endif
```

Adding Domain Principals in Windows 2000

If you plan on writing a lot of code against the Active Directory, you'd be well advised to spend some time learning about LDAP (Lightweight Directory Access Protocol). Windows provides an interface to the directory service (which uses the LDAP 3.0 network protocol) called ADSI (Active Directory Services Interface), but since the recommended provider for use with the Active Directory is the LDAP provider, cutting your teeth with a primer on LDAP programming will help you feel more confident. ADSI can be accessed from either scripts or languages such as C++, but since scripts are so much more compact, they are used here for demonstration purposes.

Here's a script that adds a user named Bob to the quux.com domain:

```
const UF_NORMAL_ACCOUNT = &H0200
const ERROR_OBJECT_ALREADY_EXISTS = &H80071392

set c = getObject("LDAP://cn=Users,dc=quux,dc=com")

set u = c.create("user", "cn=Bob")

u.put "sAMAccountName", "Bob"
u.put "userAccountControl", UF_NORMAL_ACCOUNT
u.put "description", "Bob is just this guy, you know"

on error resume next : err.clear
u.setInfo
select case err.number
  case 0
  case ERROR_OBJECT_ALREADY_EXISTS
    wscript.echo "That account already exists"
    wscript.quit
  case else
    err.raise err.number, err.description
end select
on error goto 0

u.setPassword "password"
```

The first thing to notice about this script is that I placed Bob in the Users container. This is the place where most administrators will expect to see user principals. Also note that I hung this user account directly off the quux.com domain. If I had instead wanted to place this account into an organizational unit named foo, I would have connected using the following LDAP distinguished name:

```
cn=Users,ou=foo,dc=quux,dc=com
```

The *sAMAccountName* property is required for backward compatibility with earlier versions of Windows (this is the name used in the authority\ principal form of the name, which is currently used for COM servers, as you'll recall from Chapter 9). The name must be unique within the domain, which is something I've punted on here; I'm assuming that you'll pick a name for your COM servers other than "Bob." (For a pet store application, perhaps you might pick PETSTORE_SERVICE, to identify the service principal for the application.)

Notice that I was also careful to set the *userAccountControl* property; by default this will include a flag that disables the account, and so I overrode this by clearing this flag. (I set the value so that it only has one flag—the one that indicates that this is a normal account for a user principal.)

One property that I didn't bother to set was *userPrincipalName*; if I had set this value, its natural value would have been "Bob@quux.com," but because this name cannot be used by COM+ to establish a logon anyway, I've omitted it.

Finally, notice that I was careful to reset the password. (Look at the CryptGenRandom API for a great way to generate a random stream of bits from which you can derive a password; don't simply hardcode a password as I have done!) Until you set the password, the account will be marked "User must change password at next logon," and the SCM won't be able to establish a logon session in this state. Besides, if the account is for use with a service or COM server, you'll need to know the password in order to configure your service or COM server properly.

Adding Groups in Windows 2000

In Windows NT 4, groups[2] are simple: They're always scoped by a domain (the domain on which they're created), and they can only contain principals from that single domain. Groups cannot nest in Windows NT 4. Windows 2000, with the introduction of the directory and the global catalog, makes things considerably more flexible (and accordingly more complex). After lots of experimentation and hypothesizing, I arrived at what I think is a reasonable story that explains the differences between the different types of groups in Windows 2000.

---

[2] In Windows NT 4, groups are known to administrators as *global groups,* as opposed to *local groups,* which are aliases.

A Note on Group Scope in Windows 2000

First, let me mention that this discussion assumes native Windows 2000 domains as opposed to "mixed-mode" domains in which some domain controllers are still running Windows NT 4. (In the mixed-mode case, most of the new features, such as group nesting and universal groups, aren't supported.)

There are three types of groups in Windows 2000: universal, global, and domain local. The *universal group* is the simplest to understand because its name and the names of its members are replicated to all domain controllers, and it simply works the way you'd expect it to: If you're a member of universal group Baz within a forest,[3] any logon sessions that you establish on any machine in any domain in the forest will contain Baz as one of your authorization attributes. Universal groups can contain principals and groups of any scope (except domain local) from any domain in the forest. In fact, this discussion would be really simple if all groups were universal groups, because there's not much to say about them except that they are replicated across the entire forest via the global catalog. That's the good part, and it's also the bad part. Universal groups are often overkill when more localized administration is needed. Clogging the global catalog with unnecessary baggage isn't a good idea.

Consider what would happen if you took the existing Windows NT 4 model for groups (which works pretty well in small organizations) and simply added this type of group to Windows 2000 (call it a global group for consistency). You'd advertise the existence of the group in the global catalog (in other words, the friendly name and SID of the group would be available throughout the forest). This way anyone anywhere in the forest could grant or deny access to a global group. Because a global group can be applied to objects anywhere in the forest but its membership isn't replicated throughout the forest, you'd have to rely on each authority to provide the appropriate global groups for its principals during the authentication handshake. Therefore, a global group can only include global groups and principals that the authority knows about (this is

---

[3] A forest is an Active Directory term for a group of domain trees that share a schema and a global catalog. All domains within a forest share bidirectional transitive trust relationships that (at least by default) follow the hierarchy of the domain structure. I discuss transitive trust in more detail in Chapter 7.

consistent with the model in Windows NT 4.0), but nothing prohibits global groups from nesting.

So far so good, but here's where things get a bit dicey. Because Windows 2000 allows nesting of groups, what would happen if a global group were to include a universal group? For instance, say Foo\globalgroup includes Quux\universalgroup (the authority of the universal group doesn't really matter for this discussion). Say also that universalgroup includes alice@foo.com and bob@bar.com. Now, when foo.com produced a ticket for Alice, what groups would it include in that ticket? Clearly it knows about globalgroup, because that group is defined at foo.com, and it also knows about universalgroup, because that information is replicated everywhere. No problem. But what does bar.com say about Bob? It knows about universalgroup just like foo.com does, but bar.com knows nothing about Foo\globalgroup, other than its name and SID. Therefore the resulting token for Bob would be incomplete. Is that such a big deal? Well, considering that someone could *deny* access to Foo\globalgroup, or could be auditing based on this SID, it's extremely important to the integrity of the system that tokens aren't missing any SIDs.

One way to solve this problem is to simply not allow global groups to include universal groups. However, this reduces the utility of global groups and might encourage administrators to make everything universal. Windows 2000 therefore provides this type of group (which is in fact called a *global group* and may not include any universal groups), but also provides a third type of group as well to provide more flexibility with regard to universal groups.

This third type of group is called a *domain local group*. This type of group is flexible in the sense that it can include global and universal groups as members, but in order to make this work, it is restricted in other ways. Although a domain local group can include universal groups defined by any domain in the forest, its existence is not advertised in the global catalog. Its SID will only be found in tokens for logon sessions on machines in the domain where it is defined, and thus it can only be used to control access to resources in that single domain. Table A.3 summarizes the three types of groups.

The next page includes some code that adds a global group named Surfers to quux.com (I've omitted the existence check for brevity).

Table A.3. Groups in Windows 2000

Group Type	Can Include	Visible From
Universal	Principals from any domain in the forest; other universal groups from any domain in the forest; global groups from any domain in the forest	All machines in the forest
Global	Principals from the same domain; other global groups from the same domain	All machines in the forest
Domain local	Principals from any domain in the forest; global groups from any domain in the forest; universal groups from any domain in the forest; other domain local groups from the same domain	All machines in the domain

```
const GLOBAL_GROUP       = &H80000002
const DOMAIN_LOCAL_GROUP = &H80000004
const UNIVERSAL_GROUP     = &H80000008

set c = getObject("LDAP://cn=Users,dc=quux,dc=com")
set g = c.create("group", "cn=Surfers")

g.put "sAMAccountName", "Surfers"
g.put "groupType", GLOBAL_GROUP
g.put "description", "Folks who surf"

g.setInfo
```

Finally, here's some code that uses the `IADsGroup::Add` method to add Bob to the Surfers group:

```
set g = getObject( _
  "LDAP://cn=Surfers,cn=Users,dc=quux,dc=com")
g.Add "LDAP://cn=Bob,cn=Users,dc=quux,dc=com"
```

Adding Local Accounts and Aliases

Windows 2000

Note that you cannot create local accounts and aliases on a domain controller in Windows 2000. Because local accounts and aliases are not stored in the directory, you cannot use the LDAP ADSI provider; rather, you should use the WinNT provider, which has a similar interface, but is implemented using RPC over SMB as opposed to LDAP over TCP. Here's the code for adding a local account named Bob on a machine named Wendoline (note that you don't have to be running this script on Wendoline, but you need to be able to be authenticated as an administrator or account operator on that machine):

```
set c = getObject("WinNT://Wendoline,computer")
set u = c.create("user", "Bob")
u.put "description", "Bob is just this guy, you know"
u.setInfo
u.setPassword("password")
```

Here's a script that adds an alias on the same machine:

```
set c = getObject("WinNT://Wendoline,computer")
set a = c.create("group", "Surfers")
a.put "description", "Folks who surf"
a.setInfo
```

Previous Versions of Windows NT

Although it's possible to download and install ADSI along with the WinNT provider on Windows NT 4, it's unlikely (at least as of this writing) that you'll find it roosting on the server machine when your application's install program runs, and ADSI is not currently a redistributable component. In this case, you'll need to back off and use the older Net APIs to do the same work. (It's also possible to use these older APIs on Windows 2000.) Here's an example that adds a local account called Bob and an alias called Surfers, and makes Bob a member of that alias.

```
#include <lm.h>
USER_INFO_1 ui = {0};
ui.usri1_name     = L"Bob";
ui.usri1_password = L"password";
ui.usri1_comment  = L"Bob is just this guy, you know";
ui.usri1_priv     = USER_PRIV_USER; // required!
ui.usri1_flags    = UF_SCRIPT;      // required!
DWORD nIndexOfBadParam;
NetUserAdd(0, 1, (BYTE*)&ui, &nIndexOfBadParam);

LOCALGROUP_INFO_1 gi = {
  L"Surfers",            // name
  L"People who surf"  // comment
};
NetLocalGroupAdd(0, 1, (BYTE*)&gi, &nIndexOfBadParam);

LOCALGROUP_MEMBERS_INFO_3 members = {
  L"Bob"
};
NetLocalGroupAddMembers(0, L"Surfers", 3,
                        (BYTE*)&members, 1);
```

Note that I passed NULL for the first parameter of each of the three Net functions above. If you can be authenticated as a member of either the Administrators or Account Operators alias on a remote machine, you can make these changes remotely as well; just specify the NetBIOS name of the target machine as the first parameter. (You'll need to prefix the name with two backslashes as you would with a UNC pathname.)

Privileges and Logon Rights

MTS and COM+ programmers don't have to worry about granting their server principals the right to a batch logon, because the catalog manager handles this automatically. However, if you're installing a base COM server and want it to run as a distinguished principal, you'll need to grant that principal this right.

The following helper function adjusts the security policy on the specified machine to grant a single privilege to a single SID. (Logon rights are granted the same way as privileges, the main difference between a logon right and a privilege being that the logon right never appears in a token.) The functions used here are fully documented in current versions of the Platform SDK (the LSA API used to be hidden away deep down in a little-used sample directory).

```
DWORD _grantPrivilege(wchar_t* pszMachine,
                      void* psid,
                      wchar_t* pszPrivilege) {

  LSA_UNICODE_STRING usMachine, usPrivilege;
  if (pszMachine)
    _initString(usMachine, pszMachine);
  _initString(usPrivilege, pszPrivilege);

  LSA_OBJECT_ATTRIBUTES oa = {sizeof oa};
  DWORD grfAccess = POLICY_LOOKUP_NAMES |
                    POLICY_CREATE_ACCOUNT;
  LSA_HANDLE hPolicy;
  NTSTATUS s = LsaOpenPolicy(pszMachine ?
                               &usMachine : 0,
                               &oa, grfAccess,
                               &hPolicy);
  if (!s) {
    s = LsaAddAccountRights(hPolicy, psid,
                            &usPrivilege, 1);
  }
  LsaClose(hPolicy);

  return LsaNtStatusToWinError(s);
}
```

Here's an example that grants a local account named Bob the right to a batch logon (with error checking omitted for clarity):

```
wchar_t szAuthority[256];
DWORD cchAuthority = sizeof  szAuthority /
                     sizeof *szAuthority;
SID_NAME_USE snu;
BYTE sidBob[_maxSidSize];
DWORD cbSid = sizeof sidBob;
LookupAccountName(0, L"Bob", sidBob, &cbSid,
                  szAuthority, &cchAuthority, &snu);
_grantPrivilege(0, sidBob, SE_BATCH_LOGON_NAME);
```

Table A.4 is a list of logon rights. See Chapter 4 for a description of the various types of logons and how they differ from one another; this list is repeated here solely for your convenience.

Table A.5 (starting on page 510) provides a complete list of privileges and their meanings. For those privileges most interesting to programmers, I've generally tried to provide extra information based on my own experience; often the documentation for privileges is either out of date, vague, or just plain wrong.

Secrets: The Windows Password Stash

If all your COM servers are packaged in COM+ applications (or MTS packages for earlier versions of Windows), the catalog automatically updates the Windows password stash on your behalf; all you need to do is set the `Password` attribute on the application. If, however, you are installing a base COM server that runs as a distinguished principal, you'll need to update this password yourself.

The password stash is a simple dictionary in which the keys and values are both strings; it is stored in the registry at `HKLM\Security\Policy\Secrets`. (If you run the registry editor from the System logon session, you'll see the keys of this dictionary, including what appears to be the location of the machine's password, stored in a key named `$MACHINE.ACC`.) In any case, the function

Table A.4. Logon rights

Name	Description
`SeServiceLogonRight,` `SeDenyServiceLogonRight`	Control the right to a service logon session on the local machine
`SeBatchLogonRight,` `SeDenyBatchLogonRight`	Control the right to a batch logon session on the local machine
`SeNetworkLogonRight,` `SeDenyNetworkLogonRight`	Control the right to a network logon session on the local machine
`SeInteractiveLogonRight,` `SeDenyInteractiveLogonRight`	Control the right to an interactive logon session on the local machine

you need to call to update this stash is `LsaStorePrivateData`. The COM SCM expects to see a key formed in the following fashion: `SCM:{APPID}`, where `APPID` is replaced with the AppID of the server. Normally, strings in the stash do not contain NULL terminators (they are instead length-prefixed), but COM doesn't follow this rule of thumb. (I got nailed by this in my November 1998 Security Briefs column, hence the errata on my Web site.) Thus, be sure to include the NULL terminator in both the key and the value.

Here's a helper function you can use that sets the COM `RunAs` password on any machine where you are an administrator:

```
// pass NULL for pszMachine for localhost
// pass NULL for pszPassword to remove the secret
DWORD _setCOMRunAsPassword(wchar_t* pszMachine,
                           REFGUID appID,
                           wchar_t* pszPassword) {
  LSA_UNICODE_STRING usMachine, usPassword;
  if (pszMachine)
    _initString(usMachine, pszMachine);
  if (pszPassword) {
    _initString(usPassword, pszPassword);
    // don't forget to include the NULL terminator
    // in the length calculation for the password
    usPassword.Length += sizeof *pszPassword;
  }

  LSA_OBJECT_ATTRIBUTES oa = {sizeof oa};
  DWORD grfAccess = POLICY_CREATE_SECRET;
  LSA_HANDLE hPolicy;
  NTSTATUS s = LsaOpenPolicy(pszMachine ?
                               &usMachine : 0,
                               &oa, grfAccess,
                               &hPolicy);
  if (!s) {
    wchar_t szKey[256];
    lstrcpy(szKey, L"SCM:");
    StringFromGUID2(appID, szKey + 4,
                    sizeof szKey / sizeof *szKey - 4);
    LSA_UNICODE_STRING usKey;
```

```
    _initString(usKey, szKey);

    // don't forget to include the NULL terminator
    // in the length calculation for the password
    usKey.Length += sizeof *szKey;

    // note that passing NULL for the value removes
    // the secret from the dictionary
    s = LsaStorePrivateData(hPolicy, &usKey,
            pszPassword ? &usPassword : 0);
  }
  LsaClose(hPolicy);

  return LsaNtStatusToWinError(s);
}
```

Table A.5. Privileges

Programmatic Name	Display Name
SeAssignPrimaryTokenPrivilege	Replace a process level token

Comments: Allows one to replace the token on a process with a different one. CreateProcessAsUser is implemented by creating the new process in a suspended state, and then replacing its token before resuming it; thus, you need this privilege in order to call CreateProcessAsUser. (There is no documented API to replace the process token of a running process, in case you were wondering.)

Programmatic Name	Display Name
SeAuditPrivilege	Generate security audits

Comments: A process must have this privilege in order to generate audit events in the security event log. For instance, in order to call ObjectOpenAuditAlarm, this privilege must be present and enabled in your process token; otherwise, the call will fail.

Programmatic Name	Display Name
SeBackupPrivilege	Back up files and directories

Comments: If you are granted this privilege (you must manually enable it in your token), you'll be able to open any file for read permissions (GENERIC_READ). When calling CreateFile, you must indicate your desire to leverage this privilege by passing FILE_FLAG_BACKUP_SEMANTICS via the dwFlagsAndAttributes parameter. Note that this will also allow you to access the SACL even if you don't have the SeSecurityName privilege (ask for ACCESS_SYSTEM_SECURITY permissions if you need to exercise this). Note that you can also use this privilege to gain similar access to the registry: See RegCreateKeyEx along with the REG_OPTION_BACKUP_RESTORE flag.

Programmatic Name	Display Name
SeChangeNotifyPrivilege	Bypass traverse checking

Comments: If you have enabled this privilege, you can access a file as long as you're granted access to that particular file. (In other words, you can be denied FILE_TRAVERSE access to any parent folder in the tree, but the system won't walk up the tree checking these, for reasons of efficiency.) This privilege is granted to Everyone by default, and is one of the few privileges that's also enabled by default in all tokens. As of this writing, the Platform SDK incorrectly asserts that this privilege also controls who can receive file change notifications (based on my experiments, this is not the case). However, one cannot fault the folks writing the documentation; SeChangeNotifyPrivilege certainly is a misleading name for this privilege.

`SeCreatePagefilePrivilege`   Create a pagefile

Comments: The documentation for Windows 2000 states that this privilege is required to adjust the pagefile settings; in practice, this appears to be controllec based on whether or not the user is a member of the Administrators alias.

`SeCreatePermanentPrivilege`   Create permanent shared objects

Comments: I haven't found any use for this privilege; its documentation implies control over kernel-mode components, which doesn't make sense since these components are part of the TCB.

`SeCreateTokenPrivilege`   Create a token object

Comments: Allows one to create tokens. There is no documented API for doing this, so this privilege isn't terribly interesting for folks outside Microsoft.

`SeDebugPrivilege`   Debug programs

Comments: You can normally obtain a handle to a process for all permissions by simply calling `OpenProcess`, as long as that process is running in your logon session and its DACL hasn't been adjusted manually by its creator (or anyone else for that matter). However, processes running in logon sessions for other principals will generally be off limits to you (unless you're running in the System logon session, where you can do anything you darn well please). By enabling this privilege, you can now open all processes for all permissions, including those running in the System logon session. This is pretty important if you need to debug the process, hence the name of the privilege. I find it convenient to enable this privilege in TASKMGR.EXE so that I can kill any process on my machine, even ones running in alternate logon sessions (such as hung COM servers and services).

`SeEnableDelegationPrivilege`   Enable computer and user accounts to be trusted for delegation

Comments: This privilege does just what it says; unless you have been granted this privilege, you are not allowed to change the `userAccountControl` property of a user or computer account to include the `UF_TRUSTED_FOR_DELEGATION` flag, even if the directory service ACLs grant you the right to modify that property. I found it interesting that this privilege does *not* control whether you can change the `UF_NOT_DELEGATED` flag in this same property. (This flag indicates whether the account is "sensitive and cannot be delegated.") This privilege is enabled for the Administrators alias by default in the group policy object for the *domain controllers* organizational unit of each domain, which means that each domain controller in the domain automatically agrees on this setting. (It would be awfully strange if they didn't agree, if you think about it.) This privilege was added in Windows 2000.

Table A.5. Privileges *(continued)*

Programmatic Name	Display Name
`SeIncreaseBasePriorityPrivilege`	Increase scheduling priority

Comments: This privilege is required in order to increase the working set size of a process by calling `SetProcessWorkingSetSize`. It is also required in order to increase the base priority class of a process via `SetPriorityClass`. Unfortunately, as of this writing only the first of these functions appears to check for this privilege. (I've submitted this to Microsoft as a bug.)

`SeIncreaseQuotaPrivilege`	Increase quotas

Comments: The only documentation I've found for this privilege (and I've searched far and wide) explains that it is required to call `CreateProcessAsUser` (I've verified this to be true experimentally). However, this privilege does not appear to control working set quotas, as one might assume; rather, `SeIncreaseBasePriorityPrivilege` controls this. Administrators are normally granted this privilege.

`SeLoadDriverPrivilege`	Load and unload device drivers

Comments: This privilege allows you to install or uninstall plug-and-play device drivers. It is normally granted to Administrators.

`SeLockMemoryPrivilege`	Lock pages in memory

Comments: This privilege is required to use the Windows 2000 feature called Address Window Extensions (AWE). The AWE function `AllocateUserPhysicalPages` will fail unless this privilege is present and enabled in the caller's token. Administrators and Power Users are normally granted this privilege.

`SeMachineAccountPrivilege`	Add workstations to domain

Comments: This privilege is obsolete in Windows 2000. (I was able to successfully add a machine to a domain without this privilege.) This activity is now controlled via DACLs in the Active Directory.

`SeProfileSingleProcessPrivilege`	Profile single process

Comments: The documentation for Windows 2000 states that this privilege allows you to gather performance data for processes that are *not* part of the operating system (in other words, processes running outside the TCB). See also `SeSystemProfilePrivilege`; this privilege also doesn't appear to be enforced.

`SeRemoteShutdownPrivilege`   Force shutdown from a remote system

Comments: If you've been granted this privilege on a remote machine, you can call `InitiateSystemShutdown` to cause that machine to shut down. (This privilege also controls who can call `AbortSystemShutdown` on that machine to halt the shutdown, assuming the timeout specified for `InitiateSystemShutdown` hasn't yet expired.) If you target these APIs at the local machine, `SeShutdownPrivilege` controls access instead of `SeRemoteShutdownPrivilege`.

`SeRestorePrivilege`   Restore files and directories

Comments: If you are granted this privilege (you must manually enable it in your token), you'll be able to open any file for write permissions (`GENERIC_WRITE` works fine here). When calling `CreateFile`, you must indicate your desire to leverage this privilege by passing `FILE_FLAG_BACKUP_SEMANTICS` via the `dwFlagsAndAttributes` parameter. Note that you can also change the owner of any file (even existing files) to any security principal you like using this privilege. This is clearly needed for programs that restore files. As with `SeBackupPrivilege`, this privilege will also allow you to access the SACL even if you don't have the `SeSecurityName` privilege. (Ask for `ACCESS_SYSTEM_SECURITY` permissions if you need to exercise this.) Note that you can also use this privilege to gain similar access to the registry: see `RegCreateKeyEx` along with the `REG_OPTION_BACKUP_RESTORE` flag.

`SeSecurityPrivilege`   Manage auditing and security log

Comments: This privilege is required in order to read or write the SACL of an object or to clear the security audit log. Administrators are normally granted this privilege.

`SeShutdownPrivilege`   Shut down the system

Comments: This privilege must be enabled in order for `ExitWindowsEx` to succeed when instructed to shut down the machine. (Currently, this applies to the following flags: `EWX_POWEROFF`, `EWX_REBOOT`, and `EWX_SHUTDOWN`, the three flags that cause the system to shut down.) This privilege also affects calls to `InitiateSystemShutdown` and `AbortSystemShutdown` when they apply to the local machine.

`SeSyncAgentPrivilege`   Synchronize directory service data

Comments: The documentation for this privilege in the Platform SDK states that the holder of this privilege can read all objects in the directory in order to poll for changes via an LDAP synchronization extension. The documentation also specifies that this privilege is granted by default only on domain controllers to the Administrators alias and the System logon session there. However, my own experiments show that this privilege isn't granted to anyone at all by default (at least in build 2195 of Windows 2000).

Table A.5. Privileges *(continued)*

Programmatic Name	Display Name
SeSystemEnvironmentPrivilege	Modify firmware environment variables

Comments: Firmware? Hmm. If you track down the documentation for this privilege, you'll find that this privilege is supposed to be necessary to change the environment variables for processes running in the System logon session. However, in my own tests, I've found that as long as you're granted access to the registry key where these settings are stored (HKLM\SYSTEM\CurrentControlSet\Control\Session Manager\Environment), you can make changes regardless of this privilege. I've submitted this as a bug to Microsoft.

SeSystemProfilePrivilege	Profile system performance

Comments: The documentation for Windows 2000 states that this privilege allows you to gather performance data for processes that are part of the operating system (in other words, processes running in the TCB). However, this privilege doesn't appear to be enforced; I can use the performance monitor to gather process statistics on any program in the system without having this privilege. (I happened to have a Windows NT 4 SP4 box handy and found the same was true on that platform.) I've submitted this as a bug to Microsoft.

SeSystemtimePrivilege	Change the system time

Comments: You must enable this privilege before calling any functions that adjust the system clock; otherwise, you'll be denied access. See SetSystemTime.

SeTakeOwnershipPrivilege	Take ownership of files or other objects

Comments: If this privilege is enabled, you are allowed to open virtually any object in the system for WRITE_OWNER permissions. I say "virtually" because I've never been able to open Winlogon's desktop object, even with this privilege enabled; it appears to have hardcoded limitations.

SeTcbPrivilege	Act as part of the operating system

Comments: The major documented functionality that this privilege allows is the ability to establish logon sessions (see LogonUser) and to access the credential cache of any logon session on the machine (see AcquireCredentialsHandle). You should avoid granting this privilege to user accounts; code that requires this privilege should run in the System logon session, where this privilege is granted automatically.

`SeUndockPrivilege`   Remove computer from docking station

Comments: This privilege was added in Windows 2000. As of this writing, this privilege is not documented in the Windows 2000 online help. I've always wondered how a software privilege can keep someone from undocking a computer, anyway <grin>. This privilege is granted to all Users, Power Users, and Administrators by default.

`SeUnsolicitedInputPrivilege`   Required to read unsolicited input from a terminal device

Comments: The string in the Display Name column is the only documentation I've found for this privilege; it appears to apply to Terminal Services only.

Glossary

access control entry (ACE) An entry in an access control list. See *access control list* for more details.

access control list (ACL) A data structure that contains a list of records (ACEs) indicating which principals or groups are allowed to access a resource, and in what ways. Windows also uses access control lists to specify auditing and alarm information (although as of this writing, alarms are not supported). For a Windows ACL, each ACE has the following elements:

- SID: The principal or group/alias in question
- Access mask: A 32-bit group of bits that indicates which permissions are in question
- Type and flags: Indicate whether this record grants, denies, or audits access, as well as how the ACE should be used in an inheritance scheme

See also *discretionary access control list* and *system access control list*.

access mask A 32-bit group of flags that indicates a set of permissions. For instance, when you call OpenProcess, you must specify an access mask that indicates your intentions. (If you want to terminate the process, this mask must include the PROCESS_TERMINATE permission.) Access masks are also found in access control lists.

account Each user principal has an account in the security database. Each machine principal also has an account. Each account holds security settings for the principal, the most critical being some data that can be used to authenticate the principal (a one-way hash of a password or a certificate is typical). See also *principal*.

ACE See *access control entry*.

ACL See *access control list*.

ACL editor Windows 2000 and earlier versions of Windows provide interactive editors to allow an administrator to view and modify access control lists for objects in the system such as files, registry keys, and so on. As of Windows 2000, the access control editor is a documented component that any application can use (see `ISecurityInformation` for documentation, and also see my Web site for an example). In case you're interested, Mark Russinovich has documented the Windows NT 4 ACL editor APIs in `ACLEDIT.DLL`; you can find this information at http://www.sysinternals.com.

Active Directory Microsoft's LDAP directory service in Windows 2000, which is an integral part of the domain architecture. The domain topology, user and computer accounts, groups, security policy, and so forth are stored in the directory. Windows 2000 system administrators must be intimately familiar with this data store to be effective.

alias Known by administrators as the "local group," this term refers to an authorization attribute that may be defined and granted on any machine (although Windows 2000 does not allow the definition of custom aliases on domain controllers). Aliases are often used to implement a role-based access control policy, the canonical example of this being Windows itself. Being assigned the Administrators alias on a particular machine grants you a whole slew of built-in permissions, such as the ability to install services. Because aliases are only known by a single machine (ignoring Windows NT 4 domain controllers, which replicate local authorization attributes between all domain controllers in the domain), the only tokens in which you'll find these SIDs will be on the machine where the alias is defined. Thus, if you're a member of the Administrators alias on one box, you will not necessarily be a member of that alias on another box.

asymmetric algorithm A cryptographic algorithm in which the encryption and decryption keys are different. Data may be encrypted with one key and decrypted with the other. Given one key, it is computationally infeasible to determine the other key. For instance, if Bob has a pair of keys, he can keep the encryption key secret (this is a private key), and publish the decryption key as a public key. This allows Bob to create signatures by encrypting (with his private key) a one-way hash of a message or document. If Bob gives his public key to Alice and Mary while they are having lunch together, from then on Alice and Mary can both decrypt any signatures Bob creates and verify that it was Bob who created the signature. The challenge is to build an infrastructure that allows Bob to share his public key with Alice and Mary without physically meeting them, and to inform them if his private key is ever compromised. See also *public key infrastructure*.

authentication The mechanism by which one principal proves his or her identity to another principal. This could be as simple as presenting a password to a local operating system, or as complex as using Secure Sockets Layer or Kerberos to validate a client's credentials over a public network. On the Windows platform, authentication of a principal always results in a logon session for that principal.

Authentication Service Before a client principal can authenticate with another via Kerberos, the client must first request credentials from the Kerberos Authentication Service in the form of a ticket-granting ticket (TGT). Unless the client can prove ownership of the TGT in a later request to the Kerberos Ticket Granting Service (TGS), the TGS will not issue any server tickets; thus, this initial ticket helps the client authenticate herself to Kerberos. See Chapter 7 for more details.

authority A trusted entity that vouches for the identity of a set of principals. Unless there is a path of trust from the target server principal to the client's authority (in NTLM, the server principal is always the server machine itself for the sake of this discussion), the client will not be able to be authenticated (and thus will not be able to access secured resources).

In a password-based authentication system such as Kerberos, the authority is the keeper of secrets (the authority knows the master key held by each of its principals). In a certificate-based system, the authority (also known as a certificate authority) is the keeper of a single critical secret: the private key that it uses to sign certificates. The certificates themselves are not secrets.

authorization attributes Each principal may be assigned one or more authorization attributes that indicate (in a general sense) what the principal is authorized to do. Authorization attributes include groups and privileges. Granting a privilege to a principal increases the scope of that principal's authorization in a very particular way, depending on the privilege. Granting a group assignment to a principal generally also increases the scope of that principal's authorization, but because groups can be both granted *and* denied access, in some cases adding a group assignment might actually decrease that principal's authorization. (This is somewhat counterintuitive, but may become more prevalent with the added flexibility of the group infrastructure in Windows 2000 native domains.)

Authorization attributes are discovered at authentication time, and each token holds a cached set of these attributes for efficiency.

backup domain controller (BDC)   Prior to Windows 2000, a master-slave approach was used for replicating the security database. A backup domain controller holds a read-only copy of the security database and can provide the same services as the primary domain controller (PDC), including authentication and read access to the security database. However, by virtue of the replication model, updates must be made on the PDC for the domain.

batch logon One of two daemon logon types (the other is the service logon). The COM SCM uses this type of logon session to host each COM server that runs as a distinguished principal, but you can establish a batch logon at any time by calling `LogonUser` (assuming you're running in the TCB). A token from a batch logon can be identified by a well-known authorization attribute (a group SID): S-1-5-3.

BDC See *backup domain controller*.

BUILTIN domain Although this isn't actually a domain in the normal sense of the word, it acts as a namespace for a collection of aliases that are often used as roles by the operating system to categorize principals. Examples include Administrators, Users, Power Users, and Guests. The appendix provides a list of these aliases and their SIDs. Technically, therefore, the Administrators alias is written "BUILTIN\Administrators."

certificate revocation list (CRL) Certificates issued by authorities typically have long-term expiration dates; often they don't expire for a year or two. The self-signed certificates for the major certificate authorities don't expire for several years. (The root certificate I have for Verisign, for instance, has a validity period of about 15 years.) The expiration date is actually just an optimization, because to be sure that the owner's secret key hasn't been compromised you have to check a current certificate revocation list from the authority that issued the certificate. If there were no expiration date, CRLs would grow infinitely long.

ciphertext An encrypted set of bits. Ciphertext can be decrypted into plaintext only by someone who knows the key. See also *plaintext* and *cleartext*.

cleartext A commonly used synonym for *plaintext*. See also *ciphertext*.

credentials A principal has credentials if it can prove its identity to the system via authentication. For an interactive logon, the credential consists of the cleartext password. For a logon over the network, the principal requires *network credentials,* the form of which depends on the network authentication protocol in use. A Kerberos credential consists of a ticket and its associated session key. An NTLM credential consists of a password hash. An SSL credential consist of a certificate plus a private key.

CRL See *certificate revocation list*.

cryptographic hash SHA (Secure Hash Algorithm), MD4 (Message Digest 4), and MD5 are examples of cryptographic hash algorithms. Unlike the hash algorithms you may have learned in school, these algorithms worry about someone deliberately attempting to create a collision by finding another set of bytes that hashes to the same value as the bytes protected by a cryptographic hash. Thus these hash values are typically quite long (between 100 and 200 bits is typical), and very chaotic with respect to the input. If one bit in a message changes, the hash value changes dramatically.

DACL See *discretionary access control list*.

DC See *domain controller*.

desktop A secure Win32 object that is housed inside a window station. Desktops are really only interesting in the interactive window station, where a warm human can see and touch them. The main reason to have desktops is to allow a secured user interface; press Control-Alt-Delete to get a fine demonstration. When you press this sequence of keys, the system detects your request and switches to the highly secured Winlogon desktop where you can do things such as lock the console so that your boss can't see your FREECELL high score.

dictionary attack An attack that is usually mounted on a password database that stores one-way hashes of user's passwords. Because the attacker has no chance of decrypting the passwords, he or she can only try to guess them, which is typically done using a dictionary, that is, a set of common words that users often choose for passwords. By hashing each word in the dictionary, the attacker simply needs to compare the hash values in the dictionary with those in the password file. This type of attack is made a bit more difficult by adding "salt" to the password file: including a plaintext number with each record in the file that is also hashed with the password. This keeps the attacker from being able to precalculate the hashes in advance; each word in the dictionary must be hashed with its corresponding salt value. This won't stop a dedicated attacker, but it will slow him or her down a bit.

digital certificates It's a bad idea to trust a naked public key delivered across an unsecured network link. Digital certificates are normally sent instead. At its essence, a digital certificate is a name bound to a public key, the whole package being signed by a trusted third party whose public key is often well known. See also *public key*.

discretionary access control list Also known as a DACL (pronounced such that it rhymes with "jackal"), this data structure is the most common example of an access control list (ACL, see *access control list*). The ACL is discretionary in this case because the owner of the object protected by the DACL can choose the contents of the DACL. Each entry in the DACL either grants or denies access to a principal or group, or is provided for inheritance by child objects in the hierarchy.

At the other end of the spectrum are mandatory access controls, which are used in military and governmental systems, where the system controls who can read or write information based on clearance levels. Windows does not provide mandatory access controls natively.

domain A Windows domain is a boundary for security policy, a scope for principals, and a provider of authentication services (it acts as an authority). See also *authority*.

domain account A security account for a principal that is managed and authenticated by the centralized authority in the domain. See also *local account*.

domain controller For each domain, there may be several physical machines designated as domain controllers that replicate the security database. (In Windows 2000 this database is just one part of the overall directory service being replicated by the domain controllers.) All domain controllers provide access to the security database (although in Windows NT 4, only the *primary domain controller* would accept updates). All domain controllers provide authentication services as well; thus, replication can provide lower latency and higher availability to users of the network.

downgrade attack An attack that typically occurs during the negotiation phase of a network authentication protocol. The idea is that an attacker will attempt to force the parties on either side of the wire to agree to an authentication protocol that contains a flaw that the attacker knows how to exploit. SPNEGO is an example of a network protocol that attempts to mitigate these problems.

empty DACL A DACL that contains no ACEs. Since the rule of thumb is that you're not granted access by a DACL unless an entry explicitly grants you access (either via your principal SID or via a group or alias SID), an empty DACL implicitly denies everyone all access. Be aware that DACLs don't normally stand alone, however; the owner of an object (specified in the security descriptor) has implicit permissions. Other permissions may also be conferred via privileges.

Everyone S-1-1-0. This SID is scoped by the WORLD authority, and is the same everywhere. Every token created by the LSA contains this SID.

forest In Active Directory parlance, a collection of one or more disconnected trees in the directory that share a common schema and global catalog. All domains in a forest share bidirectional transitive trust relationships.

generic permissions Permissions used as a polymorphic template for a concrete access mask that will be generated at a later time. For instance, the default DACL in a token uses generic permissions so that when a thread creates an object and doesn't specify a DACL (and no inheritable ACEs from a parent object are available), the generic DACL can be applied to that class of object by mapping the generic permissions onto concrete permissions for the class. Generic permissions are also sometimes thought of as a convenient crutch for use with functions such as `CreateFile`, where you might not feel like looking up the absolute minimum permissions that you really need for a task; this is not their intended purpose, however.

GINA Short for Graphical Identification and Authentication; a pluggable DLL (hosted in `WINLOGON.EXE`) that houses the user interface required for gathering interactive credentials. Winlogon delegates all user interface chores to this DLL. Companies developing smart card readers or bio-metric authentication equipment often replace the default GINA DLL (`MSGINA.DLL`) with their own.

group A particular type of authorization attribute that represents a logical group of principals (or other groups). It is represented by a SID just as a principal is, but it cannot be authenticated (it has no credentials) and thus is not con-sidered a principal in itself. Groups are stored on domain controllers so that they can "follow" a domain principal as he or she establishes logon sessions on various machines in the domain. See also *alias*.

identifier authority Within a SID, this is a 48-bit number that is the root scope of the SID. Generally only a few bits of this number are ever used (likely for historical reasons); see the appendix for a list of identifier authorities and some well-known SIDs that they scope.

impersonation A mechanism by which a thread in a process has its own token (apart from the process token). Typically used in a gateway component such as a file or Web server for delegating access control from the network dae-mon to a local resource manager such as the file system. Some examples of alternate access control strategies are provided in Chapter 3.

impersonation level A client-side setting supported by virtually all the secure network communication substrates in Windows: named pipes, RPC, and COM(+). The idea is that if a client allows the server to authenticate her, the server can use her logon session for good or evil by impersonating. The client can therefore limit the strength of her remote logon session to prevent the server either from delegating her network credentials or even from accessing local resources while impersonating. Considering the fact that a remote server could have been compromised, the only impersonation level that really has any meat on the network is SecurityDelegation, which, assuming all the knobs are twisted just the right ways in the security database, causes the underlying security service provider to forward the client's Kerberos credentials to the server.

impersonation token See *primary token* for a description of this token type.

inheritable ACE Both DACLs and SACLs support the notion of inheritance, in which a child object inherits ACEs from the parent object in a tree. The parent object must include inheritable ACEs to allow this propagation to occur. See Chapter 6 for a detailed description of ACE inheritance.

interactive window station Also known as Winsta0, this is the only window station on the machine (or in the Terminal Services session) to be bound to hardware. Thus, windows created by processes running in this window station can be seen onscreen, and input from devices such as a mouse and keyboard are passed to these processes. Configuring a service to "interact with the desktop" causes the System SCM to direct the service process onto the interactive window station. Configuring a COM(+) server to run as the interactive user causes the COM SCM to direct the server process onto the interactive window station.

KDC Short for *Key Distribution Center* (not Kerberos Domain Controller, as I've seen some documentation state).

Key Distribution Center (KDC) In Kerberos, a daemon that provides the Kerberos Authentication and Ticket Granting services on UDP/TCP port 88. Each domain controller in a Windows 2000 domain acts as a KDC. (The daemon actually runs inside `LSASS.EXE`; check out how much memory that puppy chews up on a domain controller if you're bored sometime.)

LAN Manager Microsoft's file server technology that has been with us since DOS days. This technology includes both a file server (the Server service) and a client (the Workstation service).

lmclient A short term that I use occasionally in this book to refer to the LAN Manager Workstation service.

lmserver A short term that I use occasionally in this book to refer to the LAN Manager Server service.

lmsession A short term that I use occasionally in this book to refer to a Server Message Block (SMB) session. Each client logon session/server host pair can have at most one lmsession, which can sometimes create race conditions between applications that share a logon session. See Chapter 8 for more details.

local account Often referred to as a "workstation account," or, heaven forbid, a "workgroup account" (workgroups have *nothing* to do with security in Windows), this is a user principal account that is not managed on a domain controller. It's possible to authenticate a local account on the wire by creating a matching user name and password on two machines, but this doesn't scale well. Local accounts are great for running daemons that don't need network credentials, because if the Windows password stash is compromised on a machine where one of these daemons is running, the only passwords that will be discovered will be of no use on the network anyway. `IWAM_MACHINE` and `IUSR_MACHINE` are two good examples that are discussed in Chapter 10.

local group See *alias*.

Local Security Authority (LSA) A daemon that runs in a process known as `LSASS.EXE` and provides authentication services for the local machine. If the machine is a domain controller, the LSA provides authentication services for all principals in the domain.

logon session After a principal has been authenticated on a machine, the LSA creates a logon session for that principal, which caches authorization attributes and credentials for the principal. There are many different types of logon sessions, but the rule of thumb is this: You must establish a logon session on a machine before being able to access any secured resources on that machine. Tokens represent the surface area of a logon session; this is the part that you can see and touch as a programmer, but becoming aware of the underlying logon session boundaries will help you become more comfortable with Windows security. Thinking about logon sessions will help you determine whether any given process has network credentials, which window station a process might be found in, and which processes might be stepping on one another when trying to access a remote file server. Thinking about logon sessions will remind you of what it takes to establish one, and thus help you debug very common COM security problems such as forgetting to grant the batch logon right to a COM server.

LSA See *Local Security Authority*.

LUID Short for locally unique identifier; a 64-bit number that is guaranteed to be unique within the following limits in space and time: The number is only unique on the machine where it is generated, and is only unique until that machine is rebooted. LUIDs are used to identify logon sessions and privilege identifiers, among other, more esoteric things.

MAC See *message authentication code*.

master key In Kerberos and NTLM, a principal's password is not used directly as an encryption key; rather, a one-way hash of that password is used. This hash is known as the *master key*. If the master key is compromised, the attacker cannot establish an interactive logon (where the original cleartext password is required), but he or she can establish network logons anywhere there is a trust path back to the authority for the compromised account.

message authentication code Often abbreviated MAC (or MIC for message integrity code), this is similar to a digital signature except that it doesn't need to be verified by several entities; rather, it only needs to be verified by the person on the other end of the wire receiving the message. Therefore a MAC uses a symmetric (session) key to encrypt a cryptographic hash of the message, as opposed to a private key. This reduces the load on the CPU. (Encrypting data with a symmetric algorithm is typically hundreds of times less CPU intensive than using an asymmetric algorithm.)

mutual authentication A form of authentication in which both principals develop trust in their peer's identity. Kerberos and SSL are examples of authentication protocols that support mutual authentication.

net send A command that you can send to NET.EXE to cause it to send a message to another machine. The messenger service listens for these messages and displays a message box containing the text for the interactive user to see.

network authentication protocol A protocol used to prove one principal's identity to another across a public wire. Unless a good protocol is chosen, there are many ways that the handshake can be attacked. Kerberos, SSL, and NTLM are examples of network authentication protocols used in Windows.

network credentials See *credentials*.

network logon See *network logon session*.

network logon session The type of logon session established after a network authentication handshake. Generally speaking, because a network logon session represents a logon for a remote client, it will *not* contain the client's network credentials, which often confuses developers new to Windows security terminology. I like to think of a network logon session as a proxy for a remote client's logon session.

nonce Rhymes with "once," and stands for a number that will only be used once. Nonces are often used in network authentication protocols to help avoid replay attacks; because the nonce will not be reused, including it in a signed or sealed message can help guarantee that an attacker isn't simply replaying a message seen earlier. In practice it's possible for a nonce to be reused (such as across reboots or machine reconfigurations), but the nonce should be generated in such a way that this doesn't happen often enough (or regularly enough) for an attacker to use this as an advantage.

noninteractive window station A window station that is not bound to hardware. Putting up a window and expecting user input is futile. `ASSERT` statements that put up message boxes in noninteractive window stations can ruin your day. Most window stations on a machine are noninteractive. Unless you're running code in the interactive logon session (or in the System logon session), you're almost guaranteed to be running in a noninteractive window station. This includes services and COM(+) servers running as distinguished principals, tasks started by the `AT` command without the `/interactive` switch, and so forth.

NSA An acronym for the National Security Agency, the military agency that is responsible for code making and code breaking in the United States.

NULL DACL When a security descriptor *has* a DACL, but the DACL is simply a null pointer. (Technically, there is no DACL data structure at all.) This indicates to the system that the access control policy for the object protected by the security descriptor is NULL; everyone is granted all access implicitly. See also *empty DACL*.

OLTP See *online transaction processing*.

one-way function (OWF) A function that takes input *X* and produces output *Y*. *Y* cannot be reversed to determine *X*. See also *cryptographic hash*.

online transaction processing (OLTP) A computer system optimized to process individual transactions in real time. This might include banking deposits, purchases at an online store, and so forth. Because of the online nature of the system, throughput and responsiveness are very important factors, and often a three-tier system is used to free up as much horsepower as possible on the back end database. COM+ (and its predecessor, MTS) was designed specifically to help build these types of systems.

organizational unit (OU) Often refers to a department in a company. In the Windows directory service, this term denotes a physical container that may hold computers and users, and that may hold a security policy that is distinct from other OUs in the domain. The one default organizational unit that you'll find is *domain controllers*. If you want to configure privileges for a Windows 2000 domain controller, generally you'll want to edit the security policy for this OU to make sure that all domain controllers are running with similar configurations.

OU See *organizational unit*.

out-of-band A term often bandied about by computer nerds (especially the subset that works at DevelopMentor) that implies information that is sent via some other mechanism or protocol than the normal mechanism by which you'd expect to get information. For instance, you can use thread-local storage to pass extra variables to a function without having to change the signature of that function. These variables are thus communicated *out-of-band* to the function.

OWF See *one-way function.*

owner The owner of an object is always *implicitly* granted READ_CONTROL and WRITE_DAC permissions to the object, and thus can read and write the DACL at will. See also *discretionary access control list*.

PDC See *primary domain controller*.

PKI See *public key infrastructure*.

plaintext A term commonly used to refer to a set of bits that form a message that is readable by anyone. See also *cleartext* and *ciphertext*.

primary domain controller (PDC) Prior to Windows 2000, which uses the multimaster replication topology of the directory service to replicate the security database between domain controllers, a simple master-slave system was used. The primary domain controller is a single machine that acts as the master and thus has the only read-write copy of the security database for the entire domain. All other domain controllers for that domain are considered backup domain controllers, and obtain read-only copies of the database from the PDC. See also *backup domain controller*.

primary group A setting in a security descriptor that fills the need for each object to have a group associated with it (for POSIX and Macintosh compatibility). It is not used by native Windows applications.

primary token Due to historical reasons, each token has a type that is either primary or impersonation. Primary tokens may be applied to processes (via `CreateProcessAsUser`, for example). Impersonation tokens may be applied to threads (via `SetThreadToken`, for example). You cannot pass one type of token where the other is required, but other than this little bit of nomenclature, these tokens are roughly equivalent from a conceptual point of view. They both refer to an underlying logon session, and they both can contain network credentials (or not). As of Windows NT 4, you can convert back and forth between these types of tokens by simply calling `DuplicateTokenEx`, so don't let this historical nomenclature confuse you.

principal An entity in a secure system that can be authenticated. Users can be principals; machines can also be principals. See also *authentication* and *credentials*.

private key In an asymmetric algorithm, there is a public key and a private key. The public key can be shared with the world, whereas the private key is known by only a single entity. Data can generally be encrypted with the private key and decrypted with the public key (or vice versa), and it is cryptographically infeasible to derive the private key from the public key. Some examples of the use of public key cryptography are provided in Chapter 10. See also *asymmetric algorithm*.

privilege An authorization attribute that doesn't pertain to one particular object; rather, it affects the application of security policy in a more general way. The canonical example of this is the "Bypass traverse checking" privilege, which determines whether a client should be granted access to a file simply based on the file's ACL alone, without traversing up to each parent directory checking for the FILE_TRAVERSE permission, one by one, until the root is reached. Because each principal can be granted a different set of privileges, security policy can be adjusted in a very fine-grained way using privileges. Privileges are granted on a per-machine basis, but with the advent of Group Policy in Windows 2000, an administrator can push a particular configuration to a group of machines (in an organizational unit or domain, for instance) and thus make sweeping policy decisions without having to roll his or her chair to each machine individually. See also *group*.

public key See *private key*.

public key cryptography See *private key*.

public key infrastructure An infrastructure consisting of mechanisms and policies that allow digital certificates to be issued and verified. This generally includes a hierarchy of certificate authorities that are responsible for issuing certificates and certificate revocation lists (CRLs). See also *digital certificate*, *asymmetric algorithm*, *private key*, and *certificate revocation list*.

realm In Kerberos parlance, a realm represents a security scope whose principals can be authenticated by a single authority (this may consist of several KDCs sharing a replicated security database). In Windows parlance, this is equivalent to a domain.

restricted token Technically (according to the documentation for the `IsTokenRestricted` API), a restricted token is one that contains a separate list of SIDs that are used to perform a second access check against any given object; only if both the normal access check and the one using the list of restricted SIDs succeeds will the overall access check succeed. Loosely speaking, this is any token that has groups marked SE_GROUP_ USE_FOR_DENY_ONLY or has had privileges removed from it, either via direct use of the `CreateRestrictedToken` API or indirectly via a job object. See Chapter 4 for more details on restricted tokens.

RID The elements that make a SID unique are its 48-bit identifier authority, followed by an ordered collection of 32-bit relative identifiers (RIDs for short). SIDs are variable-length beasts; their length varies according to the number of RIDs they have. For instance, S-1-5-32-544 is the SID for BUILTIN\Administrators. 32 is the RID for the BUILTIN domain, and 544 is the RID for the Administrators alias.

roles The operating system itself was built around the notion of roles from day 1 in the life of Windows NT. The Administrators alias is a great example of this. Rather than hardcoding the SIDs of users who are allowed administrative access to a given machine (which would be silly, given the general-purpose nature of the operating system and the fact that Microsoft actually makes money when they ship it to other companies where the SIDs will be different), the system looks for the well-known Administrators alias in order to make sweeping decisions (like who is allowed to install services). I should note that with the introduction of a directory service in Windows 2000, many of the previously hardcoded role-based checks are being removed in favor of a finer-grained, object-centric access control strategy that hinges on the directory. For instance, in Windows NT 4, Administrators and Account Operators were the two roles that were allowed to add user accounts. With the directory service in Windows 2000, these controls can be customized on a per-domain (or even per-organizational-unit or per-container) basis.

COM+ (and its predecessor, MTS) provides a role-based infrastructure that provides many of the benefits of the old role-based system in Windows, simplicity being one of the major benefits.

SACL See *system access control list*.

SCM An acronym for Service Control Manager, of which there are two on Windows: the System SCM and the COM SCM. Both act as logon session brokers; that is, they can create logon sessions in order to sandbox the services or COM servers that they start.

SD See *security descriptor*.

secure channel Generally speaking, a communication channel whose contents can be secured via the use of a MAC, encryption, or both to provide integrity and confidentiality. This requires that both sides of the channel hold a symmetric key, typically known as a session key.

You may also hear this term in conjunction with a particular SSP provided by Microsoft: SCHANNEL. This security service provider implements the secure sockets layer protocol (SSL) and its variants (PCT and TLS), and is housed in SCHANNEL.DLL.

security context An abstract term for the collection of security settings that determine the security environment in which a thread executes. This includes a logon session along with any network credentials that may be housed there, as well as a token and any authorization attributes that may be present there. This also includes settings such as the default owner and DACL in the token.

If a thread is not impersonating, it runs in the security context of the process. If a thread is impersonating, it runs in the security context determined by the token that has been placed on the thread.

security descriptor (SD) A security descriptor has four parts, three of which are interesting to native Windows programmers: the owner, DACL, and SACL. The security descriptor also houses some flags that affect the DACL and SACL (such as SE_DACL_PROTECTED, which blocks the flow of inheritable ACEs from a parent object's DACL). Each secure object in the operating system generally has an SD (although sometimes entire groups of objects, such as windows, are protected by one SD, in this case the SD of the scoping window station). See also *owner*, *discretionary access control list*, and *system access control list*.

security service provider (SSP) A part of the operating system that implements the client and server legs of a network authentication protocol such as Kerberos. By abstracting these implementations behind a common interface (SSPI on Windows, GSSAPI for the rest of the world), it's possible to build secure distributed systems using a number of different network authentication protocols.

server farm A collection of servers (typically Web servers) that have a similar configuration and perform load balancing such that one box is as good as the other for servicing any incoming request.

Server Gated Cryptography (SGC) An extension to a digital certificate that indicates it belongs to a company that has been approved by the U.S. government as being free to do business using strong cryptography, even in the face of the strict export regulations that were in force prior to January 2000. Now that virtually anyone can download strong encryption packs for their browsers, this technology isn't nearly as interesting as it used to be.

Server Manager A tool in Windows NT 4 that showed the list of machine accounts for a domain and also provided several other features, such as being able to start and stop services on any computer in the domain. These tools are now provided via Microsoft Management Console (MMC) snap-ins, but the idea is still the same. The one major difference in Windows 2000 is that machines are now first-class citizens; their accounts are no longer hidden away in a separate tool and virtually unconfigurable. Instead, machines can now be added to groups and treated as any other user principal in the domain.

service Microsoft's light-and-happy term for a daemon program or process.

service logon One of two daemon logon types (the other is the batch logon). The System SCM uses this type of logon session to host each service that runs as a distinguished principal, but you can establish a service logon at any time by calling `LogonUser` (assuming you're running in the TCB). A token from a service logon can be identified by a well-known authorization attribute (a group SID): S-1-5-6.

session key After an authentication exchange over the network, the client and server discover a session key. The session key is a symmetric key that can be used to encrypt or decrypt messages and to create or verify message authentication codes. See also *secure channel*.

SGC See *Server Gated Cryptography*.

SID An acronym for a security identifier, which is simply a variable-length number that is designed to uniquely identify something (similar to a GUID in COM). SIDs have structure, unlike GUIDs, and thus well-known SIDs can be constructed from well-known relative identifiers (RIDs). See also *RID*.

single sign on The idea that a client can log in to Windows once, providing a single password that provides access (directly or indirectly) to all resources (local or remote) that the client needs to get his or her work done. This only works if all applications the client uses smoothly integrate with Windows security (using the identification and authorization attributes in a token, for instance). Applications that provide their own logons force clients to remember alternate passwords, which generally makes them rather angry. Most native Windows applications can in fact integrate quite seamlessly with

Windows security; all that's required is learning a little bit about programming with Windows security in mind (hence this book).

specific permissions The set of permissions defined by a particular class of object. An access mask with specific permissions for one class of object will generally be quite meaningless when applied to another class of object. See also *standard permissions* and *generic permissions*.

SPNEGO An acronym for Simple and Protected Negotiation (RFC 2478), which is a way for two SSPs to negotiate the best authentication protocol between them and to have some means of securing that negotiation. This protocol is discussed in Chapter 7.

SSP See *security service provider*.

standard permissions A set of permissions that all classes of objects share, including `DELETE` and `WRITE_DAC`, among others. This simply allows some commonly used access masks to become polymorphic across all classes of objects. See also *generic permissions*.

subauthority A 32-bit value that makes up part of a SID. A variable number of these coupled with the identifier authority makes the SID unique. See also *identifier authority*.

symmetric algorithm A cryptographic algorithm in which the encryption and decryption keys are the same. These algorithms are much more suited to bulk data encryption than are asymmetric algorithms, which are orders of magnitude slower.

SYSTEM You'll often see the string SYSTEM in ACL editors (and you'll sometimes see it referred to as LocalSystem in documentation). This term simply refers to the system logon session on the local machine (S-1-5-18). You can grant or deny access to this SID, but denying it access is pretty pointless. Because it's part of the TCB, by definition any program running in this logon session can get around any access controls on the local machine (even if it takes installing a device driver that has direct access to hardware).

system access control list (SACL) The data structure that controls auditing for a given object. Because auditing policy is determined by an administrator, this ACL is nondiscretionary; you cannot read or write this ACL without a special privilege that is normally only granted to administrators (`SeSecurityPrivilege`). Just like the DACL, this ACL contains ACEs that can use inheritance, but in this case the ACEs control whether a successful or failed attempt at access should be audited.

System logon session Logon session 999, the System logon session, is the first logon session to be created on a machine and the last logon session to terminate on a machine. It hosts the majority of the user-mode operating system components, and is considered part of the trusted computing base (TCB). You can place your own code in this logon session by writing a service, but it's generally a good idea to put as little code here as possible because bugs in code in the TCB can allow an attacker to compromise the security of the machine (and if the machine is a domain controller, this compromises the security of the entire domain).

System Service Control Manager See *SCM*.

TCB See *trusted computing base*.

TCB privilege A privilege that allows logon sessions other than SYSTEM to become part of the TCB. Avoid granting this privilege; run code in the System logon session that needs to be part of the TCB.

TGT See *ticket-granting ticket*.

ticket Although Kerberos tickets contain lots of interesting things, there are really only two critical pieces of information in a ticket: the name of the principal who owns the ticket (the principal to whom the KDC issued the ticket), and a session key. Both of these pieces of information are encrypted with the target server's master key. The client presents this ticket to the server along with proof of ownership, that is, proof of knowledge of the session key, which was issued along with the ticket by the KDC to the requesting principal. See Chapter 7 for more detail.

Ticket Granting Service (TGS) Whereas the Kerberos Authentication Service issues TGTs, the Ticket Granting Service issues server tickets using the presented TGT as proof of the requestor's identity. See also *Authentication Service*.

ticket-granting ticket (TGT) The tickets issued by the Kerberos Authentication Service. See also *Authentication Service*.

token An executive object that represents the surface area of a logon session. It contains a SID identifying a security principal, a set of authorization attributes (groups and privileges), and a set of default settings (a default DACL and owner). Each process is tied to a logon session via its process token; no process can run without a token. Tokens may also be placed on threads; see *impersonation*. Tokens and logon sessions are created by the LSA. See also *primary token*.

transitive trust Prior to Windows 2000, transitive trust relationships between domains were not supported (for reasons of efficiency). Thus each domain required individual trust relationships to be set up and maintained manually in order to create a web of trusted domains. Windows 2000 uses Kerberos, which was designed with transitive trust in mind (see Chapter 7). All domains in a Windows 2000 forest trust one another automatically, using transitive trust relationships that wind through the individual trees in the forest and are bound together at the root of each tree in the forest.

Trojan horse Λ program that appears benign, but when executed does something other than what was intended. Generally it does something mean and nasty such as ask you for your password or email X-rated URLs to your family and friends.

trust accounts The LSA on each machine maintains a set of trust accounts. On a domain controller there may be several trusted or trusting domains, and thus several interdomain trust accounts. On a machine that is not a domain controller there will be at most one trust account, the account with the domain in which that machine is a member.

trusted computing base (TCB) I provided a definition of this term in the first chapter of the book, but it's so important to understand that I think I'll repeat it here so you don't have to go look it up:

> [The] totality of protection mechanisms within a computer system, including hardware, firmware, and software, the combination of which is responsible for enforcing a security policy. Note: The ability of a trusted computing base to enforce correctly a unified security policy depends on the correctness of the mechanisms within the trusted computing base, the protection of those mechanisms to ensure their correctness, and the correct input of parameters related to the security policy.

What this says in essence is that in any secure system there always has to be a core set of components that enforce the security policy, and that this core set of components must be protected to avoid compromise. Guarding the perimeter of the TCB may involve ensuring that the machine is physically secure (a bootable floppy has undone many a secure operating system), and ensuring that the operating system components themselves cannot be replaced (perhaps by applying rigid DACLs on system files and even digitally signing them). This also means not injecting buggy or malicious code into the TCB that will allow its compromise. See also *SYSTEM*.

trustee A principal, group, or alias that can be granted or denied access in a DACL. It can also mean a principal, group, or alias that can be called out for auditing in a SACL. The difference between a trustee and a principal is that a principal can be authenticated, whereas a trustee is simply a SID that is compared against a previously authenticated principal's list of authorization attributes.

use record A term I use in Chapter 8 to refer to the data structure that is created when a client uses the LAN Manager function `NetUseAdd` (or the `net use` command). This seemed clearer to me than the term "connection," which can mean many things. Each use record can specify alternate credentials, so that each *lmsession* established for that use record automatically uses alternate credentials as opposed to the default network credentials of the client-side logon session.

User Manager The tool that was used prior to Windows 2000 to configure user accounts, privileges, logon rights, and auditing, among other security policy settings.

WAM See *Web Application Manager*.

Web Application Manager (WAM) The component of the IIS implementation that allows ISAPI applications to be isolated from the core Web server process, `INETINFO.EXE`, which runs in the System logon session. The WAM implements a COM interface and thus can run in the same process as `INETINFO.EXE` or in a separate process. Remember that any code running inside `INETINFO.EXE` is code that runs inside the TCB. Consider moving Web applications out of the process to avoid encouraging attacks against the TCB of the Web server.

window station A window station provides a USER environment complete with clipboard, atom table, and a set of desktops. Each process runs inside a window station, and the windows created by that process's thread(s) live in the window station they were created in *forever*. Window handles are window station relative; you cannot send window messages across window station boundaries. This is to keep sandboxed processes (services and COM servers running as distinguished principals) from hijacking the interactive user's logon session by sending messages to windows created for the interactive user. See also *interactive window station* and *noninteractive window station*.

Windows Terminal Services Windows 2000 added support for this service, which allows a single Windows machine to host several logical sessions, each for a different remote user on a terminal who feels as if he or she is in control of the machine. Each session has its own separate namespace for objects; thus, there is an interactive window station (named Winsta0) for each session.

Winsta0 The hardcoded name of the interactive window station (see also *interactive window station*

Bibliography

Please note that I have links on my Web site (http://www.develop.com/ books/pws) so that you can read most of the articles referenced here online.

Adams, Carlisle, and Steve Lloyd. 1999. *Understanding the public-key infrastructure.* Indianapolis, IN: Macmillan Technical Publishing.

Box, Don. 1998. *Essential COM.* Reading, MA: Addison Wesley Longman.

Box, Don, Keith Brown, Tim Ewald, and Chris Sells. 1999. *Effective COM.* Reading, MA: Addison-Wesley.

Brown, Keith. 1999a. Security briefs: The Windows 2000 access control editor GUI. *Microsoft Systems Journal,* May, 85–93.

Brown, Keith. 1999b. Building a lightweight COM interception framework. *Microsoft Systems Journal,* January/February.

Brown, Keith. 1999c. Security briefs: Exploring NULL sessions and the Guest account. *Microsoft Systems Journal,* February, 79–85.

Brown, Keith. 1999d. Security briefs: Exploring security issues in three-tier web applications. *Microsoft Systems Journal,* November.

Brown, Keith. 2000a. Security briefs: Exploring handle security in Windows. *MSDN Magazine,* March, 85–90.

Brown, Keith. 2000b. Handle logons in Windows NT and Windows 2000 with your own logon session broker. *Microsoft Systems Journal,* February, 17–32.

Daily, Sean K. 1999. How to rename your NT domain: Rechristen your network without wrecking it. *Windows NT Magazine,* February. Available at http://www.winntmag.com.

Ewald, Tim. 2001. *Transactional COM+: Designing scalable applications.* Reading, MA: Addison-Wesley.

Feghhi, Jalal, Jalil Feghhi, and Peter Williams. 1999. *Digital certificates.* Reading, MA: Addison-Wesley.

Ford, Warwick, and Michael S. Baum. 1997. *Secure electronic commerce: Building the infrastructure for digital signatures and encryption.* Upper Saddle River, NJ: Prentice Hall.

Initial authentication and pass through authentication using Kerberos V5 and the GSS-API. 1999. Internet draft filed as draft-ietf-cat-iakerb-03.txt.

Kaufman, Charlie, Radia Perlman, and Mike Speciner. 1995. *Network security: Private communication in a public world.* Englewood Cliffs, NJ: Prentice Hall.

Kim, Frank. 1998. Run your applications on a variety of desktop platforms with Terminal Server. *Microsoft Systems Journal,* December.

Kindel, Charlie. 1998, January. Distributed Component Object Model Protocol—DCOM/1.0. Internet draft (expired), filed as draft-brown-dcom-v1-spec-02.txt. Available on MSDN.

Leighton, Luke Kenneth Casson. 2000. *DCE/RPC over SMB: SAMBA and Windows NT domain internals.* Indianapolis, IN: Macmillan Technical Publishing.

Microsoft Corporation and Digital Equipment Corporation. 1995, October. The Component Object Model Specification 0.9. Available on MSDN.

Private Communication Technology. 1996. Internet draft (expired). draft-benaloh-pct-01.txt.

Richter, Jeffrey. 1999a. *Programming applications for Microsoft Windows.* 4th ed. Redmond, WA: Microsoft Press.

Richter, Jeffrey. 1999b. *Programming server-side applications for Microsoft Windows.* Redmond, WA: Microsoft Press.

Schneier, Bruce. 1996. *Applied cryptography.* 2nd ed. New York: John Wiley & Sons.

Secure Sockets Layer 3.0 Specification. 1996, November. Most recent Internet draft (expired): draft-freier-ssl-version3-02.txt. As of this writing, this document is available at http://home.netscape.com/eng/ssl3/index.html.

Solomon, David A. 1998. *Inside Windows NT.* 2nd ed. Redmond, WA: Microsoft Press.

Zimmermann, Philip R. 1995. *The official PGP user's guide.* Cambridge, MA: MIT Press.

Index

Addison-Wesley Professional

How to *Register* *Your Book*

Register this Book

Visit: **http://www.aw.com/cseng/register**

Enter the ISBN*

Then you will receive:

- Notices and reminders about upcoming author appearances, tradeshows, and online chats with special guests
- Advanced notice of forthcoming editions of your book
- Book recommendations
- Notification about special contests and promotions throughout the year

*The ISBN can be found on the copyright page of the book

Visit our Web site

http://www.aw.com/cseng

When you think you've read enough, there's always more content for you at Addison-Wesley's web site. Our web site contains a directory of complete product information including:

- Chapters
- Exclusive author interviews
- Links to authors' pages
- Tables of contents
- Source code

You can also discover what tradeshows and conferences Addison-Wesley will be attending, read what others are saying about our titles, and find out where and when you can meet our authors and have them sign your book.

We encourage you to patronize the many fine retailers who stock Addison-Wesley titles. Visit our online directory to find stores near you.

Contact Us via Email

cepubprof@awl.com

Ask general questions about our books.
Sign up for our electronic mailing lists.
Submit corrections for our web site.

cepubeditors@awl.com

Submit a book proposal.
Send errata for a book.

cepubpublicity@awl.com

Request a review copy for a member of the media interested in reviewing new titles.

registration@awl.com

Request information about book registration.

Addison-Wesley Professional

One Jacob Way, Reading, Massachusetts 01867 USA
TEL 781-944-3700 • FAX 781-942-3076